WE ARE THE FACE OF OAXACA

Lynn Stephen

WE ARE THE FACE OF OAXACA

Testimony and Social Movements

May 9, 2014

Dear Kimberly,

I hope you enjoy this book. I hope your commitment and participation represents the critical voices, movement, and participation represents the critical voices, movement share to justice represent this something you share to is some thing forward over continuing amistad.

Abrazos
Lynn

DUKE UNIVERSITY PRESS   DURHAM AND LONDON   2013

Printed in the United States of America on acid-free paper ∞
Designed and typeset by Julie Allred, BW&A Books, Inc.,
in Charis and The Sans

Library of Congress Cataloging-in-Publication Data
Stephen, Lynn.
We are the face of Oaxaca : testimony and social movements / Lynn Stephen.
pages cm
Includes bibliographical references and index.
ISBN 978-0-8223-5519-9 (cloth : alk. paper)
ISBN 978-0-8223-5534-2 (pbk. : alk. paper)
1. Social movements—Mexico—Oaxaca (State)
2. Oral communication—Mexico—Oaxaca (State)
3. Asamblea Popular de los Pueblos de Oaxaca. I. Title.
HN120.029.S74 2013
303.48′4097274—dc23
2013012815

Cover photograph by Barucha Peller

CONTENTS

MAPS, ILLUSTRATIONS, AND VIDEOCLIPS

Maps

Illustrations

All photographs are taken by the author unless otherwise specified in the captions.

ACRONYMS AND ABBREVIATIONS

APPO   Asamblea Popular de los Pueblos de Oaxaca (Popular Assembly of the Peoples of Oaxaca)

ASARO   Asamblea de Artistas Revolucionarios de Oaxaca (Assembly of Revolutionary Artists of Oaxaca)

CACTUS   Centro de Apoyo Comunitario Trabajando Unidos, A.C. (Center for Community Support Working Together)

CASOTA   Casa Autónoma Solidaria Oaxaqueña de Trabajo Autogestivo (Autonomous Oaxacan House Supporting Self-Managed Work)

CCI   Central Campesina Independiente (Independent Peasant Central)

CCIODH   Comisión Civil Internacional de Observación por los Derechos Humanos (International Civil Commission for the Observation of Human Rights)

CDDHO   Comisión de Derechos Humanos de Oaxaca (Oaxacan Human Rights Commission)

CDI   Comisión Nacional para el Desarollo de los Pueblos Indígenas de México (National Commission for the Development of the Indigenous Peoples of Mexico)

CIPO-RFM   Consejo Indígena Popular de Oaxaca Ricardo Flores Magón (Council of Oaxaca Ricardo Flores Magón)

CNC   Confederación Nacional Campesina (National Peasants Confederation)

CNDH   Comisión Nacional de Derechos Humanos (National Commission for Human Rights)

CNPA   Coordinadora Nacional Plan de Ayala (National Coordinator Plan de Ayala)

CNTE   Coordinadora Nacional de Trabajadores de la Educación (National Council of Education Workers)

COCEI Coalición Obrero Campesino Estudiantil del Istmo de Tehuantepec (Isthmus Coalition of Workers, Peasants, and Students)

COCEO Coalición Obrero Campesina Estudiantil de Oaxaca (Worker, Peasant, Student Coalition of Oaxaca)

CODEMO Coordinadora Democrática del Magisterio (Democratic Council of Teachers)

COMO   Coordinadora de Mujeres de Oaxaca (Coordinating Committee of Women of Oaxaca)

COR-TV Corporación Oaxaqueña de Radio y Televisión (Oaxacan Corporation of Radio and Television)

DDHPO Defensoría de los Derechos Humanos del Pueblo de Oaxaca (Office for the Defense of Human Rights of the People of Oaxaca)

EPR   El Ejército Popular Revolucionario (Revolutionary Popular Army)

EZLN   Ejército Zapatista de Liberación Nacional (Zapatista Army of National Liberation)

FIOB   Frente Indígena de Organizaciones Binacionales (Binational Front of Indigenous Organizations)

FPCR   Frente Popular Contra la Represión (Popular Front against Repression)

FUCUPO Fusión Cívica de Organizaciones Productivas (Civic Merger of Productive Organizations)

IAGO   Instituto de Artes Gráficas (Institute of Graphic Arts)

IEEPO Instituto Estatal de Educación Pública de Oaxaca (State Institute of Public Education of Oaxaca)

IFE   Instituto Federal Electoral (Federal Electoral Institute)

INI   Instituto Nacional Indigenista (National Indigenist Institute)

LASA   Latin American Studies Association

Limeddh Liga Mexicana por la Defensa de los Derechos Humanos (Mexican League for the Defense of Human Rights)

MULT   Movimiento de Unificación y Lucha Triqui (Movement for Triqui Unification and Struggle)

MULTI Movimiento Unificación Lucha Triqui Independiente (Independent Movement for Triqui Unification and Struggle)

PAN Partido Acción Nacional (National Action Party)

PFP Policia Federal Preventitativa (Federal Preventative Police)

PRD Partido Revolucionario Democrático (Party of the Democratic Revolution)

PRI Partido Revolucionario Institucional (Institutional Revolutionary Party)

PUP Partido Unidad Popular (Popular Unity Party)

SARH Secretaría de Agricultura y Recursos Hidraúlicos (Ministry of Agriculture and Hydraulic Resources)

Sección 22 Local 22

SEP Secretaría de Educación Pública (Ministry of Public Education)

SIPAZ Servicio Internacional por la Paz (International Service for Peace)

SNTE Sindicato Nacional de Trabajadores de Educación (National Union of Education Workers)

TMA Transferencia de Medios Audiovisuales a Organizaciones y Comunidades Indígenas (Tranference of Audiovisual Media to Indigenous Communities and Organizations)

UABJO Universidad Autónoma "Benito Juárez" de Oaxaca (Autonomous Benito Juarez University of Oaxaca)

UBISORT Unidad de Bienestar Social para la Región Triqui (Unity for the Well-Being of the Triqui Region)

USEM Unión Social de Empresarios Mexicanos (Social Union of Mexican Businesses)

UTE Unión de Trabajadores de la Educación (Union of Education Workers)

VOCAL Voces Oaxaqueñas Construyendo Autonomía y Libertad (Oaxacan Voices Constructing Autonomy and Freedom)

ABOUT THE WEBSITE

*W*e are the Face of Oaxaca is a book designed with integral digital content through an accompanying website found at http://faceof oaxaca.uoregon.edu. The website features twenty-six video testimonies of people who were interviewed for the book and hundreds of photographs, maps, and documents. Section 1 of the website, "Rights Histories in Oaxaca," contains videos of Oaxacan intellectuals and movement leaders describing rights histories in the state. Section 2, "Timeline of the 2006 Social Movement," features short videos of key events to help readers better visualize and feel the experiences of those who were caught up in the movement. Sections 3–7 ("Human Rights Violations in Oaxaca," "Media, Gender, and Indigenous Radio," "Economics and Politics of Conflict," Indigenous Activism in Mexico and Transnationally," and "Youth Organizing and Art") contain digital content that is linked to specific parts of the text in the book. Beginning in chapter 2 of the book, there are embedded links to the digital content of the website that correspond to specific areas of text. If viewing electronically, readers can access a link by clicking on the doi number shown in the text. This link will take readers directly to the digital content references—whether it be a video testimony, photograph, or map.

For example, in chapter 9, in a section that describes the origins of the artist collective known as Asamblea de Artistas Revolucionarios de Oaxaca (Assembly of Revolutionary Artists of Oaxaca, or ASARO), readers can click on a link labeled

✳ VIDEOCLIP 9.1: http://dx.doi.org/10.7264/N3RB72JW

and be taken to video testimony of Mario Guzmán describing how ASARO got started and the challenges it has faced.

If readers choose to visit the accompanying website as a stand-alone platform, they can access each of the seven topical areas of the website and then select buttons to view related video testimonies, documents, maps, and photographs. The website is bilingual in Spanish and English. The website is particularly useful for providing students, community members, and others with direct access to the testimonies, ideas, and photographs of the people profiled in the book.

ACKNOWLEDGMENTS

When I arrived in Oaxaca City in the summer of 2006 with several colleagues from the University of Oregon, I did not imagine that six years later I would be writing acknowledgments for a book about a social movement that transformed the city and many people in it. I am grateful to the Center for the Study of Women in Society at the University of Oregon and to my colleagues Gabriela Martinez, Stephanie Wood, Analisa Taylor, and Judith Music for financial and emotional support during the summer of 2006 and afterward related to this project and more. I had with me my two sons, Gabriel and José, who were six and fourteen. We had never shared such an intense experience as living in Oaxaca during the summer of 2006. The atmosphere was electric with hope, fear, joy, sadness, violence, repression, and amazing acts of courage, humility, and cooperation all at once.

I have spent part of every year for the past twenty-five years in Oaxaca, often with my children and my partner, Ellen Herman. I am grateful for our long-standing community of friends and compadres and our children's father, Alejandro de Avila, who have shared their lives with us and opened up their hearts and homes. Without this community in Oaxaca, I do not believe this book would have been written. In the process of working on this book and the website that preceded, my community of friends grew much larger.

I first want to thank the more than eighty men and women who spoke with me, many on multiple occasions, and who agreed to be audiotaped and videotaped. I cannot acknowledge them all here, as some did not want to have their identities revealed, but a surprising number did, and their names appear in the chapters that follow. Ramiro Aragón Pérez, Ruth Guzmán Sánchez, and their extended families were extremely helpful and important in shaping this project as well as in providing crucial connections.

Yésica Sánchez Maya provided crucial interest and support in the project in its early phases and provided valuable feedback about initial interviews, the website, and also connections to other participants. Her work as a human rights advocate and the way she and others employ testimonies in their work was an intellectual and moral inspiration. José Antonio Altamirano was extremely generous with his time over several years, helping to connect me to members and leaders of Sección 22 and members of the Asamblea Popular de los Pueblos de Oaxaca (APPO). Lucero Topete was very generous with her time in helping me to connect to business owners and entrepreneurs in Oaxaca. Debbie Poole, Chacho Renique, and their son, Lucas, were steadfast friends and colleagues as we together accompanied the processes of the movement and its aftermath from 2006 on. Gaspar Rivera Salgado, Centolia Maldonado, Odilia Romero, and Rufino Domínguez Santos of the Frente Indígena de Organizaciones Binacionales provided important support in helping me to set up interviews and to collect materials related to indigenous participation in APPO outside of Oaxaca City, primarily in Juxtlahuaca, Huajuapan de León, and Los Angeles. Roberto Olivares provided insights and connections to explore the role of community radio and video in the movement and after. Kevin McClosky, César Chávez, Itandehui Franco Ortíz, and Ed McCaughlin shared information and images and helped me to strengthen my analysis of the role of stencil, graffiti, and graphic arts in the social movement of Oaxaca.

Dear friends and colleagues in Oaxaca, including Margarita Dalton, Julia Barco, Salomon Nahmad, and Conchita Nuñez, and longtime friends in Teotitlán del Valle, including Petra Bautista, Paco González, Josefina Jiménez, and others who wish not to be named, provided crucial insights, support, and often interviews for this project. Leticia Aragón Ramírez and her family in Arazola and her brother Saúl Aragón received me, my students, and my son warmly in their homes on numerous occasions and generously shared their perspectives with me in interviews and in conversation. Juana Rodríguez and Sandra Ramírez provided important friendship and support to me and my family throughout the time I was working on this project in Oaxaca.

I also want to acknowledge the important roles that my students have played in this project. Jesse Nichols worked tirelessly as an undergraduate at the University of Oregon for a year and a half with me to edit and subtitle video clips that are available through this book and the website that preceded it. Jesse also accompanied me to Oaxaca to record additional interviews, return transcripts, and discuss the website design and content with people. Mauricio Magaña began his own research in Oaxaca in 2007 and provided important help transcribing interviews and also sharing ideas and analysis about the movement. Iván Sandoval Cervantes has provided important help transcribing interviews and also translating things I have written into Spanish, which allowed me to share my writing with many in Mexico and elsewhere. Anna Cruz and Suzy Chavez also provided important assistance in transcribing interviews. Michelle Goris provided additional editing and subtitling of video interviews done with members of ASARO and I thank her for that work.

Karen Estlund, Head of the Digital Scholarship Center of the University of Oregon Libraries provided crucial help in setting up the new website that accompanies this text.

Colleagues at the University of Oregon in anthropology, Latin American studies, ethnic studies, women's and gender studies, the School of Law, and elsewhere who have provided important intellectual ideas, discussion, and support for this project include Carlos Aguirre, Michael Hames-García, Ernesto Martínez, Sandra Morgen, Lamia Karim, Frances White, Madonna Moss, Heather McClure, Carol Stabile, Pedro García-Caro, Cecilia Enjuto-Rangel, Lise Nelson, David Vazquez, and Amalia Gladhart. Alice Evans, Eli Meyer, Peggy McConnell, and Feather Crawford, who worked with me at the Center for Latino/a and Latin American Studies, provided ongoing logistical support, editing assistance, and other forms of encouragement for this project in various stages. Cecelia Hagen also provided important editorial assistance while I was writing the manuscript.

Karen Brodkin and Carollee Howes provided wonderful friendship, intellectual discussion, and use of their home in Mapleton, Oregon, as a place to relax, think, write, and have fun. Guadalupe Quinn, Ken Neubeck, and Patricia Cortéz are important friends and colleagues in Eugene who keep me engaged with the Latino immigrant community. Larry Kleinman and Ramón Ramírez and other friends in Pineros y Campesinos Unidos del Nordoeste (PCUN) and the CAPACES Leadership Institute (CLI) in Woodburn, Oregon, also provide this important connection. Lynn Smith and Tom Sears have provided important spaces for singing, playing music, and relaxing through the choir we participate in at the Unitarian Universalist Church in Eugene.

This project also benefited from financial support from the Center for the Study of Women in Society and from research funds provided by the College of Arts and Science and the Office of the Vice President for Research and Innovation at the University of Oregon. I gratefully acknowledge this support. The University of Oregon also provided generous support for my sabbatical year during 2011 and 2012, which allowed me to write. I want to particularly thank the dean of the College of Arts and Science, Scott Coltrane, for his ongoing encouragement, support, and interest in my research.

A generous fellowship from the Center for U.S.-Mexican Studies, where I was in residence from September 2011 through June 2012, made it possible for me to complete this book. The director of the Center, Alberto Díaz Cayeros, and my colleagues there, Danny Zborover, Maylei Blackwell, María Teresa Sierra, Claudia Rodriguez, Miles Rodríguez, Héctor Tajonar, and Javier López, provided friendship, important suggestions for improving my manuscript, and a valuable intellectual space for exchange through our writing group and other activities. Greg Mallinger was an all-around wonderful person who helped me with many different things in relation to my residency at the Center. Justin Levitt provided important basic templates for the maps used here, which were finished by George Chakvetadze. Joyce Qaqundah, along with other members of the choir we sang in, was a wonderful friend who provided encouragement and joy.

Colleagues at other universities provided important opportunities for me to share my work in talks and conversations that were crucial to being able to write and finish the manuscript. I thank the following individuals and institutions for invitations to give talks about my research related to this project: Timo Schaeffer, the Simon Frazier University Latin American Studies Student Union and Latin American Studies Program, the University of British Colombia Latin American Studies Program, and CIPO-Vancouver; Marisol de la Cadena and the Hemispheric Institute of the Americas, University of California, Davis; Tony Lucero and María Elena Gracía and the Latin American Studies Program at the University of Washington; Amparo Hoffman-Pinilla and Sonia Ospina and the Research Center for Leadership in Action, New York University; Patricia Zavella, Jonathan Fox, and the Chicano/Latino Research Center at the University of California, Santa Cruz; Elizabeth Kuznesof and the Center of Latin American Studies at the University of Kansas; Dorothy Hodgson and the Institute for Research on Women at Rutgers University; Ingrid Kummels and the Latin American Institute at the Frei Universität Berlin; Edgar Talledos and the Seminario Permanente de Estudios Chicanos y de Fronteras at the Universidad Nacional Autónoma de México (UNAM); Arturo Escobar, Paul Leslie, Lou Perez, and the Department of Anthropology and the Institute for the Study of the Americas at the University of North Carolina at Chapel Hill; Cristina Oehmichen, Hernán Salas, and the Instituto de Investigaciones Antropológicas of the UNAM; Jorge Vargas and the School of Law at the University of San Diego; Rachel Sieder, Aída Hernández Castillo, and Natalia de Marinis at CIESAS, Mexico City; Nancy Postero and the Anthropology Department at the University of California, San Diego; and Ramona Pérez and the Center for Latin American Studies at San Diego State University.

I gratefully acknowledge permission from Latin American Perspectives and Sage Publications to reprint parts of "Testimony and Human Rights Violations in Oaxaca," *Latin American Perspectives* 38(6): 52–68, November 2011; to Critique of Anthropology and Sage Publications to reprint parts of "Karen Brodkin and the Study of Social Movements: Lessons for the Social Movement of Oaxaca, Mexico," *Critique of Anthropology* 30(1) (2010): 1–29; to the University of Pennsylvania for permission to reprint parts of "The Rights to Speak and to Be Heard: Women's Interpretations of Rights Discourses in the Oaxaca Social Movement," in *Gender at the Limits of Rights*, ed. Dorothy Hodgson (Philadelphia: University of Pennsylvania Press, 2011), 161–79; to Latin American and Caribbean Studies (LACES) for permission to reprint parts of "Indigenous Transborder Citizenship: FIOB Los Angeles and the Oaxaca Social Movement of 2006," forthcoming; to Palgrave Macmillan for permission to reprint parts of "Testimony in Truth Commissions and Social Movements in Latin America," in *Pushing the Boundaries of Latin American Testimony: Meta-morphoses and Migrations*, ed. Louise Detwiler and Janice B. Breckenridge (New York: Palgrave Macmillan, 2012), 109–30; to New York University Press for permission to reprint parts of "Community and Indigenous Radio in Oaxaca: Testimony and Participatory Democracy," in *Radio Fields: The Anthropology of Radio in the Twenty-first Century*, ed. Danny Fischer and Lucas Bessire (New York: New York University Press, 2012), 124–42.

I want to extend a special thank you to my editors Valerie Millholland and Gisela Fosado at Duke University Press. This is the third book I have produced with Valerie, and her never-ending enthusiasm, support, creativity, friendship, insights, and love for Mexico and Latin America are much appreciated. Gisela provided wonderful ongoing support, advice, and encouragement, particularly as we navigated the new path of producing an electronic book version with integral digital content. I am grateful also to the two anonymous reviewers whose careful reading of the manuscript and insightful suggestions made the book better.

I thank Alejandro de Ávila for his ongoing interest and support of this project and the love and knowledge he shares with our children. To my sons, José Angel and Gabriel, who accompanied me on important parts of the research and writing, I thank you for your company, patience, and love. To my life partner, Ellen Herman, I offer my profound appreciation, gratitude, and love for all we have been through and all she has given me in supporting my work for this book and every day as we continue the journey of life together.

1

Testimony

Human Rights and Social Movements

I am a woman born in Oaxaca of Zapotec and Mixtec blood. We Oaxacan women ask that a woman be treated with the same rights as a man. Our mission as women is to create, educate, communicate, and participate. That is why we are here occupying the state radio and TV station. . . . From the countryside to the city, we Oaxacan women are tired of bearing alone this burden of the repression we are experiencing from the long line of people who have governed us and from our current governor, Ulises Ruiz. . . .

We went out into the streets on the first of August to tell Ulises Ruiz that he had to leave Oaxaca. We are women who don't usually have a voice because we are brown, we are short, we are fat, and they think that we don't represent the people, but we do. WE are the face of Oaxaca. . . . It is too bad that the government doesn't recognize the greatness, the heart, and the valor of the women who are here. We are here because we want a free Mexico, a democratic Mexico, and we have had enough. . . . They will have to take us out of here dead, but we are going to defend the TV station and radio.

—Fidelia Vásquez, testifying inside the Corporacíon Oaxaqueña de Radio y Televisíon after women took it over, August 5, 2006, Oaxaca, Oaxaca

---

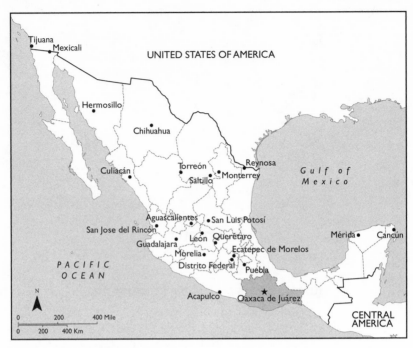

Map 1.1 Oaxaca, Mexico. DOI: 10.7264/N3C8276G

A majority of the indigenous, rural, and urban inhabitants in Latin American countries receive news and culture through oral and visual media: radio, television, videos (commercial and self-produced), and sites like YouTube. Oral testimony is a long-standing form of political participation in indigenous and rural communities. Most basically, testimony refers to a person's account of an event or experience as delivered from the lips of a person through a speech act. It is an oral telling of a person's perception of an event. It signifies witnessing, from the Latin root *testis*, or witness. As indicated by Fidelia's testimony, there are also important performative and public aspects of oral testimony.

This book seeks to illuminate the relationships among oral testimony, rights claiming, and identity formation in contemporary social movements. Examining these relationships can provide a crucial window on the continuing importance of culture in politics and on the ways social movements organize and engage with states. Testimony and rights claiming permit silenced groups to speak and to be heard, to enact alternative visions for political and cultural participation, and to formulate new, hybrid forms of identity. Oral narrative can play an important role in creating an individu-

Map 1.2 Primary locations in Oaxaca named in the text. DOI: 10.7264/
N37H1GGR

al's political identity, as well as in contributing to other kinds of identities. These identities become shared in specific times and places by a group of individuals and can sometimes help to create new cultures that influence how to do politics, defend rights, and engage with the state.

This book centers on a social movement in Oaxaca, Mexico, and the emergence in June 2006 of the Asamblea Popular de los Pueblos de Oaxaca (Popular Assembly of the Peoples of Oaxaca, APPO). A coalition of over three hundred organizations, APPO disrupted the usual functions of the Oaxaca state government for six months. It took over state radio and TV stations and began to construct a more inclusive and participatory political vision for the state, until the Mexican federal police force intervened. A complex mixture of movements—including those of teachers, indigenous peoples, women, students, peasants, and urban neighborhoods—had coexisted in Oaxaca for several decades and was the political soup out of which the Oaxacan social movement of 2006 emerged. The state of Oaxaca is also characterized by the strong presence of sixteen different indigenous languages and long traditions of community assemblies that use personal testimonials as an integral form of political participation. This social movement relied heavily on oral testimony, which was heard in marches and rallies, in grassroots video productions, on the state and commercial radio and TV stations that were taken over by the movement, and in nightly

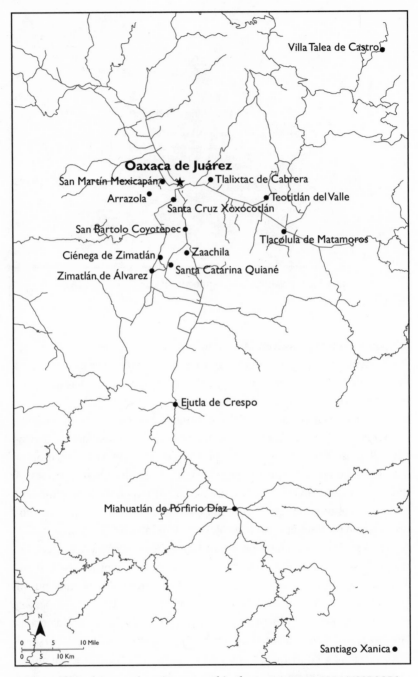

Map 1.3 Central Oaxaca locations named in the text. DOI: 10.7264/N33R0QR1

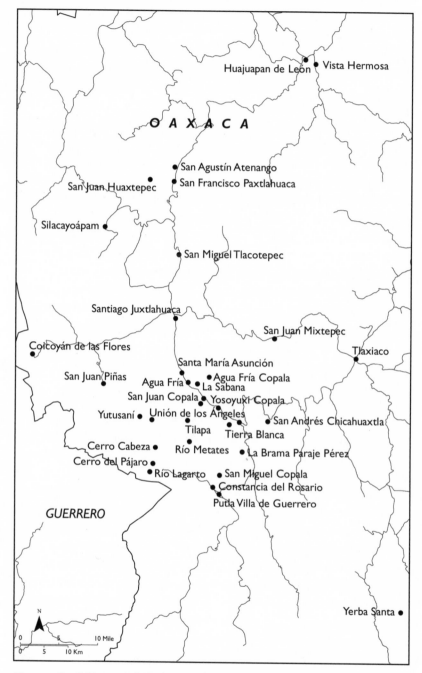

Map 1.4 Juxtlahuaca and Huajuapan de León and Mixtec Baja region of Oaxaca. DOI: 10.7264/N300001D

conversations at the hundreds of neighborhood barricades constructed throughout the city.

The movement was met with strong repression. In the course of just six months (June–November 2006), at least twenty-three people were killed, hundreds were arrested and imprisoned, and over twelve hundred complaints were filed with human rights commissions. Since then the violence has decreased and human rights violations have continued. The state government repression of the Oaxacan social movement in 2006 involved explicit strategies of targeted assassinations, torture, fear and intimidation through unjustified detentions, and the leveling of false charges against those detained. It also included militarization of Oaxaca City and other regions by unmarked paramilitary convoys and marked police and military vehicles, the targeting of movement leaders and others on a website identifying them as "already eliminated" or needing to be eliminated, and the photographing and videotaping by security forces of movement participants in public marches and occupations. The electoral victory of an opposition alliance in July 2010 and the governorship of Gabino Cué Monteagudo (whose term ends in 2016) in Oaxaca may provide a path for reconciliation for some, but they also create an expectation for significant change in the way Oaxaca is governed and a new notion of who "counts" politically, economically, and socially.

The "official" story of what happened in Oaxaca between June and November 2006 looks quite different from what was experienced by the participants. It goes something like this: In May 2006 a large group of teachers who belonged to Sección 22 (Local 22) of the Sindicato Nacional de Trabajadores de Educación (National Union of Educational Workers, SNTE) and were part of an independent movement within the larger national union engaged in their annual sit-in, where they tried to negotiate higher salaries for themselves and better conditions for schoolchildren. Governor Ulises Ruiz Ortiz, who had been generous in bargaining with them the previous year, decided that enough was enough. He gave the teachers a reasonable offer and ordered them to go back to their classrooms. Instead of accepting the offer, the teachers dug in. In order to keep peace and to guarantee that the state's children received an education, the governor sent in state police to remove the teachers from their occupation in the historic center of the city. The teachers got angry over this response and fought back. The police were not successful in removing them from the center. In the process, the police inadvertently tear-gassed and wounded some innocent bystanders. This angered other people in the city. There were many police hurt as well.

While the teachers remained in the center of the city, they exploited the anger of the innocent bystanders who were wounded and tear-gassed. This generated sympathy for the teachers' cause, and they were able to take advantage of the discontent to build alliances with other organizations whose leaders were also waiting for an opportunity to gain a broader audience. The teachers and the new alliance of radical organizations known as APPO called for the governor to resign, but there was no reason for him to do so; he was established and worked to negotiate with APPO and the teachers. Instead of negotiating, APPO illegally took over public buildings and TV and radio stations, vandalized the city, and caused a great deal of insecurity. Radical elements began to take over APPO, and it was necessary to increase security around the city in the fall of 2006. Throughout this period appeals were made to the federal government to intervene and help calm down the escalating conflict. After an American journalist was killed in October 2006, it became necessary for the federal government to solve the problem. They sent in the Policía Federal Preventitativa Federal or the Preventative Police (PFP), who restored order and security in the city.

While this "official" story was widely disseminated in Mexico and elsewhere, it is not the story I am going to tell. Rather, my purpose is to share the untold story of the 2006 social movement as experienced by those who participated in it and were strongly affected by it, whether or not they were directly involved. While the significant scale of the violence and the high number of human rights abuses, cases of torture, and assassinations would suggest the necessity for a national truth commission to investigate what happened, such a national commission has not been created. There were national and international delegations that wrote reports about what happened, and the human rights cases were reviewed by Mexico's Supreme Court. While the court did find that there were human rights violations committed in Oaxaca during 2006, it has no power to sanction and punish those who committed the abuses. There is currently an investigative Oaxaca state commission, La Fiscalía de Investigaciones en Delitos de Trascendencia Social (Office to Investigate Crimes of Social Significance) which is examining the assassinations, arrests, and human rights violations committed in 2006. However, it must follow all legal processes and function on the basis of evidence. Because much of the evidence linking people from the administration of Ulises Ruiz Ortiz to crimes committed has been destroyed, and at least two people who headed up security and policing operations in 2006 have been murdered, the work of the Fiscalia is slow and will take a long time to develop. In August 2012, Governor Gabino Cué Monteagudo presented the Oaxaca state congress with an initiative to create a truth commission which would investigate human rights violations committed against APPO during 2006 and 2007. As of this writing the commission had yet to be named and to begin to work. The work of truth commissions can be important in ultimately changing the "truth" of what happened in conflicts such as this one. In addition, however, unlocking the voices of the unofficial story is crucial to changing the established "truth" of what happened and also in the production of the history and social memory associated with the events of 2006.

It is my contention that much of the knowledge, experience, and insight about the social movement of 2006 and its consequences now and in the future can be found in what we might call the testimonial archive and in testimonial performance. Oral testimony allows people to bear witness, archive their memories of wrongs committed, and represent personal histories within complex identity categories of race, ethnicity, gender, and class. My examination here of the role of oral testimony in human rights work, Latin American truth commissions, and social movements relates to important larger questions about memory and the ways that history and truth are understood and interpreted. These larger questions include the following: Who defines legitimate speakers? Who defines history? Who controls and legitimates social memory, and how? How do we understand and interpret "truth," whether in a legal context, in the construction of local, regional, or national histories, or in the formation of identity and social movements?

Testimonials in Human Rights Work and Latin American Truth Commissions

The practice of oral testimony has been broadly defined by Shoshona Felman and Dori Laub as a form of retrospective public witnessing of the shattering events of a history that is "essentially not over and is in some sense brought into being by the (itself interminable) process of testimonial witnessing" (1992: xvii, xv; see Sarkar and Walker 2010: 7). Since the 1980s Latin American truth commissions have placed individual oral testimonies that are focused on specific cases, individual victims, and individual perpetrators in opposition to the collective experiences of victims that are related to structural and systemic violence (Taylor 1994: 197; Grandin and Klubock 2007: 4–6). The contemporary truth commission form, as documented by Grandin and Klubock (2007: 1), begins in 1982 in Latin America with the establishment of Bolivia's Comisión Nacional de Desaparecidos (National Commission of the Disappeared), followed by the Argentine Comisión Nacional sobre la Desaparición de Personas (National Commission on Disappeared People) in 1983. Some later commissions added the terms *reconciliation* and *historical clarification* to their titles, suggesting not only the documentation of human rights abuses but also a process of healing, forgiveness, and national unity—ideas that are included under the concept of transitional justice.[1] This justice, of course, usually came with impunity for the perpetrators of violence. Eight different truth commissions have functioned in Latin America: Argentina's Commission on the Disappeared (1983), Bolivia's President's National Commission on Inquiry into Disappearances (1982), Chile's National Commission for Truth and Reconciliation (1990), Ecuador's Truth and Justice Commission (1996), El Salvador's Commission on the Truth for El Salvador (1992), Guatemala's Historical Clarification Commission (1994), Peru's Truth and Reconciliation Commission (2000), and Uruguay's Commission for the Investigation of the Situation of the Disappeared and Related Events (2000); (Arias and del Campo: 2009: 9).

The impact of these commissions in eight different countries over almost two decades cannot be underestimated in terms of their role in rewriting national histories. As such, truth commissions are important archives of historical materials that are and will be continually drawn upon to interpret periods of brutal violence and dictatorships as well as the "democratic transitions" that followed, usually accompanied by neoliberal economic development policy as part of the healing process. As characterized by Grandin and Klubock, "truth commissions work, at least in theory, similar to other myths and rituals of nationalism, to sacramentalize violence into a useful creation myth" (2007: 3). Thus truth commissions can work to paper over past atrocities in the name of "getting over it" and "moving on" to "prioritize catharsis and forgiveness over punishment" (5). In sum, they may or may not function to punish the perpetrators of human rights violations.

While I do not disagree with this analysis, in this book I am concerned with a different dimension of truth commissions, one that centers on the testifier as an active social agent engaged in a personal and collective performative act that can potentially broaden the meaning of truth to advance alternative and contested understandings of history. While Grandin and Klubock point out that "in the case of commissions whose charge is both truth and reconciliation (Chile and Peru, for example) and forgiveness in the case of South Africa, it might be argued that the goal of reconciliation imposes profound obstacles to the production of historical truth" (2007: 6), we might also question whether any process can produce a homogeneous historical truth equally believed and understood by all. Part of what happens in the process of truth commissions, with their inclusion of people who have been literally silent and invisible in officially sanctioned spaces of legality, is that these people and others close to them have the experience of speaking and being heard, of asserting their dignity through the process, and also of becoming cognizant of their rights to speak and be heard—processes that are at the heart of how testimony counts in social movements.

As suggested by Kimberly Theidon (2007: 456), one of the important purposes of truth commissions is the rewriting of national narratives so that they are more inclusive of groups that have been historically marginalized. Theidon points out rightly that such forums usually have a focus on victims, are victim-friendly and victim-centered—producing a narrative standard that many may feel compelled to follow. Fiona Ross (2003: 178–79) has made similar observations in her analysis of the South African Truth and Reconciliation Commission, as has Julie Taylor in her discussion of Argentina's truth commission. Taylor argues that truth commissions tend to transform individuals, political activists, and others into either "innocent or transgressing individuals with individual rights and obligations" or "victims" (1994: 197–98). But victim narratives in court may be recast elsewhere with very different meanings.

In her analysis of the focus groups and public assemblies conducted by the Peruvian Truth Commission in Ayacucho in 2002, Theidon found a preponderance of witness testimony in public arenas about rape and sexual violence that primarily followed a victim narrative. But when the same women entered into conversations with Theidon and her research team outside of official venues, they always located sexual violence within its broader social contexts: "They detailed the preconditions that structured vulnerability and emphasized their efforts to minimize harm to themselves and to the people they cared for. With their insistence on context, women situated their experience of sexual violence—those episodes of brutal victimization—within womanly narratives of heroism" (2007: 265). In other words, we cannot read the larger social impact of people's statements in truth commissions simply in terms of what is said within the courtroom or the official forum. The same people are circulating their testimonials in forums outside of the courtroom, where they may be expressed and interpreted quite differently. For this reason, it is important to consider the testimonials that are given during truth commissions or in other public forums in a broader context.

Giving testimony affects the people who provide it, both in and outside of the courtroom. Because truth commissions function within national legal systems and rely on both eyewitness and third-person testimonies—which were particularly useful because of women's extreme reluctance to report on rape in Guatemala, Peru, and South Africa (Theidon 2007: 458; Mantilla 2005: 3)—the courtroom becomes a platform for speaking, giving juridical recognition to the voices of victims, and validating their right to talk both inside of and outside of the courtroom (Jelin and Kaufman 2000: 94). As Rachel Sieder states, "The legal system is converted into a contested site of meaning over state accountability and citizen's rights as the dominant ideas and values that underpin the law provide a framework for advancing alternative understandings—of history, democracy, rights" (2001: 204). In his magisterial trilogy *The Memory Box of Pinochet's Chile*, Steve Stern (2004, 2006, 2010) argues for "the study of contentious memory as a process of competing selective remembrances, ways of giving meaning to and drawing legitimacy from human experience." He writes, "In the approach I have taken, the social actors behind distinct frameworks are seeking to define that which is truthful and meaningful about a great collective trauma" (2004: xxix). For Stern, the point of oral history and the testifying process is not simply to establish the "factual truth or falsehood of events . . . but to be able to understand what social truths or processes led people to tell their stories the way they do, in recognizable patterns" (2006: xxviii). If truth commissions are looked at as important arenas for oral expression bound to larger contexts, then we can broaden our view of the impact of testimonials.

Through this process, oral testimony has become a vehicle for broadening historical truth by opening up the range of who can legitimately speak and be heard and, ultimately, who participates in the construction of shared social memory. It is interesting to note that in truth commission court hearings, the evidentiary standards are flexible. This in turn requires a flexing of the notion of truth, moving away from strictly empirical, material evidence to incorporating other forms of information and broadening how we think of truth and perhaps come to acknowledge multiple truths. As Theidon points out, "While legal standards of proof might disallow 'hearsay' or anecdotal evidence, truth commissions can work with other evidentiary standards to establish historical truth" (2007: 458). In Peru, for instance, third-person testimonies were permitted; Theidon notes that the majority of information about rape and sexual violence came through third-person testimonies in which women talked about what they had heard or seen happen to others, not to themselves. Theidon and others have interpreted this as evidence of the self-censorship and community gender policing that has permeated many public hearings in truth commissions (see 2007: 458; Ross 2003: 169–70).

Recent discussions regarding the role of testimony in documentary films also centers on what kind of "truth" is captured through testimonials in film. This discussion is useful for interpreting testimony in courtrooms and social movements as well. In implicit dialogue with the Rigoberta Menchú controversy of the late 1990s that was launched by David Stoll's (1999) book *Rigoberta Menchú and the Story of All Poor Guatemalans*, José Rabasa suggests that all "forms of collecting testimony are by definition forms of engaged dissemination of truth" (2010: 234). In his analysis of different documentaries about the massacre of forty-five indigenous Tzotzil men, women, and children by paramilitaries in Acteal, Chiapas, in 1997, Rabasa suggests that simply including a testimonial in a documentary "necessarily involves recognition of its veracity. . . . Testimonial documentaries are therefore political interventions in the context of a disputed truth" (234). Instead of returning to the overworked conversation about Stoll's book, Rabasa turns to a different critique of testimony written by Beatriz Sarlo (2005), who suggests the epistemological limits to knowing the past in Argentina through the use of testimonies in Argentina's truth commission. While Sarlos's critique comes from a deconstructionist framework in which the certainty of all knowledge is questioned (whether from an empirical point of view calling for "evidence" or from belief in the truth of testimony), Rabasa suggests that we not enter into the trap of determining "the truth." Instead he suggests that we "observe that testimony partakes of other forms of knowledge besides those based on fact and falsification or even on experience. . . . The point is that mistaken memories, amnesias, and other such aporia should not entail the dismissal of testimony, but rather a redefinition of epistemological terms that would no longer call forth factuality as the ultimate criterion" (2010: 235). This is an important contribution to the argument I am making here. I argue that to take testimony seriously is to acknowledge that it is a form of knowledge production and part of the epistemologies that engage a mixture of forms of archiving including oral, visual, and textual information. Rabasa suggests that testimonial film can sidestep the framework that revisionists attempt to impose about "fact checking" not by an immediate, innocent, and iconoclastic expression of truth but by taking full advantage of what he calls the "fabric of testimonial film" (235). His strategy for interpreting documentaries about the Acteal massacre comes from Bruno Latour. Interpreting Latour, he states, "Belief is bound to the iconoclastic destruction of the icon. Fetish and fact can be traced to the same root. The fact is that which is fabricated and not fabricated. . . . But the fetish too is that which is fabricated and not fabricated. . . . Rather than seeing these audio-visual texts as truthful representations of the community of martyrs . . . we ought to underscore that these documentaries . . . fabricate and not fabricate . . . the truth of Acteal by . . . a variety of means" (237).

If we take Rabasa's insights into consideration when looking at testimonials, we can consider them orally based information sources that can produce partial insights that broaden the range of perceptions and experiences included in the historical record. If understood in this way they become very useful in complicating the texture of national histories and truths. Here testimonials become an important resource for broadening the story about the social movement of 2006 in Oaxaca. Rabasa's suggestion, like that of Theidon, is that we evaluate testimonials not in terms of themselves but as part of a broader social and historical context. When we do, our definition of *truth* is necessarily multiple and complicated.

Testimonials and Social Movements

Prior to the Spanish conquest, indigenous peoples in Mexico had several types of writing that have since been found in codices, maps, and glyphs on architecture. Recent research on indigenous literacies during the colonial period suggests that we discard the notion that indigenous literacy was either lost to what became an entirely oral circulation of indigenous languages or that indigenous peoples are only recently shifting from an oral to a written culture. Joanne Rappaport and Tom Cummins's recent research on how Andean peoples received and subverted the conventions of Spanish pictorial and alphabetic representations suggests a broad understanding of literacy that links alphabetic, pictorial, oral, and corporeal elements, including oral performance. Citing Diego Valadés's extensive book on memory, *Rhetorica christiana* (published in 1579), they point out that his "'visual alphabet' is not directed toward reading or writing a text, but instead is meant as a tool for recalling from memory texts that can be recited out loud. The alphabet and literacy were thus something visual and very much part of orality. The two forms of literacy, visual and alphabetic, were thus mediated by orality, a practice common to Spaniards and natives alike" (Rappaport and Cummins 2012: 8).

Historians such as Mark King and John Monighan have suggested that Mixtec codices—which are nearly half of the surviving books we have from before the Spanish conquest—can be treated as scripts or scores for performances (King 1994: 102–3): "Mixtec books represent sacred texts or scripts for the performance of elite histories, including the ancient, mythic past, especially the genealogy-based stories with which we are all most familiar. These scripts were written in what was thought of as an ancient elite-class dialect" (105). Monaghan writes:

> In determining how the information contained in the codices may have been broadcast, it should be pointed out that the codices were, in all probability, based on oral traditions. . . . King (1988) forcefully argued that they were produced with the intention of being read aloud. This suggests that the information within the codices was made available to wider audiences through their presentation in a public form, and that we should be looking at these documents not solely as comic strips to be read, but also as scripts to be performed. (1990: 133)

Elizabeth Hill Boone writes about "performing histories." Focusing on Aztec pictorial histories, she states, "Aztec pictorial histories were read aloud to an audience, they were interpreted, and their images were expanded and embellished in the oration of the full story. The pictoral histories were painted specifically to be the rough texts of a performance" (1994: 71). The pictorial signs in the histories, she states, were reduced to their most essential and basic visual forms. The location of events, their participants, and time were reduced and abstracted, signaling to the reader and performer what should be emphasized. The performance of the histories, according to Hill Boone, was flexible and "permitted embellishment and variation in the telling" as interpreters told or sung pictorial histories to an audience (72).

The contents of the codices were likely performed for multiple audiences. One audience may have been composed of elites in order to establish the legitimacy of one family's claim to a territory and the governing power that went with it. According to Fray Francisco de Burgoa's description of Mixtecos during the seventeenth century, Mixtec elites would recite from the codices in assemblies: "They used to hang some of these papers extended as tables of cosmology in their main rooms as a sign of greatness and vanity, honoring themselves by dealing in their assemblies with such matters" ([1670] 1989: 210).

The work of these anthropologists suggests the long-standing ways oral performance and different forms of literacy are interconnected in indigenous communities and histories. The notion that indigenous languages are "merely oral" is linked to the emergence of mestizo nationalism. Following independence and the creation of nationalist cultures in Latin American countries like Mexico, Guatemala, Peru, Bolivia, and Ecuador that had large indigenous populations, "indigenous languages became oral in a new way, defined not only by their oral transmission practices but also in contrast with Spanish. . . . Ideas that indigenous languages were just dialects and hence 'cannot be written down' found increasing traction" (Faudree 2013: 51–52). Until national programs of *indigenismo* abandoned their assimilationist tendencies in the late 1970s and 1980s in Mexico and elsewhere and began to legitimate the teaching of reading and writing in indigenous languages in schools, indigenous and other rural communities were lettered in Spanish. The transmission of history and local knowledge and the administration of indigenous rituals, systems of governance, and law, however, continued to be done orally in hundreds of indigenous languages in Latin America. We must remember, however, that this orality is linked to a history of pictorial, alphabetic, and visual literacy.

In fact one could argue that for a significant part of the twentieth century in Latin America, the archiving of knowledge and history took place orally not only for indigenous peoples but for many others as well. In Mexico, for example, only about 15 percent of the population was literate in 1910. By 1940 literacy campaigns raised this rate to 41.7 percent overall. But literacy rates in the heavily indigenous South remained lower. In 1940 the literacy rate in Chiapas was 21.2 percent and in Oaxaca 20.2 percent. In 1960 the literacy rate in Chiapas was up to 39.3 percent and in Oaxaca 40.9 percent (all figures from Greer 1969: 468). In 2000 Chiapas had a literacy rate of 77 percent (Speed and Leyva Solano 2008: 21) and Oaxaca of slightly below 77 percent in 1999 (Corbacho and Shwartz 2002: 19). These continued to improve in the twenty-first century. By the year 2000—with the exception of females in Guatemala and Bolivia—approximately 90 percent of Latin Americans could read and write, primarily in Spanish (UNESCO Institute for Statistics 2002). Nevertheless the data from Chiapas and Oaxaca suggest that even when national literacy rates became high in Latin America during the twentieth century, for significant numbers of people—particularly women and everyone in heavily indigenous parts of Latin America—the oral transmission of knowledge continued to be important.

Given the long history of oral knowledge transmission in Latin America and its continued importance, the role of oral testimony in more contemporary social movements should come as no surprise. What is interesting, however, is a lack of analytical discussion about the ways oral testimony functions in contemporary Latin American social movements. One of the most useful sources of analysis comes from performance studies, which focuses on the testimonial as an event that joins together memory and knowledge replication. Dori Laub, one of the coeditors of a 1992 book on testimony, writes, "Knowledge in the testimony is . . . not simply a factual given that is reproduced and replicated by the testifier, but a genuine advent, an event in its own right" (65). Sarkar and Walker observe that testimonials are performative "with regards to the truths and memories of testifying and witnessing" (2010: 10).

My argument here about the role of testimony in Latin American social movements, particularly those bound directly or indirectly to indigenous contexts, is that because indigenous languages have a long history of being used orally, performatively, and even in writing (at least by elites) until the mid-1800s, we need to center an analysis of testimonials in a space that considers them in all of these dimensions. The work of Diana Taylor in performance studies is particularly useful here. Taylor locates some of her discussion in the strain between the concepts of the archive and the repertoire:

> The archive includes, but is not limited to, written text. The repertoire contains verbal performances—songs, prayers, speeches—as well as non-verbal practices. The written/oral divide does, on one level, capture the archive/repertoire difference I am developing in so far as the means of transmission differ, as do the requirements of storage and dissemination. The repertoire, whether in terms of verbal or nonverbal expression, transmits live, embodied actions. As such, traditions are stored in the body through various pneumonic methods, and transmitted "live" in the here and now to a live audience. (2003: 24)

In moving away from the notion that writing is equivalent to memory and knowledge—an idea developed during the sixteenth century as a part of colonial regimes' focus on writing and printing (Anderson 1983: 67–82; de Certeau 1988)—Taylor proposes that performance studies allow us to "take seriously the repertoire of embodied practices as an important system of knowing and transmitting knowledge" (2003: 26). "Traditions stored in the body through various pneumonic methods" refers to the ways that memory is written onto and stored in the body through devices such as song, dance, chant, movement, and other oral and physical techniques that trigger associations and assist memory. For example, in the social movement of 2006, the chant "Ya cayó, ya cayó, Ulises ya cayó" (He is gone, he is gone, Ulises is already gone), chanted while moving the right hand up and down, is a pneumonic method associated with the memory of large crowds gathered in marches and rallies seeking the ouster of Oaxaca's governor. In indigenous and other social movements tied to contexts in which knowledge production and transmission happen partially or even primarily through oral testimony, Taylor thus suggests that we look at the performance of repertoires as forming part of the knowledge archives. Pushing against the idea prevalent in some strains of cultural studies to turn everything into a text, she suggests that we pay attention to the repertoire. She goes further by suggesting a new methodology for helping us to understand testimonials as they are narrated in real time and space and points out that they take on second, third, fourth, and even infinite lives through their travel in the press, on the Internet, radio, and television, in gossip, and in other forms of human codification. Testimonials as recorded and disseminated by human rights workers are excellent examples of oral narratives that are important parts of knowledge archives.

It is important to acknowledge that the methodology I have used here—recording testimonies on audio and video—is not the same as what happens in a face-to-face encounter in the performance of testimony. Digitizing testimony, while offering a greater degree of connection with and access to the embodiment of testimony, nevertheless freezes the moment out of context and makes it portable and replicable. Textualizing testimonies, as I have done in this book, does the same. While this may be so obvious it need not be mentioned, it is important to acknowledge what the research method does to the material. I believe, however, that the use of video in recording testimony allows us to begin to see the emotional power of the speech act of testifying and to begin to appreciate how important such acts are in social movements such as the one described here.

Collaborative Methods:
A Framework for Working with Testimonials

Being present in Oaxaca during the explosion of the social movement in 2006 forever changed my perspective of the city, the state, and my place in it. The longevity and intensity of my emotional, family, and friendship ties there, in conjunction with both the amazing events and the frightening repression, produced a powerful need to tell the stories of what happened. To narrate. To testify. To witness. Like a spectacular storm that produces rippling effects of water and wind present for centuries in the geological record, what happened in 2006 is a part of the social and political record of Oaxaca. In that archive are recipes for new ways of organizing driven by social media; for horizontal relationships and forms of decision making; for the rights to speak and be heard; for participatory democracy; for women transforming public and commercial media; for embodied critiques of power; for hybrid forms of urban racial and ethnic identity; for indigenous and nonindigenous alliances; for creative strategies for claiming rights; for occupying metaphorical and physical space; and for challenging inequalities.

One of my strongest motivations for writing this book, and for creating the initial website that preceded it (Making Rights a Reality: Oaxaca Social Movement, 2006–Present http://www.mrarOaxaca.uoregon.edu/) and which is incorporated into this book's website, was to support human rights work in Oaxaca. Because I have been working in Oaxaca since 1983 and spend one to two months every year there, it is home for me. A large group of *comadres, compadres*, godchildren, old and dear friends, longtime academic colleagues and collaborators, and family place me in an extended network of wonderful people, communities, and institutions. While I do not have Mexican citizenship, I feel a profound sense of cultural citizenship through my life in the city and state of Oaxaca. As defined by Richard Flores and Rina Benmayor (1997), cultural citizenship involves everyday activities through which marginalized social groups can claim recognition, public space, and eventually specific rights. Renato Rosaldo (1997) is interested in the concept of cultural citizenship as a way to help develop full democratic participation. While I by no means consider myself to be part of a marginalized social group in either the United States or Mexico, because I am not a Mexican citizen my rights of political expression are significantly limited there.

Article 9 of the Mexican Federal Constitution guarantees the right of peaceful association for any licit purpose, and Article 6 assures freedom of expression, but these guarantees do not apply to foreigners. As noted by the Mexican legal scholar Jorge Vargas, foreigners are prohibited from getting involved in any political associations or activities: "Pursuant to Article 33 of the Federal Constitution, the Federal Executive is empowered with exclusive and absolute authority to deport from the Mexican territory, 'immediately and without any previous legal action,' any foreigner whom the Mexican immigration authorities or agents deem to be engaged in any political activity" (2008: 848). Vargas notes the expulsion of European nationals and Americans who attempted to document human rights violations in Mexico (849). Foreign researchers are thus bound to tread carefully in their public interactions with the press and media in relation to political demonstrations and marches and in how they express their observations in any public forum. A rule of thumb that I learned while participating as a Mexican government–credentialed electoral observer in 2000 applies to many situations: describe what I observe but refrain from public political pronouncements in the press or other forms of media. I must note that for foreign academics working in the United States, the same restrictions apply, and that those colleagues often identify as cultural citizens of the United States in the same sense I am talking about for myself in Mexico. For me and others working as foreigners but identifying as cultural citizens of Mexico, the question becomes how to enact a politics of accountability while simultaneously dealing with our professional and academic roles as anthropologists.

The anthropologist Vivian Newdick explored this issue in her dissertation on the relationships between law, governance, and social movements centered on Tsotsil and Tseltal-Maya women's activism in Chiapas from 1994 to 2011. She writes, "In posing the question of the relationship between my positionality, my participation in (and disassociation with) Zapatista autonomy, and how this shapes my ethnography, I would propose to retain the idea of 'accountability' despite the dynamics of association and disassociation in which I have taken part. This question foregrounds various problems, various other questions: how is one accountable to a set of ideas, rather than a group of people?" (2012: 16–17). Centered on the interrelated members of three families who have lived in seven different villages and many of whom parted ways with the Zapatistas, Newdick's ethnography was challenged to figure out what accountability means under shifting circumstances, shifting relationships with the actors she spent the most time with, and in relation to a member of the high command of the Ejército Zapatista de Liberación Nacional (Zapatista Army of National Liberation, EZLN) who told her "it was better that they didn't approve [her] project since now they wouldn't be controlling what [she] wrote" (17). Ultimately Newdick decided that her accountability was to a political process that cannot be reduced to particular people. While her discussion is unusual in North American ethnographies, our Latin American colleagues have much to teach us on issues of accountability.

The Colombian anthropologist Myriam Jimeno has articulated the tension inherent in the dual position of being a researcher and a fellow citizen with those who are subjects of inquiry. She describes of the history of Colombian anthropology since the mid-1940s:

In countries such as Colombia, anthropological practice is permanently faced with the uneasy choice between adopting dominant anthropological concepts and orientations or modifying them, adapting them, rejecting them, and proposing alternatives. The need to adapt the practice stems from the specific social condition of anthropologists in these countries; that is our dual position as both researchers and fellow citizens of our subjects of study, as a result of which we are continually torn between our duty as scientists and our role as citizen. (2006: 59)

Her point is that political neutrality is impossible and accountability to political processes is inevitable when one identifies as a citizen in the shared polity of the people one is researching. This shared interest in the political implications and influence of research leads to a set of questions that are quite distinct from the position of researchers who consider themselves "outsiders" in relation to their research projects and who perceive that they move in and out of "the field."

The shared experiences of anthropologists who conduct their studies among those with whom they share citizenship—not just legal but cultural and political citizenship in terms of "considering political communities and systems of rights that emerge at levels of governance above or below those of independent states or those that cut across international borders" (Bauböck 2003: 704)—have much to offer us in terms of rethinking our methods. The lessons learned from de-centering the notion of the field and seeing ourselves as always "in the field" can work not only for those who conduct research at home in the context of their daily lives but also for those who conduct their research elsewhere (see Uribe 1997; Stephen 2002: 13–15). Operating as citizens not only of individual or multiple nations (in a legal and cultural sense) but also as citizens of the planet in our role as anthropologists is one way to open up our thinking. Most of us don't push hard enough in terms of how we position ourselves in the sociopolitical proximity of our subjects in the globalized Americas.

While there is perhaps a fuzzy boundary between the practice of anthropology as a discipline and the social action we take as citizens (cultural or otherwise; Jimeno 2006: 61), it is important to acknowledge differences of power, positioning, and exit that distinguish me from people in Oaxaca. As someone who has conducted research in Oaxaca over the past twenty-five years as well as in Oregon with many Oaxacans who live there, I am a transborder researcher with a visa. I can come and go when I please and I have *permiso* (legal authority) to return to Oregon when things get dangerous or difficult in Oaxaca. Most people in Oaxaca don't have that ability. Oaxacans have to stay and try to survive—as attested to by many whose stories are told here—or leave and struggle to survive in the United States.

Unlike most of my Oaxacan counterparts, I am working in the multisited field of a transborder ethnographer. One dimension of this is recognizing that I am never "in" and "out" of the field. My life in Oregon and in Oaxaca is part of one field (see Stephen 2002: 7–15). Another is the ongoing difference that all researchers experience in that they are "conducting research" and not just "living life," as those around them are in a field context. Thus as a transborder researcher I am at least doubly different from those I am working with: I choose when to come and go in and out of places and countries, and I am engaged in the particular project of research. We could add to the list other dimensions of difference such as class, race, ethnicity, and nation, which all, in one form or another, make me distinct from those I was working with in the creation of this book. However, these differences and my privileged position as researcher with a visa to come and go do not erase my capacity and responsibility to engage in a politics of accountability with those around me. Although I am prohibited from producing public political analysis, my role as an anthropologist facilitated the documentation and dissemination of the points of view of those around me. As someone deeply committed to what I have elsewhere labeled ethnographic collaborative research (Stephen 2007b: 321–25), I wanted to know how a direct defiance of the subject-object dichotomy could change the way I approached my research topic (Hale and Stephen 2013: 21).

In my role as a co-initiator and co-coordinator of the first phase of the Otros Saberes (other knowledges) project of the Latin American Studies Association (LASA), I spent many hours contemplating the lessons of collaborative research. Conceived as a LASA project in 2004, Otros Saberes has a primary goal of promoting "collaborative research between civil society– and academy-based intellectuals focused on research topics of interest to both, giving priority to topics to which the civil society organizations in question assign special importance" (Hale and Stephen 2013: 3). These lessons came home to me as I contemplated my course of action in relation to the social movement of Oaxaca in 2006 and beyond. Important questions included the following: What happens if I subject my ideas about researching the Oaxacan social movement to a horizontal dialogue with protagonists? What kinds of suggestions and insights will I receive? What research problems will those in and around the social movement consider to be important, and why? How can I create the best conditions for people in and around the social movement to assert their knowledge, analysis, and political judgment at each stage of the process? (see Hale and Stephen 2013: 21).

I was in Oaxaca in July and August 2006 with the intention of filming a wide range of activities, including weddings, *mayordomías* (sponsorship of a cult celebration for the local saint), local dances, the process of communal labor known as *tequio*, and medical plant use for a course I was to coteach with four Mixtec community outreach workers titled Indigenous Immigrants in Oregon. We had mapped out the curriculum and planned to show short video clips in relation to particular units. I was also visiting with a group of colleagues from the University of Oregon who were seeking to forge stronger links between the university's Center for the Study of Women in Society and several institutions in Oaxaca. Because of the social movement and my longtime connection to many who were getting involved, I began to film events and conduct interviews, and a new research project quickly emerged.

My experience in the Otros Saberes project and prior collaborative research projects in Oregon led me to discussions with observers, activists, and participants of the Oaxacan social movement, as well as with citizens who opposed the movement about what kind of research project to engage in, what methods to use, what results would be desirable, and what kind of collaborative process could work for carrying it out given the constraints of time, resources, and location. Initial conversations focused on the urgency of responding to human rights violations, such as those documented in chapter 4 here, and the need to disseminate points of view that were being shut out of the mainstream media. Because I was in Oaxaca with a video camera for another project, the camera, in addition to my notebook and digital voice recorder, became a research tool. In July and August 2006 I filmed events and interviews and recorded testimonies, primarily with people I had known through my long history of research in Oaxaca. In many cases, these long-term friendships led to the recording of other testimonies. Some of the initial recordings were linked to documenting the cases of Ramiro Aragón Pérez, Juan Gabriel Ríos, and Elionai Santiago Sánchez, the assassination of José Jiménez Colmenares, and other human rights violations. Human rights workers such as Yésica Sánchez Maya of the Liga Mexicana por la Defensa de los Derechos Humanos (Mexican League for the Defense of Human rights, Limmedh) and others working on these cases were video-recording testimonies which were then disseminated through the press, on YouTube, and on organizational websites. This practice of knowledge production had some clear results: (1) the views of those who were survivors of human rights violations were directly accessible; (2) recording and putting testimonies on the Internet provided an alternative source of information to the mainstream media, which largely ignored the overall conflict in 2006; (3) dissemination of the testimonials legitimized the experiences of those who suffered from repression and human rights violations, particularly in their own families and communities; and (4) public recognition of rights violations made those who provided the testimony vulnerable to further repression by those they implicated in a climate of impunity.

In thinking with others about what kind of venue or product would work best to rapidly and effectively provide documentation of the 2006 social movement and the repression that accompanied it, we came to the conclusion that a multipronged approach would be best. The urgency of the human rights violations and the later political asylum case of Ramiro Aragón Pérez and his wife, Ruth Guzmán Sánchez, encouraged me to think about using a publication platform on the Internet that would center on the initial events and testimonies we had recorded in 2006.

With these ideas in mind, I returned to the University of Oregon in the fall of 2006 and began to transcribe the audio recordings and log the video we had recorded. In May 2007 the social conflict in Oaxaca moved into the orbit of my daily life. I began to work with Ramiro Aragón Pérez, Ruth Guzmán Sánchez, and their children on settling into a new life in the United States after fleeing from Mexico. Subsequently I worked to support their application for political asylum. We decided that recording further testimonials from their family members, human rights workers, and others could be useful for supporting their application and the applications of others who might follow. We also decided that we would create a number of products and work in different venues to disseminate information about their case and other human rights violations. We decided to create a DVD and a website and to give talks together at conferences and other venues. Importantly, we decided that we needed to produce educational tools that would provide information and background about the larger context of the 2006 movement. With these ideas in mind, during the summer of 2007 I returned to Oaxaca with a video camera and audio recorder. I recorded about thirty more testimonies from Ruth and Ramiro's family members, teachers, and others who were illegally detained, tortured, and imprisoned for their political activities, as well as from women who had participated in the takeover and reprogramming of radio and TV stations. I also began recording testimonies from those who were not a part of the social movement but were strongly affected by it, including working-class mothers and housewives, middle-class professionals, students, business people, and artisans.

After discussion in Oaxaca during the summer of 2007 about the different questions the project would try to answer, the kinds of testimonials we wanted to include, and the other kinds of background information that were necessary, I began to work closely with Ruth, Ramiro, and several University of Oregon students and a colleague to design a website. We decided that we would initially edit the video testimonials to a length of six to seven minutes, which would permit them to be posted on YouTube. The methodology we developed—in consultation with human rights workers, teachers, and others in Oaxaca—was that we would prepare draft versions of the testimonials, subtitle them, copy them to DVDs, and then review them with the people who provided them. We also decided to transcribe each interview in its totality, both to facilitate our editing process and to offer a complete transcript to all of our participants. In addition, we decided to make an initial website design and to share it with people from the organizations we had worked with as well as the people whose testimonies would be featured. We posted some of the draft video testimonials on a closed channel on YouTube that could be accessed only with a password. This allowed us access to draft videos from any place with a computer so that we could share them with people and make changes and corrections. Once we made the corrections we would remount the video testimonials on the closed channel so our participants could see the final result and provide their approval.

During the summer of 2008 I returned to Oaxaca with Jesse Nichols, who was an undergraduate at the University of Oregon at the time. Jesse had carried out an internship previously with Mal de Ojo TV (roughly translated as Evil Eye TV), an Oaxaca NGO formed in 2006 as a coalition of independent, indigenous, and community media workers who had a long history of collaborating with indigenous communities in the production of community video and radio. They dedicated themselves to covering the social movement in its repression. He was skilled in editing and subtitling and went on to assist with some of the filming and much of the subtitling for the videos included on the website. For several weeks Jesse and I met with all the people whose video testimonials I had recorded. We showed them the results and gave them a copy of their transcript if they wanted it. We also showed participants the initial website design and solicited their opinions and suggestions.

This step in our methodology proved to be of crucial importance: not only were we able to discuss personally with everyone what their video testimony would look like and make any changes they wanted, but we were also able to get a broad set of opinions and ideas about how to improve the website. Many of the people we interviewed suggested additional people we might include. They also pointed out that viewers who were not familiar with the social movement needed more context than our website initially included. They suggested we provide a video timeline of events from 2006 and beyond and that we provide viewers with information about other social movements that were part of the story of APPO and the broader 2006 movement. This led us to videotape interviews with experts and leaders in indigenous movements, the teachers' movement, women's movements, and human rights movements and with those who played key roles in local community TV and radio production as well as in the creation of popular media. We also added video testimonials of indigenous participants in the 2006 movement and went to Juxtlahuaca to videotape testimonials from Mixtec and Triqui participants in APPO Juxtlahuaca and from those who worked with them.

The Frente Indígena de Organizaciones Binacionales (Binational Front of Indigenous Organizations, FIOB) was instrumental in helping us to set up and schedule these interviews in several communities. Because of the conflict that emerged in Triqui communities following the declaration of San Juan Copala as an autonomous municipality (discussed in chapter 8), we did not post all of our interviews because of risks they might pose for the interviewees. The FIOB also facilitated video recordings that I did in Los Angeles in the fall of 2008 to profile the transnational organizing links between Oaxaca and Los Angeles in 2006. The FIOB was extremely generous in sharing photographs and other documents about APPO Los Angeles and in providing suggestions for improving the website and its content. For the last set of testimonials, recorded in 2008, we relied primarily on telephone and email consultations and posted drafts of the videos on the closed YouTube channel for participants to review, suggest changes, and give final approval.

In addition to preparing the website, we also produced a DVD focused on the cases of Ramiro Aragón Pérez, Juan Gabriel Rios, and Elionai Santiago Sánchez. We gave copies to all of the participants in Oaxaca who wanted them as well as sharing them in venues in the United States. A copy of this DVD, along with a set of transcripts from related interviews, a dossier of photographs, and related documents, was submitted to U.S. Citizenship and Immigration Services in the Department of Homeland Security in January 2008 as a part of Ramiro Aragón Pérez and Ruth Guzmán Sánchez's political asylum application.

From January 2008 until May 2009, I worked intensely with a team of students—the website designer Alina Padilla Miller (a graduate student in the University of Oregon's School of Journalism and Communication), Jesse Nichols, the translator Magali Morales (who produced the Spanish text on the website), Josúe Gómez (a former graduate in anthropology at the University of Oregon who helped with translation and subtitling), and my colleague Professor Gabriela Martínez from the School of Journalism and Communication (who provided technical expertise).[2]

Once we had received approval from all the participants for the final drafts of their video testimonials, we completed the site. On May 29, 2009, the website Making Rights a Reality: The Oaxaca Social Movement 2006–Present was launched in a public celebration that included Ramiro Aragón Pérez, Ruth Guzmán Sánchez, and some of their family members. An electronic announcement of the website launch was sent to over five hundred organizations, communities, and individuals in Mexico, the United States, and Europe.

After the website was launched, I continued to discuss it with the people who had participated in it and others who had reviewed it in Oaxaca. I received many ideas for how to improve and broaden the project. Since most of the participants were interested in seeing a book produced as well, I set about to concentrate on that project. The conversations and connections I made through the process of working with people on the website resulted in further suggestions for interviews and the video and audio recording of more testimonials.

During the summers of 2009, 2010, and 2011 I continued to interview and record testimonials. Most of these are not included in the website but became important sources of insights and information for this book. I interviewed local business owners, people involved with the Catholic Church, teachers, artisans, participants in subsequent radio station takeovers in Oaxaca, and others active in creating new community radio stations. I also spoke with participants in barricades, youth activists, and academics. I ended up with a corpus of more than eighty audiovisual interviews with testimonials embedded in them.

In most of these interviews, I framed the discussion by using a life history approach. I first spent considerable time having the participants tell me about significant events and periods in their life, from early childhood to the present. Later in our conversation, I embedded questions about their particular role or observations about the 2006 social movement. Interviews usually lasted at least one hour and often extended to three or more hours. In some cases, the interviews involved multiple sessions.

As I moved into the third year of interviewing and recording testimonies, I realized that the form of providing testimony—of witnessing, of retelling events and experiences of 2006—was a visceral and emotional experience for everyone I talked with. The urgency with which everyone talked about the social movement and conflict of 2006 almost always resulted in long stretches of reflective narration and the recall of events, feelings, and emotions, which included a strong identification with being Oaxaqueño (Oa-. xacan), interpreted, of course, from many different perspectives and with multiple meanings. One of the most interesting results of the 2006 social movement was the unification of many different sectors of Oaxacan society under the political identity of *el pueblo de Oaxaca* (the Oaxacan people). The hybrid ethnic, class, and generational differences that came together in APPO and the related movement created a new sense of who is Oaxacan, as reflected in the testimony of Fidelia that begins this chapter and became a kind of mini-mantra and analysis for the processes and experiences represented here.

As I immersed myself time and time again in the narratives I had recorded, shared as transcripts with our participants and edited as videos, I was struck by the fundamental importance of testifying—not only for individuals but also for the social movement. This importance was evident in video recordings of public events and radio broadcasts as well. The power of oral testimony was amplified not only emotionally for those who did the telling and listening but also through its reproduction in multiple forms as it was recorded, broadcast, textualized, and then disseminated along multiple transmission channels. I was observing a form of knowledge production that drew from oral archives of knowledge and then reproduced them in conjunction with written and visual forms.

The Structure of This Book

A number of scholars have recently observed the importance of understanding literacy not only as reading and writing but also as involving interpretations of the spoken word, paintings, gestures, and visual and design elements (Rappaport and Cummins 2012). Ethnohistorians have long emphasized the importance and overlap between pictorial, textual, and oral modes of knowledge codification, production, and reproduction (Barton Kranz 2010; Burkhart 2010; Salomon and Niño-Murcia 2011; Schroeder 2010). While some of this work has been applied to understanding indigenous communities from the colonial period to the present, a broader understanding of literacy and knowledge production can easily be applied to other social groups and processes. As I hope to show in the subsequent chapters, oral testimony and the many forms of capturing it (visual, textual, and audiovisual recordings) and retransmitting it are a part of a broader literary tradition that is crucial to human rights work and social movements. The power of convocation found in testimony is its ability to move listeners and readers into a relationship as witnesses to the testimony givers. Testimony allows listeners to "be there" and to experience the reactivation of past events by making them present once again (Taylor 2003: 32). Thus the theoretical innovation I am arguing for here—centering the role of oral testimony in human rights work, social movements, indigenous and other forms of participatory democracy, and community radio—emerges precisely from the particular collaborative methods used in this project. By following the methodology of human rights workers and building on it to create a knowledge product engaged with and driven by the concerns of participants in the social movement and others, we illuminated the theoretical innovations reflected in the chapters that follow (see Hale and Stephen 2013).

Chapter 2 traces the emergence of APPO and the broader social movement to prior movements, including the teachers' movement of Sección 22, urban popular movements, peasant movements, indigenous movements, and women's movements. The chapter explores the continuities and differences between past social movements in the state and that of 2006, suggesting that the 2006 movement draws heavily on the experiences and knowledge of the democratic teachers' movement.

Chapter 3 provides a detailed ethnographic account of the local and national conditions that led many people to lose faith in the Oaxaca state government and join together to try to run the city and some regions of the state themselves. Special attention is paid to the vacuum of power left by an unresolved presidential election for several months as well as the initial event that detonated the social movement through a botched attempt by poorly trained state employees and police to evict teachers and other protesters from the historic center of Oaxaca City. This chapter sets the scene for examining in detail in subsequent chapters the profound changes that were experienced in many parts of Oaxacan society during the six months the social movement prevented the state government from operating.

Chapter 4 documents the severe repression unleashed on many participants in the 2006 social movement. The chapter highlights the cases of three individuals who were detained, tortured, and falsely charged and imprisoned as a window on the hundreds of human rights violations committed that affected many individuals and families. Theoretically, the chapter explores the ways that rights discourses from local, national, and international arenas were mobilized in the movement and led to ironies and unfulfilled expectations about punishment for the perpetrators on rights abuses. It also explores the kinds of tools and options survivors of human rights abuses can turn to when judicial systems don't provide justice. Ethnographically, the chapter operationalizes some of the ideas of the performance theorist Diana Taylor through an analysis of a press conference held by Elionai Santiago Sánchez and Juan Gabriel Ríos in which they testify in the *zócalo* (center plaza) of Oaxaca city about being detained, tortured, incarcerated, and served with trumped-up arms possession charges. I analyze the press conference using the idea of a scenario proposed by Taylor (2003: 28–33) which is particularly useful for demonstrating the performative aspects of testimony, how it connects listeners and tellers, and the ways testimony is replicated and travels.

Chapter 5 highlights one of the longer term outcomes of the 2006 Oaxaca social movement: the proliferation of indigenous and community radio stations. The chapter explores the relation of testimonials broadcast as part of community radio and the enactment of participatory democracy in indigenous and other rural communities through the form of governance known as the *asamblea* (assembly). Testimonial speech acts on the air and in the deliberations of indigenous community assemblies are important aspects of the ways the decision-making processes and dynamics of the 2006 social movement live on in media and governing practices in Oaxaca. After tracing the history of indigenous and community radio in Mexico and some of the challenges to it, the chapter analyzes several contemporary examples, including Radio Zaachila, which emerged in 2006. I argue that to explain the widespread adoption of radio within indigenous communities and the links between radio and indigenous autonomy we have to look at the intersection of political history, contemporary radio technology, and indigenous cultural styles of doing politics.

Chapter 6 documents the process by which several hundred women took over state and then commercial media (radio and television), opening up key cultural, political, and communication channels—literally and symbolically—that permitted new voices to be heard, new faces to be seen, and alternative models of governance and political participation to move temporarily into the mainstream. Through their experience running radio and television stations these women came to a gendered local vernacular of rights talk that became accessible to many other women and men in the city. The chapter also highlights the crucial security and information role played strategically by movement-controlled radio as repression of the movement increased and terminated with occupation by federal police forces after six months.

Chapter 7 focuses on the severe economic downturn that resulted from the social conflict of 2006 and its impact on those who make their living from tourism, roughly 77 percent of those in and around Oaxaca City (Ramos Sánchez 2007: 29; INEGI 2000). While it might be expected that artisans, merchants, and business owners would uniformly condemn the social movement, that is not the case. This chapter highlights the varied opinions of artisans and small merchants about the movement, including weavers from Teotitlán del Valle and the producers of *alebrijes* (painted wooden animals) from Arrazola. Some of them roundly condemn the movement and blame APPO for the ongoing economic disaster they have experienced; others are more sympathetic. The chapter also documents the efforts of independent businessmen who identify themselves as "civil society" to promote dialogue between APPO and state and federal governments. While they had little success with the state government, their conversations with APPO produced some interesting exchanges with some surprising shared ideas. Ultimately their efforts to broker a peaceful turnover of the city were not successful, but their perspectives have much to tell us about how those who have privileged economic, social, and cultural positions use their social capital to be heard. Their continued belief in the rule of law and the importance of voting and electoral processes contrasts with the projects of some of the youth who participated in APPO.

Chapter 8 draws attention to pan-ethnic indigenous organizing and indigenous-nonindigenous alliance building which occurred as part of the movement in rural Oaxaca and transnationally between Oaxaca and California. This discussion is strongly informed by indigenous claims to local governance and legal autonomy through customary indigenous law and systems of governance known in Mexico as *usos y costumbres* (roughly translated as "customs and traditions"). Oaxaca state, like Colombia, Bolivia, Ecuador, and other Latin American countries, has changed its constitution to honor indigenous customary law.

The organization of APPO Juxtlahuaca provides an example of a regional attempt at alliance and governance across indigenous ethnic groups and with mestizos. The most striking outcome of this alliance came through the emergence of the declaration of the Autonomous Municipality of San Juan Copala in January 2007. Related to but driven by separate dynamics from those that produced APPO in Juxtlahuaca, the conflict surrounding the autonomous municipality suggests the difficulty in forging solidarity within the Triqui ethnic group because of decades of state and elite attempts to divide communities and pit them against one another in the coffee and land markets. A second example of alliances comes in an examination of APPO Los Angeles, which allowed indigenous immigrant Oaxacans in the United States to connect with their families and communities in Mexico through financial and political support. There alliances with local Latino, Chicano, Anglo, and left organizations also proved temporary. The chapter suggests the limits and possibilities for cross-ethnic alliances both in Mexico and the United States.

Chapter 9 documents how the life on the barricades in 2006 fomented a new political culture among youth unified around the concept of autonomy. Characterized by horizontal relationships, consensus decision making, mutual aid, self-empowerment, and self-sufficiency, this culture of politics blends ideas from anarchism with popular understandings of how indigenous systems of justice and governance work. Decision making and political participation through community assemblies is emphasized as a way of keeping the 2006 social movement's legacy independent from political parties and formal electoral politics. Two organizational spaces, Voces Oaxaqueñas Construyendo Autonomía y Libertad (Oaxacan Voices Constructing Autonomy and Freedom, VOCAL) and Casa Autónoma Solidaria Oaxaqueña de Trabajo Autogestivo (Autonomous Oaxacan House Supporting Self-Managed Work, CASOTA) are highlighted as examples of how the concepts of autonomy and assemblies work in practice. The chapter briefly examines youth organizing through the production of public art using graffiti and stenciling and the creation of movement icons such as La Virgen de la Barrikada. The images produced by youth artists first on the public walls of the city of Oaxaca and then in galleries across Mexico and internationally are important visual and textual elements in the construction of social memory about the movement of 2006. In addition, the visual symbols and elements combined in the distinctive genre of stencil art developed in 2006 also contribute to the building of a popular political identity built around "the people of Oaxaca" as cross-class, multiethnic, and multigenerational.

The conclusion offers a theoretical discussion of some of the lessons learned from Oaxaca about engaged politics, participatory democracy, and concepts of citizenship. The power of testimony as a strategic and ideological tool in a wide range of venues in the movement suggests the importance of reexamining how we think about the production, distribution, and dissemination of knowledge. As a form of communication that also intensifies and highlights emotion, the testimonial became a vehicle for the recuperation of personal and collective dignity, distinct from rights. Using Chatterjee's (2004) concepts of civil society (as the political realm of educated elites) and political society (those excluded from civil society who use their status as population groups to claim entitlements granted to them though processes of governmentality and policymaking), I argue that the Oaxaca social movement illustrates the importance of nonelectoral forms of political participation and process that are being emphasized by many movements around the world today which complicate electoral politics and conventions. I invoke Saskia Sassen's discussion of how concepts of citizenship are being changed both inside and outside of nation states through processes of globalization. Following Sassen (2006: 321), I suggest that new types of political subjects, such as many of those in the Oaxaca social movement, are increasingly important as the growing distance between states and individual citizens produces new possibilities.

The Oaxaca Social Movement in a Larger Arch of Social Protest

In December 2011 *Time* magazine named "The Protester" as "The Person of the Year."

> Is there a global tipping point for frustration? Everywhere, it seems, people said they'd had enough. They dissented; they demanded; they did not despair; even when the answers came back in a cloud of tear gas or a hail of bullets. They literally embodied the idea that individual action can bring collective, colossal change. And although it was understood differently in different places, the idea of democracy was present in every gathering. The root of the word democracy is *demos*, "the people" and the meaning of democracy is "the people rule." And they did, if not at the ballot box, then in the streets. (Stengel 2011)

In his article in *Time* Kurt Anderson (2011) gives readers a global tour of protests in 2011, beginning in Tunisia and then Egypt, where people took to the streets to unseat despotic rulers. He then moves to Los Indignados of Spain and to Greece, where protests centered on unemployment, a lack of opportunity, and lackluster politics. He spends considerable time discussing the

Occupy movement in New York, where the phrase "We are the 99%" was coined. Text messaging, Facebook, YouTube, and Twitter were the social media motors behind mass protests and occupations that brought people together to defy political and economic authority around the world.

The anthropologist David Graeber, one of the architects of the Occupy Wall Street movement, argues in his book *Debt: The First Five Thousand Years* that we are only now seeing the first planetary administrative system with the primary purpose of protecting the interests of creditors through institutions like the World Bank, the International Monetary Fund, corporations, and financial institutions. Such institutions have lost their moral authority, according to Graeber, in part through anticorporate global social movements and also through the banking crises and the threat of global economic collapse (Graeber 2009: 8; 2011a). While such larger structural circumstances are crucial to understanding the dynamics behind the protests of Los Indignados in Spain, the difficult living conditions in Oaxaca, and the impetus behind the Occupy movements, they do not really tell us what the protests are about for those who live them and what they mean.

Javier Auyero suggests that in our analysis of social protest we need to dig deeper. In his book *Contentious Lives*, he focuses on the experiences and understandings of two women (Nana and Laura) who participated in the two-day protests in Santiago de Estero, Argentina, in 1993, which were linked to attempts to reduce public unemployment, and in the six-day roadblock in the southern Argentine oil towns of Cutral-co and Plaza Huincol in 1996 that resulted in part from the effects of privatization of the state oil company. Concerned with the ways that their roles in the protests affected their daily lives, Auyero argues that to view the protesters only as antistructural adjustment protesters would be insensitive to local political dynamics and to "be ignorant of the indigenous meanings with which participants imbue the protests. Protesters . . . are indeed in search of their jobs and salaries, but they are also in search of dignity" (2003: 7–8). He suggests that the uprisings are not only about structural adjustment but are "also about other 'local' issues such as government corruption and residents' dissatisfaction with their elected representatives—the uprisings are as much about politics as about the economy" (7). Auyero's insights in analyzing Argentine social protests of the 1990s ring true for the Oaxaca social movement described here.

Auyero, like other sociologists (Goodwin, Jasper, and Polletta 2001; Polletta 2002) who have focused on the emotions involved in passionate (collective) politics suggests that "the way in which people live and feel collective struggle is crucial to understanding what a protest or social movement is about" (Auyero 2003: 205). Individual and collective emotional energy in the creation of affective solidarity—amplifying an initiating emotion and transferring it into a sense of collective solidarity—is a key component in building sustainable social movements (Juris 2008: 65). The tool of testimony is an important part of harnessing emotion and building it into a sense of collective solidarity and human dignity.

The Oaxaca social movement of 2006 can be seen as part of an arch of social protest in the Americas with new technological and organizational forms that begins to bubble in the 1990s. Some points along this arch include (1) the Zapatista movement that erupted in 1994 and forever changed the Mexican political landscape for indigenous peoples; (2) the *piqueteros* movement of Argentina beginning in the mid-1990s, which went from roadblocks to occupations of streets, bridges, and buildings and the formation of cooperatives as a part of the unemployed workers movement of Argentina, which continues today; (3) the "Battle of Seattle" of 1999 in which at least forty thousand protesters occupied Seattle intent on derailing the World Trade Organization Ministerial Conference and who set off a series of protests in subsequent years at organizational meetings of the WTO, IMF, World Bank, Free Trade Area of the Americas, and others; (4) the fight against water privatization in Cochabamba, Bolivia, in 2000, when protesters successfully stopped Bechtel Corporation from taking over public water systems and kept water in the public sector; (5) the massive immigrant rights protests in dozens of U.S. cities in 2006, when hundreds of thousands turned out to protest anti-immigrant legislation; and (6) the Occupy movements of 2011, held in thirteen Latin American countries as well as in Canada and the United States.

Perhaps the strongest thread connecting these movements is the way they have challenged traditional authority and forms of participation in governance. In many of these social protest movements there is strong resistance to Western liberal forms of political organization, whether political parties or traditional leftist unions or organizations. There is resistance to vertical authority and power structures and an embrace of more horizontal and consensual forms of decision making. In the case of the Occupy movement of 2011, the organizational form is driven by the concept of the general assembly, which is based on the idea of a carefully facilitated group discussion and decision-making process in which decisions are made by consensus. Voting, majority rule, and *Robert's Rules of Order* are out. If there is an impasse in decision making, smaller groups of people will undertake the task of working on the problem and returning to the larger group with a proposed solution. Consensus rules, no matter how many hours it takes. U.S. analysts attribute the structure and process of the general assembly to contemporary anarchist activism (Bennett 2011). Others have pointed out the continuity between this form of governance and indigenous forms of political governance and autonomy, perhaps most strongly disseminated through the autonomous Mayan communities of the Zapatista movement, which have functioned by consensus decision making for two decades (Earle and Simonelli 2011). Interestingly, many more people are paying attention to the process of inclusive democratic consensus because of the Occupy movement. A look into the social movement of Oaxaca and at other social movements in the Americas from the 1990s to the present reveals this tendency as a key part of many movements. While traditional political analysts are frustrated with the lack of "specific" demands from some of these movements,[3] perhaps the real radical elements are the political processes they represent, the tactics they use, and the theoretical models behind their ideas. As Walter Mignolo (2011: 239, 234–35) argues in his discussion of the Zapatistas' theoretical revolution, ideas such as "the return to human dignity," "the right to be different because we are all equals," "a world composed of multiple worlds," and "to rule and obey at the same time" can be motors for decolonial options and thinking which can challenge the dark heritage and consequences of Western modernity experienced by many. In the broadest sense, the arch of social protest in the Americas from the 1990s onward can be seen as educating the world about new logics of democracy, participation, and human worth and dignity. Such political processes are important complements to formal political systems, which cannot be abandoned as they can offer the possibility of real change when the right coalition of forces unites at the right time. When formal political systems stagnate and are incapable of change, innovative social movements and political processes such as those highlighted here are the lifeblood of political engagement for many people.

2

Histories and Movements

___

Antecedents to the Social Movement of 2006

*Flyers, lightning meetings in markets and public places, painting the
walls of the city, demonstrations, sit-ins in front of City Hall, and the
commandeering of buses . . . were carried out. . . .*

*The students and their representatives . . . used the university radio
to contradict the propaganda of the bus company owners and they also
used sound systems installed in cars, which permitted them to inform
the inhabitants of the city of what they were doing. They accessed the
press through taking out ads and also disseminated documents and
manifestos of the workers.*

— Martínez Vásquez 1990: 156

If one does not read this quote carefully, it might appear to be a description of the Oaxacan social movement of 2006. It is not; it is a description
of actions carried out in Oaxaca thirty-three years earlier by students and
by an urban popular movement known as the Coalición Obrero Campesino
Estudiantil de Oaxaca (Worker, Peasant, Student Coalition of Oaxaca, or

COCEO). The date is January 4, 1974. With COCEO is a wide front of students known as the Frente Popular Estudiantil; they are engaging in actions to support the workers of Choferes del Sur (Drivers of the South, primarily bus drivers and employees) who are protesting rising bus fares. Several weeks earlier, on December 13, 1973, the same groups mobilized ten thousand people to support the demands of the bus drivers.

The state of Oaxaca has a distinguished history of social movements, particularly during the last three decades of the twentieth century. The emergence of APPO and the broader social movement of 2006 are strongly linked to this history. What histories and experiences of previous social movements—particularly the teachers' movement, popular urban movements, peasant movements, and indigenous movements—are necessary to understand the strategies, tactics, and emergence of APPO and the wider 2006 social movement in Oaxaca? What are the similarities and differences between the previous social movements and that of 2006? These are the questions this chapter attempts to answer.

Education in Oaxaca and the History of Teachers Organizing

The teachers' movement in Oaxaca was the backbone of APPO and has been strongly tied to many other social movements in the state. The importance of the teachers' movement is marked by the fact that Sección 22 is the only organization capable of generating simultaneous coordinated action in all of the municipalities in the state of Oaxaca. And because teachers live and work in the poorest and most marginal of Oaxaca's communities, they tend to "identify strongly with the communities where they work and they become not only activists in their union but also become spokespersons for communal demands as well" (Hernández Navarro 2011: 368).

Teachers have historically been involved in a range of community and social movements, ever since education was formally institutionalized after the Mexican Revolution. Public education was consolidated in Mexico in 1921 under President Alvaro Obregon, who created the Secretaría de Educación Pública (Ministry of Public Education, SEP). As part of a nationalist strategy to consolidate the Mexican Revolution and build a nation of mestizos (people who are a mixture of Spanish, indigenous, and African heritage), education became one of the primary routes for "civilizing" and assimilating Mexico's rural and primarily indigenous peasants. The focus of SEP educational programs in the 1920s was to integrate individuals into the market economy and communities into the nation (see Vaughn 1982). Oaxaca saw a 27 percent increase in its state primary school enrollment between 1920 and 1928 (Vaughn 1982: 156).

During the 1930s, under President Lázaro Cárdenas, the promotion of socialist schools as well as accelerated agrarian reform and the organization of the Confederación Nacional Campesina (the National Peasants Confederation, CNC) were key pieces in a government-run campaign to create a national popular culture around the Mexican Revolution, with the Mexican government as its main beneficiary (see Vaughn 1997). I have documented elsewhere how the figure of Emiliano Zapata and other aspects of the Mexican Revolution became part of a nationalist campaign to build the political party of Cárdenas in the 1930s and ensure values that inspired loyalty to the government (see Stephen 2002). Rural schoolteachers were primary actors in promoting a popularized Mexican Revolution that emphasized phrases such as "the proletarian cause," "the land belongs to everyone, like the air, the water, the light, and the heat of the sun" (Stephen 2002: 44–45).

In Oaxaca, as well as elsewhere, the ideas of socialist education were disseminated wherever there were schools. The First Congress for Socialist Education was held in the city of Oaxaca on February 25–28, 1935. Publications such as *El Socialista* were produced to help spread socialist ideals. Teachers in Oaxaca were organized primarily by the Sindicato Único de Trabajadores de le Ensenañza (Sole Union of Education Workers). After a teachers' strike in 1937, officials from the Oaxaca state government and the federal government signed an agreement that brought all Oaxacan teachers under the secretary of federal education. Oaxacan teachers not only continued to promote socialist education in the late 1930s but also worked as agrarian activists (Stephen 2002: 54–55). Thus teachers in Oaxaca and other states have a long history of working simultaneously as educators and activists.

In 1943 the Sindicato Nacional de Trabajadores de Educación (National Union of Education Workers, SNTE) was founded and came to represent all educational workers in Mexico's primary and secondary schools. With closed-shop representation of all education workers, SNTE quickly followed in the pattern of other government unions: the organization came to be very closely tied to government policy priorities and was part of a well-oiled vote-delivery machine that was formally affiliated with the Partido Revolucionario Institucional (Institutional Revolutionary Party, PRI; see Cook 1996). While there were several attempts by reform movements within SNTE to democratize it, all failed until 1979, when dissidents formed the first reform caucus in SNTE history.

The Emergence of CNTE and the
Democratic Teachers' Movement

In understanding the history of the movements that define the APPO of 2006, the democratic teacher's movement of Oaxaca is key. The backbone of the APPO from 2006 to the present, the Coordinadora Nacional de Trabajadores de la Educación (National Council of Education Workers, CNTE) became one of the primary organizing hubs not only for teachers, but for a wide variety of other movements in the 1980s, 1990s, and beyond. The strategies, structure, processes, slogans, persistence, and high number of people with intergenerational organizing experience found in CNTE make it the nest out of which many other movements have hatched and been nurtured.

In December 1979 the CNTE was founded in Tuxtla Gutiérrez, Chiapas, with the strong participation of teachers involved in regional movements in Chiapas, Tabasco, La Montaña de Guerrero, and La Laguna (Hernández Navarro 2011: 19). These teachers were looking for a pay raise of 30 percent and wanted to democratize SNTE. According to Luis Hernández Navarro (2011: 20; see Street 1992: 89), there were many bilingual indigenous teachers active in the formation of CNTE, as well as those who worked in areas with strong *caciques* (local political bosses) or peasant struggles. The power of CNTE, as Hernández Navarro (2011: 20) states, comes from its capacity to mobilize and to maintain relative regional autonomy.

In her close analysis of the origins of CNTE within a wider examination of how the teachers' movements of the late 1970s and early 1980s transformed the Mexican state's educational bureaucracy, Susan Street suggests that prior struggles against the antidemocratic tendencies of SNTE were important.[1] In CNTE teachers developed tactical and organizational strategies that were integral to the success of their democratic projects in the 1980s. These included "the use of the direct strike (that the law prohibited for workers of the state), the exercise of union autonomy at the delegational and sectional levels, respect for the collective decisions taken in assemblies, an emphasis on mobilizations at the base more than personal relations of leaders as a way to pressure for their demands, and the development of a politics that links with other groups and social movements" (CNTE 1982, cited in Street 1992: 92).

Street states that while the importance of CNTE leadership obeying the base allowed the movement to be unified in its respect for ideological and political diversity, it did not result in a unified national program. The CNTE thus emerged more as a unified space for planning, strategic actions, and negotiating rather than a formal national organization (Street 1992: 95). This resulted in a sort of organic unity of the movement that always functioned as an assembly of delegates and a space for deliberation (Arriaga 1981; Street 1992: 94). "CNTE lived up to its name. . . . It coordinated struggles. It promoted massive mobilizations and carried out political work in the states where there was real or potential discontent" (Street 1992: 95). Both Street and Hernández emphasize the importance of how the teachers who formed CNTE interpreted democracy: to them, it meant their direct participation in their immediate and local circumstances. The local form of organization in CNTE, usually known as *consejos centrales de lucha* (central councils of struggle), was where teachers participated intensely. Each council, itself made up of different groups, developed its own ideas about strategic actions and what kinds of struggles to take on and where they should be fought (Street 1992: 95). Democracy was defined by CNTE as "establishing the mechanisms which guarantee the participation of the base in the union leadership, decision-making, and the validation of each of these" (CNTE 1982, quoted in Street 1992: 98).

The participation of Oaxacan teachers in CNTE came slightly later than that of neighboring Chiapas. Rogelio Vargas Garfías (real name), who has been a teacher for thirty years in Oaxaca, participated in the founding congress of CNTE in Chiapas in 1979. He has been an active participant in the teachers' movement in Oaxaca and at the national level through CNTE. At the time we spoke in 2007, he generously shared his experiences and analysis of how Oaxaca had participated in CNTE and in the struggle to democratize the larger educational workers' union (SNTE). Rogelio has dark curly hair, an ample mustache, and a friendly manner and smile. He sits at a desk, relaxed, in a dark T-shirt as we discuss his personal history and participation in CNTE. His narrative captures some of the most important parts of the formation and trajectory of CNTE in Oaxaca and also offers insights into some of the structure, tactics, and tensions that emerged in APPO.

✳ VIDEOCLIP 2.1: http://dx.doi.org/10.7264/N3QJ7F75

CNTE . . . picks up on all of the experiences of the years leading into the 1970s, including the struggle of teachers, of railroad workers, of the students of 1968, and electricians. . . . CNTE follows from all of these social struggles to improve life and work conditions in Mexico and from all of the pressure they faced and continue to face from the charro *[sold-out] leaders of the* SNTE—*from corrupt leaders who simply serve the Mexican state. All of this made it necessary* for teachers in 1978 and 1979 to take the initiative to identify themselves inside of SNTE with a distinct organization. They did this in order to pull together the protests of education workers in different parts of the country and also to confront the state policies inside of SNTE.

CNTE began with a very legitimate protest on the part of teachers in the southeast of Mexico. At that time, teachers were experiencing very intense repression linked to union charros [leaders bought off by the state officials], and teachers also had very little control over what they did due to the policies of the SEP. All of the state policies were implemented inside of the SEP by supervisors, by sectoral bosses, and the union leaders, who were all in the service of the state. . . . SNTE was very antidemocratic in its practices.

CNTE came out of the struggles of teachers in Tabasco and Chiapas. In this part of the country, the living and working conditions were deteriorating seriously. They decided to protest and called the attention of the rest of the country to the southeast. And although we were a small group of teachers in Oaxaca, we went to the event that was the founding of CNTE in 1979.

Oaxaca wakes up to this national movement in May of 1980. . . . This is because the first leaders of SNTE's Sección 22 in Oaxaca were members of the PRI. So, due to their political formation, they were strongly opposed to the integration of Oaxaca into CNTE. Initially Oaxacan teachers were fighting a strong internal battle within Sección 22 in order to be able to join CNTE. It wasn't until 1983, when we won Oaxaca's first democratic congress of Sección 22, that we made the decision to join CNTE. Here in Oaxaca we consulted with the teachers in the base of Sección 22 to ask whether they were in agreement that we should join CNTE. The answer was a resounding "Yes! We want to enter CNTE with all that we have."

In the 1980s, CNTE fought its strongest battles against union corruption, against the state, and we were able to mobilize almost all of the country. There were strikes all over the country called and directed by CNTE. This was a decade in which CNTE really consolidated itself.

The 1980s were very intense years of confrontation here in Oaxaca as well, with hired gunmen, paid assassins, and killers who were sent by the national union, the state government, and the national government. They saw Sección 22 in Oaxaca as a major threat. . . . In Oaxaca, dozens of people were assassinated in the 1980s, but since 1989 we have been able to have various sectional executive committees that are democratic. There were also other teachers' unions on the path to democracy as well at that time.

By 1989, both Sección 22 in Oaxaca and CNTE at a national level were consolidated. What this means is that by 1989, half of the teachers in the *country are with CNTE and the other half are with the charro unions of SNTE. In the 1990s the solidarity of CNTE began to come apart at the national level, as happened in a lot of social movements. Those who were directing CNTE began to stop focusing on CNTE as a united movement with a democratic assembly and a flexible program of struggle, and they began to focus on their regional spaces of power and also their part in the struggle for power within CNTE.*

In Oaxaca, perhaps more than other states, we have found a way to coexist with all of the different political and ideological currents that you can imagine within Sección 22. This has been to the point that we can have very large conflicts between the different political ideologies within Sección 22, but at the same time we have a strong unity in defense of the process that we have been carrying on for twenty-eight years of struggle.

The base of Sección 22 jealously guards and obligates its leaders to respect the agreements made at the base level. The base demands that their leaders be the custodians of the key work done in the 1970s by so many teachers and pass on the gains to today's teachers and to the people of Oaxaca. Other states in Mexico have not gone through this same kind of process and history. It is because of this that I believe that the Mexican state and the corrupt leaders of SNTE see Oaxaca as a grave threat. The secret of Oaxaca's success is that although we coexist with all of these different political ideologies here, in moments of grave danger, we are unified against a common enemy.

During the past twenty-seven years, CNTE has gained control of key locals in Mexico City, as well as in the states of Michoacán, Chiapas, Guerrero, Tlaxcala, Zacatecas, Morelos, Baja California Sur, Sinaloa, Durango, and Oaxaca, with representation growing in other states. According to Chiu Velásquez, the public spokesperson for Sección 22 whom I interviewed in 2006, "Now there are 1,400,000 workers in SNTE, and about 45 percent of these are with us in CNTE." That is about 630,000 workers. An earlier estimate from 1997 puts the numbers of CNTE workers at 250,000 (Monroy 1997: 2).

The power of CNTE extends not only to the large number of teachers within its ranks but also from its ability to capture and wield power in institutions that control education in Oaxaca. In 1992 then-governor of Oaxaca Heladio Ramírez López announced the creation of the Instituto Estatal de Educación Pública de Oaxaca (State Institute of Public Education of Oaxaca, IEEPO). Sección 22 was successful in penetrating the structure of this administrative institution, and in 2003 was reported to occupy sixty-seven positions in the state administrative structure of education (Náthan Pérez 2003). According to observers such as Cuauhtémoc Blas López, this turned the union members into bosses and employees at the same time and put them in charge of supervising themselves, "severely affecting the quality of education" (2007: 45).[2] While many in the union would certainly debate this assertion, having significant inroads into the IEEPO certainly helped to consolidate the ability of Sección 22 and of CNTE to politically pressure the governors of Oaxaca—usually successfully, at least until 2006, when Ulises Ruiz Ortiz refused to negotiate.

Since the formation of CNTE, indigenous teachers have been a large part of its membership. In states like Oaxaca, indigenous teachers are a majority of those involved in the dissident movement. Previously, bilingual indigenous teachers were paid less than nonindigenous teachers and were employed by the Instituto Nacional Indigenista (National Indigenist Institute, INI). In the 1980s and 1990s CNTE in Oaxaca was a major player in forcing the Ministry of Education to expand bilingual education. Since 1994, under CNTE control and guidance, the Oaxacan state Indigenous Education Department has been developing and putting into use textbooks in Oaxaca's sixteen indigenous languages (Monroy 1997: 11–12). Bilingual indigenous teachers are in every community and hamlet throughout the state.

Another group with significant representation in CNTE is women, who account for at least 60 percent of all teachers nationwide and thus are a majority of members of CNTE (Monroy 1997: 6). While no precise figures are available, it appears that the percentage of women teachers in Oaxaca is similar to that nationwide. In Oaxaca this translates into very significant representation in the dissident movement by indigenous women, who have been vocal in protesting discrimination, sexual harassment, and racism both in the union and elsewhere. (This theme is further discussed in chapter 6.)

Members of CNTE have extensive organizational experience and a complex system of grassroots democracy. The basic organizational forms are the "struggle committee," regional "central councils of struggle," and "brigades" of teachers who carry information and support from one area to the next. In addition to these parallel structures, which are not official in SNTE, CNTE has a four-level pyramid of elected officials. From the bottom up, this is (1) the individual school committee, (2) the local executive committee, (3) sector committees, and (4) zone committees. The highest authority is the assembly, which is a meeting of all elected representatives. The decision-making process of the assembly is based on the practice of the *consulta*: delegates must go back to their local areas to hold debates and conversations (consultas) before voting and adopting a decision in the general assembly (Monroy 1997: 13). This structure has strongly influenced APPO as well. It also reflects forms of decision making in many indigenous communities, where decisions are made according to the sentiment of the asamblea, not by individual officials.

The Organization and Structure of Sección 22 of Oaxaca

Since 1983 Sección 22 in Oaxaca has been unique in its ongoing ability to maintain a commitment to the project of democratization and its ability to evoke widespread, coordinated action to pressure the Oaxacan state and federal governments.[3] Interviews I did with teachers active in Sección 22 reveal personal histories entwined with the struggles of the union. Many teachers come from families where one or both parents or other relatives were teachers, so they essentially grew up in the movement. Others did not have such a direct relationship growing up, but when they entered normal school to be trained as teachers and began to work in rural schools, their commitment to the union struggle often intensified. Many of the interviews also underscore how profoundly their experiences as teachers in extremely marginalized rural and often indigenous communities influenced their ideas about education and politics.

Participation in Sección 22 begins at the workplace. Each school participates in a higher level *delegación* (delegation or local instance of representation). The delegaciones feed into thirty-seven different sectors. Each delegación elects a representative who goes to the asambleas of its own sector and also to congresses of Sección 22, called *congresos secionales*. The state-level congress of Sección 22 has about eight hundred representatives, who all have the right to debate and vote. Most representatives come to statewide congresses with agreements from their sector about what their priorities and strategies are.

Esteban Manuel Rodríguez (real name), who teaches at a *telesegundaria* (middle school with a televised curriculum),[4] explained to me how representation in Sección 22 works and how everyone has the opportunity to participate in Sección 22. He is further profiled below.

My workplace gives me the space to participate in the union. All of the workers from my school can become members of Sección 22, to be unionized. How? Our Sección 22 is organized by sectors and then by delegations. There are thirty-seven sectors, and each sector has different delegations. In my case, my school belongs to Delgación D2–87 of telesegundarias. In this delegation, all of us can vote, we can all belong, and we can all participate. When they first called us to assemblies of our delegation, I tried to pay close attention to what was being presented. It was a little hard for me to participate initially because I needed to understand the context. Then after I went to three or four assemblies I got over my fear and I started to share my point of view in the asamblea. In my delegation there were four hundred people that included men, women, administrators, and teachers. After I participated for several years, my compañeros had confidence in me and they elected me to represent the delegation at a higher level. I represented my delegation in CNTE at the state level. At the state level congresses of Sección 22 there are eight hundred representatives.

Portraits of Two Teachers: Esteban and Carmen

Understanding the history and struggles of unionized teachers within CNTE and Sección 22 can give us some insights into the kinds of experiences and socialization teacher activists had in the 2006 movement. But it is also important to look at personal histories, particularly the experiences that all teachers have in their first and often subsequent postings in marginal, rural areas. Because seniority allows teachers to have more choice about where they are assigned, newly minted teachers often receive assignments in the most isolated areas of the state of Oaxaca. The portraits I provide here are of two teachers who were active participants in the 2006 movement. One is Esteban Manuel Rodríguez, introduced earlier. We will return to Esteban's narrative later in this chapter as well. The other is Carmen López Vásquez (real name), who came to occupy a key role as the most consistent presence in Radio La Ley, which was occupied and run by the social movement from August through November 2006. Here Carmen's personal history and her work as a teacher are introduced. In chapter 4, her participation in the radio station is discussed in more detail.

Esteban Manuel Rodríguez

Born on December 26, 1975, in Zaachila, Oaxaca, into a family of nine children, Esteban did not come from a family of teachers. His father was a small-scale merchant and his mother worked at home. He completed primary school in Santa María Arevalo Trinidad de Zaachila and then was able to keep studying through a telesegundaria. In high school he went on to pursue a specialized course of study in information technology. He was able to get a nonteaching position in a school and entered Sección 22 as a unionized educational worker in 1995. He then left briefly for six months to work for a soft drink company, El Rey. Six months later, at the age of nineteen, he was offered a teaching job in a telesegundaria in the region of Putla de Guerrero. After teaching in San Juan Copala in the Triqui zone of Oaxaca, he was able to enter a rural normal school as part of a special program and receive training as a teacher. Once he graduated, he went on to found a telesegundaria, where he still works.

Esteban has a wide-open face and slightly curling hair. He is relaxed and sits easily in a simple wooden chair before a table. The first couple of buttons on his white shirt with blue stripes are open, and he rests his hands in front of him. As he begins to talk about his first teaching experiences, his expression intensifies and his hands begin to move as he speaks.

In order to get to Zaragoza Santa Cruz I first went to Putla de Guerrero. There I had to change to a pickup truck and ride in the back for more than nine hours. The rainy season was almost over, but it was still raining. It took the driver about ten hours to get from Putla to Zaragoza Itundujia. The road, as is characteristic of our state, ran through a lot of forests. It was a coffee zone where people also exploit wood. There are incredible plants and animals there, including deer.

When I first got there, I reported to the principal of the school and he told me what my work would be and introduced me to my colleagues. I was in this community for one year, and then I went to another community, called El Rincón Zocotiaca. This is a community that is near the entrance to the district of Putla de Guerrero, but toward the coast, in the direction of Pinotepa Nacional. Unlike the first community, people here spoke Spanish. It was a community that was very poor and had a lot of people migrating to the United States. This is very characteristic of towns like this one. A lot of young people were using drugs and dedicating themselves not to a career but to criminal activities like robbing people, serving as assassins, and other criminal things. . . . What I remember about this community was that we were successful with the soccer team. I took charge of the soccer team, and we practiced at six in the morning, before dawn, and we were always working on our soccer. When we had a competition, our community's team took first place. This gave a lot of satisfaction to the parents and the students. It was a great thing that we achieved for that community.

The other thing I remember about this community is that during my last days there, Hurricane Paulina touched down there and it destroyed all of the roads. In order to leave, we had to walk for eight hours before we even reached a main road, which was also in terrible shape.

After that, they sent me to the community of San Juan Copala, which is now famous for all of the problems that it has had for so many years. The majority of people there only spoke the Triqui language. . . . In San Juan Copala,[5] *we teachers didn't get involved in the conflicts in the community, but the communication there was very cold and very tense. We didn't have the kind of open relationship there that we usually have in other communities with the parents. In other communities the parents organize events with the teachers. In this community the parents only participated if they were obligated, forced to do so. So we really didn't interact with people much and we couldn't offer help. . . .*

At the time I was there it was only the MULT that was in charge.[6] *The other organizations that emerged in 2006 were not in existence yet. When I was there, there was only one organization and it maintained everything in a very tense situation. The community was also extremely poor.*

After his year in San Juan Copala, Esteban was able to enter the Escuela Normal Federal Superior de Oaxaca, which allowed him to receive a teaching certificate and move up to other levels beyond technical administration. But it was only through a special program that he was allowed to enter. He remembers that he and other students who entered the program were marginalized as students.

We didn't have a classroom. They just gave us some seats in a hallway. We put in our own money to seal off the hallway and to create a classroom so that we would have better conditions to learn. Even so, they still marginalized us. But in spite of everything we provided an example of how, if you want something badly enough, you can succeed.

Esteban did not have an inherited teaching position, or *plaza*, because no one in his family was a teacher. He finished the program in 2001 with a specialty in telesegundarias. "With 60 percent of our education completed, they opened up the doors for us. They assigned us a formal position with a number which we could present to our supervisor so that we could go and work in a school as a teacher." For Esteban, this was a major accomplishment. The first position he held as a teacher required that he literally build the school he was going to teach in, with help from the people of the community.

They sent me to the community of Río Nube in San Lorenzo Texmelucun. This is a community where 100 percent of the people speak Zapotec. Even the kids speak Zapotec. People dress very simply and they have a very high level of poverty. Apart from this, they also had a long history of a land conflict from more than eighty years ago and with more than one hundred deaths. The conflict is with the municipality of Santo Domingo Teojomulco. The result was a history of a lot of death, a lot of widows, and a lot of orphaned kids.[7]

When I went to work there, there was no transportation. There only was a microbus that took people from Oaxaca to another community, called Santa Cruz Zontepec in the Chatino region. When the weather was bad and the microbus would get stuck on bad roads it could take people two or three days to get home. The other thing was that this bus also brought basic products to the small stores. If it didn't come, then there would not be any food.

The houses in this town were very simple. The roofing was corrugated aluminum or clay tiles. The walls were made out of cane and mud. People had lots of children, and basic sanitation was lacking. The bathrooms were near the kitchens. The animals were also very close to where food was prepared. Kids would defecate outside of the houses. People had very little to eat. . . . The agrarian conflict also resulted in a lack of food. When it was time for Teojomulco to bring in their harvest, there were no crops. There was no corn, no beans because the enemy town had come and cut down the whole crop.

So the situation there was very extreme. There was a lot of alcoholism and drug addiction in the town as well. The elderly would get sick from simple disease and they would die. Why? Because there were absolutely no services in this community. There was one clinic in the municipal center to attend over seven thousand people spread out into seven communities. Most of these smaller communities had between six hundred and a thousand inhabitants, and there was only one clinic for all of these people.

The schools in places like this are in horrible conditions too. Often there are not even classrooms for schools. When I got there to start the telesegundaria, I had to start out in a space in the primary school. I began to build with some laminas [corrugated aluminum made from pressed cans] I borrowed. . . . We adapted a classroom in the primary school for sixteen students. We made a table out of boxes. Then we had a wood table made from the wood from this region. We also had to improvise our seats for the first year as well because there were not any.

During the second year we decided that in order to set up the school we needed a space. We began to work with the authorities to acquire land. We bought a piece of land. The next year we had to get the equipment to prepare the land. We leveled the land, cut down trees, and the following year we had the equipment come again. So it was this work with the community, little by little, with the support of the parents' committee, the community's authorities, and all the parents that we were able to build three classrooms, an administrative office, and a basketball court, and prepare the ground. We had to work with everyone again to get computers, and now there are actually thirty computers in the schools with a satellite signal. Now we are in the process of building a media lab for the communities that we have.

. . . We finished the building in 2004. The students had to wait four or five years for their school to be finished. After all that time they finally had an adequate space to receive their classes in.

And we also want our students to be able to come to school wearing shoes. Very few of them have shoes because they can't afford them. We can't ask parents to pay for or supply them with books or notebooks because there is no stationery store or bookstore. There is no place to buy these things. Every time the parents have to go to the city to buy these things it is very expensive.

The state that students there arrive in also affects their educational processes. They often arrive without having eaten anything. Their stomachs are empty. When they come to class they are sleepy and they are thinking more about eating than studying. We have to consider these conditions when we think about education—even the kind of vocabulary students are exposed to in Spanish.

. . . In this community the daily reality of the local agrarian conflict also entered the classroom. The kids would always comment in class, "They killed my dad, they killed my uncle, and they killed my cousin, because today there was an armed confrontation." They would say, "Well, we had to leave in the middle of the night" or "We were with my family, camped out for three days to guard our borders from the other town." This produced a very tense atmosphere. A lot of nights you could hear shooting going on or the bells would be ringing to call people out to defend their lands. So what this meant in school is that the kids were all preoccupied with these other problems instead of how to get ahead and how to engage with their education.

Carmen López Vásquez
Carmen is perhaps best known as "Maestra Carmen," one of the primary voices heard on Radio La Ley 710. This is the station that was taken on August 21, 2006, after the governor destroyed the transmission towers of the

Corporación Oaxaqueña de Radio y Television (Oaxacan Corporation of Radio and Televisión, COR-TV). Renamed La Ley del Pueblo, this radio station had the longest life of all of those taken by the movement in 2006. Apart from her role in the media and as a representative in APPO's governance structure, Carmen has had a long and distinguished career as a preschool and elementary school teacher and activist in Sección 22. Born in the 1960s, Carmen came of age in Oaxaca's premier rural normal school and was part of the movement to democratize CNTE. As with Esteban, Carmen's experiences growing up in rural Mexico and working there as a teacher have been formative in her ideology and politics.

I spoke with Carmen on three occasions in 2010 and 2011. She has an animated, engaging presence accentuated by her curly reddish hair and long fingernails. I sat facing her and was immediately taken by her passion and emotion for the movement she participated in. She is small in size but not in presence; her narrative moves in waves of intense concentration as she recalls details of particular events. Here I concentrate on her childhood and first experiences as a teacher. We will return to her testimony in several other places in the book.

I am Oaxacan, originally from San Pedro Jicayán, an indigenous municipality. I was born in the district capital of Santiago Jamiltepec on the coast of Oaxaca. My mother is from San Pedro Jicayán, and my father is from the Mixteca region of Oaxaca. Because of work [her mother was a teacher], my first years were spent in different locations on the coast of Pinotepa Nacional. When I was six years old we came to live in San Pedro Jicayán and it was there that I first went to school.

I only spoke Spanish, but because San Pedro Jicayán is a community where about 99 percent of the population speaks Mixtec, I had to learn how to speak. So, when I was six years old I learned how to speak Mixtec. The entire time I was in elementary school I lived in San Pedro Jicayán. When it was time for me to attend secondary school, I had to leave the town and go to study in Pinotepa Nacional. Now looking back, I really think that it was the six-year period I spent living in that Mixtec community that gave me the basis for developing a consciousness about the social reality we live in.

LYNN: *Could you tell us a little bit about the specific experiences you had that you remember as foundational in this consciousness?*

CARMEN: *Well it was a community where* caciquismo *[political bossism] was protected by the PRI, as has been the case for many years in Oaxaca. Actually* they had been in power for eighty years. The PRI, as the government political party, really treated people in this indigenous community like third- or fourth-class citizens. There were a lot of daily injustices that I observed there. . . . For example, the family of caciques there used the majority of the peasant men to work in their properties for really miserable salaries. Their salaries were so low that they couldn't have any quality of life. In San Pedro Jicayán there was staggering poverty. The kids were barefoot and malnourished. If they had a tortilla and beans to eat that was a lot. Sometimes they would go all day without eating. A lot of people didn't have land to work, either.

The mestizos who lived there were called gente de razón [the people who know, who are knowledgeable, literally "people of reason"], and the indigenous people, who they said were sin razón [without reason, ignorant, without knowledge], were practically treated like animals. They had fewer rights than mestizos and their situation was extreme. Most did not go to school. There were only a few of us who were able to go and study. This experience really marked me. I remember thinking as a kid, "How is it possible that this is happening to other human beings?" They were human beings just like me.

. . . After I studied secondary school in Pinotepa I didn't go to high school. We had a plan of study for those who wanted to be teachers that involved us going directly to the rural normal school, which was Escuela Normal Vanguardia in Tamazulapan, in the Mixtec region. It is one of sixteen such schools that still exist in the country that are a product of the Mexican Revolution.

LYNN: *How did you know to go there?*

CARMEN: *It was my mother. She was a municipal teacher first, working in literacy campaigns. Then she had to leave her teaching position, but she was a person who always identified with the struggle against injustice, whether it was injustice against her neighbors or against others. . . .*

I started at the normal school in 1980. You studied for four years. It was a very important experience for me and also very satisfying. The students were organized, and they defended their demands inside of the school. We had a democratic culture in the school. We had asambleas [meetings] and also a student organization.

I immediately identified with the student organization and I started to participate. This is how I first became an activist. I then became the president of our committee of political orientation and then I became secretary-general of the student committee. Because we developed a strong student movement in school, as was the case in most of the normal schools, we became identified with those struggles. We didn't just focus on demands inside of the school, but

we also aligned ourselves with peasant movements and other social move-
ments that were being repressed at that time by the state and federal govern-
ments. There was so much repression against what we were doing that I had
to leave school for one year, and so it took me until 1985 to finish.

LYNN: *So your time in the normal school coincided with the democratization*
of Sección 22?

CARMEN: *Yes, in terms of the timing. I formally joined Sección 22 in 1985,*
when I graduated from the normal school. At this time, all of us who gradu-
ated from rural normal schools had the automatic right to a teaching post or
plaza. When you finished the normal school you got your plaza, they sent you
to work, and they immediately paid you for your first two weeks. But even
before this period I knew about the teachers' struggle because of my mother,
who was very involved in the teachers' movement since 1980. Because we were
students in the normal school in Tamazulapan, we participated in the first
marches that Sección 22 made to Mexico City.

I was nineteen years old when I finished normal school, and now I have
been working as a teacher for twenty-five years.

My first teaching post was in a community that was very, very isolated.
There were no roads, no electricity; there was not even any place for me to
stay. It was called Coyché, in the municipality of Jamiltepec. It was a place
where the horses would sink up to their knees in mud during the rainy season.
And horseback was the only way to get there.

When I arrived there, it was up to two of us to teach the first through sixth
grades. It was a very wonderful experience that also made me strong. It also
prepared me in some way to participate in a longer social struggle. It was part
of the service I gave. I see social struggle not just as a pure political struggle,
but also as an act of love and of service. I believe that real politics is about
serving humanity, helping humanity to grow and prosper.

For Carmen, her childhood experiences in extremely marginal indigenous communities were fundamental in forming a consciousness about the different kinds of hierarchies, discrimination, and injustices that existed in Oaxaca. When she went to a rural normal school these ideas were further crystallized and were fused with her organizing experience as a student activist. Moving into her own teaching position and beginning to be active in Sección 22 provided the track for her further political development and eventual involvement with APPO.

While teachers such as Carmen and Esteban and others in Sección 22 were crucial participants in APPO, other historical social movements were important in the ability of APPO to take shape in 2006.

COCEO, COCEI, and Other Movements Topple a Governor and Rework Oaxacan Politics in the 1970s and 1980s

Of special note in the story of APPO are the urban, student, indigenous, women's, and peasant movements that have flourished in Oaxaca over the past thirty years. Analysts of the 2006 movement have pointed to the 1970s and 1980s as crucial years in the formation of a constellation of movements that worked in coalition over a period of time and were instrumental in fashioning a new relationship between the state and Oaxacan society and gave increasing bargaining power to social movements.

The student movement of Oaxaca that began in the 1970s was a crucial source of support for a variety of movements that defined the state in the 1970s, particularly COCEO. Like many parts of the world, Mexico City was the site of a growing student movement in the summer of 1968. Tired of authoritarianism, the movement built on the discontent of high school and university students who protested police violence after soldiers blasted through the door of a prep school, killing students. Students from the Universidad Nacional Autónoma de México (National Autonomous University, UNAM) and other area schools began to organize protests against repression and violence. The police seized the UNAM and then another university amid student resistance. Several days later students organized a new protest shortly before the Olympic Games in the Plaza de Las Tres Culturas in the neighborhood known as Tlatelolco. They were met by government troops, who fired on them for two hours. Newspaper reports suggested that hundreds were killed (see Poniatowska 1975).

After the massacre in Tlatelolco and the scattering of student activists to many corners of the republic to carry on their struggles, Oaxaca, like other rural states, became a site of popular organizations. In 1970, as noted by Gerardo Renique, radicalized students in Oaxaca turned the Federación Estudiantil Oaxaqueña (Oaxacan Student Federation) into a more political organization and worked with other organizations to protest the high cost of living, organize resistance to increased bus fares, and demand democratic rights. A *bufete popular* (people's attorney's office) provided free legal advice to labor unions, peasant organizations, and other movements. In

1971 the student movement was able to achieve considerable educational reforms that resulted in the autonomy of the university, known since that time as la Universidad Autónoma "Benito Juárez" de Oaxaca (Autonomous Benito Juarez University of Oaxaca, UABJO).

In 1972 the student movement was divided: one part joined the guerrilla struggle, and the other formed COCEO and related organizations.[8] In its founding document, COCEO stated that it:

> proposes to convert itself into an instrument of the united combative popular forces of the democratic and progressive sectors . . . and as a front which . . . should obey the demands of the base and the general demands which mobilize the masses as well as those of the participating organizations. The front should respect the autonomy of its participating members and push for democratic discussions in the decision-making processes related to tactical decisions brought about through consensus in order to lead people in unity in practice. (Martínez Vásquez 1990: 133n11; see also Yescas Martínez 1979)[9]

The group lent support to local peasant movements that carried out significant land invasions in Oaxaca in the mid-1970s. The region of Zimatlán was the epicenter of a series of land invasions that also included Tlalixtac de Cabrera, La Ciénega, Santa Catarina Quiané, el Faro, Xoxocotlán, and San Martín Mexicapan. All of these regions had a high level of participation in agriculture, an increase of population over time that caused plots to become smaller or nonexistent for each successive generation, and a low level of other employment options (see Zafra 1979; Martínez Vásquez 1990: 139–42).[10] Links to the student groups in Oaxaca were important to the people from the land-invasion communities because it helped them obtain legal advice as well as economic resources, help making posters and flyers, and improved access to the press (Martínez Vásquez 1990: 143).

The property owners who were the subjects of the land invasions insisted that the state remove the invaders and formed an association of "small landholders" to pressure government leaders. The response of Governor Fernando Gómez Sandoval, however, in the cases of Ciénega and Quiné, was to buy the lands from the landowners using a government credit program, turn over the lands to the invaders, and suggest that they pay for them later. This response came after the owners presented *certificados de inafectabilidad*, which were legal documents that permitted landowners to not have their property touched for agrarian land redistribution as specified under Article 27 of the Mexican Constitution. None of the peasant groups accepted the condition of paying for the invaded lands (Martínez Vásquez 1990: 145). Governor Gómez Sandoval was accused by landowners of being "soft," and they later joined merchants in supporting a new candidate for governor, Manuel Zárate Aquino, who came into office promising to take a *mano duro* (hard line) against social movements. In several communities, the struggle for land was translated into a movement for control of municipal governments.[11]

At the same time that local peasant land invasions and COCEO were gaining success in the central valleys of Oaxaca, a new organization was launched in the isthmus of Tehuantepec, the Coalición de Obreros, Campesinos, y Estudiantes del Istmo (Isthmus Coalition of Workers, Peasants and Students, COCEI). This new coalition combined claims to land, credit, wages, benefits, municipal services, and Zapotec cultural identity to create a unique form of organization (see Rubin 1997; Campbell 1994; Campbell et al. 1993). While COCEI began by joining together some of the same sectoral elements as COCEO, it endured much longer and, in retrospect, can be seen as a pioneer in the struggle for indigenous autonomy and territory that is strongly tied to the production and reproduction of a specific indigenous ethnic identity and culture. COCEI was also successful in winning municipal elections in the early 1980s, as described later in this chapter. Both COCEO and COCEI had major impacts on Oaxaca politics.

The years 1973 and 1974 were contentious for independent labor unions in Oaxaca. At the national level as well as in Oaxaca, labor conflicts were at an all-time high in 1974. During a three-month period in 1973, three new independent unions (Oaxacan municipal workers, meat workers, and bus drivers) were formed in Oaxaca. These unions and others participated in strikes the following year (Alafita Méndez 1979: 264).[12] Most of the strikes centered on wage increases.

Not only because of the legal advice it provided through the students' bufete juridico but also through the widespread political support it generated for strikers and their demands, COCEO became a major resource for independent labor unions. As noted at the beginning of this chapter, the tactics and strategies used by COCEO and other movements have some important similarities with actions and tactics taken by APPO and Séccion 22 in 2006, such as the claiming of public space through demonstrations, marches, and sit-ins, the use of graffiti, and the distribution of flyers and leaflets. COCEO also used the university radio station to create an alternative message and give voice to the demands of the workers and peasants they were supporting. Mobile brigades drove through the city broadcasting the latest demands and updates through speakers mounted on cars, typically VW *bochos*, or Bugs. And buses were commandeered to protest fare increases and inflation. All of these tactics were seen in 2006 as well.

By the fall of 1974 Oaxaca City had significant daily political activity. The government of Gómez Sandoval signed an agreement with meat workers in partial recognition of their demands. This, along with the concession made to those who had occupied land, pitted landowners and merchants against the state government and made it necessary for President Luis Echeverría to put in a new governor who would not concede to social movements. Echeverría thought he had found the right person in Manuel Zárate Aquino, who promised to "make sure that people obeyed the law" and to "put an end to the disorder that has characterized our city and that has wounded our dignity with all of the acts of vandalism and abuse" (referring to the meetings, demonstrations, graffiti, and flyers of the popular organizations; Martínez Vásquez 1990: 167).

Putting things "in order" entailed widespread repression under Zárate Aquino, who instituted a program of co-optation and repression. Independent labor unions were continuously intimidated by official state sectoral unions such as the CNC and the Confederación de Trabajadores de México (Mexican Workers Confederation), whose leaders called for "punishment for the agitators" of independent unions in Oaxaca. Governor Zárate Aquino began an explicit campaign using radio and the media to link COCEO student leaders to guerrilla groups. He also sent in the army to impose order "in the city halls of Zimatlán, Zaachila, Santa Gertrudis, Xoxocotlán, and Juchitán, where land invasions and attempts by movement organizers to win election to municipal city councils and mayoralties had taken place. Landowners, merchants, and businessmen—the political class of Oaxaca— came together to support the state government" (Martínez Vásquez 1990: 169–70). Some of the tactics used were imprisonment of urban movement leaders, assassination of peasants and peasant leaders, and use of the army to intimidate rural communities. The most dramatic expression of state authority against the popular movements came in July 1975, when two thousand people were detained for invading private lands under the leadership of an independent peasant federation.[13]

In 1976 Oaxaca became further polarized. Governor Zárate Aquino decided to consolidate his political support and suspend civil liberties, such as the right to assemble. Demonstrations continued in Oaxaca, Juchitán, and Tuxtepec despite the prohibition, and members of the student movement and others continued to paint public walls, hold public actions, and disseminate their demands. On January 8, 1977, the central building of UABJO was taken over by a group of people that included the owners of the bus company Estrella del Valle y Pacifico, a state representative, women devoted to La Virgen de la Soledad (Oaxaca's patron saint), family members of the head of the local House of Representatives, government bureaucrats from several offices, the leaders of the Partido Acción Nacional (National Action Party, PAN), and even the governor himself (Martínez Vásquez 1990: 187). The Fusión Cívica de Organizaciones Productivas (Civic Merger of Productive Organizations, FUCOPO) was formed out of this group that occupied the university building and became the primary instrument for the organization of the political and economic elite of Oaxaca in support of the state government. An anticommunist campaign grew in Oaxaca, targeting the student, labor, and peasant movements. The campaign was fueled by two local papers, *El Imparcial* and *Noticias*, as well as by stories on the national news show *24 Horas*, anchored by Jacobo Zabludovsky.

In response, organizations that had supported one another and suffered ongoing repression of their leaders under Zárate Aquino formed the Frente Popular Contra la Represión (Popular Front against Repression, FPCR). Members included COCEO and COCEI, among others. Their demands focused on continued respect for individual democratic rights, a resolution of the ongoing conflict regarding leadership of UABJO, and the removal of the governor (Daria 2010: 24; Ruiz Cervantes 1978: 64–67).

Determined to shut down the increasingly unified movements, the state government escalated its tactics to include the assassination of some participants in the demonstrations. This tactic was also used in the repression against APPO in 2006. In February 1977 two children were killed in front of the city hall of Juchitán. The following day, the mutilated bodies of three peasants who had participated in the demonstration appeared a hundred miles from Juchitán. Witnesses stated that they had been tortured (Martínez Vásquez 1990: 191).

By February 1977, the FUCOPO, which supported the Zárate Aquino government, had run out of patience. The leaders organized a general strike (which they called a suspension of business activities to avoid using the word *strike*) to try to get the federal government to intervene in the polarized city of Oaxaca and shut down the social movements—another tactic repeated in 2006 by Governor Ulises Ruiz. They published a leaflet on February 25:

The organizations that make up the FUCOPO have agreed to carry out a suspension of business activities for the period of 48 hours beginning on the 28th of this month of February, inviting the people in general to unite themselves in this suspension [strike] so that our state can return to legality. . . .

Concretely we ask: first, the detention of delinquents who, disguised like students, peasants or workers, have intervened in our economic activities. We also ask for the detention of the intellectual authors of these activities who have devoted themselves to subverting order in our state.

Secondly: we ask that notification be given immediately of the determinations necessary to resolve the problems that are behind this violence in the countryside, in industry, in the student sector and in general.

Third: We ask that the federal government support and back the determinations of our state government . . . in order that we achieve these objectives previously noted. (Mártinez Vásquez 1990: 192)

Demonstrations in Mexico City in February 1977 called for the *desaparación de poderes*, the disappearance of government powers in Oaxaca that had the support of various political parties. In Oaxaca on March 2, 1977, police fired into a demonstration close to the zócalo; twenty people were wounded, one of whom died. This was just days after the slaughter on February 27 in San Juan Lalana of twenty-seven peasants by local police forces and paramilitaries in the service of local caciques. On March 3 the army began patrolling the city, concentrating in places where student activists were headquartered. On the same day, the governor was called to Mexico City and the leaders of COCEO and COCEI were summoned by the *secretaría de gobernación* (secretary of the interior) to Mexico City. The Oaxaca state legislature held a special session and, by the end of March 3, the Comisión Permanente de la Legislatura (Permanent Committee of the Legislature) read a text asking the governor to take a leave of absence. Manuel Zárate Aquino stepped down.

Oaxaca state senator Eliseo Jiménez Ruiz was appointed governor. This marked a downturn in the popular movement of the 1970s, with the exception of COCEI in the Isthmus. Jiménez Ruiz, a Mexican army general, had led a successful campaign against the Ejército Guerrillero de los Pobres (Guerrilla Army of the Poor), led by the schoolteacher Lucio Cabañas in the state of Guerrero (Reneque 2007: 5). Ruiz devoted himself to a systematic campaign against the 1977 social movements and also focused on dismantling the Unión del Pueblo (People's Union) and its guerrilla forces. By 1979 COCEO was gone, the Unión del Pueblo no longer existed, and COCEI had experienced significant repression in the Isthmus.

Ironically COCEI was able to leverage at the national level the political reforms that had been instituted under the Echeverría government in 1977. These reforms permitted local political organizations to get onto municipal ballots by aligning themselves with a national political party. COCEI aligned itself with the Partido Comunista Mexicano (Mexican Communist Party) and in 1981 won municipal elections, making Juchitán the first and only city in Mexico with a government that was both leftist and indigenous. Juchitán was governed by COCEI from 1981 until 1983 under the leadership of Leopoldo de Gyves, a student activist in COCEI. Through its program of *ayuntamiento popular* (people's government) COCEI engaged in several reforms, including an ambitious cultural project that centered on using the Zapotec language in arts, music, poetry, and literature; an attempt to regain land lost to peasants by initiating land occupations; the formal recognition of local peasants; the development of beneficial public works projects; a literacy campaign; the start-up of a local radio station; and building clinics and schools. (For detailed descriptions, see Rubin 1997; Campbell 1994; Martínez López 1983; Monsiváis 1983; Iturbide et al. 1989.)

By 1983, under the administration of President Miguel de la Madrid, there was less tolerance of leftist movements. Elements within the Oaxaca state government as well as within the press began to push for withdrawing recognition of the popular government of Juchitán. At the end of July 1983 two people were killed in a bitter confrontation between COCEI and local PRI politicians. In early August the Oaxacan state legislature withdrew recognition of the COCEI government and put in a new municipal government. These actions were accompanied by the arrival of federal army and state police forces that occupied the city.[14]

In 1986 COCEI entered the municipal elections again and joined a coalition municipal government. In 1989, after winning again, COCEI governed jointly with the PRI. COCEI won subsequent victories in 1992, 1995, and 1998. In 2002 it lost local elections for the first time in two decades and didn't regain power until 2005, forming a problematic alliance with the local Partido Revolucionario Democrático (Party of the Democratic Revolution, PRD). In 2007 COCEI abandoned its alliance with the Oaxaca PRD and joined with the Partido del Trabajo (Workers' Party), which many believe is simply an extension of the PRI. With this alliance, COCEI was able to hang onto the municipal government until 2010, when it lost to the PRI. The PRI is in power until 2013.

The successful organizing campaigns of COCEO in the 1970s that partially contributed to the resignation of Governor Zárate Aquino and of COCEI in the 1980s, which resulted in Mexico's first socialist municipal government, foreshadow the emergence of the APPO in 2006. The legacies of these organizations can be seen in some of the goals, tactics, demands, and strategies of APPO in 2006.

Rights Discourses and Social Movements in Mexico and Oaxaca

While the democratic teachers' movement and the urban, peasant, and indigenous movements are important elements underlying the Oaxacan social movement of 2006, the later movement can also be understood as part of a historical process of the globalization and institutionalization of rights discourses. Major rights discourses have had legislative and policy impacts in Mexico, and the active claiming of rights has unfolded by a wide range of organizations in Oaxaca.

In Mexico three kinds of rights (cultural, agrarian, and human) have come to be recognized in legislation since the 1990s, and nongovernmental and civil society organizations have emerged in relation to these rights. Cultural rights are recognized to some degree in the Mexican Constitution through the 1990 rewriting of Article 4, which states:

> The Mexican nation has a multicultural composition originally found
> in its indigenous peoples. The law protects and promotes the devel-
> opment of their languages, practices, customs, resources, and specific
> forms of social organization and guarantees their members effective
> access to the full range of the state's legal authority [jurisdiction].
> In the agrarian judgments and legal proceedings they are part of,
> their own legal practices and customs shall be taken into account in
> establishing the law.

The San Andrés Accords that were signed in 1996 by the Zapatista Army of National Liberation with President Ernesto Zedillo would, if they had been made law, have recognized traditional indigenous systems of governance and justice, provided indigenous peoples with the opportunity to design their own economic development plans, and provided opportunities for indigenous organizations and communities to build larger political blocs. Instead of implementing these accords, however, the government of Vicente Fox facilitated much weaker legislation, passed in April 2001, that granted states the right to limit indigenous rights proposals, confined "indigenous autonomy to communities within single municipalities, denied constitutional recognition of indigenous peoples as subjects with the right to decide upon their own forms of governance and development, and maintained a paternalistic relation in which the federal government would provide social services to indigenous communities" (Harvey 2001: 1048).

Agrarian rights were articulated under the rewritten Article 27 of the Constitution, which facilitated but did not require the privatization of land held communally in social tenancy. Invoking Emiliano Zapata's dictum "The land belongs to those who work it," the neoliberal governments of Carlos Salinas and Ernesto Zedillo harnessed "land and liberty" to a modernist discourse of individual rights. Slogans such as "Defend your rights to your individual parcel" and "Guarantee your individual freedom" were associated with the government surveys that accompanied the agrarian counterreform (Stephen 2002: 62–63). While the rights granted were centered on the individual, reactions to the government effort to encourage privatization of communally held land recentered discourses of collective and indigenous rights in Oaxaca and elsewhere.

Human rights discourses were institutionalized at the national level with the establishment in 1990 of the Comisión Nacional de Derechos Humanos (National Commission for Human Rights, CNDH). CNDH has some two hundred lawyers working full time (Dezalay and Garth 2002: 231) and, in addition to handling thousands of complaints every year, maintains relationships with other human rights entities abroad and an ever-growing number of such organizations in Mexico. A few years after CNDH was established, state-level counterparts were set up. The Comisión de Derechos Humanos de Oaxaca (Oaxacan Human Rights Commission, CDDHO, originally known as the State Commission of Human Rights) was established by law in 1993. Its website stated in 2008: "With the creation of this commission the necessity of the people of Oaxaca to have their rights and liberties guaranteed as well as the prompt and impartial procurement of justice is satisfied." The specific human rights mentioned are "the right to life, to physical integrity, equality, liberty, dignity, and judicial security of all persons, property, as well as the greatest possible efficiency in the provision of public services" (CDDHO 2008).

After the repression of 2006 and 2007 and more than twelve hundred human rights complaints, national and international pressure was put on the state of Oaxaca to reform the way the state office to defend human rights functioned. In April 2011, under the administration of newly elected governor Gabino Cué Monteagudo, the Oaxacan Constitution was reformed to create the Defensoría de los Derechos Humanos del Pueblo de Oaxaca (Office for the Defense of Human Rights of the People of Oaxaca, DDHPO). It had a broader mandate than CDDHO in terms of the rights it was supposed to protect and reflects discussion of rights that were articulated in the 2006 social movement. They include the right to life, to physical integrity, to freedom of expression, to freedom of belief or religion, to not be discriminated against, to judicial security, to property, to not be deprived of liberty in an arbitrary manner, to identity, to sexual preference, to health, to be heard and defended in a trial, to education, to not be tortured, and reproductive rights (DDHPO 2012). In 2012 legislation was passed to make DDHPO fiscally, administratively, and politically independent of the governor and state government.

A major increase in the number of organizations carrying out work that they called human rights monitoring and defense emerged in the 1990s in Oaxaca. The defense of the human rights of indigenous peoples in Oaxaca is rooted in the experience of the 1980s and dedicated to gaining power at the municipal level, defending indigenous land rights, promoting community-based grassroots development, and establishing links with national networks and movements for indigenous rights and self-determination (see Stephen 2002: 235–37; Rubin 1997).[15] Initially organizations at the grassroots level focused on indigenous and peasant rights, but because their work made them subject to harassment, death threats, illegal detention, and imprisonment, they became increasingly concerned with the defense and protection of their members. In the 1990s, with the militarization of several regions of Oaxaca, specific human rights organizations such as the Flor y Canto Center for Human Rights, the Siete Principes Center for Human Rights, and the Oaxaca Network for Human Rights were formed. The Bartolomé Carraso Regional Center for Human Rights links a number of such organizations and is mainly supported by the Catholic Church. These groups have undertaken campaigns to defend the rights of communities and individuals in the face of military and paramilitary occupation and harassment as well as individual cases of detention, torture, and illegal incarceration (see Stephen 1999). In 1998 the Liga Mexicana de Defensa de los Derechos Humanos (Mexican League for the Defense of Human Rights, Limeddh) formalized its statutes in Oaxaca and quickly became one of the foremost human rights groups, particularly in relation to indigenous communities. Limeddh also played a major role in defending the human rights of Oaxacans in 2006 and after, as described in chapter 4.

Women's committees within mixed organizations, women's organizations, and later networks of women's groups have also played important roles in integrating agendas of indigenous rights, human rights, and cultural rights with gender concerns. Historic groups such as Grupo de Estudios Sobre la Mujer, Rosario Castellanos A.C. (Women's Studies Group Rosario Castellanos), which began in 1977, have been pivotal in bringing women's rights to state and city politics and in pushing for legislative reforms that focus on reproductive rights and domestic violence.[16]

In the 1990s many indigenous, peasant, urban, student, and other organizations had women's committees that functioned as internal human rights committees had in the 1980s. In 2003 women's groups from around the state, including independent groups such as the Grupo de Estudios Sobre la Mujer, Rosario Castallanos A.C., and the women's committees and caucuses of other groups, formed the Huaxyacac Collective. The purpose of this alliance-building network was to pressure candidates in the 2004 elections (in which Ulises Ruiz was "elected" governor of Oaxaca) to sign the Oaxaca Agenda for Gender Equity, which would have obligated Oaxaca to adhere to the UN Convention for the Elimination of All Forms of Discrimination against Women, ratified by the Mexican Senate in 2001 (Dalton 2007; Magaña 2008). The collective pressured the Ruiz administration to take action on the alarming number of femicides in the state, which it estimated to number 351 between 1999 and 2003 (Davies 2006). From 2006 on, the collective was an active member of APPO.

Summary

A study of the rich history of social movements that have characterized the state and city of Oaxaca since the 1970s reveals some important continuities with the social movement of 2006. First, the critical role played by the democratic teachers' movement, as represented by Sección 22 as the "spine" of APPO, draws on the structure, discipline, and statewide convocational power of the teachers. The organizational model of APPO, as discussed in the next chapter, is strongly influenced by the structure of CNTE, organized by workplace-based committees gathered into local delegations that then elect representatives to a statewide assembly. CNTE congresses of Sección 22 have approximately eight hundred participants. The initial statewide assemblies of APPO had hundreds of representatives as well.

The mandate that leaders respond to the base is also clearly influenced by the political culture of CNTE, by the governance style in indigenous communities where community authorities elected in asambleas are expected to respond the mandate of the asamblea (see chapter 5), and by the neo-Zapatista ideology of *mandar obedeciendo* (lead by obeying), which implies that leaders should follow the will of the larger group they represent. The importance of granting autonomy to local organizational groups, as is the case for CNTE delegaciones, is also reflected in the structure of APPO. This became one of APPO's weaknesses because of the independent actions of groups that organized in neighborhoods around physical barricades, known as *barricadas*, to prevent the entry of paramilitaries into neighborhoods. This process is described in the following chapter.

One of the weaknesses noted in CNTE, in the analysis of Susan Street, could also be applied to APPO. Because CNTE functioned primarily to coordinate strategic and negotiation activities, it never developed a unified ideology that translated into an alternative education program at the national level. While the Oaxaca Sección 22 of CNTE has maintained much more unity than other sections, this national problem of unity for CNTE can also be seen in APPO. As long as the governor of Oaxaca held power and was repressing the groups that were aligned in APPO, they worked in unified ways to coordinate strategic actions. Other than the shared demand to remove Ulises Ruiz as governor of Oaxaca, the more than three hundred organizations in APPO did not have common, future-looking ideological goals and programs. Attempts were made to craft such goals, such as the Foro Nacional: Construyendo La Democracia y La Gobernabilidad (National Forum: Constructing Democracy and Governability), held on August 16 and 17, 2006, which brought together Sección 22, APPO, municipal and agrarian community authorities, and civil society organizations in an attempt to create a series of initiatives for redefining governance in Oaxaca (see chapter 8). Because of the repression and jailing of many APPO participants in November 2006, it took almost a year and a half to reconstitute the APPO statewide assembly. Many of the proposals had languished by that time.

The tactics and strategies used by participants in APPO, Sección 22, and the barricades, as described throughout this book, clearly draw many lessons from the movements of the 1970s through the 1990s. Demonstrations, marches, the occupation of government buildings and public spaces, public graffiti, the use of radio and other media, and the importance of localized modes of participation are clearly reflected in the 2006 movement. Many of the strategies and tactics seen in 2006 echo those used by previous movements. The escalation of violence and the polarization of Oaxaca in 2006 also echo the mid-1970s, when movement leaders were assassinated, activists imprisoned, and organizations routinely intimidated and harassed by the press. In 2006 the confrontation reached more extreme levels and the arrival of federal troops produced a different result. In addition, other forms of organizing that focused on autonomy, decision making by assembly, and the use of popular religious symbols and other forms of public art and media distinguish the movement of 2006 (discussed in chapter 9).

While Manuel Zárate Aquino was partially successful in organizing the economic and political elite in alliance with the state government through the creation of the FUCOPO, ultimately the group's pressuring of the federal government to retake control of the state resulted in his removal and the imposition of a new, harder-line governor: Eliseo Jiménez Ruiz. The militarization of Oaxaca City and some other parts of the state ultimately resulted in the downturn of COCEO and other movements, except COCEI. Governor Ulises Ruiz Ortiz was in power in 2006, when the Federal Preventative Police arrived and shut down APPO, arrested and imprisoned hundreds, and likely disappeared others. He served until the end of his term in December 2010.

Perhaps the greatest source of the continuities between the 1970s and the present in Oaxaca are found in the legacy of activist experience and struggle, which spans four generations. The socialization of the goals, ideology, strategies, and tactics of many movements has been passed on to multiple generations throughout the state. This collective experience and knowledge, along with Oaxaca's traditions of indigenous and organizational governance by assembly, are perhaps the most important legacies from the earlier decades, and they were instrumental in the political events of 2006.

3

The Emergence of APPO and the
2006 Oaxaca Social Movement

On July 30, 2006, the popular park in Oaxaca known as El Llano or Parque Benito Juárez was the site of a cultural and physical battle for symbolic and material space. Unable to carry out the official Oaxaca state folk celebration known as the Guelaguetza at the site of its outdoor stadium, members of the governor's cultural staff were attempting to produce a smaller scale version in the Llano. Protesters from APPO, Sección 22, and others quickly gathered with people from nearby neighborhoods to encircle and drive out the dancers, musicians, and cultural administrators who were attempting to carry on their Guelaguetza celebration.

Guelaguetza refers to the institution of reciprocal exchange in Zapotec, but in the hands of the state it came to refer to a commercialized festival of folkloric dances and gift showering, with a high admission price. The state-sponsored Guelaguetza, which has its origins in the Homenaje Racial (ethnic/racial homage) of 1932, was described as "a great festival of the races" (Poole 2004: 76–77). It was to "consist of 'Racial Ambassadresses' and their indigenous entourages, supposedly representing a discrete cultural territory within the state." One of its main features was to be entourages made up of "men and women who still conserved the autochthonous garments of their race" (76–77). This event, which marked the four-hundredth anniversary of Oaxaca as a city, was a way for the post-revolutionary state to consolidate a state "culture" but also to define Oaxaca as consisting of "different regional races" (78).[1] The first Guelaguetza stadium, known as Rotonda de la Azucena (Rotunda of the White Lilies), had also been built in 1932. The inaugural Homenaje Racial also included the presentation of representatives from the seven regions of the state who demonstrated their music, dances, and customs (Rivas 2011).

From the 1930s through the early 1970s, this event had been loosely organized; dancers performed in the Rotonda Azucena, which was on El Cerro Fortín near the center of the city. Many elderly Oaxacans and people from nearby communities remember coming to sit with their families on blankets or *petates* (palm mats) and eating food they had brought with them while they watched the dancers. They remember the event as free and relatively informal. In 1974 a new auditorium was built by the state government of Oaxaca and inaugurated by then-governor Fernando Gómez Sandoval. Funding for the auditorium came primarily from the federal government, which contributed 8 million pesos to the state's 250,000 pesos (Rivas 2011). Beginning that year, admission was charged for entry. In 1999 the auditorium was officially named the Auditorio Guelaguetza.

Many locals have never attended the event since the 1970s because of its high price tag. By the twenty-first century, ticket prices had become prohibitive even for middle-class Oaxacans. A description of the 2008 official Guelaguetza stated that ticket prices were about 400 pesos (approximately U.S.$40) for each performance (Oaxacalive.com 2008). In 2006 the closure of the Guelaguetza stadium by APPO was the beginning of a battle for control of public space. In conjunction with Sección 22, APPO held the first Guelaguetza Popular, or People's Guelaguetza, in the soccer stadium of the UABJO on July 23 and 24, 2006.

※ VIDEOCLIP 3.1: http://dx.doi.org/10.7264/N3KS6PHF

This event, which partially paralleled the structure of the official Guelaguetza, also involved presentations of dances, music, and customs of the seven Oaxacan regions. The presentations were augmented by anti–Ruiz Ortiz slogans and other social movement symbols and chants. Attended by over twenty-five thousand people in 2006 and continuing on an annual basis, this cultural conquest of space was continued at a different event in the Llano on July 30, through an APPO protest.

What began as about ten contingents of official state dance troops and bands in the center of the park ended with their withdrawal and a complete occupation of the park by hundreds of APPO and Sección 22 support-ers carrying wooden sticks and metal rods and shouting "Ya cayó, ya cayó, Ulises ya cayó" (He has already fallen, he has already fallen, Ulises has al-ready fallen). An APPO supporter climbed to the top of a statue of Oaxaca's native son Benito Juárez, the Zapotec lawyer from Guelatao, Oaxaca, who became president of Mexico. From atop the statue the supporter waved and shouted "Ya cayó, ya cayó." He was almost ripped from the statue by the official Guelaguetza defenders but escaped after being surrounded by a cir-cle of APPO supporters. The park divided into two contingencies that were shouting slogans at each other. Eventually the official dancers withdrew and APPO supporters spread out over the entire park, controlling the space.

✳ VIDEOCLIP 3.2: http://dx.doi.org/10.7264/N3G15XS1

How did APPO, Sección 22, and many unaffiliated people come to lose faith in Oaxaca state governance and decide to try to run the city them-selves? What kinds of political conditions and histories produced an open-ing that allowed the Oaxacan social movement to flourish and grow for a six-month period in 2006 and then be shut down in November 2006 by military and police occupation? These are the questions this chapter will attempt to answer. More extensive analysis and descriptions of particu-lar events and aspects of the 2006 movement will come in the subsequent chapters.

Oaxaca's State Governments and Social Movements, 1986–2006: Combining Negotiation and Repression

Beginning in the mid-1980s, state governments in Oaxaca began a process that some have called governmental hybridization: combining the creation of more formally democratic institutions and forms of governance with au-thoritarian practices. While this was modeled at the national level to some degree in the presidency of Luis Echeverría, it did not become a common practice in Oaxaca until the administration of Heladio Ramírez López, who governed from 1986 through 1992 (see Durazo Herrman 2010). Ramírez López had been a PRI senator from Oaxaca and had spent time promoting proposals at the national level to recognize Oaxaca's multicultural character (Hernández Díaz 2007: 49). In 1990 Ramírez López proposed two modifica-tions to the Oaxacan Constitution. One was to Article 16, to recognize the pluriethnic composition of the state of Oaxaca due to the presence of the state's sixteen different ethnic groups. The other change was to Article 25, which established "respect for the traditions and democratic practices of indigenous communities" (Acevedo Conde and Pardo 1993; Florez Cruz 2002: 176–78; Hernández Díaz 2007: 49). The reforms were approved by the Oaxacan Congress and made Oaxaca the first state to have constitutional recognition of indigenous people and their internal norms. As pointed out by Jorge Hernández Díaz (2007: 49), this constitutional change outlined a new formal, legal relationship between indigenous communities, the state, and the larger society, predating similar reforms made at the national level several years later.

Ramírez López also was able to partially integrate Sección 22 of SNTE into a relationship with the government through the creation of the Instituto Estatal de Educación Pública de Oaxaca (IEEPO), as discussed in chapter 2. By granting teachers access to the state administrative structure of education and raising their salaries using resources from the federal education program, Ramírez López began what became a negotiating pact with the teachers, which was followed by each subsequent administration until that of Ruiz Ortiz in 2006. As discussed by Martínez Vásquez, in their part of the bargain teachers agreed to mediate between the government and Oaxaca's myriad social movements. This change empowered Sección 22 not only in relation to the state but in relation to other social movements as well. The government also sought to expand its influence among urban unions through "the clientelistic distribution of material resources and operating permits" to taxi drivers and street vendors and in markets (Durazo Herrmann 2010: 97).

The government of Diódoro Carraso Altamirano (1992–98) started out following a track similar to that of Ramírez López's: initiating governmental reforms in the arenas of indigenous and human rights and continuing some engagement with social movements. His government initiated the first state human rights commission in Oaxaca in 1993. In 1994 the Congress of Oaxaca approved further reforms to recognize indigenous *usos y costumbres* (customary forms of governance and justice). On the birthday of Benito Juárez, March 21, the state government announced the Nuevo Acuerdo para los Pueblos Indígenas (New Agreement for Indigenous Peoples), which focused on three areas of indigenous rights: the administration of justice, resolution of agrarian conflict, and respect for customs and traditions. The changes were legislated through new laws and a further modification of Article 16 in the Oaxaca Constitution (Hernández Díaz 2007: 50).

The reforms in Oaxaca were pushed by indigenous intellectuals and others who were close to the governor (Anaya 2002a: 105–6).[2] According to

Hernández Díaz (2007: 51), while the PRI supported the reforms, the PRD did not have a clear position as a political party, and the PAN was clearly opposed. He and others (Anaya 2002a; Recondo 2002) suggest that the PRI supported this initiative because as political parties began to enter into municipal elections in Oaxaca, the PRI began losing power. By 1995 opposition candidates for the state senate received more votes than the PRI in seventy-six Oaxacan municipalities (Hernández Díaz 2007: 51). By supporting the usos y costumbres legislation in Oaxaca, which would forbid the entrance of political parties into *municipios* opting for customary forms of governance based on community-wide assemblies, the PRI hoped to stem the tide of Oaxacan voters opting for the PRD and PAN.

While Carrasco Altamirano's administration began with some positive attempts to continue the dialogue with social movements, this all changed when an armed organization called El Ejército Popular Revolucionario (Revolutionary Popular Army, EPR) made its first public appearance in Aguas Blancas, Guerrero, to commemorate a massacre of peasants that had been carried out by the Mexican Army.[3] In August 1996 EPR mounted two attacks in Oaxaca and five other states. The first attack occurred at 10 p.m. in Tlaxiaco, Oaxaca, sixty miles west of Oaxaca City, where men armed with AK-47s attacked the city hall and killed two police officers, according to some reports (Ruiz Arrazola et al. 1996). The bloodiest attack occurred in the resort town of Huatulco, where a significant number of gunmen arrived and began spraying the post office, police station, and other government buildings with gunfire. According to one report, three police officers, two sailors, two guerrillas, and two civilians were killed (Pennick 2009). After that, Carrasco Altamirano's relationships with social movements, human rights groups, and indigenous groups deteriorated significantly. From the fall of 1996 to the present, the Zapotec-speaking Loxicha region of the Sierra Sur of Oaxaca has been the target of ongoing militarization and repression, which was particularly intense under the remainder of his term.

Between October and December 1996 most of the members of the municipal government of San Agustín Loxicha were arrested as suspected members of EPR, including the mayor, city council members, judges, and the heads of committees. They had been elected in 1995, in accordance with the new Oaxacan legislation that legitimized indigenous rights and customs in governance and justice. Interestingly the previous community authorities were indigenous caciques who were aligned with the PRI and the reactionary peasant organization Antorcha Campesina, known for dividing and harassing independent peasant organizations and for paramilitary violence.

In the fall of 1996 more than two hundred Zapotec indigenous people, in-cluding teenagers, were imprisoned after raids in which the Federal Judicial Police entered houses and rounded people up while the army maintained watch. Several people were also disappeared, according to an organization formed later of families of prisoners (Elizalde 1999). In 1997 the governor let it be known that he could not guarantee the safety of anyone who visited the region, effectively giving the army and Federal Judicial Police free rein in the Loxicha region. That same year, fifteen human rights workers I in-terviewed expressed grave concern about the isolation of the area and esti-mated that up to five thousand army troops were installed in the region. An analysis I carried out of the testimonials of thirty-seven Zapotec men from ten communities in the municipality of San Agustín Lochixa who were in-carcerated in Ixcotel Prison reveals that many were tortured and that more than half spoke only Zapotec and were unable to understand most of the charges against them. Also, many were detained while their families were present and were threatened with the sexual violation of their wives and children (see Stephen 1999: 830, 831).[4]

In the fall of 1998 some three thousand citizens from the twenty commu-nities associated with the municipality of San Agustín Loxicha were pushed by the state government to elect new authorities because the leaders they had elected in 1995 under usos y costumbres were still in jail. The newly elected mayor was a former state policeman who was implicated by Mexi-co's Comisión Nacional Para Derechos Humanos (National Commission for Human Rights, CNDH) in the murder of another community member. Thus, although the community had been able to take advantage of the new laws instituted by Governor Carrasco Altamirano, the benefits were short-lived as their traditionally elected officials remained in jail and the PRI returned to power. This case also suggests the specifics of state policy which com-bined negotiation and the granting of some new rights with repression.

During the last year of the Carrasco Altamirano administration, deten-tions were carried out in other places in the state as well, targeting other indigenous leaders and organizations. In April 1998 sixteen members of the Consejo Indígena Popular de Oaxaca "Ricardo Flores Magón" (Popular Indigenous Council of Oaxaca "Ricardo Flores Magón," CIPO-RFM) were arrested in Tuxtepec by more than five hundred elements of the judicial po-lice, preventative police, and army. CIPO-RFM had teachers from Sección 22 such as Raúl Gatica Bautista among its founders.[5]

The year 1998 also marked a transition of the governorship of Oaxaca to José Murat, who used Oaxaca's continued support of the PRI at the state level to leverage party resources from the national level. Murat initially also sought to renew the state government's social pact with some social movements by integrating as many of them as possible into the Oaxacan PRI (Santibáñez Orozsco 2004). He also helped to legitimize Sección 22's annual sit-in on teacher's day, May 15. Many municipalities, however, were not under PRI control. The COCEI continued to rule in Juchitán, in conjunction with the PRD. The city government of Oaxaca was headed by Gabino Cué Monteagudo, who won under the banner of the Convergencia Party after the PRI refused to let him run. During Murat's tenure as governor, with municipalities electing their local officials outside of the party system under usos y costumbres and the government of Oaxaca's two largest cities being run by opposition parties, the PRI was continuing to lose ground in the state, a trend I observed in the Loxicha region.

In August 2000 I was assigned as an official electoral observer in the municipality of San Agustín Loxicha, along with four other people. We received training by the Instituto Federal Electoral (Federal Electoral Institute, IFE) in Mexico City and were credentialed by the federal government. We set out from Oaxaca City the night before the 2000 presidential elections in a van and, after many hours on bumpy dirt roads, arrived at midnight in the municipal center of San Agustín Loxicha. When we entered the community we had to pass through three different *retenes*, or roadblocks—one by the army, one by the Federal Judicial Police, and another by an unspecified (probably municipal) police group dressed in black and holding machine guns. We were lodged in a building next to the city hall. The municipio building sported a jeep with a mounted machine gun on its roof for all to see. Early the following morning, I observed local police disguised as market vendors keeping track of the comings and goings of locals. The only political posters I observed in San Agustín and in several other small towns we were in were from the PRI. My assignment was to watch the polls and observe vote counting in several small hamlets outside of the municipal center. To our surprise, while there was no official presence of any party other than the PRI, the PRD won in the smaller communities by significant majorities. This happened without anyone's uttering a word—even in places where heavily armed police officers and unauthorized PRI representatives intimidated voters (see Global Exchange and Alianza Cívica 2000: 13–15). The 2000 presidential election marked the downfall of the PRI in Mexico with the victory of the PAN presidential candidate, Vicente Fox Quesada. In the state of Oaxaca, however, the PRI remained in power and repression against social movements was ongoing.

Under Murat, persecution of social movements continued in the state of Oaxaca, and armed confrontations remained on the upswing with the participation of paramilitary groups. For example, in 1999 a new armed group with the name Consejo Regional Obrero, Campesino y Urbano de Tuxtepec (Regional Workers', Farmers', and Urban Council of Tuxtepec), appeared with powerful weapons. It was rumored to be a paramilitary group. Two and a half years later, in 2002, the Consejo assaulted forty-six members of the CIPO-RFM in the Sierra Norte of Oaxaca.

In 2002 Raúl Gatica Bautista and other CIPO-RFM members became permanent targets of government repression, and CIPO-RFM members on the town council of Putla de Guerrero and others in Puerto Escondido were arrested (CIPO-RFM 2003; SIPAZ 2010a: 6). In the face of ongoing repression throughout the state, human rights organizations as well as other organizations in Oaxaca formed a statewide coalition that served as an important basis for future networking.

Violence continued that year in other parts of the state. On May 31, 2002, twenty-six farmers from Santiago, Chiltepec, in the municipality of Santiago Textitlán, were ambushed and assassinated in Agua Fría in the northern Sierra of Oaxaca. The people arrested for the assassinations were from Santo Domingo Teojolmulco. This armed confrontation was part of an ongoing conflict in the region, partially described by Esteban in the previous chapter. Here, as elsewhere in the state, the government of Murat did nothing to intervene or try to resolve the conflict. The ongoing violence in the Sierra Sur region, in the Triqui zone in the western part of Oaxaca, and elsewhere was an indicator of the historical tensions and deep divisions at the local level that were found throughout Oaxaca. Throughout the state, in locations both near and far from the capital, ongoing violence was part of the fuel that allowed the demands of APPO to resonate far outside of the capital in 2006.

On January 25, 2003, alarmed by the ongoing repression against groups like the CIPO-RFM, a large forum was held in Tuxtepec to protest repression and paramilitarism. Two months later, one of the CIPO-RFM leaders, Raúl Gatica Bautista, was detained by federal police. In September 2004 the sit-in staged by members of the CIPO-RFM in front of Santo Domingo Church and the Oaxaca city hall was forcibly evacuated by two hundred officers using tear gas, high-powered hoses, and pumps—some of the same techniques used to evict teachers in 2006. Gatica continued to receive death threats and was under arrest orders throughout the administration of Murat. That same year, the Comisión Interamericana de Derechos Humanos (Interamerican Human Rights Commission) asked both the Oaxaca state government and the Mexican federal government to institute precautionary measures to protect the physical integrity and legal security of Gatica Bautista and other leaders of CIPO-RFM. Neither government responded.

Murat's clear policy of repression against social movements that would not engage in clientelistic relationships with the state government also consolidated the authoritarianism of Oaxaca's subnational regime (Martínez Vásquez 2007: 23). Martínez Vásquez (2007: 25) provides further evidence of the downward spiral of clientelism that flourished under Murat and continued in the following administration. Under Murat, public administration positions were reserved for loyal friends and colleagues, not those who were best qualified; public works contracts were rewarded to contractors who demonstrated political loyalty; municipal governments that did not support the governor received few resources and were audited. Dozens of municipal administrations that were not politically loyal to the governor were replaced (thirty-eight between 2002 and 2004). Martínez Vásquez states that, under Murat, "the management of social programs, financial resources, public sector jobs, concessions and licensing of taxis and buses, housing programs, scholarships, cement, bricks, roofing, sewing machines—all were used with the intention of guaranteeing political clients, grateful followers, and votes" (25).

According to Martínez Vásquez, Murat also distanced himself and burned bridges to the traditional political classes of Oaxaca. This included many important members of the PRI, such as Diódoro Carraso Altamirano and the former governor Jesús Martínez Alvarez, who left the PRI and helped to form the Partido Convergencia por la Democracia (Convergence for Democracy Party) in 2001, which successfully brought Gabino Cué Monteagudo to the mayoralty of Oaxaca City.

In 2004 Oaxaca's mayor Gabino Cué Monteagudo was able to capitalize on the political alienation and economic difficulties associated with the Murat administration and successfully created one of the strongest coalition campaigns for governor ever seen in Mexico. He drew the Partido Convergencia por la Democracia, PRD, and PAN all together into the Coalición "Todos Somos Oaxaca" ("We are all Oaxaca" Coalition). According to Cué Monteagudo's (2004) book, *Oaxaca: Transición democrática o regresión autoritaria (La lucha contra el fraude y la elección del estado en el sur de México)*, the elections for governor were full of classic irregularities, including intervention by a host of government entities, from the governor himself to the state electoral commission to the state-owned Corporación Oaxaqueña de Radio y Televisión; cybernetic fraud, including *caerse el sistema* (system crash), as seen on television, during which the election results were changed; the use of public resources to buy votes; and much more. Cué Monteagudo received more than 450,000 votes in 2004. According to his government's website, the candidate who came closest to this number was Héctor Sánchez López in 1998. An opposition candidate, Sánchez López received approximately 320,000 votes (Gobierno del Estado 2010). It may have been Hector Sánchez López with 40,000 votes—along with electoral fraud by the PRI—who was responsible for the victory of Ruiz Ortiz in 2004 as the PRI-backed governor of Oaxaca.[6] The abstention rate also contributed to the contested nature of the election, as 48 percent of eligible voters did not vote (Martínez Vásquez 2007: 33).

Ulises Ruiz Ortiz did not waste any time in making clear his stance toward those who criticized his government. On his first day in office he approved the takeover of the offices of the Oaxaca newspaper *Noticias*, using an invented labor dispute to justify occupation of the newspaper's offices by a government-linked organization.[7] Newspaper employees were held hostage in the offices for thirty days, then were violently removed (SIPAZ 2010a). The newspaper's offices were then closed for almost a year and left in the possession of *porros* (paid thugs; Martínez Vásquez 2007: 36). Censorship of the press was accompanied by continued harassment and repression of the leaders of a wide range of organizations.[8] According to Martínez Vásquez (2007: 40), even the Catholic Church was scorned by Ruiz Ortiz's government. By May and June 2006, a large segment of Oaxacan society disliked Ruiz Ortiz and his government.

The Oaxacan Teachers' Movement in 2006

As many, including the leadership of Sección 22, have observed, the Oaxacan teachers' movement has been marked by competing leftist ideologies and organizations. The competition for leadership has centered on the secretary-general level, which provides influence at the national level inside of SNTE. Influence also means access to the considerable resources allocated for public education in Oaxaca through IEEPO. Competing currents can be traced to significant rifts in the union but were also evident in the fracturing of APPO during 2006.[9] As noted by James Daria (2010: 95), the leadership of the *secretaría-general* of Sección 22 clearly demonstrates these competing tendencies. In 2004 Enrique Rueda Pacheco was elected *secretario-general* of Sección 22 through the unification of seven different groups.[10] Although this bloc was in agreement, a dissenting bloc within the union united by two former secretarios led to an internal division in the union that later resulted in the consolidation of a new union, Sección 59 (95–96).

In 2005 Ulises Ruiz Ortiz responded within five days to the annual strike of Sección 22 and conceded the major issue they were pushing for: raising salaries to a higher level.[11] While in 2004 the union had demanded that all teachers' salaries be raised to the highest level, this demand had not been met by the previous governor. In 2005, however, Ruiz Ortiz worked out a deal with Sección 22 leadership that allowed most teachers to significantly increase their pay. As Daria notes, "For a new elementary teacher who would normally make 4,516 [pesos] per month . . . given the negotiations of 2005, the teacher made an extra 1,026 [pesos] a month" (2010: 156). This amounted to a 23 percent raise.

The union believed it had achieved significant economic gains for individual teachers in its short-lived negotiations with Ruiz Ortiz. The relative ease of the negotiations raised doubts on the part of some union members and resulted in internal accusations of corruption against Rueda Pacheco and other union officials. Not all of the agreements negotiated were fulfilled by Ruiz Ortiz in 2005, however. Members of Sección 22 held demonstrations to pressure the state government to meet its promises, but to no avail. According to Daria, Sección 22 leaders then decided that the lack of action was the fault of the director-general of IEEPO. They urged Ruiz Ortiz to remove him. The governor refused and undid the pact that had informally allowed Sección 22 to have significant control of IEEPO's administration. Eventually Ruiz Ortiz met Sección 22's demand for the removal of the IEEPO director-general and moved forward with dispersing the state government's part of the increased salary payments.[12]

On May 1, 2006, the Executive Committee of Sección 22 gave its annual list of demands to the state government. Moving Oaxacan teachers to the highest level of salary through a rezoning process was at the top of the list. Other demands included more teachers' positions, longer hours for secondary schools, loans for teachers, housing for teachers, and scholarships, uniforms, shoes, and school materials for poor students (Martínez Vásquez 2007: 60).

From the moment Sección 22 initiated the negotiating process by presenting its demands, things did not go well. Instead of responding rapidly, as happened in 2005, the governor began a media campaign against the movement and its leaders. Enraged by media spots such as that of a group of kids shouting to their teachers, "Maestro al salon/no al plantón" (Teachers, go to your classroom, not to the sit-in/occupation), Sección 22 went on strike on May 22. Again Ruiz Ortiz's response was to deny their requests. He offered a little more than half the amount he had the previous year in salary increases. He also threatened to not pay teachers for the days they were on strike if they did not return to the classroom (Martínez Vásquez 2007: 62).

This did not go over well with the union leadership. They responded by stating that if Ruiz Ortiz would not meet the teachers' demands and the increasing demands made by the larger civil society in Oaxaca, the union would call for his removal as governor. With no response forthcoming from the state, the teachers of Sección 22 did not take long to ratchet up the tension. On May 3 members of Sección 22 "opened up" the center of the city by removing the bases of parking meters and the stanchions that blocked the entrances to the streets in the historic center. The occupation grew, and a veritable tent city emerged in Oaxaca's center.

In response, the state congress issued a statement on June 1 that threw down the governor's gauntlet and clearly challenged the teachers' actions. It read in part:

> We ask that the State Government suspend the salaries of those teachers who persist in being absent from their teaching positions . . . that the Instituto Estatal de Educación Pública de Oaxaca [IEEPO] proceed to deliver notifications of unemployment to those teachers who continue in labor strike and. . . . declare that their contracts are rescinded without any responsibility of the federal and state government . . . and that the national security forces, within the scope of their competence, proceed without delay to evict people from the public roads and federal buildings, establishing protection to impede further occupation attempts. (Martínez Vásquez 2007: 63)

The situation quickly escalated, with Sección 22 calling for its first *mega-marcha* of 2006, an event that put the governor on trial in a *juicio político* (political trial). Ruiz Ortiz responded by giving the teachers just three days to return to work or lose their salaries for the days they had not worked. He also threatened to withdraw the funds for raises. But instead of returning to work, the teachers proceeded to organize another, even larger march. This one included neighborhood organizations, unions, and some of the communities that had suffered repression at the hands of Ruiz Ortiz. The number of marchers was estimated at 200,000 (Martínez Vásquez 2007: 63). The governor began circulating rumors of impending arrest orders for movement leaders.

June 14, 2006: The Detonator

The megamarches and growing tent city of Sección 22 in Oaxaca's center vibrated with energy. Men, women, and children were camped in and around the ten-block area of the zócalo. Groups of teachers lived, slept, and held meetings with others who worked in the same region of the state, and representatives from each of the different regions in which teachers worked and organized joined them. For example, teachers representing communities on the southern coast were camped out under the old municipal building on Oaxaca's zócalo. Whole families were living in the open air as the rainy season began in earnest that June. Under makeshift tarps, under cardboard, or under the *corredores* (sheltered outdoor corridors) of colonial buildings, thousands were cooking, eating, sleeping, and holding daily meetings in and around the city. Many were also housed as guests with the families of teachers who had relatives in Oaxaca City.

On June 14 Ruiz Ortiz attempted to violently evict the teachers and their families. More than three thousand poorly trained local and state riot police used tear-gas bombs, severely beat people, arrested dozens of Sección 22 activists without charging them, seriously damaged the Sección 22 Radio Plantón station and headquarters, and burned the teachers' belongings. The attack left several hundred people wounded. Conchita Nuñez (real name), a teacher, sociologist, and member of Sección 22 described June 14 as follows:

What happened was that the governor made an error in judgment. He didn't calculate the reaction to what happened in the zócalo because of his disrespect, his feeling of omnipotence. So what happened? Well, the governor didn't think what happened next would happen. But the teachers have an enormous capacity to regroup and to organize themselves. This comes from twenty-six years of struggle. There is some purpose to these twenty-six years of struggle. When those poor police came they were almost poisoned by their own tear gas because they were sent unprepared . . . as we say, sent to the war with no rifle. Not only were the teachers affected by the tear gas, but the police were too. They sent them in without gas masks. They were more afraid than the teachers . . . you could see it. When the teachers realized that they were a larger and stronger force in terms of numbers and actual physical presence, they started to come out of the buildings, to move. Some stayed inside, for example in the union headquarters and other union buildings. They were the ones who suffered the most . . . children, women, indigenous women, this was terrible. I saw how they came out with their eyes red, suffocating, the teachers were vomiting. Everyone was really affected by the gas. It was terrible. It was horrible to witness. Some people said "They [the police] didn't have weapons." But I said to myself, "Why is it that tear gas is not a weapon? It can kill people." Like the compañero who was hit in the head with a gas grenade and he was just about to die when I saw him. He didn't die in the end, but he was just about to and he is still recovering. He has a major head injury and he is still in really bad shape.

Esteban Manuel Rodríguez, introduced earlier, also recalled that day:

I was on the corner, in front of the city hall, in the heart of the zócalo. We were with my delegation at dawn and there were already a lot of rumors that they were going to forcibly evict us. A lot of people had gone home to their houses, but a lot of people also stayed who belonged to all different regions of Oaxaca. In the case of our delegation, we stayed until the end of what happened [on June 14]. . . . So at dawn there was the sound of a tear-gas bomb detonating where the cathedral is. The police came from there, and we began to advance. A lot of compañeros came from different streets. We realized what was going on when we heard about it on the radio. On the radio [Radio Universidad, which had been taken over] there was an announcement asking the people to confront the onslaught of the state.

When we heard this, a lot of us returned to support what was happening. From four in the morning until seven in the morning there was a lot of tear gas, shots fired, tear-gas bombs thrown, and helicopters in the sky shooting at the multitudes. A lot of teachers, men and women, were beaten. And we have people who lost family members who were disappeared. They are still missing. Right here in the center of town, they entered Radio Plantón [Sección 22's radio station], and they beat the people working in the station and destroyed a lot of the infrastructure and materials. . . . They were trying to destroy the movement.

This very difficult morning went by, and in the course of the day, we were able to push back this army, the police who came to forcibly evict us. We repositioned ourselves in the zócalo. Then a call went out over the radio for people to come and help us. . . .

LYNN: On which radio did they make this announcement?

ESTEBAN: It was the university radio, which was named Radio del Pueblo. This radio had been taken over by a part of the movement . . . so it was on this radio that they called to people to come out. People started to arrive and come to our aid.

Widespread Support for Teachers and the Birth of APPO

In Oaxaca, as in most of Mexico, teachers are highly respected members of local communities and neighborhoods. While many end up teaching in schools outside of the towns where they grew up, they live in the communities where they teach and are often very involved in community activities. For the many women who are public school teachers, their social, economic, and personal independence puts them in a unique position, as they are often single when they begin their jobs and function as autonomous individuals. If they have children, they may bring their children and spouse with them to live where they teach. Others return home for the weekend. In many communities where women still have to ask their husbands for permission to leave their homes to go to the market, run an errand, or to take the bus to a larger city, female schoolteachers offer a role model of an independent woman who is involved not only in education but in grassroots organizing as well. Such women may face a difficult double standard if they are unmarried and have to take care to guard their reputation, while men do not. Nevertheless the more than forty thousand female teachers who are members of the CNTE in Oaxaca have significant experience as public figures and participate in a wide range of community and political activities. Those who return year after year to educate the children of one community can become cherished local citizens, forming deep friendships with the local families whose children they have educated. In these relationships, they are often highly respected and admired.

Because higher degrees of education often are correlated with respect, social status, and a higher standard of living, Oaxaca's teachers are treated with respect and dignity by most people. Thus the spectacle of three thousand police gassing, beating, chasing, and rounding up teachers like criminals resulted in a very strong reaction from urban Oaxacans. In addition, the June 14 eviction attempt also affected a large segment of the population of Oaxaca City, who lived near the center. Tear gas entered their houses, children and the elderly got sick because of the gas, people were hit with gas canisters and other projectiles that resulted in concussions, and some were beaten up, even though they had nothing to do with Sección 22's occupation of the zócalo. The governor's miscalculated move to dislodge the teachers converted many in Oaxaca who had been indifferent or even hostile to the annual protest of the teachers to become active sympathizers, at least temporarily.

The day after the attempted eviction of the teachers from Oaxaca's center, Sección 22 organized its third megamarch, to take place within a few weeks. This one drew nearly half a million people into the street and was followed by a meeting on June 17 to which a large number of social justice organizations, unions, and other groups were invited. One of the leaders, Enrique Rueda Pacheco, explained, "We wanted to take the union's 26 years of experience and apply it to society at large" (Gibler 2009: 147). The leaders of Sección 22 saw a unique opportunity to extend their movement to many of the groups they had been building alliances with, as well as others.

Calling the meeting La Asamblea Popular del Pueblo de Oaxaca (People's Popular Assembly), APPO was born on June 17, 2006. There were 365 organizations involved in its formation (Hernández Navarro 2011: 374). The new organization was open to all who could agree on one demand: the ouster of Ulises Ruiz Ortiz as governor. Composed of neighborhood, rural, and indigenous communities, APPO was formally consolidated on June 20, with a slight change in the name to La Asamblea Popular de los Pueblos de Oaxaca (The Popular Assembly of the Peoples of Oaxaca—plural). Indigenous participants emphasized the importance of recognizing the different indigenous peoples present in Oaxaca. The word *pueblos* has multiple levels of meaning, including "towns," "communities," and "peoples." The indigenous autonomy movement emphasizes the importance of recognizing the diversity of Mexico's indigenous peoples (Stephen 2002: 330).

The rich, preexisting mix of urban, rural, and indigenous social movements and organizations that dates to the late 1970s is, of course, behind the appearance of APPO in 2006. In fact the teachers of CNTE have been involved in many of these organizations, while simultaneously working as educators. Thus the seemingly "instant" network of organizations, communities, and movements that came together to form APPO has deep roots in the democratic teachers' movement and in other social movements in Oaxaca, as discussed earlier. However, new forms of organization also emerged in the process of organizing in 2006, such as neighborhood associations, youth collectives, and barricades, some of which built on prior forms (Magaña 2013).

July 2006: National Politics and Elections in Mexico

One of the elements that allowed APPO to impede the Oaxaca state government from functioning for almost six months was the presidential election of 2006. While the attention of the nation was on the close race between the PRD candidate Manuel López Obrador and the PAN candidate Felipe Calderón, a political opening was created. It made the repression in Oaxaca invisible in the national press, but it also allowed APPO to develop rapidly, without federal intervention—at least until November 2006. The election also made evident the erosion of support for the PRI in Oaxaca.

Governor Ruiz Ortiz was famous within the PRI for his ability to deliver votes. Many have suggested that this was due to the use of classic vote-manipulation techniques, such as those described for the 2004 gubernatorial elections in Oaxaca, or because he laundered state funds into the 2006 campaign of PRI presidential candidate Roberto Madrazo (see Martínez Vásquez 2007: 85–87; Gibler 2009: 144–45). Ruiz Ortiz promised to deliver one million PRI votes from Oaxaca for Roberto Madrazo in national elections on July 2, 2006. In response, APPO called for a *voto de castigo* (punishment vote), urging all Oaxacans to vote against the PRI. And they did. The PRI lost nine of eleven congressional seats in the state, and Gabino Cué Monteagudo won a record 600,000 votes as a federal senate candidate, as did Manuel López Obrador as presidential candidate. Both Cué Monteagudo and López Obrador were from the Coalición Bien de Todos (Coalition for the Good of All) (Martínez Vásquez 2007: 86). The PAN candidate Felipe Calderón received 226,304 votes and the PRI candidate Roberto Madrazo received 428,026 votes, far less than the million Ruiz Ortiz had promised.

While the results were clearly differentiated in Oaxaca at the presidential level, this was not the case nationally. On July 2 the IFE announced that the race was too close to call and that the official count would be released on July 5. Both of the leading candidates, Calderón and López Obrador, declared themselves winners. On July 6 the IFE announced a final vote count, giving Calderón of PAN a lead of 0.58 percentage points for a razor-thin victory. López Obrador immediately mobilized the PRD to demand a vote-by-vote recount. This was accompanied by a campaign to present evidence of widespread fraud to prove that López Obrador was the *presidente legitimo* (legitimate president) of Mexico. The PRD presented hundreds of boxes of evidence and demanded a full recount. A series of large demonstrations culminated on July 20 at the zócalo in Mexico City. The establishment of *plantones* (encampments) in the zócalo and the Paseo de la Reforma snarled Mexico City traffic for many weeks. With the arrival of torrential rains in late July and early August, López Obrador's protests continued to draw most of the national media attention.

While the encampments and rallies were going on in Mexico City, the Tribunal Electoral del Poder Judicial de la Federación (Electoral Tribunal of the Federal Judiciary) was examining the evidence presented by the PRD to document widespread vote fraud. On August 5 the Tribunal met and de-

Figure 3.1 APPO occupies Teatro Alvaro Carillo, August 2006.
DOI: 10.7264/N3QN64NG

clared that there was sufficient legal justification to order the recount of
11,839 ballot boxes in only 155 districts (9.2 percent of the total vote), not
every vote, as had been requested by the PRD (Herrera and Zárate 2006).
The recount continued through August, and final results were announced
on August 28. On September 5 the Corte Federal Electoral (Federal Electoral
Court) declared Calderón the official winner. According to the final count,
he received 35.89 percent of the votes (15,000,284 votes), and López Obrador received 35.31 percent (14,756,350 votes), a difference of 243,934 (or
0.58 percent; Clarin 2006).

As national attention focused on the unclear electoral results during the
two-month period when no one was sure who the next president would be,
APPO decided to move forward with a strategy of incapacitating the state
government by occupying both state and federal administrative buildings.
For example, in August 2006 it occupied the Alvaro Carillo Theater; on the
outside of the theater they hung a banner with a picture of Ruiz Ortiz and
graffiti that read, "Sección 22, APPO, Comunidad de Oaxaca, por inutil y
asesino" (Sección 22, APPO, the Community of Oaxaca, useless and assas-
sin) (figure 3.1).

The building occupation strategy was implemented in late July, after
the successful completion of the first Guelaguetza Popular. John Gibler provides a lively description of this process, which I watched unfold. Gibler is

describing daily occupations by teachers and local residents of government buildings:

> They sat in front of the state legislature, in front of the governor's office, and in front of the state courthouse. They sat in front of the state treasury. They created "mobile brigades" by driving around in commandeered city buses to smaller state office buildings like the state archives and the department of motor vehicles, where they spray-painted the walls and then—after calling all the employees out—jammed the door locks with toothpicks, glue, and spray paint.
>
> Within a matter of days, tens of thousands of schoolteachers and APPO members forced the state government into roaming exile. (2009: 153)

Growing Tension and a Turning Point

By the time I arrived in Oaxaca in July 2006, the teachers and those affiliated with APPO controlled the center of the city. By the end of July, my daily walks through Llano Park and the city center involved observation of commandeered buses, noting which buildings had been occupied and closed up, and registering the presence of new encampments that were appearing well outside the city center, including in the Llano and other public spaces. I began to videotape regularly after the encounter in the Llano described in the opening of this chapter. I also started recording testimonials of people I met at events and around the city. Watching and filming with a local friend, I found myself documenting an amazing day-by-day shift in the control of public space in Oaxaca City.

Through my friend, I came to know several other women who were committed APPO activists and who encouraged me to keep filming. They were most interested in having me document and write about their activities and disseminate information outside of Oaxaca about what was going on. They felt, they said, "invisible, unheard, and unseen." This is how my role as one of many people who were asked to accompany the movement and to document its events began. At one point in July, in the Llano by my rented apartment, I was filming another APPO rally when shots were fired in the air at the edge of the park. APPO supporters chased down the shooters, detained them, and then took them to the UABJO Law School two blocks from the zócalo, where they were tried in a people's court. After many hours, they were finally turned over to federal police, with signs around their necks labeling them traitors.

The conflict deepened. Not only were APPO members and the teachers controlling large sections of the city and public buildings, but they had also formed their own police force, called the Honorable Cuerpo de Topiles de la Asamblea Popular del Pueblo de Oaxaca (Honorable Police Force of the Popular Assembly of the Peoples of Oaxaca) and la Policía Magisterial de Oaxaca (Teachers' Police of Oaxaca). These police forces had begun to detain people who acted against APPO and the teachers and to try them in people's courts. The Oaxaca municipal police refused to leave their barracks and attack their fellow citizens; most of them spent July and August playing basketball and hanging out in their barracks.

On August 1 a women's march organized by APPO, Sección 22, and other groups turned into a month-long occupation of COR-TV. I had begun to visit the station regularly in order to observe and record some of what was happening. On August 10, after filming the radio show of a friend, Conchita Nuñez, on Radio Cacerola, I started to walk toward a large march that was approaching the state TV and radio station. On her radio show, Conchita had announced the disappearance of Ramiro Aragón Pérez (real name), a biologist, and two teachers, Elionaí Santiago Sánchez (real name) and Juan Gabriel Ríos (real name), who had disappeared with them. Their families had been looking for them all night and through the day. (Their stories are documented in chapter 4.) Their names, as well as the names of others who had disappeared or were imprisoned, were featured prominently in the march.

I walked with Domingo, a new friend who was a teacher and who had just finished a twenty-four-hour security shift at the TV and radio station buildings. APPO supporters and members of Sección 22 were on detailed security shifts at both the stations and transmission towers in order to ensure the safety of those inside and maintain the integrity of the installations. Radio Plantón had already been destroyed on June 14, and Radio Universidad, which had been used by APPO sympathizers in June and July, was attacked and disabled on July 22 by gunmen who fired machine guns into the station. The radio was disabled for one day, and volunteers got it up and running again in less than twenty-four hours (Gibler 2009: 153).

On August 10 we watched the march approach and pass by us for about eight minutes. Then, as I watched through the camera lens, people turned around two or three blocks away and started running back. Confusion reigned. It was clear that something terrible had happened. Domingo commented, "Some kind of provocation." For about ten to fifteen minutes the march stalled. A large space opened in the middle. Some people didn't move. Then part of the march began to come forward. Domingo and I walked around the edge of the march and began to double back to the middle, where we had seen the people running. As we were walking, I smelled smoke. Suddenly we saw a huge crowd and an ambulance with a bloodied person inside. Everyone was clearly upset and in shock. We asked a woman, "What happened?" With tears in her eyes she responded, "There has been a death. Someone has already died. The bullet went into his heart. They didn't want to take him in an ambulance. They took him to a clinic nearby, where he died. There were various shots and there are others wounded."

Later we found that the person who died was José Jiménez Colmenares, a mechanic who had been marching with his wife, a teacher, and his children. Four suspected shooters were surrounded and detained by APPO and Sección 22 police. One remained in a building attached to a medical clinic. When he did not emerge, enraged people from the march set fire to the building. The four who were detained were put in a local bus that had been commandeered by APPO and driven to the state television and radio station, where I had just been. Domingo and I watched the bus go by as we walked toward the site of the shooting.

August 10, 2006, became a turning point for me and many others in Oaxaca. At that time, there was very little press attention outside of Oaxaca about what was going on. A situation that resembled what many saw beamed around the world—monks in Myanmar protesting in the streets and being detained and shot at—was not visible, even in the Mexican press. The international press did not begin to write about the repression in Oaxaca until Bradley Will, an independent American journalist who worked for Indymedia, was shot and killed on October 27, 2006, in Santa Lucía del Camino, just outside of Oaxaca City. That same day, three Oaxacans were also killed: Emilio Alonso Fabián, Esteban Zurita López, and Eudoxia Olivera Díaz.

After August 10 the conflict became further polarized. People became much more fearful, and the stakes for participating in any kind of public political action became much higher. If you could be shot at while walking in a peaceful protest march, then anything was possible. The state governor appeared on TV in Mexico City to assure the nation that everything was under control in Oaxaca, yet he and his staff could not set foot in the city of Oaxaca or in other parts of the state. APPO supporters, who were controlling the state senate, the offices of the governor, the state TV station, and other installations, redoubled their security measures and prepared for further repression. The Oaxaca city police refused to leave their barracks and attack their fellow citizens. Increasingly, unofficial "police" without uniforms, who traveled in convoys of pickup trucks, began to patrol neighborhoods and intimidate anyone who appeared to be associated with antigovernment activities or who simply "looked suspicious." Not only were people shot at during protest activities, but they were also detained unofficially at night and tortured. Later they might appear in jail.

Barricades

After witnessing the violence firsthand, I was afraid to be out after dark. Usually my children and I would walk down to zócalo or go to the local park to play, eat some ice cream, and hang out with the Oaxacans. We were not the only ones abandoning the streets at dusk. Many people saw the convoys of ten to twelve pickup trucks with un-uniformed (and sometimes masked) men riding around their neighborhoods and sporting high-powered rifles and machine guns. These were paramilitary convoys that went on nightly rounds and harassed young men and others they thought looked suspicious. My family, like many others, became increasingly nervous as the conflict heightened.

The response in many neighborhoods was to construct barricades to impede the entrance of the convoys, known as *caravanas de la muerte*. The barricades also became "the most decentralized, horizontal form of protest" in the social movement (Gibler 2009: 166). They became the basis for new neighborhood councils that joined APPO, as well as sites where young people got to know one another and spawned new groups, such as CASOTA and VOCAL (described in detail in chapter 9). These were particularly important places for the birth of new forms of political organization that incorporated youths and others who were left out or marginalized by the formal assemblies and political practices of APPO (see Magaña 2013).

Serving as central gathering points where people came together at night to provide security to their neighborhood and companionship to one another, the barricades became ad hoc cultural centers, serving as important sites for debates, the sharing of testimonials, and the development of ideas. When people recall listening to the radio and talking to one another at the barricades and in their neighborhoods, they are describing what Karen Brodkin (2007: 140) would likely call a public working-class and resistant political subjectivity. By creating narratives, listening to others' narratives, and then bringing them to the table in a public discussion, people were crafting a shared public political culture. As I have written about elsewhere, such political cultures do not necessarily focus on one set of answers but focus on an agreed-upon set of questions to ask and debate (see Stephen 2001). The work of testimony and narrative in the space of the barricades became one of the primary vehicles for creating shared and contested identities and political ideologies that began to fundamentally reshape how people thought of themselves as citizens and what seemed possible in terms of democratic models of government and participation.

In some cases, the groups of neighbors who came together to form a barricade in 2006 continued to work together and formed neighborhood associations. Such was the case for the Barricada Santa María, which was organized after the governor ordered the transmission tower of COR-TV destroyed on August 21, 2006. In August 2010 I had a long conversation with about twelve members of the Barricada Santa María. They gathered in the patio of the home of one of the key members and shared their experiences of life in the barricade. Since all wanted to remain anonymous to protect their identities, they are identified here only by gender and a number. I include a small section of our discussion. The exchange was very animated, and I seldom interrupted to ask questions.

WOMAN 2: *We would say, here in our barricade, that we were to arrive at ten o'clock at night. Then we would start to arrange our firewood to make the flame that would go all night long so we would have light. We would sit in a circle and tell each other about what had happened that day. We would all participate in that dialogue for some time. We also had a two-way radio. We would call one another on the two-way radios and talk to the other nearby barricades. If we needed help with something we could always call on them. There would generally be three or four people here and maybe more. If we had something happen where we felt that we needed more people, then we would call on the radios to where there were more people concentrated and get reinforcements for our barricade.*

So that is what we did in the barricades. It was where people who didn't know one another made friendships. We also shared some really sad moments together in our barricade. For example, when we listened to the news and heard that someone got hurt. Or we could get really happy when we heard other people talking about what they were doing and thinking. We got a lot of inspiration here in the barricades.

But we also shared terrible moments, like when the reporter Brad Will was killed. We were here together in our barricade when we heard about that. . . . This was a moment of great sadness we all shared here, together.

MAN 1: *I want to add something. This is what the barricade looked like. We each would bring one, two, or three stones, and we would look for some big stones as well. We had sticks and sometimes we would buy some fireworks that we would use in case something dangerous was going on and we needed to signal other people. The fireworks were our way of communicating. To defend ourselves we only had sticks. Some of us had slingshots, others had machetes, but we didn't have any guns. Sometimes we would light big fires as well as a way to let other people know that we were here. Our barricade was protected by men, women, and children as young as seven or eight years old, and by the elderly as well.*

Why were people willing to do this? Because we were living through a very difficult moment with our government. The repression was very bad. The governor said that he was not going to tolerate marches or occupations, but it worked out just the opposite. That is because once people saw the repression and because people didn't have enough to live on, once they saw how those people in the government took money and then they put the money in their own pockets . . . that is when people could not go along with this. . . . Now I would like someone else to explain a little bit about how we were organized.

MAN 2: *Well, it's important to know that we didn't all just decide to show up at ten o'clock for the barricade. It was more organized, and there was a pro-cess. We had a meeting and we decided that we would participate together as a colonia [neighborhood]. Then we all pitched in some money and we bought a megaphone and some two-way radios. We also all pitched in money to buy fireworks. So these were some of the operative elements of the barricade.*

So if it was my turn to work the megaphone, I would call people . . . and say, "Good evening compañeros. We invite everyone from this neighborhood and nearby neighborhoods, all who have conciencia y dignidad *[conscious-ness and dignity], we invite you to come to the barricades. If you have not participated before, we invite you to come."*

That is how it started. When the repression and the tension mounted, then we started to have a more fixed schedule. We started first at nine o'clock, then at ten o'clock. We also talked with people from other neighborhoods and organized with them. People decided where they were going to put up the barricades.

MAN 3: *Yes, people would come and sometimes we would divide up the time in terms of who would be there. A lot of people spent the entire night on the barricades. Others had to go home to bed at a certain point because of health problems. But a lot of us would stay until six or seven in the morning.*

MAN 2: *We would be there all night. And we had lots of ways of communi-cating with other barricades. Apart from cellular phones and radios, we also had lights. And whistles. When there was an emergency situation we would use whistles. And if it was a really difficult situation we would use the alarm sound from the megaphone—the siren. At one point we decided that we needed to organize ourselves among the barricades. So we worked to be able to provide radios to other barricades, particularly those that had very few people. We would patrol our area and then send a signal from a very powerful light that we had and communicate to the other barricades.*

The other important thing about the barricades is that we shared a lot together. We would listen to protest music together, and on some nights we would get together a big group of people, say eighty or ninety people from our neighborhood. It was like a big family. Before the barricade started, none of us knew one another. People didn't necessarily go to meetings. We had not par-ticipated in anything together. Then people started to arrive at the barricade with coffee, with baskets of bread, tamales, and all kinds of food. They would give it to the people who were manning the barricade. It really was the kind of sharing we had never had an opportunity to experience.

Structure, Governance, and Political Plan of APPO

While APPO began as a quickly assembled group of organizations that Sec-ción 22 invited to come together in June 2006, by that August it began to resonate well outside of Oaxaca and to include representation from in-digenous communities, feminist and ecological organizations, and human rights groups, as well as participants from the Zapatista La Otra Campaña, who had been present since June (Esteva 2008: 25). In communities such as Santa Cruz Amilpas, Zaachila, and Miahuatlán, local authorities declared themselves part of APPO. On August 16 and 17 APPO sponsored a forum ti-tled El Foro Nacional: Construyendo la Democracia y la Gobernabilidad en Oaxaca (The National Forum: Constructing Democracy and Governability in Oaxaca), which was attended by more than fifteen hundred representa-tives from throughout the state and elsewhere.

The forum was divided into three areas of discussion: (1) the well-being of all people in the state, including issues of sustainable development, so-cial stability and justice, and the guarantee of a range of economic, human, social, cultural, and ecological rights; (2) the formation of a unified pro-gram of political action that would fortify the structure of APPO and build alliances, calling for deposing Ruiz Ortiz, installing a transitional popular government, organizing a new constitutional congress to revise the Oaxaca state constitution, and widening APPO's impact through further discussions with indigenous communities and other sectors; and (3) the development of policies to promote respect for diversity in Oaxaca, including ethnic origin, sexuality, religion, and physical disability, and to include women in all areas of decision making. This part of the discussion also suggested the promotion of migrants' rights, the rights of indigenous women and children, the rights of homosexual couples, and educational forums on a variety of rights (APPO-CODEP 2006).

I attended the forum in its entirety and was struck by the respect and patience that participants demonstrated. In the third discussion roundtable, which had to do with diversity, I was amazed and delighted at the range of people in the room. Men and women representing a number of indigenous ethnic groups and communities from around the state spoke, as did out gay men and lesbians and people who were physically handicapped. When people did not understand the topic at hand or were struggling to understand concepts or experiences that were new to them, they would ask others to explain it to them. When a Zapotec woman from the Sierra Juárez was struggling to talk in Spanish about her negative experience taking her child to a local clinic where the nurse could not communicate with her, a young woman raised her hand and asked her, in Zapotec, if she could help by translating. The woman nodded and the translation proceeded. When a young urban woman who identified herself as lesbian began to talk about the discrimination she faced in the city of Oaxaca, an older man raised his hand to ask if she was born that way and why she faced *mal tratos* (bad treatment). She stopped and explained her experience to him. In my experience, such political and cultural openness is very rare in Oaxaca, and I had never been in a forum in any country where these kinds of exchanges could take place.

In October 2006 APPO and Sección 22, along with indigenous authorities and organizations, NGOs, academics, artists, and representatives from the Catholic Church and local businesses, participated in La Iniciativa Ciudadana de Diálogo por la Paz, la Democracia y la Justicia en Oaxaca (The Citizen's Initiative for Dialogue for Peace, Democracy, and Justice in Oaxaca).This initiative attempted to negotiate between the Oaxaca state government, APPO, and the Mexican federal government. This broadened the network that APPO participated in and helped to build the movement outward. (This effort is discussed in more detail in chapter 7.)

On November 10–12 the Congreso Constitutivo (Constitutive Congress) of APPO took place in Oaxaca City. Representatives from Oaxaca's eight geographical regions, as well as delegates elected from various sectors—including merchants and artisans, the judiciary, civil society organizations, popular community governments, unions, Christian-based communities, transportation workers, women, barricade groups, neighborhoods of the city of Oaxaca, youths, students, political prisoners and exiles, indigenous communities of the Central Valley, and Sección 22—were all in attendance. Gustavo Esteva (2008: 29) puts the number of representatives at the first APPO congress at 260. The program focused on generating a structure of representation and governance that would serve the interests of the diverse peoples of Oaxaca, creating a plan of action that would get Ruiz Ortiz out of office and work toward a new constitution and form of governance that would be "participatory, inclusive, horizontal, and plural." The new government would hold accountable those responsible for human rights violations, torture, repression, and assassinations, and help to strengthen popular governance in the state, as well as nationally and internationally (APPO 2006).[13] Finally, the congress approved the official APPO logo.

Further Violence and the Shutdown of the 2006 Social Movement by the Federal Preventative Police

At the end of September 2006, Oaxaca was further militarized, with the marines running an exercise with, helicopters, armed vehicles, and almost one hundred soldiers in the coastal region. On October 27, when the reporter Bradley Will and three Oaxacans were killed, more than twenty-four people were also wounded in a day of multiple confrontations. Three days later, on October 30, approximately 4,500 soldiers from the Federal Preventative Police arrived in Oaxaca and carried out an operation that resulted in multiple deaths, woundings, and detentions. Oralia from the Santa María barricade vividly remembers the experience of trying to resist the onslaught of the PFP. When I interviewed the people involved in maintaining the Santa María barricade, she pushed her way to the front of the group to speak:

Well, when the conflict got really big in October we started to get really afraid. On October 30 or 31 the PFP came into Oaxaca. I will never forget that. When they arrived, everyone came out. Even those people who never came to the barricades went into the streets to say, "It isn't possible that the people in power are doing this to our people." I even saw some neighbors here who were supposedly with the PRI go into the street and come to defend the barricades.

A lot of people were really angry. We had so much anger when we saw those Federal Preventative Police coming into town. When we went to protest their presence, they threw gas at us. We were down by the river Atoyac, and we were trying to keep them from entering the city and our neighborhoods. But we couldn't. They had big tanks. They had tear gas, which they shot right into our eyes. They also sprayed our eyes with chili powder. My whole body hurt after this. We tried to defend our neighborhood, but we were impotent in the face of so many police. There were thousands of them. They had tanks, guns, gas, and they were ready to kill us, to disappear us. They had to work hard to enter the city of Oaxaca. I am proud that they saw many, many men, women, and children there trying to stop them. We were combative and they suffered losses, as did we.

After this confrontation APPO and Sección 22 relocated their encampment in UABJO and in front of the Santo Domingo Cathedral. Radio Universidad became the primary communication forum for the movement from October 30 until November 25, when the PFP carried out a final repressive clean-up operation that resulted in the imprisonment of more than two hundred protesters. "Many detainees have reportedly been subject to ill-treatment, torture, and denial of access to family and independent legal counsel. Many were also not apparently involved in violence and evidence against them was reportedly fabricated" (Amnesty International 2007b: 7). Only two days after their arrests, detainees were moved from the Miahuatlán, Oaxaca, prison to a prison in San José del Rincón, Nayarit, far away from their families, lawyers, and Oaxaca human rights organizations.

After Felipe Calderón was sworn in as president of Mexico on December 1, 2006, amid much protest, the federal government made further efforts to hobble APPO. On December 4 Flavio Sosa, who was one of 260 representatives to the APPO assembly, was arrested along with three other APPO activists in Mexico City, where they had gone to engage in talks with the government. Sosa was imprisoned for more than a year and a half in a maximum-security prison known as Almoloya de Juárez in the state of Mexico. On December 16, 2006, the PFP left the center of Oaxaca, and different bodies of state police began to take over the militarization of the city. This militarization continued throughout the term of Governor Ulises Ruiz Ortiz.

Summary

This chapter has outlined the factors that led to the social movement of 2006. A rich and complex history of social movements in the state, a governor who broke the historical pact between the state government and Sección 22 in an annual negotiation ritual, an escalating level of repression against opposition movements and individuals who disagreed with the governor, and a national election aided by a temporary vacuum of power at the federal level of government—all of these elements were the kindling for this social movement. The metaphorical match that lit the fire of social rebellion that resulted in the formation of APPO was the botched attempt by poorly trained state and local police forces to evict teachers from their occupation of the zócalo and surrounding blocks in June 2006. During the six months that Sección 22, APPO, and their supporters severely impeded the state government from operating, profound changes took place in many parts of the fabric of Oaxaca society. The remainder of this book attempts to analyze those different spaces of change, the processes that individuals and groups underwent in those spaces, and the critical role that oral testimony played in enacting alternative visions for political and cultural participation and in the formulation of new, hybrid forms of identity. At a larger level, the following chapters highlight the critical role that oral narrative can play in creating political and ethnic identities in individuals. Oral narratives can also be shared in specific times and places and sometimes help create new cultures of how to do politics, defend human rights, and engage with states.

4

Testimony and Human Rights
Violations in Oaxaca

During June through November 2006, the legitimacy of the Oaxaca state government was strenuously questioned in a massive assertion of rights. These assertions came in the form of megamarches of thousands, the creation of APPO, the occupation of state and federal buildings and offices, the takeover of the state's television and radio station, the construction of barricades in many neighborhoods, and regional movements throughout the state. APPO interrupted the usual functions of the state government for six months and began to construct a parallel police force, constitution, and state assembly structure geared toward a more inclusive and participatory political vision. It was met with strong repression. At least twenty-three people were killed, hundreds were arrested and imprisoned, and over twelve hundred complaints were filed with human rights commissions.[1]

In the course of the events of the summer and fall of 2006, the biologist Ramiro Aragón Pérez and the teachers Elionai Santiago Sánchez and Juan Gabriel Ríos were falsely charged, tortured, and imprisoned. Ramiro, against all odds, eventually received political asylum in the United States, while Elionai and Juan Gabriel were tried, found guilty of the invented crimes, and fined. Their testimony and that of others was crucial in helping their claims to achieve legitimacy in the Mexican and international press and in the broader communities.

Both Mexico and Oaxaca have formally established human rights commissions, as described in chapter 2. CNDH and CDDHO are intended to serve as alternative legal systems guaranteeing rights such as "physical integrity, equity, dignity, and judicial security" and the "impartial procurement of justice" (CDDHO 2008). However, these commissions are not integrated into the larger Mexican judicial system, and they have no power to punish perpetrators of human rights abuses (see CNDH 2007: conclusions, pt. 6). At the surface level this can be viewed as problematic; at a deeper level it might be viewed as dangerous or even unethical. What does it mean to create expectations of rights and impartial justice when the courts may be acting primarily in response to the political demands of those in power? How can rights abuses be documented and perpetrators held accountable in this situation? What kinds of tools and options can survivors of human rights abuses turn to when human rights commissions and judicial systems do not provide justice? The story of the illegal detention, torture, and imprisonment of Ramiro, Elionai, and Juan Gabriel, and their appeals for justice and defense of their human rights, shed light on these questions.

Theorizing Human Rights and the Social Movement of 2006

While the Mexican Constitution provides for freedom of speech, rights for women, and racial equality—with specific mention of indigenous peoples— these rights are juxtaposed with a contradictory reality in Oaxaca (see Martínez Vásquez 2007; Hernández Navarro 2007; Stephen 2007). There a long-standing political elite has maintained control of politics and economics through a regional political culture that is built on a discrepancy between claims to equal citizenship for women, indigenous people, and the poor and the lived reality of people who lack the resources, public spaces, and power to exercise such rights. Awareness of the struggle for rights by these silenced sectors is at an all-time high because of the rights discourses being conducted by federal and state human rights commissions and by social movements and nongovernmental organizations.

As Mark Goodale has suggested for Bolivia, human rights consciousness in Oaxaca came to "serve as a kind of normative standard against which social and economic relations can be measured (and resisted if needed)" (2007: 157). Human rights, and more specifically indigenous rights, women's rights, and the rights of the poor, are expressed as an idea, "as a kind of floating signifier that represents a new form of human dignity and moral worth." Thus human rights "can reinforce—and embolden—existing normativities, even if their provisions or rules or 'laws' do not, strictly speaking, conform to specific human rights instruments" (160). Rights discourses, an important strategic resource for social movements in Oaxaca since the late 1980s, came to the fore in 2006 and 2007, when a repressive political system made it increasingly dangerous to express the fundamental rights that are guaranteed by the Constitution and the international accords to which Mexico is a party (see OAS 1969; United Nations Office of the High Commissioner for Human Rights 1966; LASA 2008: 153–54).

The rights claims expressed in the testimony of survivors of human rights abuses in Oaxaca in 2006 reflect "human rights in a connotative sense of 'human rights'—in which reference is made to a moral universe in which each person is granted dignity and respect—and a denotative sense, in which gestures are made toward specific perceived human rights provisions" (Goodale 2007: 149–50). As Goodale and others have noted, when individuals express their rights claims as part of a larger testimony, they do not distinguish between these senses of the term, nor do they necessarily distinguish between ways of claiming rights that are specifically legal or extralegal. As discussed by Speed in relation to the Zapatistas, conceptualizations of rights can emerge "in their exercise, not as designations from God/nature or the state/law" (2007: 184).

In the cases explored here, testimony became the primary vehicle for legitimizing the victims' claims. The forums in which they testified outside of Oaxacan courtrooms included radio, video, rallies, and press conferences. Through such forums the life of a testimonial can extend far beyond one event, one telling, or one text in terms of how it travels and works and may resignify "the truth" and the official and unofficial versions of history. Testimonials can have influence in many venues outside of their origin.

While all three men appeared before judges many times, their courtroom testimony was not taken seriously and was trumped by police testimony. It was outside the courtroom that it gained credibility and traction. This has often been the case in Latin America, where human rights violations were first documented by social movements and human rights organizations such as the Comité de Madres Mons. Romero (Monsignor Romero Mothers' Committee) of El Salvador (Stephen 1994), the Mothers of the Plaza de Mayo of Argentina (Bouvard 1994), and the Coordinador Nacional de Viudas de Guatemala (National Committee of Widows of Guatemala; Schirmer 1993). Only later was the testimony of members of these organizations integrated into truth commissions and commissions of inquiry. In these more official venues, as well as others, testimony represented the right of "recountability" (see Arias 2001; Beverly 2004), which, according to Richard Werbner, is "the right, especially in the face of state violence and oppression, to make a citizen's memory known and acknowledged in the public sphere" (1998: 1). Fiona Ross describes "this coming-to-voice in a public sphere" through testimony as holding "the promise of new subjectivities in the aftermath of disrupted social formations or in establishing fresh forms of sociality" (2002: 27). The use of testimony in grassroots venues can help to build legitimacy with a larger public that may then transfer to more formal legal spaces.

In the trial of nine men who ruled Argentina from 1976 to 1982 and were accused of "organizing and ordering massive kidnappings, torture, and killing of anonymous individuals" (Jelin and Kaufman 2000: 93–94), testimony was a crucial part of the process, particularly in the absence of substantial material evidence. The use of testimony as a political strategy for more than three decades by the Mothers of the Plaza de Mayo had helped to establish it as a legitimate source of information in the formal court proceedings. As Jelin and Kaufman point out, because the construction of juridical proof was based on the testimony of victims (military records having been mostly destroyed), "this implied juridical recognition of their voices and their right to talk." In the courtroom, testimony is broken down into specific components that fit into the judicial framework: "the requirement of personal identification, the pledge to tell the truth, the description of circumstances, and relationship with the case" (94). Testimony in court legitimizes the testimony that is often already circulating in society. While the disappeared, for example, can cease to exist as subjects of rights, since they are not present in the court as "victims" converted into witnesses, the testimony in court of those who have been searching for them is legitimized through its entry into the legal record. When opportunities to testify in such legal forums are lacking—as in the case of human rights abuses committed in Oaxaca—the use of grassroots venues for documenting abuses is an important part of building a record for eventual legal proceedings. In demonstrations and meetings and on the radio, testimony that has been circulating on the street, in the markets, in social interactions, and in people's homes becomes legitimized by being incorporated into the official records and disseminated to the larger listening community. While testimony givers in such situations are not necessarily subject to a pledge to tell the truth, the requirements of identification, location in a larger social field and community, and the description of circumstances and relationship with the case are similar to those in legal proceedings.

Ramiro Aragón Pérez, Elionai Santiago Sánchez, and Juan Gabriel Ríos: Three Cases of Human Rights Violations under Conditions of Repression

Ramiro Aragón Pérez worked for Grupo Mesófilo, an NGO dedicated to the sustainable management of natural resources and improving the quality of life in the villages and indigenous *ejidos* (communally owned and managed lands) of Oaxaca. He was not a political activist or a member of APPO or Sección 22. At approximately 1 a.m. on August 10, 2006, he was forcibly detained, along with his brother-in-law Elionai Santiago Sánchez and Juan Gabriel Ríos, primary school teachers and members of Sección 22, in San Felipe del Agua. They had gone there in search of two childhood friends of Ramiro's who had disappeared the day before in the company of the teacher and longtime activist Germán Mendoza Nube. Noticing a car following them, they turned around to go home but were blocked by another vehicle, a truck. Five men got out of the two vehicles and proceeded to ask them for their identification and question them about what they were doing. After finding on Elionai an identification card that identified him as a teacher and a flyer from a leftist organization in Oaxaca, the men bound the friends' hands and beat them for more than thirty minutes.

In an interview in July 2007, Ramiro described the experience, as he had done earlier for staff members of Limeddh, Amnesty International, the press, and others:

They threw us in the truck, and we started to drive, and they started beating us again. They threatened to kill us, told us that they were going to rape us and that after they raped us they were going to go to my house and do the same thing to my family. They took all of my documents and had my address. . . . Then they began to pull me by the hair. One of them asked one of the others for a knife to cut my hair, but they didn't give it to him because he would have done something crazy. In that moment they were really enjoying themselves in their fiesta of violence. It was a party for them. They were beating us and kicking us. Wham! They would hit us and then say, "Hey, look, this fucking guy is squirting blood all over me. He got my new shirt all bloody." They were really enjoying it, and we were bleeding all over the place. Then one of them took a cigarette and burned me with it on my face. . . . They cut my neck and pulled out a lot of my hair. They were playing with us, and having an orgy of violence and laughing. They were putting into practice what they had learned in their courses. . . . Then they asked for the glass that they cut Elionai with, and the other guy wanted to cut my throat, but he didn't have time.

They stopped then, and we got down. Then they pushed us into the back of a police truck. There we saw a policeman. They kept on driving. We were really beat up and wounded. My face was really swollen, and they were braking suddenly and jumping over these speed bumps while we were still tied up. . . . We had no idea where we were. Finally, they stopped and they put us in a jail. We asked the jailer, "Where are we?" He said, "You are in Ejutla." They threw us into that jail at about three-thirty in the morning.

✳ VIDEOCLIP 4.1: http://dx.doi.org/10.7264/N3B85623

Back in Oaxaca City, Ramiro's, Elionai's, and Juan Gabriel's families were increasingly worried. Ruth Guzmán Sánchez began to feel alarmed early on the morning of August 10, when her husband, Ramiro, and her brother Elionai did not come home.

She was supposed to go to Santa María Ayoquesco to work, and Ramiro was supposed to be at home taking care of their two young children. She went down to the zócalo where the organizing headquarters for the APPO and other organizations were. At 9 a.m. Yésica Sánchez Maya, director of Limeddh, arrived. Ruth told Yésica that Ramiro, Elionai, and Juan Gabriel were disappeared, as they had not been seen since early the previous evening and did not return home or to any of the places where they usually hung out or worked. Ruth spent the day in the zócalo with the families of other people who were missing or imprisoned. They reassured her, telling her that her husband, brother, and family friend would be found. Ruth recalled in an interview with me in July 2007 that one person even told her, "Be patient, they have to invent false charges for why they arrested them. After they do that, they will appear." At 7 p.m. on August 10, Ruth received her first news. She recalled:

I was there in the zócalo when one of the women who was there received a call. I was watching her as her face got all serious. . . . Then she called me over and said to me, "They are in Ejutla. They say that they were very badly

beaten, but they are okay, they are alive." . . . Oh, I was so glad to hear that.
. . . About twenty minutes later we got another call and they told us that José
Colmenares [killed in a march on August 10, 2006] was dead. I was feeling so
great when I heard my husband, brother, and friend were alive, and then this
news. They told us that he had just been killed in the march. I felt really sad
after that.

. . . A little bit later, Yésica Sánchez Maya called me and said that they
knew where Ramiro was, but that I couldn't go there right now.

✳ VIDEOCLIP 4.2: http://dx.doi.org/10.7264/N36H4FBC

Yésica, a young human rights defender working for Limeddh, was
among the first people to see Ramiro, Elionai, and Juan Gabriel. She viewed
what happened to them as part of a new strategy of selective repression designed to intimidate people who were participating or sympathizing with
APPO. She noted that on August 9, Mendoza Nube of FPR was kidnapped
while in his wheelchair, and that very early in the morning on August 10,
Ramiro, Elionai, and Juan Gabriel were kidnapped, tortured, temporarily
disappeared, and falsely charged. Later that day, José Jiménez Colmenares
was assassinated in an APPO march. She says of the day she first found the
three in jail:

Ramiro, Elionai, and Juan Gabriel were detained and we didn't see them until
the night of August 10. I'd had several meetings with the ministerio público
[public minister/public defender], and I told him that I had reports of three
people who had been detained. I described what they looked like to him. He
told me that he didn't have any report at that time of people who had been
detained. Then I went down to the zócalo for a rally for the detained that was
being organized when he called me back. He said, "I just got word of three
people. Tell me their names. . . ." I told him the names: Ramiro Aragón Pérez,
Elionai Santiago Sánchez, and Juan Gabriel Ríos. He said, "Yes, yes, yes.
That is them. But you know what, looking at the medical reports, I am afraid
for their lives." I said, "What do you mean?" He said, "They are in terrible
conditions in the jail where they are. We need to get them out of there and
transfer them to the Procuraduría General de la Republica (Federal Attorney
General's Office)."

We went into the municipal jail in Ejutla, and when I first saw them it
left a very strong impression on me. I don't think I was prepared to see people
bleeding, people who were anxious to see their families, and also to see the

horrible conditions they were in. Ramiro was outraged. He said, "Yésica, loan me your camera. I have to take photographs. Look where they put us. They have us by excrement, sleeping on the floor, and bleeding all over."

✳ VIDEOCLIP 4.3: http://dx.doi.org/10.7264/N32R3PMN

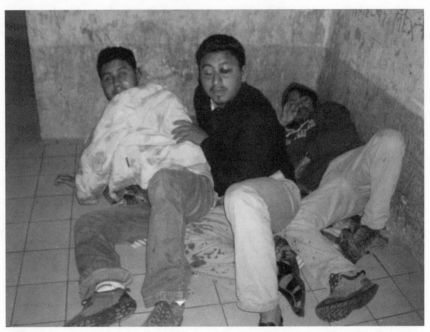

Figure 4.1 First encounter with Ramiro, Elionai, and Juan Gabriel after they are found in jail in Ejutla de Crespo. DOI: 10.7264/N3KW5CXR

  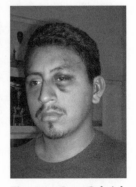

Figure 4.2 Ramiro shortly after he is first found in jail. DOI: 10.7264/N36Q1V51

Figure 4.3 Elionai with his sutured ear. DOI: 10.7264/ N32Z13FP

Figure 4.4 Juan Gabriel with bruises. DOI: 10.7264/N3Z60KZ9

Yésica returned to the zócalo where Ruth had been waiting to hear from her. After waiting until 11 p.m., Ruth went with family members to San Bartolo Coyotepec, where she was told she could get more information and speak with people from the Procuraduría General de la República (Federal Attorney General's Office). Ruth recalled:

By ten o'clock the next morning we were there in the jail in Ejutla. I thought for sure that we would all get to see them, but only my mother and Ramiro's dad got in to see them. . . .

Then they told us what the charges were. They told us that Ramiro could not get out on bail and that my brother and Juan Gabriel could, and we needed 12,000 pesos [about U.S. $1,200] for each one of them. We were able to get this money together very quickly by everyone helping out. We needed 24,000 pesos [about U.S. $2,400]. . . .

We waited there all day, all afternoon, and all night. Finally my little brother came out at three in the morning. His face was really swollen. I didn't cry very much because I was so angry. I also really wanted to see my husband. A woman who worked there who was in solidarity with APPO helped me get to see him. She told me, "Stand here. He is going to pass by here in ten minutes."

So that is how I got to see Ramiro. He was behind bars and we couldn't touch each other. . . . It was surreal. He was so badly beaten and he told me, "I am okay. Don't worry about me." I cried a little bit. He told me to call a lot of people, which I had already done. Then they told me we had to leave, and we left with my brother and Juan Gabriel.

From the jail in Ejutla de Crespo, Ramiro was transferred to a jail in Zimatlán de Álvarez, south of Oaxaca City. When he passed through the federal attorney general's office in San Bartolo Coyotepec earlier on August 12, he was charged with possession of a *mosquetón*, a 1924 musket that was for the exclusive use of the Mexican armed forces. He was also charged with possession of bullets that were not compatible with the gun. Juan Gabriel and Elionai also faced invented weapons charges. All three men vehemently denied these charges.

Ramiro's father, Victorino Aragón, was among the first to see his son. Along with his wife, Victorino camped out in front of the jail in Zimatlán where Ramiro was held until he was released at the end of October 2006.

In an interview with me in July 2007, Victorino reflected on what had happened to his son and his and his wife's experiences with the people of Zimatlán de Álvarez:

When the judge sentenced my son Ramiro to prison, there were two different elements involved. One was the gun and the other was the bullets that the police turned in. My son was not carrying either. When the judge scrutinized the gun and the bullets, she did something which might be legally acceptable, but which does not make rational common sense. She said, "This gun is for exclusive use of the army and the bullets are not compatible with the gun. So my decision is that you are free on account of the bullets, but I sentence you to prison for the gun." And it goes on from there. . . .

There is tangible evidence that my son was tortured. An official representative from a human rights organization told me, after seeing my son, "There is visible evidence that there is a cigarette burn." . . . But this is not given any importance by the state. Never did anyone say that Ramiro had been tortured. . . .

After my son was transferred to Zimatlán de Álvarez, we received unconditional support from the people there. . . . They gave us economic support, they brought us food, clothing, bedding, and emotionally supported us. We set up a loudspeaker system there and we announced all of the news about what was going in Oaxaca. We let them know all about the case of my son Ramiro.

I also can't complain about his treatment in the Zimatlán jail. The people who took care of him there understood that this was an injustice. They were employees of the judicial power and had to do their job, but they treated us with respect, allowed us to see him, and made sure that he was living in good conditions.

✳ VIDEOCLIP 4.4: http://dx.doi.org/10.7264/N3Z31WJ0

The hotly contested national presidential election in August 2006, and the period of more than a month afterward during which votes were being recounted, focused the national attention on the election rather than on the violence in Oaxaca. Manuel López Obrador, who was ultimately declared the loser to Felipe Calderón by less than 1 percent of the vote, organized a massive campaign of resistance, taking over much of the center of Mexico City. In Oaxaca the state government had begun to escalate its repression efforts through the use of paramilitaries. During the three months that Ramiro was in jail, he kept up with the movement by listening to Radio Cacerola and other radio stations that APPO took over. From his jail cell he heard López Obrador talking on the radio. He said of this experience:

He was talking on the radio and he was saying, "Vote by vote, ballot box by
ballot box, we will go." . . . It sounded absurd to me—knowing that we were
part of a terrible violation of human rights going on, really revolting, and in
the meantime here they are worried about voting, saying "ballot box by ballot
box." This was what the political parties were saying, and I was asking, "Why
did I go to vote? What did it matter?"

For Ramiro, this absurd moment captured the contradiction of legal
rights versus the actual rights that he and many others were living. While
one had the right to vote and participate in a democracy, freedom of assembly was disregarded. Marchers were shot, and civilians looking for friends
in the night could be arbitrarily detained, beaten, tortured, and imprisoned
on false charges. For him, Juan Gabriel, Elionai, and others, the rights guaranteed under Mexican law became meaningless. Legal protections had no
meaning in Oaxaca in 2006. The CNDH (2006: 5) report concluded that
twenty people had been killed, 370 injured, and 349 imprisoned between
June 2 and December. While the Supreme Court later named a special commission to investigate the violation of human rights in Oaxaca, that commission had no authority to punish anyone found guilty. In the meantime,
those who had been falsely imprisoned had witnessed a justice system in
crisis.

For example, the policeman who accused Ramiro of carrying a weapon
reserved for the army stated in a preliminary hearing that Ramiro had been
found running through the street with a gun and had been in a street fight.
The swelling and contusions left from the severe beating he had received
were attributed to this supposed fight. When the firearm he was charged
with possessing was tested for fingerprints, his prints were not found on
it. The judge found the evidence inconclusive and sent him back to prison.

Ramiro was freed at the end of October as a result of an agreement
worked out between Carlos Abascal, who had been secretary of the interior
in the Vicente Fox administration, and Enrique Rueda Pacheco, the secretary-general of Sección 22. Early in the morning of October 30, Ramiro
was flown by small plane to Mexico City and released in a press conference
that included representatives of APPO, Sección 22, and the federal Ministry
of the Interior. He received no documentation, and all of the false charges
were left on his record. He fled for safety to the United States with his wife
and children. Although he has reported his case to the federal and state human rights commissions, no action has been taken to investigate his illegal

detention, torture, and imprisonment, and he fears that he may be attacked or arrested if he returns to Oaxaca.

Juan Gabriel, who had been teaching in a small town in the district of Sola de Vega, was an active member of Sección 22. He had been tear-gassed during the attempt to dislodge the teachers from the central plaza on June 14 and had been actively participating in the sit-in and occupation of the plaza that followed. In his testimony on July 2007, he emphasized that it was when his tormenters found flyers advertising an APPO march and a small biography of Joseph Stalin on his fellow teacher and friend Elionai that they decided to beat them up. The right to free speech was clearly violated in his description of their detention:

I have been an active sympathizer and participant in our [teachers'] struggle, but I have never been a leader or part of another organization. I am part of Sección 22, of course, but I don't belong to any other organization. Something important that happened is that when they found a socialist piece of literature on my friend Elionai, that was what made them really beat us up. Why were they so violent toward us? The torture lasted a long time. Then one of them said, "Who wants to put out my cigarette? Stick your tongues out. I want to put out my cigarette." I stuck out my tongue and so did Ramiro, but they decided not to burn my tongue. Instead they began to burn Ramiro in the chest with the cigarette. They grabbed him by the hair and began to pull his hair and beat him up around the face. They beat him really, really badly around the face—his face was terribly hurt. They began to beat me too, from behind, beating me on the ears with their hands open. This resulted in the rupture of my eardrum. It made a terrible sound, and then I had a terrible pain. It was really, really ugly. Then they grabbed me by the neck and began to beat me on the face. I don't know what they were hitting me with, something really hard, like a bottle. I still have a scar where they broke open my eyebrow and a lot of blood poured out. At that point the pain was so terrible that I just became resigned to it and gave up. . . . I was tied up, and they continued to beat me. I couldn't do anything, being tied, and they were verbally assaulting us too, telling us they were going to do [to us]. I have never felt so afraid in my entire life.

✳ VIDEOCLIP 4.5: http://dx.doi.org/10.7264/N3TB14TN

While Juan Gabriel was being beaten, Elionai was being strangled and cut with a broken bottle. Elionai had been teaching elementary school in the southern part of the state. Like Juan Gabriel, he was an active member of the teachers' union and had supported the occupation of the plaza. He had also been caught in the state police attempts to evict the teachers from the center of the city and had gone on to support other actions that the teachers and APPO undertook. He had helped to guard the transmission towers of the television and radio station and had attended conferences, marches, and other activities. Though not a leader, he had felt confident of his ability to participate freely:

After the attempt to remove the teachers from the plaza a lot of activities started. But our spirits were very, very high because we [the teachers] had tremendous support from the people. People would arrive in the plaza with blankets, with food, with money to support us. This kind of experience really made a difference and motivated us. We realized that our struggle was supported by the people of Oaxaca. There were marches that came down from the different neighborhoods in the city, and people came to tell us that we were not alone. Little by little there were more and more activities, like conferences, talks, other things. I was really into it because my family was participating too. My mother, my sister, we had grown up in this atmosphere, because my mother is a teacher too, and she had suffered a lot in the past as well. We were also really angry about what had happened with the attempted eviction and how people were treated.

✳ VIDEOCLIP 4.6: http://dx.doi.org/10.7264/N3PK0D3B

Confident that he could freely exercise his rights to free speech and free assembly, Elionai had spoken with the many different people who congregated daily in the plaza. Many groups from a wide range of leftist and progressive perspectives had set up booths there, and thousands of teachers were sleeping and living in and around the plaza in what became a tent city. Hundreds of meetings, exchanges, cultural events, and activities were going on. Many of the groups that established a presence there set out books, brochures, DVDs, CDs, and other materials for sale or for small donations. Elionai had bought a book and was distributing flyers for an APPO march. When the men who detained him and the others found a biography of Stalin and an APPO flyer on him, the three of them were immediately tagged as suspicious and treated as if they had no civil or human rights. Elionai offered this testimony in July 2007:

They had Ramiro on one side and Juan Gabriel on the other, and they pushed me up against the side of a truck with my hands up in the air. They patted me down, like a routine check, and then they stopped and said, "What's this?" They found my teacher's ID and a book, a biography of Joseph Stalin that I had bought from a stall in the plaza. I saw a red book that said Life and Works of Joseph Stalin, *and I bought it. I had this with me, and I was also passing out the last accords of* APPO, *which said that they were going to have a march for children. . . . So I had these documents, and when they found them, their attitude changed. One of them said to me, "What are you doing with Stalin? Now you are going to really get fucked up, teacher. What are you doing here? What are you looking for?" I told them, "I am just moving about here freely. We were looking for a place to eat." "Looking for a place to eat at this hour?"*

They kept asking us what we were really doing. After that they stopped asking me anything. They took my cell phone, all of my documents, my credit card, only leaving me my teacher's ID. Then they tied us up with really heavy rope. . . . They were beating me really hard in the front of my body, and another person was beating me on the neck. The blows were really hard, and I asked for help, but who was going to help me? . . . Then they started to pull on a rope. The one who was behind me began to strangle me. I tried to grab it. . . . For a while I was able to use my hands on the rope to keep them from strangling me. . . . "Talk! Talk! Talk!" they kept saying. They were telling me that I was guilty of something. I don't know what their intentions were. . . . Then they grabbed me by the hands, and I heard them break a bottle. They said, "Now we are really going to fuck over the three of you." Then I heard Ramiro and Juan Gabriel screaming, and I felt really bad. I started to get really very, very nervous, hysterical, and I started to scream. Their screams were really terrible. . . . After they broke the bottle, that is when I thought, "Now they are going to kill me." And they said to us, "Now you are going to die." . . .

I thought they were going to cut my throat or something, but no. I started to feel an intense pain in my ear, and I felt lots of blood flowing. I said, "Oh, no, they are going to cut my ear." I started to scream because the pain was unbearable. That's all I remember, because after that I received a blow that rendered me unconscious. Then I only remember vaguely that they loaded me into a new truck, a Nissan that the State Preventative Police used. Then I remember that Ramiro was beside me. I touched his hand and he moved. The three of us were there. I remember thinking, "Well, at least all three of us are alive."

Elionai grimaced as he retold this to me. He then described the false weapons possession charges he received, which stated that he had a gun for the exclusive use of the army and National Air Force. Elionai and Juan Gabriel both received federal charges for weapons possession, which put the three men in the custody of the Federal Attorney General's office. Elionai and Juan Gabriel were released on 12,000 pesos bail each (about U.S. $1,200) on August 12. Ramiro remained in jail.

Elionai's Testimonial in Action: Analysis of the August 12, 2006, Press Conference at Which He First Testified

Diana Taylor (2003: 28) proposes that, instead of privileging texts and narratives, we look at what she calls "scenarios" as meaning-making paradigms. If we think about testimonials given at truth commissions and in social movements within the framework of these scenarios, we can better understand the emotional and social power of oral testimonials in these two contexts. Taylor describes six characteristics of a scenario, which I summarize here (29–32): (1) a scenario involves a scene as a physical environment, such as a stage or place; (2) it requires viewers to deal with the embodiment of the social actors; (3) by including both action and the formulaic structure of performance, scenarios suggest certain outcomes yet allow for reversal, parody, and change; (4) because of the multiplicity of forms of transmission (telling, reenactment, mime, gestures, dance, singing), a scenario can draw from written and oral archives and repertoire; (5) the frame of the scenario forces us to situate ourselves as participants, spectators, or witnesses, to "be there"; (6) the scenario usually works through reactivation of past situations and memories to make them present, constituting a "once-againness."

I take these six elements as a basis for analyzing the press conference where Elionai first gave his testimony. Just hours after his release, he and Juan Gabriel appeared at a press conference in the central plaza in Oaxaca to publicly testify about what had happened to them and to ask for help in securing the release of Ramiro, who was still being held in jail. Before more than a hundred people and surrounded by television, radio, and print journalists, they shared their stories. They were accompanied by Yésica Sánchez Maya, the human rights worker who had found them in jail, and Ruth Guzmán Sánchez, Elionai's sister and Ramiro's wife. The award-winning journalist Hermann Bellinghausen covered the story. He wrote the following description of their appearance and the response to their testimonials at the press conference.

The teachers were severely beaten on the face and on their bodies. Their eyes were swollen, and they had wounds on their faces and signs of lacerations on their backs. They had cut Elionai's ear with glass so much that it was almost mutilated. He had dozens of sutures from various wounds in his ear. It looked as if they had sewn it back together in a big hurry. They [Elionai and Juan Gabriel] showed their clothing with huge blood stains on them. Their blood. In their testimony, the teachers told that besides severely beating Ramiro as they did them and even worse, they also burned his forehead with cigarettes. . . .

[Elionai stated]: "One of them grabbed me from the back seat and grabbed my ear and I didn't know what happened until I felt that blood that filled up my throat." He raised the jacket he was wearing, with a blood stain that covered almost half of it. He raised his shirt and showed his torso. He showed his ear. His face already said everything. "What bad people they are!" exclaimed a voice from the public which had gathered in front of the old city hall. (Bellinghausen 2006, my translation)

Physical Environment
The press conference took place in the zócalo of Oaxaca, in front of the old city hall, which had been taken over by the APPO movement. In their occupation of major city buildings, APPO had converted the zócalo into its logistical center, with a press tent, a medical tent, a media tent, and other public spaces. It was the place where news was often shared for the first time with reporters and the public. Late-night strategy sessions took place in the zócalo and in dozens of surrounding locations when the streets were occupied by thousands of teachers and others. The zócalo is a traditional place for crowds to gather to watch performances, listen to music, and meet family members. During 2006 it was the news and event center for APPO.

Embodiment
This is a case of a corporal as well as a oral testimony regarding the torture that Elionai and Juan Gabriel suffered. The men are showing their physical wounds to the press with gestures and facial expressions as well as verbal descriptions.

Structure of Performance
The press conference follows a format that people expect. Here that includes oral and visual testimonies of what happened, additional testimony

from Ruth, and sharing a letter signed by intellectuals and nonprofit organizations addressed to President Vicente Fox calling for Ramiro's release. At its end the event moves out of the structure of a press conference and into a rally when Juan Gabriel cries, "There have been others before us and there will be others. This is what we cannot permit anymore." In this way the structure of the press conference morphs into an emotional rally that then motivates people to work to free Ramiro and other political prisoners.

Multiplicity of Forms of Transmission

At the press conference, Elionai's testimony is transmitted orally and corporally. Subsequently, however, the testimony from this one event gives rise to multiple forms of transmission through different outlets, including the national TV network Televisa, Radio Cacerola (a station run by APPO, which took it over from the state public radio and TV network; see Stephen 2011), the national newspaper *La Jornada*, the local newspaper *Las Noticias*, and the retelling of the event by those who saw or attended the press conference. Additionally, the testimonial has been partially transcribed by the Limeddh (2006) and put on its website. Subsequently it has been repeated in various publications of Amnesty International (2007a) and other human rights organizations (see United Nations General Assembly 2007: 209–16) and then video-recorded again and put on another website (Stephen 2009a). The initial scenario not only brings together multiple forms of transmission but gives birth to others, bringing together the repertoire of knowledge that Elionai and Juan Gabriel provide and then serving as the basis for different forms of oral, visual, and textual archiving.

Observers, Readers, and Listeners as Witnesses

The people at the press conference are clearly situated as witnesses and testifiers. Bellinghausen's written account of the press conference includes two remarks by audience members (one cited here) and provides a sense of presence. Elionai's and Juan Gabriel's retelling of what happened to them connects the audience members and motivates some to act as the press conference transforms into a rally, which then also results in the formation of a commission to free Ramiro. This commission functioned at a high level for several months and resulted in dozens of activities and actions aimed at freeing Ramiro and other political prisoners. In this sense, "being there" is highly emotive for observers (see Juris 2008). This sense of connection is also conveyed to those who read Elionai's testimony or watch it on video.

Reactivation of Past Events

Related to the witnessing dimension of the scenario of Elionai's testimony at the press conference, the retelling of past events here brings them into the present, constituting what Taylor calls a "once-againness." Testimony has the ability to reactivate not only past events but the emotions linked to them; in this way, testimony attaches those past emotions of the tellers to the present emotions of the listeners. In social movements, this can be a particularly powerful dimension of testimonies, as they reconnect listeners, readers, and observers to events that have already happened but that, through testimony, become alive again and motivate some to want to act.

Analysis

The analytical and methodological framework of the scenario, as suggested by Taylor, permits us to see how testimonials function in particular contexts and also to begin to see how they are connected to broader social contexts. Here we have observed how a testimonial can be linked to organizing actions in social movements, such as the commission to free Ramiro from prison. Elionai's testimony can also be connected to providing new and more complex versions of Oaxacan history about the social movement of 2006. Until December 2010 the state government of Oaxaca was completely unwilling to take seriously or even listen to testimonies such as that of Elionai and of hundreds of others, including the families of the twenty-three people who were killed in 2006. The governor dismissed the reports of Amnesty International and other human rights groups as "tainted" and took no action to investigate murders and abuses.

In 2010 the state of Oaxaca elected and installed a new governor, Gabino Cué Monteagudo, who pledged during his campaign to investigate the assassinations and human rights abuses of 2006 and to punish the guilty (Galo Samario 2010). Some senators in the state legislature and social movements called for an Oaxacan truth commission to investigate the crimes and assassinations that occurred in 2006. But when he gained the governor's seat on December 1, 2010, Cué Monteagudo initially discarded the idea of a truth commission. In March 2011 he created the Fiscalía de Investigaciones en Delitos de Trascendencia Social (Prosecutor's Office to Research Crime of Social Significance) and charged it with investigating the killings, torture, and other violations of human rights activists who participated in the social movements of 2006. He also appointed a citizen committee, made up of Oaxacan experts in law and the defense of human rights, to oversee and monitor the actions of the Fiscalía (Vélez Ascencio 2011). Later he back-pedaled to some degree. In August 2012, Cué Monteagudo sponsored state legislation for the formation of a state-level truth commission to investigate human rights violations in 2006 and 2007, which has yet to be implemented as of this writing.

In the investigative process, perhaps the testimonies of those who suffered human rights abuses will finally have an officially sanctioned legal forum. Elionai's testimonial, seen through the elements of a scenario analysis, permits us to see how a testimonial can extend far beyond one event, one telling, or one text in terms of how it travels, works, and may come to resignify "the truth" in official and unofficial versions of history. Perhaps these testimonials will be a part of "the truth" arrived at by the Fiscalía and the future truth commission in Oaxaca. (This Prosecutor's Office is further discussed in the conclusion.)

Elionai and Juan Gabriel were tried and convicted of the charges of illegal weapons possession. After they had exhausted their appeals, they paid large fines and received three-year suspended sentences. If they are ever arrested again for any offense, the three years will be added to whatever new jail time they receive. This has effectively silenced them and kept them from going to any political demonstrations or events. This solution has been used with many others who were falsely charged as well. The worst of this terrible experience for the two men has been the psychological damage it has caused them. For Elionai, his experience of torture and detention has affected his daily life. He continues to be afraid to go out alone:

Sometimes in the mornings I don't want to wake up because I still know what happened to me. . . . I stopped doing a lot of things that I used to do before: visit places, go to the movies, read books. I stopped doing these things because it seemed like they didn't have any meaning. Sometimes I even have a moment when I feel peaceful, and then I feel guilty because I am having a peaceful moment because so many people are suffering.

Human Rights Organizations' Reports on Violations in Oaxaca during 2006 and 2007

The Latin American Studies Association (LASA) sent an investigative delegation of five academic experts to Oaxaca in June 2007. They wrote an extensive report focused on violations against freedoms of inquiry and expression in the city of Oaxaca. The principal finding of this delegation was that "repression, violations, and a general atmosphere of threats extended broadly among researchers, teachers, cultural workers, and intellectuals associated with universities, schools, nongovernmental organizations, and similar institutions. These violations and threats are deeply disturbing as specific cases and chilling in their implications for democracy in Mexico" (LASA 2007).

Amnesty International (2007a) also carried out an investigation and issued a report on the human rights violations committed in Oaxaca between June 2006 and April 2007. A section of that report, titled "Arbitrary Detention, Torture, and Fabricated Charges," discusses the disturbing evidence compiled not only by Amnesty International but also by other human rights organizations of arbitrary arrests, incommunicado detention, ill treatment, and torture. The report goes on to specify that while state and federal authorities deny arbitrary arrests, false charges, and imprisonment to deter political activists and others

> in many cases documented by AI, criminal charges were based on the statements of arresting officers. In a number of cases prosecutors and judges do not seem to have taken even steps to corroborate the statements or assess whether the suspect's involvement in offences has been adequately demonstrated. In virtually all cases documented by AI, the arrest, whether carried out with or without a warrant, was conducted in an arbitrary manner. In many cases police did not identify themselves, inform the suspect that they were under arrest or make them aware of their rights. They also often failed to ensure communication with family or grant immediate access to effective legal counsel and medical attention.

Amnesty International's findings were corroborated by the report of a European-based human rights commission, Comisión Civil Internacional de Observación por los Derechos Humanos (International Civil Commission for the Observation of Human Rights, CCIODH), based on interviews with 420 individuals from Oaxaca.[2] The CCIODH's conclusions, like those of Amnesty International and others, suggest that state and federal police forces in Oaxaca carried out arbitrary and illegal detentions frequently and on occasion massively against the civilian population. Some of these detentions were also carried out by people dressed as civilians who were working with police forces. The CCIODH report stated that the rights of the detained were not respected; they were not notified of the crimes they were charged with, were not advised of their rights, and were left incommunicado, and no one was notified of their detention. In addition, the CCIODH found that when people were transported while under detention, their rights were gravely abused as they suffered physical torture such as beatings, stabbings, burnings, and electric shocks. Testimonies also suggest men and women were raped while in detention. People who participated in transporting those who were illegally detained included police forces and persons who were armed but did not wear uniforms. They were the custodians of the detained until they were deposited in prisons.

Based on their extensive interviews, the CCIODH also concluded that the rights to a fair defense and legal process were denied to many of the detained. Many did not have access to a lawyer of their choice. Many of the detained were assigned lawyers from the government who acted in defense of the state. Long and inexplicable delays were found in the processing of many cases. These reports suggest patterns that are illustrated in the cases of Ramiro, Elionai, and Juan Gabriel.

The Ironies of Rights and Political Asylum

For Elionai, Juan Gabriel, and Ramiro, the rights they are guaranteed in the Mexican Constitution and through international rights agreements ring hollow. Their feelings might be summarized by the words of Shannon Speed, speaking of the Zapatista movement's experience: "Rights-based claims can be seduced into a system where legal process is an empty signifier for the resolution of immediate conflict, while the heavier architecture of power that created those conflicts remains unquestioned" (2007: 180). For the three men, the power of the human rights discourses they interacted with is double-edged. A sincere belief in the moral authority of human rights gave them and many others the confidence to support a powerful social movement that swept through the city of Oaxaca like wildfire in the summer and fall of 2006. Their disbelief at the false charges, the torture, the apparent impunity of those who acted against them, and the total stagnation of the Mexican justice system has left them in a state of suspension. Juan Gabriel and Elionai are out of jail and were reporting to a judge, and Ramiro has fled the country, but all three men are still imprisoned by fear, doubt, and anger. As of the writing of this book, Juan Gabriel and Elionai had finished their requirement to report to a judge, but remain incredulous at the process they went through. Juan Gabriel explains:

In spite of the fact that we have demonstrated that our fingerprints were not on those weapons, that we demonstrated that we were tortured—because we have submitted torture charges—that I was beaten so badly my eardrum broke, that one of us had cigarette burns on his chest, that we were terribly beaten, that we were treated so horribly in order to make us completely afraid—in spite of all of this, nothing has happened with our cases. We continue to be accused. . . . This has also affected our families, like Ramiro's wife, Ruth, and our families. We had to come forward and make public denunciations about what happened, to do interviews with the press, to go to the official human rights offices of the government, to go to the Limeddh, Amnesty International, and the international human rights organizations. We had to do this because we had to declare what had happened. We had to declare again and again what happened. We have pictures, infinity of photos showing what they did to us, and in spite of all this the government says, "You are accused of a crime, you are guilty, and that's the end of it."

Oral testimony is crucial for documenting human rights abuses that gain little or no traction in the legal system. Not only does testifying provide psychological relief for survivors of human rights abuses, but oral testimony can be the foundation for building an alternative archive of violations. This archive can then be mobilized through the media, the Internet, and human rights organizations to defend those survivors. In Ramiro's case, the alternative archive of testimonials compiled by the teachers' union, Amnesty International, and other groups was critical in helping to legitimize his case for political asylum in the United States.

The experiences of Juan Gabriel, Elionai, and Ramiro can be multiplied by hundreds to include all of those who were treated similarly by state police and security forces in 2006 and 2007. The families of those imprisoned and assassinated will never forget how their loved ones were treated. The discourses of human rights that helped them to take to the streets and take over large parts of the city are connected to a very present moral outrage that is going to fuel future actions in the city of Oaxaca. When the disconnect between consciousness of rights and the inability to act on them is clear and long-lasting, movements for social justice are likely to emerge. Elionai's words in a July 2007 interview point to fertile ground for such a movement:

All of this that happened to us and many others has resulted in a lot of disillusionment and sadness for everything that happened. . . . After the death of

José Jiménez Colmenares we understood what was going on. There were more than twenty other deaths after that. This has put us in a situation of despair with the Mexican system of justice, the federal as well as the state. Our justice system is controlled by a government that is super-corrupt. We are profoundly disillusioned with the system we live under. We have seen so many injustices committed in the light of day, and now this situation has become normalized. It is still happening. Just yesterday there were more detentions, more tortures. We have seen how this works right here in Santa Lucia. We saw the same police running with weapons [a reference to the death of Bradley Will and others on October 28, 2006].

We want to get rid of this whole system, this system of assassins. The only way we can really relax and calm down is if this government leaves. Until there is justice for all of us, the tortured, the unjustly imprisoned, for the families of those who were assassinated, until all are punished, all of these who carried out these acts against the people—until that happens, we cannot rest.

In May and June 2007 Ramiro and his family came directly into my orbit. He and a member of my family knew one another, and through this tie, I began to talk with him, his wife, Ruth, and their extended families in Oaxaca. They were all trying to draw continued attention to his case and those of Elionai, Juan Gabriel, and others and to receive recognition, restitution, and justice from the Mexican legal system. On July 31, 2007, Governor Ruiz Ortiz dismissed the Amnesty International (2007a) report that documented "grave violations of human rights" between June 2006 and April 2007, describing it as "one-sided." According to Amnesty International's secretary-general Irene Khan:

> The meeting with the state authorities was disappointing. . . . The governor and his colleagues refuse to recognize that serious human rights violations have taken place. One year down the road they appear not to have drawn any lessons from the prolonged crisis to improve the protection of human rights. Although they claimed to have opened investigations, they could not provide any tangible proof of progress in bringing to justice those responsible for criminal offences in the context of the protests or human rights violations. (Amnesty International 2007b)

Oral testimony from Ramiro, Elionai, Juan Gabriel, and many others was part of this report, and it was partly because of this testimony that Ramiro received political asylum in the United States in July 2009. A report based on data from the U.S. Department of Justice (Michel 2009) states that of the 75,000 Mexicans who requested political asylum in the United States between 1998 and 2008, only 548 (fewer than 1 percent) received it. During the last year for which there are complete data, 3,229 Mexicans applied for political asylum, and 109 (3.3 percent) received it.

If a political asylum case can hold up and receive a positive decision by the U.S. Department of Justice and the U.S. Department of Homeland Security, it should certainly receive similar treatment by the Mexican justice system. So far there has been no investigation of the people who abducted and tortured Ramiro and his companions, and no compensation for the emotional and physical damage they suffered or for the time they spent in prison on false charges. While free in the United States, Ramiro is still waiting for justice in Mexico. In July 2009, upon hearing the news that he and his wife had received political asylum, he shared his thoughts with me in an interview:

RAMIRO: *On July 10, I received a letter from the Department of Homeland Security of the United States that announced that my petition for political asylum had been approved. So I am now here legally and form part of a group of people who are exiled from Mexico for political reasons. I am now a political refugee with asylum here in the United States.*

LYNN: *On the day you received that letter, what were your first thoughts, your first emotions?*

RAMIRO: *Well it was interesting. First, I felt a feeling of confidence and of victory that we had finally been listened to. I felt like our version of what happened in Oaxaca in 2006 was seen as the truth. It is a shame that it is in another county [outside of Mexico] where this has taken place. We have been found innocent, but the Mexican state has treated us like common criminals. . . .*

So now, fortunately, due to all of the documentation of our cases, of our torture and disappearance, and of the falsification of the crimes that we did not commit—thanks to all this—an official in the United States believed our version. . . . So we have to thank all of the coverage of the alternative media sources, the academic groups and others who came to Oaxaca to report on our case. . . . What was so evident for people here was not evident in Mexico. In October of 2006 they let us out of jail, but there are still outstanding arrest orders for us. Our legal process continues in Mexico, and nothing has been solved. In fact that is the primary reason we had to leave Mexico.

LYNN: *Now that you have this good news about receiving political asylum in the United States, what do you want the government of Oaxaca and the federal government to do? Are there outstanding charges against you and damages that you suffered?*

RAMIRO: *Yes, there are a lot of reparations that need to happen. Most of all we feel the moral outrage of it all. And from there we need to see the complete exoneration of all the invented charges that were served up to us [Ramiro, Elionai, and Juan Gabriel]. . . . There also is a federal charge against me that was invented. The real problem is that the justice system in Mexico is being used illegally to incriminate people.*

LYNN: *Are there more specific things that need to happen?*

RAMIRO: *State authorities have to acknowledge that the version of the police who were accusing us is completely false and invented. There needs to be an investigation against the people who did this to us. This investigation should look into who were the people who kidnapped us. Were they part of a paramilitary group? Who were the people who turned us in to state police? And we need to have an investigation of the people who stole my car. They robbed with violence, kidnapped us, and tortured us with impunity. There needs to be an investigation of all of this. I am not going to do it. The Mexican state needs to do it and work through the justice system to find out who was responsible. . . .*

The underlying issue is that we need to reform the Mexican judicial system. For example, how is it possible in Mexico that the accused are never even seen or interviewed by the judge? The judge only reads everything that is written or told by the police, not the version that I or someone else wrote, and then sits in his office, reads the case, and based on the law makes a decision. It is so easy in this system to criminalize just about anyone. There has to be a change in this system. For example in Chile there are three judges who listen and then make a decision, all three of them. There are direct interviews where the accused gets to face the judge. We need changes like this to diminish the illegal use of our justice system. . . .

Finally, I want to say that even though Mexico has signed all the possible international human rights declarations, they are never applied inside of the country. There is a huge hypocrisy on the part of the state by saying that they are ready to sign human rights conventions of all kinds, but they do not want to produce the conditions inside of the country to comply with the content of these agreements.

In the absence of a functioning justice system, human rights are documented and defended by grassroots organizations. In the cases discussed here, dissemination of testimony on the radio, on television, on the streets of Oaxaca, and through organizations such as Limeddh and Amnesty International was critical in granting the testimony legitimacy and the weight of truth. While transformation of Oaxaca's justice system does not seem possible at the moment, the political and cultural space that opened in Oaxaca for six months in 2006 created a deep synergy between rights discourses that had been circulating for almost two decades among a limited public and the majority's long-standing tradition of testimony. The verdict is still out on the outcome of the Oaxaca social movement of 2006, but we can already clearly see the resonance of rights discourses with a cultural form that empowers those who have been silenced, because it makes what they have to say understandable to others who are hearing their voices for the first time.

5

Community and Indigenous Radio in Oaxaca

Testimony and Participatory Democracy

This chapter uses ethnographic analysis of the takeovers of Oaxaca radio stations in 2006 and of the subsequent changes in indigenous community radio stations to explore the connection between radio practices—and in particular the testimonials they broadcast—and the enactment of participatory democracy. While testimonials are often inaudible within the cultures of mainstream political parties, the halls of state assemblies, and conventional Mexican media, they are central to models of decision making in local social movements in Mexico. When political discussion hit the airwaves following the occupation of radio stations in Oaxaca, testimonials were widely broadcast, and they continue to be programmed on indigenous community radio broadcasts there. During and after the 2006 social movement, indigenous and grassroots radio stations became important arenas for a transformative kind of cultural politics that determines "the meanings of social practices, and moreover, which groups and individuals have the power to define these meanings" (Jordan and Weedon 1995: 5–6).

The dynamics of deliberation in community radio programming and in indigenous community assemblies are facilitated by exposure to testimonial speech-acts, both on the air and in face-to-face gatherings (Brodkin 2007; Polletta 2002; Stephen 2005a). The format of indigenous and grassroots radio programming is linked to this speech genre and and has implications for participatory democracy. I argue that indigenous radio has flourished in Oaxaca partly because listeners are accustomed to and comfortable with the testimonial format these stations often feature. Radio broadcasts amplify and intensify this communicative genre's popular appeal.

The testimonial genre is deeply rooted in the decision-making processes of community assemblies, in which formalized interactional styles are purposefully used to solicit and emphasize shared opinions while accommodating divergent ones. When used in local deliberative processes, testimony provides a model for radio programming, as happened after the takeover of COR-TV in Oaxaca. Links connect the oral nature of radio, the growing presence of radio testimonials in Oaxaca, programming formats, and the decision-making forms of community assemblies. Efforts to explain the widespread adoption of radio within many indigenous communities, or to understand how such radio practices relate to discourses of community autonomy, must begin by taking seriously this intersection of technology, political history, and cultural style.

Testimonial Formats on the Radio and in Community Assemblies

Rights in Oaxaca are often grounded in claims to indigeneity, gender, or a universal humanity. In each case, all rights are held to depend first on the right to speak. And in Oaxaca, as elsewhere, the right to speak begins with *actually speaking*, with thinking of oneself as someone who can speak about experiences of injustices. The right to speak relies on a sense of membership within a larger community of similar speakers that have similar rights. *Being heard* involves having access to public spaces and channels of communication that cuts across different social sectors, cultural groups, and venues. The rights to speak and to be heard are foundational rights. A public deliberative space was created by radio call-in and on-air testimonies that occurred during the takeover of COR-TV in 2006 by women in Oaxaca City, which we can compare to the testimonial dynamics in an indigenous community assembly. Contemporary indigenous community radio stations have drawn from the 2006 radio takeovers to make a similar testimonial format central to their programming.

On August 10, 2006, the road leading up to the occupied COR-TV and radio station was lined with several public buses and cars that had been commandeered by the movement and were spray-painted with references to APPO, Sección 22, and the inevitable fall of Governor Ulises Ruiz Ortiz (e.g., "Ya cayó," "He has already fallen"). A crowd of about a hundred people from the neighboring community of Telixtlahuaca gathered outside of the station. Other small delegations lined up as well. The women occupying the station had decided to open up the airwaves to on-air testimony of the injustices suffered and to different visions of how to improve the state of Oaxaca. Speakers came not only from Oaxaca City but increasingly from more distant communities. Individuals and groups would come to the station, register with the women, and receive a time to speak. There were often long lines of people waiting for a chance to speak on air and preparing their statements for the radio.

While I was waiting to clear security to go inside the station, the members of the delegation of the Organización de Mototaxis de Oaxaca (Organization of Mototaxis of the State of Oaxaca) were outside practicing their testimonial before going on the air.[1] Here is part of their statement:

We want to let you know that we are part of the Organization of the Mototaxis of the State of Oaxaca. We have been the victims of indifference on the part of state and city authorities. We want to inform you that like many organizations here, we have not been listened to by the municipal president Jesús Angel or by the governor of the state Ulises Ruiz, nor by the secretary of state Jorge Franco. We have in our possession applications for licenses that were received and stamped by people who have deceived us, telling us to come back on many occasions, which we did. When we arrived no one would talk with us. . . .

We have a presence in six neighborhoods in Oaxaca and we know that those in power are protecting the interests of other taxi owners who have thirty or forty taxis. Because our cabs bear the insignia of APPO, they have threatened us. We want to let you know that from this moment we are here to say that if anything happens to our drivers, we will hold the governor of the state, Ulises Ruiz, the municipal president Jesús Angel, and the ex-secretary of state Jorge Franco responsible.

Concerned with the safety of their drivers who were in taxis bearing the APPO logo, the delegates were also publicly documenting corruption on the part of state officials who, they argued, favored another taxi union over theirs because it was associated with the PRI, which was the party of the

governor. Their testimony of corruption and favoritism was a theme repeated many times by a variety of groups on the renamed Radio Cacerola.

After I secured permission to enter, I and others were ushered in through
a courtyard where many women were sorting the food, clothing, and blankets that had been provided to those who spent long days and nights occupying the station. We were escorted upstairs past the television studios
and into the radio station. Two young women were serving as engineers
and another was emceeing a call-in show that was receiving cell-phone updates about a large march winding its way to the center of the city. In the
studio, two women were preparing to begin a testimonial segment about
the current social movement and how it had affected them as women. Pilar
Montenegro began to speak about her experience of the attempt to force
the teachers from the center of the city, which she watched from inside her
home. Her dark hair hung in a curtain over her face as she leaned down to
speak into the microphone:

---

*For those of us who live in the historic center of the city, we experienced this
terrible day from the intimacy of our homes. I think I first opened my eyes
early that morning hearing someone saying, "Fuck your mother." I heard
someone else screaming from the street about what was going on. I was able
to go down to the street in that moment in my pajamas. I got to the corner of
Avenida Morelos and Avenida Juárez and there was a group of heavily armed
police. I was terrified and I ran back to my house because I couldn't believe
the level of aggression that was going on at this point.*

*So we lived through the attempted desalojo [eviction] from our home.
The teachers began to leave, and my family went down to the street. We went
down to be with the teachers because not only was it an invasion against
democracy and the right to freely demonstrate, as the teachers were doing
with their sit-in, but it was also an invasion into our homes. We went out
because we didn't want to permit this violence. . . .*

*You are never prepared for this kind of violation, and that is what we
mothers felt in the historic center. Our kids were asleep at this hour when it
happened. The only thing we could think of to do was to put up handwritten
notices that said that we repudiated the attempt to dislodge the teachers in
this manner and we united ourselves with the teachers as they attempted to
retake their area of occupation in the center. Later we brought them coffee,
some bread, and things to eat. . . .*

*It felt like the city was raped. The center was pulled apart, beaten,
wounded. It was this sensation you would feel walking downtown. We walked*

on Morelos Street past the store called the Gem Palace and we saw little blankets, baby shoes, and a sheet. I took a picture there because I had such a strong feeling about that spot where a small child had been. It made me feel really sad. We saw a lot of things like that in the historic center on that day that we will not forget for decades.

Pilar's graphic imagery of the pillage of downtown Oaxaca by state police captures the fear and sense of violation and invasion felt by many. The power of the images she paints in her personal testimony resulted in many callers contacting the radio station during the broadcast, identifying with and echoing her feelings.

Through testimony about her experience, Pilar also places herself physically in the center of the city as a resident and then as someone who experienced the repression of June 14. She goes on to identify her solidarity with the group of teachers occupying the city center and to describe her presence as one who interacts with them, offering them coffee and food. The last part of her testimony grounds her as a part of the larger entity of "the city," which she characterizes as being oppressed and victimized—raped, pulled apart, wounded, beaten—a metaphoric woman who has been violated. By using this metaphor to include not only herself but also a much broader group of people who live in the city, Pilar emphasizes a shared sense of suffering and community. People who called in identified with both the physical and social suffering outlined in Pilar's call and underlined the connections between the individual suffering of teachers and their families and the structural violence that was all around them, in both the past and the present. Pilar's testimony and the shared community expressed by the callers connected such experiences of violence to "a language of dismay, disappointment, bereavement and alarm" (Kleinman et al. 1997: xi). After she finished her testimonial and had listened to those who called in, Pilar told me that she felt a great sense of connection to all of the women who had called in to share their stories: "I don't feel alone. We are all here together." Through the testimonial experience, she felt connected to a larger community.

If we look structurally at what happened, the airing of her testimonial legitimates her as a speaker who is given the right to speak and the right to be heard. Those listening are her shared speech community, as are those who are present in the station. This genre of radio broadcast places and legitimates the speaker in much the same way as community assemblies do. Consider the following description of such an assembly in the Zapotec community of Teotitlán del Valle (where I have worked since 1983; Stephen

2005): inside the building labeled Salon de usos multiples, Xa Guiea—(Hall for Multiple Uses [in Spanish] of Teotitlán del Valle [in Zapotec]), about two hundred people have assembled. The crowd is primarily men, with perhaps ten to fifteen women present, all speaking in Zapotec. There are also men standing at the back of the room. This community assembly has been called to elect slates of new officials to various civil *cargos* (positions) in the civil government.[2] The meeting begins with a roll call in which each of six different neighborhoods of the community (*secciones*) are called out and people stand, state their name, and report, "I am present." In this way all publicly identify themselves and where they live in the community. After the official agenda items are read in Spanish by the *síndico* (trustee), who serves as the chief fiscal officer for the community, discussion rapidly switches into Didxsaj (Zapotec). People begin their statements in third-person formal Zapotec and include ceremonial forms of address that connote humility before the public assembly and great respect for all present.

Point 3 on the agenda is the naming of new municipal *policía* (police). This turns out to be the most heated and heartfelt part of the discussion, as the naming of a new slate of young men to the position of policía generates a lot of commentary about how to deal with issues of security and the greatly increased sense of danger in the community. Even those who have been absent for some time and are returning to the community with somewhat rusty Zapotec resume use of the ceremonial form of Zapotec as best they can.[3] As the síndico begins to call out names of people proposed to be policías from different neighborhoods, people begin to raise their hands to speak. A microphone is passed around, and one by one people begin to testify about the difficulties that the police have had in controlling violence and crime in the community. A man who is about forty stands up. He has on a Los Angeles Raiders jacket and gently takes the mike in his hand. He begins to speak in a soft voice, looking slightly downward while facing the local authorities, a posture that denotes respect.

I humbly ask you for permission to speak to you. I pay my respects to all of our authorities and appreciate the importance of their responsibility and appreciate their service. I also know that things are not safe around here anymore. We are worried about the gang problems and our young people. They are on the streets and they are even breaking into people's houses and robbing them. How can our police deal with this? We also have a problem with drugs in our community.

Another, younger man, dressed in jeans and a black baseball jacket, stands next. He begins:

I humbly agree with my fellow citizen and request permission to speak to you. The work of the police is very hard these days. I think that we need to think about how they are being trained. We expect a lot from them. They used to be auxiliary police and just carry canes.[4] Now they have pickup trucks and they take great risks when they are called on to go to violent situations. They need more help. It is a very hard job. I have done it.

He continues to speak for another five minutes.

From this point on more people raise their hands and begin to interject testimonials, often speaking for five to ten minutes at a time. While this appears to disrupt the process of naming the individuals who will assume the positions of municipal police, no one seems to mind. Instead the process opens up a broad conversation about crime, safety, and what the police actually are able to do. This continues for more than an hour. When it seems all who wanted to have spoken, the síndico moves back to the process of naming new police. The assembly goes on until about 1 a.m. At different points in the meeting people stand one after another to offer testimonials about what they have experienced and how they feel in relation to different themes of discussion. This style of interaction produces an assembly that often lasts for three, four, or five hours, and sometimes even longer.

In this community assembly and through Pilar's on-air testimony with call-in respondents, speakers anchor themselves as legitimate members of a shared community by locating themselves in a specific place (in the community assembly as part of a particular neighborhood in Teotitlán del Valle, and on Radio Cacerola as a resident of the historic center of Oaxaca City), by identifying themselves with their names, and by describing experiences that they have shared with those they are speaking to. Once they are located, testimonial speakers proceed to deploy their rights to speak and to be heard by a larger public.

Not only do decisions about whether or not to have a radio station begin in a community assembly, but community radio stations in indigenous communities can take on some of the functions of community assemblies in terms of creating shared spaces for public discussion and forging agreement across different perspectives, which are usually expressed in personal testimonials. Juan José García, a Zapotec videographer and radio producer who works for the Oaxacan NGO Ojo de Agua Comunicación and who provided technical assistance during the radio takeovers,[5] explicitly notes the centrality of testimonials not only in community assemblies, but also in the broadcasts of Radio Cacerola in 2006. He was interviewed in December 2009 by Mauricio Magaña as a part of some shared interviews we conducted in 2009 and 2010:

During the process [in Radio Cacerola], people could express themselves
freely and a lot of people responded to this—not everyone, but the radio
did open things up to a certain point. People called in from all over on their
phones. They sang on the radio. They raised their voices against the govern-
ment and the rich. There was a whole oppositional discourse and an attitude
of challenging the status quo. But there were also many people detained and
it was hard to even go out on the street. In response to this, a lot of people
were interviewed. They gave their testimony on audio and on video. There
were a lot of testimonies about aggressions of the state against the people.

During 2007 and 2008 Juan José and others logged and edited hundreds of hours of video and audio testimonials about government repression and human rights violations that had been recorded during the radio takeovers. These testimonials were then submitted to the Mexican Supreme Court for a hearing on Oaxaca. The audio testimonials that were broadcast on the radio as well as on video and collected by Mal de Ojo TV have become key evidence for claiming and documenting human rights violations by the Oaxacan state government and associated institutions during the political upheavals of 2006.

The State and Indigenist Radio Policy:
INI, the EZLN, and La Ley Televisa

Before discussing some of Oaxaca's newer indigenous and community radio stations, it is important to understand their historical link to the radio programming begun by the National Indigenist Institute (INI) in 1979. The first INI radio station was set up in coordination with the Comisión del Río Balsas (Rio Balsas Commission) in Tlapa, Guerrero. The Commission was part of the Secretaría de Agricultura y Recursos Hidraúlicos (Ministry of Agriculture and Hydraulic Resources, SARH), which was linked to many rural development projects in the 1970s and 1980s. At the time the radio station was created in Tlapa, 85 percent of the population spoke Nahuatl, Mixtec, or Tlapanec, with 55 percent not fluent in Spanish (Castells Talens 2004: 112; SARH 1977: 2–3). The station, XEZV, was called La Voz de la Montaña (Voice of the Mountain).[6]

Subsequent INI-sponsored radio stations were often linked to *centros de coordinación indígena* (centers for indigenous coordination, CCIS). The first was established in 1951 in San Cristóbal de las Casas, Chiapas. By 1970 INI had set up three more CCIS in indigenous areas of Mexico, including in the state of Oaxaca (Wortham 2013). As Wortham points out, many of the people who were trained by INI as cultural promoters later became bilingual teachers and were transferred in 1970 to the Ministry of Education. Some, however, remained in radio. From 1971 to 1988 INI opened seventy-nine new CCIS. The growth of the INI indigenous radio system is linked to this period of expansion (Wortham 2013). Between 1979 and 1988 INI launched seven indigenous radio stations: Tlapa de Comonfort, Guerrero (XEZV, 1979); Nacajuca, Tabasco (XENAC, 1981); Peto, Yucatán (XEPET, 1982); Tlaxiaco, Oaxaca (XETLA, 1982); Guachochi, Chihuahua (XETAR, 1982); Cherán, Michoacán (XEPUR, 1982); and Las Margaritas, Chiapas (XEVFS, 1987); (Olvera Romero 2008: 80–81).

During this time INI faced sharp criticism from anthropologists such as Arturo Warman, who then went on to direct the INI (Warman et al. 1989).[7] Ideas about cultural diversity and plurality, which had been part of the critique against INI since the 1970s, were adopted in the 1980s by some of those inside the institution. They were also adopted by a growing indigenous rights movement that began to get significant traction at the regional level in the 1980s and gained major political ground after 1994, in the wake of the Zapatista movement.

Between 1988 and 1994 INI added another eight stations to its network, undergoing a significant period of expansion. An important factor in the growth of INI radio stations during this period was the support they received from President Salinas de Gortari's (1988–94) antipoverty program, known as the Programa Nacional de Solidaridad (or Solidarity). As discussed by Wayne Cornelius, Ann L. Craig, and Jonathan Fox (1994: 3), the program had two foci: (1) material support, including social services and infrastructure provision as well as poverty alleviation; and (2) institutional relations, including the rearrangement of state-society relations, and support of the PRI. The building of additional INI radio stations fell potentially under both of these foci, although primarily under the latter. The expansion of INI radio stations, which was broadcasting in twenty-eight different indigenous

Table 5.1 INI Radio Stations

Call sign	Launched	Transmitting from	Coverage	Languages	Frequency
XEZV	May 10, 1979	Guerrero (Tlapa de Comonfort)	Guerrero Oaxaca Puebla	Nahuatl Mixtec Tlapanec	800 AM
XETLA	Sept. 15, 1982	Oaxaca (Tlaxiaco)	Oaxaca Guerrero Puebla	Mixtec Triqui	930 AM
XEPUR	Oct. 2, 1982	Michoacán (Cherán)	Michoacán	Purepecha	830 AM
XETAR	Nov. 11, 1982	Chihuahua (Guachochi)	Chihuahua Sinaloa Durango	Tarahumara Tepehuano	870 AM
XEPET	Nov. 29, 1982	Yucatán (Peto)	Yucatán Quintana Roo Campeche	Yucatec Maya	730 AM
XEVFS	Apr. 17, 1987	Chiapas (Las Margaritas)	Chiapas Guatemala	Tojolabal Mam Tseltal Tsotsil Popti	1030 AM
XEANT	Sept. 28, 1990	San Luis Potosí (Tancanhuitz de Santos)	San Luis Potosí Hidalgo Querétaro Veracruz	Nahuatl Pame Wastek	770 AM
XEGLO	Nov. 18, 1990	Oaxaca (Guelatao de Juárez)	Oaxaca Veracruz	Zapotec Mixe Chinantec	780 AM
XEZON	Nov. 20, 1991	Veracruz (Zongolica)	Veracruz Oaxaca Puebla Tlaxcala	Nahuatl	1360 AM
XEOJN	Dec. 14, 1991	Oaxaca (San Lucas Ojitlán)	Oaxaca Puebla Veracruz	Mazatec Cuicatec Chinantec	950 AM
XEJMN	Apr. 3, 1992	Nayarit (Jesús María)	Nayarit Jalisco Durango Zacatecas	Cora Huichol Tepehuano Nahuatl	750 AM

Call sign	Launched	Transmitting from	Coverage	Languages	Frequency
XEJAM	May 5, 1994	Oaxaca (Santiago Jamiltepec)	Oaxaca Guerrero	Mixtec Amuzgo Chatino	1260 AM
XEQIN	June 15, 1994	Baja California (San Quintín)	Baja California	Mixtec Zapotec Triqui	1160 AM
XECTZ	Aug. 21, 1994	Puebla (Cuetzalan)	Puebla Hidalgo Veracruz	Nahuatl Totonac	1260 AM
XEXPUJ	Jan. 22, 1996	Campeche (Xpujil)	Campeche Quintana Roo	Yucatec Maya Ch'ol	700 AM
XEETCH	Feb. 19, 1996	Sonora (Etchojoa)	Sonora Sinaloa Chihuahua	Mayo Yaqui Guarijio	700 AM
XECOPA	July 17, 1997	Chiapas (Copainalá)	Chiapas Tabasco	Zoque Tzotzil	1210 AM
XETUMI	May 12, 1998	Michoacán (Tuxpan)	Michoacán Edo. de México Querétaro	Mazahua Otomi	1010 AM
XECARH	Aug. 1, 1998	Hidalgo (Cardonal)	Hidalgo Querétaro Veracruz San Luis Potosí	Ñha-ñhu Nahuatl	1480 AM
XENKA	June 15, 1999	Quintana Roo (Felipe Carrillo Puerto)	Quintana Roo	Yucatec Maya	1030 AM

Note: Now known as the Sistema de Radiodifusores Culturales Indigenistas, INI stations are run by the Comisión Nacional para el Desarollo de los Pueblos Indígenas de México (National Commission for the Development of the Indigenous Peoples of Mexico, CDI). The CDI handles many functions that were carried out by INI until 2003, when the CDI was created and INI abolished. This list does not include Nacajuca, Tabasco (XENAC, 1981), which went off the air in 1990 and lost its broadcasting license in 2001.

Source: Wikipedia 2011. This information is licensed under the Creative Commons. I use it here with correct attribution. Another webpage that leads readers to the current radio stations sponsored by Mexican government is the public-access website of the Comisión Nacional para el Desarollo de Los Pueblos Indígenas, http://www.cdi.gob.mx/index.php ?option=com_content&view=category&id=71.

languages by 1994, also supported the state's promotion of the pluricultural composition of the Mexican nation (as written into the revised Article 4 of the Mexican Constitution in 1992) and allowing indigenous organizations and communities to independently manage their resources and development planning and projects. The anthropologist Arturo Warman headed the INI from 1988 until 1992. His long-term promotion of indigenous autonomy and self-organization was a good match for the ideology of the Solidarity Program and a similar political current that was strong within INI at that time (see Fox 1994: 190). With a budget that grew eighteen-fold between 1988 and 1991, to U.S.$140 million (Fox 1994: 188), INI became a significant source of economic development. By 1994, the year the Zapatista rebellion broke out in Oaxaca, INI was managing fifteen radio stations. Table 5.1 depicts the evolution of INI stations from 1979 through 1999, listing them by call sign, launch date, place of transmission, area of coverage, languages used in broadcasting, and frequency.

A turning point in both the structure and the functioning of INI occurred in 1994. According to Wortham's analysis of the internal politics of INI and its investment in the transference of power and resources to indigenous communities, the 1992 departure of Arturo Warman, who was a strong advocate for INI's radio programs, was a major blow, as was the termination of a program titled Transferencia de Medios Audiovisuales a Organizaciones y Comunidades Indígenas (Transference of Audiovisual Media to Indigenous Communities and Organizations, TMA). The upper-level INI managers who came after Warman highlighted the underlying paternalism of INI's basic model, that indigenous peoples are beholden to INI's benevolence for their access to audiovisual media (Wortham 2013). The challenge to INI's right to manage indigenous radio stations came from the Zapatistas, as well as from other indigenous organizations and leaders.

Part of the Zapatistas' agenda was to establish indigenous community radio as a collective right of indigenous communities, which could use the power of radio to fortify indigenous autonomy through the arena of cultural rights. The San Andrés Accords on Indigenous Rights and Cultures, which was negotiated in 1996 between the EZLN and the Mexican government, included a section that dealt specifically with communications media. The document made explicit reference to turning over control of state-run radio stations, which were administered by the INI, to indigenous communities. The accords also laid out specifics for empowering indigenous communities with rights within the area of communications. Document 2 of the accords, section III, item 8, titled, "Communications Media," states:

It will be proposed to the respective national authorities that they pre-pare a new communications law that will allow the [*pueblos indígenas*] to acquire, operate, and administer their own communications medias.

The federal and state governments will encourage the conversion of the National Indigenous Institute's communications media into indigenous communications media. . . . The Federal government will recommend to the respective authorities that the seventeen INI (National Indigenous Institute) radio stations be turned over to the indigenous communities in their respective regions with the transfer of permits, infrastructure, and resources. . . .

It is necessary to create a new legal framework in the area of communications that may consider the following aspects: the nation's multiculturalism; the right to use indigenous languages in the media; the right to rebuttal; guarantees to rights of expression, information, and communication; and the democratic participation of the [*pueblos indígenas*] and communities in relation to the authorities who decide on matters of communication. (San Andrés Accords on Indigenous Rights and Culture 1996)

Following the signing of the San Andrés Accords, six other INI radio stations were created between 1995 and 1999 in the states of Campeche, Sonora, Chiapas, Michoacán, Hidalgo, and Quintana Roo. None of the new stations came under the independent control of indigenous organizations and communities.

Wortham documents the success of Radio XEGLO, "La Voz de la Sierra," in Guelatão, Oaxaca, as an INI radio station whose operators believed they were able to maintain relative independence and control over their station's content. Because they broadcast in Zapotec, Chinantec, and Mixe, opera-tors thought they could effectively evade government pressure (Wortham 2013). According to Jaime Martínez Luna, one of the founders of XEGLO who was interviewed by Wortham, INI stole some of the successful outreach strategies the station used, "such as community advisory councils made up of community authorities, community correspondents whose job it was to assure community representation within the radio, and community-based radio production centers (CPS), that produced multi-lingual, diversified programming from throughout the region" (100). According to Luna, many of the correspondents were able to count their work at the radio station as part of their community service, and radio production was considered "a part of rotating community obligations or cargos" (100).

While the EZLN and other indigenous organizations struggled to get the San Andrés Accords legislated, INI was one of the few doors open for the creation of licensed stations. But INI administrators began to decrease the autonomy of the network of indigenous radio stations, severely undercutting the ability of operators to program and operate their stations independently. Wortham reports that by the end of 1994, "INI installed cut-off boxes at all its stations allowing the signals to be cut remotely from INI's office in Mexico City" (2013: 101).

In Guelatão and elsewhere, radio operators sympathized with the Zapatista movement and pushed to have their radio stations transferred to indigenous control. Through the use of the INI cut-off box XEGLO in Guelatão was taken off the air numerous times. Its Zapotec director, Aldo Gonzalez, was eventually forced to resign after he became an advisor to the EZLN (Wortham 2013: 101). Luna, who was set to step into the radio director position at XEGLO, was passed over and subsequently left the station, a pattern repeated elsewhere. In 1997 the Mixe leader Adelfo Regino Montes worked with XEGLO operators to get INI to transfer the station over to local indigenous control, but their efforts were briskly dismissed. According to Regino, INI director Carlos Tello told him that "radio stations were a matter of national security and could not be in the hands of the pueblos" (Wortham 2013: 104). Such experiences led to the proliferation of independent media projects in indigenous communities in Oaxaca and elsewhere.

As Wortham (2013) points out, contemporary indigenous radio also shares a partial lineage with *video indígena* (indigenous video) and *radio indígena* (indigenous radio), which were created from the 1950s through the 1990s through the now defunct INI as a part of top-down development process. Wortham documents how video indígena and other skills linked to radio broadcasting were originally taught in Oaxaca, in part by video instructors who were paid by INI. Instructors and students trained by INI's TMA program went on to found the Centro de Video Indígena in Oaxaca and then the NGO Ojo de Agua (Wortham 2013). Wortham's work shows the important history of state-indigenous community relations as part of the evolution of indigenous and community radio and video.

Since 1998 Ojo de Agua has provided a production facility and space that allows indigenous and other media producers of radio, video, and television to do their work without depending on state sponsorship for existence (Wortham 2004: 365). Although it shares some history with INI's audiovisual project, Ojo de Agua in Oaxaca was explicitly formed to be independent of government sponsorship and is linked to the staff's "overt support of indigenous self-determination and the government's obvious retreat from the idea of transferences that originally underwrote INI's" TMA program (Wortham 2013: 115).

The efforts of indigenous peoples and organizations to get the San Andrés Accords legislated ended in bitter disappointment. After a national bus tour in 2001 by the EZLN to raise awareness about the importance of the Accords, the Mexican Congress passed a greatly watered-down version of the original that omitted many of the concrete proposals, such as that for media. The 2001 legislation also left most of the specifics about the implementation of indigenous rights to individual state legislatures. While the national legislation on indigenous rights states that it aims "to establish conditions for villages and indigenous communities to acquire, operate, and administer mass media," indigenous access to media was to be granted "in accordance with existing laws" (McElmurry 2009: 4).

The limitations inherent in this phrase prohibited significant reforms that would give better access and control of media to indigenous communities. This became particularly evident in 2006, when the ruling party (PAN) passed a modification to Mexico's Federal Telecommunications Law and Federal Radio and Television Law that clearly favored corporate media and severely disadvantaged community radio and other forms of grassroots media. The law established that radio and television enterprises that hoped to gain access to new parts of the TV and radio spectrum would be granted licenses through a process of competitive public bidding. While this was supposed to facilitate much-needed transparency in the process of granting media licenses, it placed poorer community radio stations at a clear disadvantage. Since the bidding process contains no consideration of social or cultural reasons for granting licenses, few indigenous radio stations outside of the INI-controlled network of stations currently have licenses. Operating without a license makes them, technically, illegal. In 2007, following the new federal telecommunication and radio legislation, the Comisión Nacional para el Desarollo de los Pueblos Indígenas de México (National Commission for the Development of the Indigenous Peoples of Mexico, launched seven ten-watt high-frequency FM stations in Yucatan, Veracruz, and Michoacán (SIMO 2011).[8]

Eugenio Bermejillo, the coordinator for Boca de Polen, a network-building organization that supports community radio stations, estimates that there are 150 to 200 community radio stations in Mexico, and that only 15 to 20 percent of them are licensed by the Mexican government (McElmurry 2009: 4). The majority are unlicensed, "pirate" radio stations, seen by the

Mexican government as operating outside of the law. This makes them vulnerable to equipment seizures under the General Law of National Goods, which defines radiophonic space as a public good possessed by the nation, something that cannot be used without legal permission (Prieto Beguiristáin 2009: 2).

Community Radio and Participatory Democracy

The process of legitimizing those who have no voice in formal, electoral political systems through testimonials is connected to the larger project of creating a public, political culture of participatory democracy—something that is scarce in much of contemporary Oaxaca. Both the format and the content of broadcasting on Radio Cacerola in 2006—and subsequently on other community radio stations—contributed to a new understanding of how politics should be defined in Oaxaca and what kinds of participatory processes matter. The Zapatista movement, publicly launched in Chiapas in 1994, has provided a pioneering model of participatory, public political culture that has come to influence other parts of Mexico.

The Zapatista model of good-governance councils expands the structure of the community assembly described earlier to include a networked, regional seat of governance that operates outside of the political party system. In August 2003 the Zapatistas announced the creation of five *caracoles* (literally "spiral shells" but meaning points of communication) that are the seats for five Juntas de Buen Gobierno (Good Governance Councils). Each of the five Juntas includes one to three delegates from each of the already existing Autonomous Councils in each zone. There are approximately thirty Zapatista Autonomous Municipalities in Rebellion, each with their own autonomous councils that feed into the five Juntas. Autonomous councils are charged with governing Zapatista territory in rebellion under the logic of *mandar obedeciendo* ("rule by obeying"; see Cerda García 2011: 131–50 for a detailed discussion of Zapatista governance at the local and regional levels).

Relevant to our discussion is the Zapatista model of public decision making. A keystone of good governance holds that authorities carry out consensual decisions, instead of making them independently. Decisions come after a careful deliberative process that does not involve a strict consensus but bears some resemblance to what Francesca Polletta describes as the deliberative and experimental model of decision making. Polletta encountered this model in a range of U.S. social movement organizations that she has studied from the 1960s to the present:

> By talking issues through, people with very little experience of political decision-making learned to identify the costs and benefits of alternative options and gathered the information needed to make judgments. Reasoning together about options and solutions led to new conceptions of self-interest and new perceptions of strategy. By rejecting conventional criteria and promoting new ones—this was the experimental part—activists helped legitimate new kinds of leadership and development for holding leaders accountable to their constituents. (Polletta 2002: 209)

Although Polletta studies movements such as the Student Nonviolent Coordinating Committee, founded in 1960 as part of the civil rights movement, and the Direct Action Network, a spin-off of the 1999 Seattle World Trade Organization demonstrations, the process she describes as deliberative and experiential bears some kinship to the model of the assembly found in indigenous communities in Chiapas and Oaxaca, although there are local variations. The central, shared element in cultures of participatory democracy is the acknowledgment that unity in decision making comes through "recognizing the legitimacy of different opinions as well as shared ones" (Polletta 2002: 210). Polletta suggests insightfully that what distinguishes this model of decision making from majoritarian voting is "its emphasis on having participants make their reasoning accessible and legitimate to each other. Solidarity is re-created through the process of decision-making, not its endpoint" (210). In this deliberative model of reasoning, which is a part of the political culture of indigenous community assemblies and of some social movements, the speech-act of testimony plays an important role.

The testimonial positions the speaker as one who is speaking from a personal perspective within the context of larger, shared structural, political, economic, and cultural circumstances. Its synthetic ability to simultaneously profile a distinct perspective and opinion within a larger context of shared circumstances makes the testimonial a natural vehicle of expression in cultures of participatory democracy. Indigenous community radio—which often mirrors the process of decision making and the culture of participation described earlier—provides one of the most important forums for realizing local aspirations for a public culture of participatory democracy. An example from Radio Zaachila, founded in 2006, brings home this point.

Adán López Santiago, one of the founders of Radio Zaachila and elected as *presidente municipal* of Zaachila (mayor) in 2010, was an avid participant in the social movement of 2006. We spoke in July 2010, shortly after his election. He was dressed in a plain white cotton shirt, open at the neck, with his long black hair gathered in a ponytail at the nape of his neck. He speaks with confidence and clarity. He was trained as a teacher and began his first job in 1987 in Santa María Ecatepec, Yautepec, in southeastern Oaxaca. He has continued his studies and traveled to Austria, Germany, France, Spain, Japan, and Argentina to network and learn more about community radio. He described the participation of people from Zaachila in APPO and the social movement of 2006 with a great deal of animation:

The central part of the philosophy of this movement was absorbed in Zaachila. We took over the presidencia municipal *[mayor's office], but we didn't forget that there was a movement in the city of Oaxaca. The people of Zaachila participated there a great deal. Every time they needed us, we were there. When they needed our support, buses of people would come to Oaxaca City from Zaachila. People in the movement were always expecting the people from Zaachila to provide reinforcements. The women of Zaachila played an important role because they provided food for people who were in the occupations [of buildings], in barricades, and they also brought firewood, and anything else that was needed for the barricades in different parts of the city.*

Radio Zaachila has worked to forge a strong connection between the participatory culture of local asambleas and radio programming. Adán explained:

The assembly is a historical element here in how we organize ourselves in Zaachila. We have thought of a series of assemblies as where we make decisions, not just the idea of one big assembly of all of the community. There are ejido assemblies where decisions are made, there are neighborhood assemblies where decisions are made, and there are organizations that have assemblies to make decisions. Right now we are thinking that the assembly model is fundamental to the way we make decisions in Zaachila. When we arrive at agreements, anyone who does not agree with the outcome has to consider the fact that the decision was made by the entire assembly. If people disagree, they have to share their point of view in the assembly. So for us, the model of the assembly is fundamental.

There is a strong link between the ways that testimony and face-to-face participation work in community assemblies and in community radio. In the organizing that has taken place in Zaachila to prevent a highway project known as Libramiento Sur from going through, there is a direct connection between the radio station and the assembly of *ejidatarios*.[9] Adán spoke emphatically about the importance of community radio in the effort to prevent construction of the Libramiento Sur in Zaachila territory:

We are convinced that our territory is a historical construction created by our ancestors. . . . When our territory is being invaded, we go out and we defend it. Recently the state government has wanted to trespass on our territory with a new highway which is called the Libramiento Sur. So we got together and we went and pulled up the stakes that were marking the topography of where the road was supposed to go. We began to work with others and started a group of organizations that allowed us to stop the Libramiento Sur. We started an organization that we call the Consejo de Pueblos en Defensa de la Tierra y el Territorio, which is against the Libramiento Sur.[10]

We defended our territory with mobilizations, press conferences, and seeking legal injunctions for the process. We have made a national campaign about this and the radio has played a very important part of this process and in creating consciousness about defending our territory.

Expanding Indigenous and Community Radio in Oaxaca

I have suggested that the takeover of commercial and state-run TV and radio stations in the Oaxacan social movement of 2006 is related to the history and ongoing expansion of indigenous and community-based radio. Since 2006 at least ten new community-based radio stations have formed in Oaxaca, in addition to those already in existence.[11] Through direct social action, the right to speak and the right to be heard that anchor face-to-face testimonials have come to define an emergent set of regional radio practices. I have argued that such community media practices are guided by indigenous political cultures, which are often self-consciously aimed at building consensus capable of accommodating different perspectives. This overlap of radio technology and local political culture has made Oaxacan community radio particularly suitable for expressing the complex and multiple subject positions of its practitioners. Moreover I suggest that grassroots social movements gain greater public traction through their use of testimonials in both radio and local politics.

The emergence of community radio networks has indelibly shaped the form of political participation in Oaxaca. Community radio stations provide important roles in communication, community building, and the promotion of local cultural forms. These roles include hosting a call-in show that indigenous migrants in the United States can use to communicate with their relatives, broadcasting local dance and music performances, and airing programs to discuss health, education, and human rights. Community radio stations are often considered to be sources of cultural revitalization.

Radio Jën Poj, Tlahuitolpec, Oaxaca
One of the community radio stations that existed in Oaxaca prior to 2006 is Radio Comunitaria Jën Poj ("energy of the wind" in the Ayuujk or Mixe language), which was formed in August 2001. In 2004 Radio Jën Poj received a license, making it one of the very first indigenous community stations in the state to operate legally. José Guadalupe Díaz, who participates in Radio Jën Poj, wrote the following on the radio station's website about its history:

> Radio Jën Poj was born in August 2001 in the heart of the Mixe community—Ayuujk in our language—Tlahuitoltepec, Oaxaca, when Mixe studentes, professionals, and community members came together to build a radiotransmitor. Now it is a space where colective thought is transformed into winds of words that for a long time had been held back and restricted and today can be heard by men and women throughout the region.
>
> We want to contribute to the development of the community through communication spaces and media that lead to the participation of its inhabitants and responds to their needs and expectations in a non-profit relationship and with a cultural linguistic perspective. (Jën Poj 2013)

Radio Jën Poj is run primarily by students from the community but includes many other people in an open-mike program where anyone can speak. The community authorities ask the radio station to cover local cultural events and to provide a public forum for discussion of issues such as the lack of water. In their coverage of events and their open-mike forum, the core group of young people who run the station also interview and bring in the perspectives of many others. As a result, many people in the community are tuned in to the station on a daily basis, according to Roberto Olivares of Ojo de Agua Comunicación, who regularly visits the community.

Radio Totopo, Tehuantepec, Oaxaca

In the Zapotec Isthmus of Tehuantepec, where there are more than twenty radio stations, Radio Totopo (meaning "baked corn tortilla," a hallmark of the Zapotec Isthmus food culture) broadcasts in Zapotec. First on the airwaves in 2005, Radio Totopo is located in a neighborhood known as the Barrio del Pescador (fisherman's neighborhood), one of the oldest and most marginal neighborhoods of Juchitán. Local residents who volunteer there receive support from others in the form of food and small donations. The station includes musical programming from a group of young people, Alcoholics Anonymous programs broadcast in Zapotec, the promotion of local events, and an ongoing project to use words in Zapotec that people have forgotten and replaced with Spanish.[12]

Radio Didhza Kieru, Talea de Castro, Oaxaca

Further north, in the community of Talea de Castro, a collective of six women and five men runs an indigenous community station called Didhza Kieru, Zapotec for "Our Words," that transmits in Zapotec fifteen hours a day. This collective is recognized and supported by the local authorities in the municipality and by the assembly of communal land holders (see Ojo de Agua Comunicación 2009). The station is acknowledged as part of the structure of local governance and recognized within the same political and cultural structure that houses community assemblies. It exists in parallel with the assembly, and working in the station is recognized as a form of contributing service to the community as part of a civil cargo or volunteer community governance position (as described in note 3).

Radio Zaachila, Oaxaca

Radio Zaachila, located in a municipality famous for its twelfth-century royal Zapotec settlement, is home to one of the Oaxacan radio stations that was born out of the 2006 social movement and that recently received a federal license. Begun at the end of July 2006, Radio Zaachila, at 94.1 FM, has a signal range of about fifteen kilometers. It grew out of the social conflict that came to a head in June 2006. According to some members of Sección 22 based in Zaachila, the local police joined forces with state police on June 14, 2006, to evict the teachers from the center of Oaxaca City. Unhappy with this action as well as other activities of the presidente municipal, José Coronel Martínez, members of APPO and Sección 22 occupied the

city hall and removed Coronel Martínez. This action is similar to what occurred in other municipalities in Oaxaca in 2006.

Adán López Santiago talked to me about the founding of Radio Zaachila:

LYNN: *How was the radio born?*

ADÁN: *The radio really emerged as a part of the movement. We conceptualized the radio as a medium which was necessary to accompany the social
movement. . . .*

*We brought a transmitter to Zaachila and we began to broadcast. . . . In
the beginning we didn't have fixed times for our programming. It was inter-
mittent. Our main idea was to inform people about what was happening every
day, what actions were planned. Later, when there were not as many activities
in the city from the movement, we decided we needed to provide regular programming and give our listeners a specific orientation.*

By 2007 Adán and others involved in running the station began to think
more specifically about what kind of radio station they wanted to have. This
period of reflection resulted in specific lines of programming and planning,
as well as a political strategy for creating the conditions that would allow
the station to continue into the future and be supported. In these discussions, one central focus was the concept of local Zaachila identity and how
it was to be represented on the radio station. The founders also identified
what kind of radio station they wanted to be and what that meant in their
local context. Adán related:

*We talked about what was going on in the social movement in Zaachila . . .
and we came to the conclusion that we wanted to be a community radio
station . . . not a cultural radio, not a commercial radio, not a political radio,
and not an "indigenous radio." We wanted to be a community radio empha-
sizing to our community what we had to offer to people in Zaachila about
their own identity. So from this moment on, the concept of identity was very
strong. We began to work and think about how to consolidate our concept of
what our local identity is.*

While Adán stated that the group of Radio Zaachila operators did not
want to create "a political radio," one part of their work was to create the
political circumstances necessary to allow the station to thrive. In part this
involved gaining support at the level of the municipal (county) government.

While they were successful in having the presidente municipal deposed in 2007, the next elections were won by a PRI candidate. Some of their political work involved not only questioning the ability of this mayor but also building a positive dialogue around revitalizing the culture of Zaachila.[13] Adán talks passionately about different forms of cultural revitalization and defense of territory, both of which are important to community identity and are promoted by the station:

We can revitalize some of the culture that we have lost. . . . We have some primary activities that we do during the year and support that are part of that. The first is that we support a fiesta that we call de Concheros. This is a fiesta where the community goes in a procession to the mountains to gather particular red and yellow flowers and then we return and walk around the community with these flowers. The procession ends in the church. While the Catholic religion is predominant here, not everyone is Catholic, so we try to emphasize the cultural part of this celebration for everyone.

Another activity we engage in is Buinza, which is the celebration of the dead at the beginning of November.[14] In this celebration we talk about our beliefs that people disintegrate [descarnar] little by little and that there are four levels to this.

We believe that someone dies and then part of their head decomposes, then there is a level where the feet touch the ground and they keep going down into the ground and the body decomposes until the whole thing is inside of the interior of the earth. . . . This signifies our conceptualization of death as the way that we also revitalize the earth. We all return to the ground and we disintegrate into the ground. These are the ideas of our ancestors that we want to help to spread. The mother earth is where we are received when we die. So on the first of November we celebrate this and we remember the dead who are not with us anymore.

Another fiesta that we have is the fiesta of corn. We give thanks every December 30 to nature, which has given us corn. We are people of corn. We have created our own world, our own gods, and our basic philosophical ideas begin with the cultivation of corn. If you don't eat corn in Zaachila, then you are not Zachileño.

In February 2010 Radio Zaachila received its federal license, giving it permission to operate for twelve years. From that point on, Radio Zaachila has operated with a higher level of security that has permitted it to continue to develop the projects and support for cultural revitalization and defense of territory. The station is not without local opponents, however: on November 18, 2008, two of the operators were victims of attempted shooting in their homes. The local mayor at the time, Noé Pérez Martínez, who was affiliated with the PRI, had publicly demanded the closure of the station, accusing it of "sickening the minds of the people in the community" (Jiménez 2008). Despite such threats, Radio Zaachila has continued to thrive.

Summary

The perseverance and proliferation of community radio—particularly in indigenous communities—illuminates the changing political cultures and spaces of participatory democracy in Oaxaca. Meanwhile these same traits of community-based radio have provoked ongoing efforts by the government to control and eliminate it. In 2008 the Asamblea de Radios Comunitarios y Libres de Oaxaca (Assembly of Free and Community Radio Stations) was formed in response to such repression. Composed of twenty-two Oaxacan community radio stations, along with three international radios, representatives from eight universities, and a wide range of NGOs, this assembly was formed just one day after federal and local police sacked the community radio station known as La Rabiosa, a Mixtec station based in the town of Huajuapan de León. Despite a concerted effort by the regional government to raid radio stations and harass its practitioners, community radio in Oaxaca continues to grow.

While the analysis of social movements and politics tends to focus much attention on marches, the control of physical space and buildings, and ultimately the movement's ability to cohere over time and to influence the outcome of electoral politics, the cultural spaces of community-based media such as television, grassroots-produced videos, and radio are equally informative for such analyses. The maintenance and proliferation of community-based radio, particularly in indigenous communities in the state of Oaxaca and elsewhere, has created fertile ground in which nonmainstream political processes, strategies, and ideas have continued to exist and grow. I have suggested that a longer view of the antecedents and legacies of the Oaxacan social movement of 2006 reveals that community-based radio is a vital technology for shaping the form and content of political agency in Oaxaca. The next chapter uses an event-centered analysis to examine the women's takeover of state and commercial media in Oaxaca during 2006 and the kind of political subject formation and gendered rights discourses that emerged during the process.

6

The Women's Takeover of Media in Oaxaca

Gendered Rights "to Speak" and "to Be Heard"

This chapter highlights the process by which several hundred women in Oaxaca City, from different types of backgrounds, took over state and then commercial media for a period of several months. While doing this, they also came to a gendered analysis of human rights. Their thinking centered on what they called the rights "to speak," "to be heard," and "to decide who governs" (see Poole 2007a, 2007b; Spivak 1988).

What is important about this process is that these women are departing significantly from the use of an outside interlocutor in order to take their stories out into the world and be heard. They do not depend on others to transcribe, translate, and contextualize their stories. They are their own witnesses and tell their stories directly to each other and others on the air. In describing the mechanics of *testimonio,* John Beverly writes, "Because in many cases the direct narrator is someone who is either functionally illiterate or, if literate, not a professional writer, the production of a *testimonio* generally involves the tape recording and then the transcription and editing of an oral account by an interlocutor who is a journalist, ethnographer, or literary author" (2005: 547). These women activists take the use of testimonio to a new place. They voice their own identities, political stances, and analyses for the world after they initiate the action of taking over the media.

The Latina Feminist Group describes how they created their own testimonio process in which "the personal and private became profoundly political" as they framed their own testimonies in a series of encounters with each other (2001: 13). The process they discuss bears some kinship to what happened inside of COR-TV during its occupation by women in Oaxaca over a three-week period The Latin Feminist Group states, "Testimonio engaged us at a deeper level than we had found in other feminist and womanist circles and in our own respective national communities. Our intense conversations, shared laughter, and emotional solidarity and bonding ultimately built trust, *confianza*" (15). Like the process described by the Group in the production of their book, Oaxacan women who occupied state and commercial media were transformed. When they didn't return home, they disrupted the gender relations in their family's daily lives. They had to negotiate with husbands, mothers-in-law, children, and others to support them and complete the tasks they were leaving undone in their absence. When they spoke on the air and received support from others in the station or family members, they began to trust themselves and others. When hundreds of outside delegations arrived to be heard on the air, the women helped to facilitate their testimonios and connected to the visitors emotionally. The women described here are moving far beyond their personal stories to share their analysis and put forward their demands—without interlocutors.

Some women in the group that took over the media were feminists who had participated for decades in women's movements in Oaxaca. The majority, however, were women from Sección 22, from local *colonias* or neighborhoods participating in APPO, or from indigenous or other grassroots organizations; there were even women who had not previously participated in political organizations. Thus a majority were not intimately familiar with gendered categories and analysis.

More specifically, the appropriation of human rights discourses became gendered through the process of the media takeover. Through their experience running state television and radio stations and, subsequently, commercial stations, the women who held the stations produced a gendered local vernacular of rights talk that then became accessible to many other women and men in the city. Women who had previously been silenced and who characterized themselves as "short, fat, and brown" and "the face of Oaxaca" were now allowing new voices to be heard and new faces to be seen and permitting silenced models of governance and democratic participation to move into the cultural and political mainstream. Beyond this, the occupation of several radios stations played a critical strategic role in helping the Oaxaca social movement endure and resist repression for six months before federal forces shut it down at the end of 2006.

The Women's Takeover of Public Radio and Television Stations

On August 1, 2006, between 2,500 and 5,000 women participated in a march known as La Marcha de las Cacerolas (the March of the Pots and Pans).[1] They brought cooking pots and utensils to bang them with while shouting slogans in support of the Oaxaca movement. They called for the ouster of the governor, justice for those who had been arrested and detained, and fulfillment of the teachers' original demands.

✳ VIDEOCLIP 6.1: http://dx.doi.org/10.7264/N3JS9NC2

According to Conchita Nuñez (real name), a longtime feminist and a member of Sección 22, the idea of the march was "to make women visible by the banging of pots and to assemble all kinds of women. . . . I remember that there were even some sex workers who participated in the march. The idea was not to take over the state and radio TV station. The idea was to arrive at the zócalo and make a lot of noise. After we got downtown they started to talk about going to the station." Later Conchita recalled that she thought it was a strange strategy, because during the Pinochet regime in Chile it was the women who were supportive of the dictatorship and on the right of the political spectrum who marched in the streets with pots and pans. Most women in this march, however, were not familiar with the march in Chile and thought it was a good way to call attention to their presence. They were making *ruido de mujer* (women's noise), as one of them later told me.

Another participant, Mariana Gómez, recalls that the several hundred women from the march who decided to go to the state television and radio stations didn't decide to take over the stations, but merely wanted to have some time on the air. Once they were at the station and were denied air time and not given any forum, they then decided to take over. She recalled:

When we got there some women asked for some time on the air to tell the truth about what was happening. First they told us to wait. Then they told us

*that we would be able to go on the air, but to come back later. Then they cut
off the transmission signal and they started to take out pieces of equipment
while we were there—like cameras and other stuff. They told us to come back
again in a little while. So we just said that we were not going to move until
they gave us permission to go on the air. They didn't make any move toward
letting us get on the air, so we said, "You know what, we are going to occupy
the station." We had a meeting on the patio of the radio and TV stations and
decided to take them over.*

In the 1990s, COR-TV, which is equivalent to state-run public broadcasting systems in the United States, had a director who was well known
for his support for public media and was also a reporter. Under him, people in Oaxaca became accustomed to programming content that reflected
a wide range of concerns from across the state. There was programming in
indigenous languages, and all of the different ethnic groups in Oaxaca were
represented. According to Roberto Olivares, a member of the Mal de Ojo
TV Collective and a longtime independent filmmaker and journalist whom
I interviewed, COR-TV would "even go out and record the community's fiestas or broadcast on traditional indigenous medicine. People got used to
it being an effective public media." In the late 1990s and early twenty-first
century COR-TV was taken over by other directors and became like other
public broadcast media in Mexico, which "are media in the service of governors and those in power, . . . more instruments of propaganda than public
media," according to Roberto and many others. Thus by 2006 COR-TV and
radio functioned primarily to applaud the actions of the governor and to
prepare the public for upcoming governmental campaigns. For many Oaxacans, the memory of an alternative vision for these public media was still
alive—one in which a wide range of people shared their perspectives and
where the rich and complex indigenous cultures of Oaxaca were prominently featured. In the early years of the twenty-first century, COR-TV went
from being the voice of many to the voice of one: the state governor.

Another participant in the march, Catalina Ruiz, recalled the diversity of women who went on the march. For her, the idea that COR-TV was
publicly owned media was an important part of her rationale for why the
women were justified in taking it over. For many women who were part of
the takeover decision, being denied the chance to share their perspectives
and speak on a public television station was pivotal in how they came to
view their right to hold the station and open up the airwaves. They were

familiar with the television and radio stations' more open past history; this, along with their determination to have their perspective aired, formed their first conceptual moment of analysis in terms of their rights "to speak" and "to be heard." Catalina is a working-class Oaxacan woman who has successfully navigated the non-profit world as a staff person. She is a sharp dresser with impeccable hair and make-up who looks directly at the people she talks to. The women's march and take-over was an emotional high point for her and she talked about it with passion, moving her hands and body to emphasize her points. She stated in an interview in 2006:

> There was a call that went out over Radio Universidad that said, "All of the women, let's go and march with our frying pans, our pots, our casserole dishes." The big surprise was when we arrived at where the march started and there were hundreds and hundreds and hundreds of women. From women with long braids and aprons on with a pot in their hands and a daughter at their side to old women, to women from the middle class, the poor, and intellectuals. . . . Everyone was saying that we had to get on the TV and radio to communicate our demands that the governor leave his office. . . . Well, unfortunately they didn't give us permission to do this. We said, "This media is ours. It is paid for by money from our taxes. We pay for it every time we buy something. It is supposed to be public, to be ours. So now since it is ours, we are going to keep it and run it."

Before the first television broadcast by the women who occupied COR-TV, a young woman announced over the public radio station that was a part of the complex taken over that she and a larger group of women had just taken over the TV and radio station: "We have taken over Channel 9. Right now we are seeing if the technicians are going to stay and if they can make an agreement to help us with our television transmissions. . . . We are waiting to see if they will answer the call of the people to stay and help us with our transmissions. If not, we will be calling for other technicians to come and help us with our TV transmissions. . . . All of the workers who are here have been treated well." Once they decided to hold the station, the women held the employees in the station and insisted that they put them on the air. The technicians agreed, and the women had their first TV broadcast. Like many in Oaxaca, I was surprised to hear the kinds of voices and programming that began to flow out of the state radio station and then, less than a day later, on the television station as well.

For the first two days after they had taken possession of COR-TV the women barely slept, and there was a great deal of tension in the air. No one was sure if the police would try to storm the station, if the transmission towers would be shot down, or what would happen. Shortly after they took the station, APPO and Sección 22 responded by sending groups of people to guard the station and assure the safety of the women inside. Then the women organized themselves into work brigades: staffing security posts in and around the station and the transmission towers, programming the radio and TV, handling the food and cooking, receiving and organizing the visiting individuals and delegations that came to get on the air, and taking care of outreach and contact with movement activists to monitor events, marches, and security concerns. The approximately three hundred women renamed the TV station Televisión para el Pueblo Oaxaqueño (Television for the People of Oaxaca) and the radio station Radio Cacerola, or Pots and Pans Radio, in reference to the August 1 march that led to the takeover.

The physical strain of working constantly, getting little sleep, interacting with hundreds of people who came every day to be on the air, and dis-

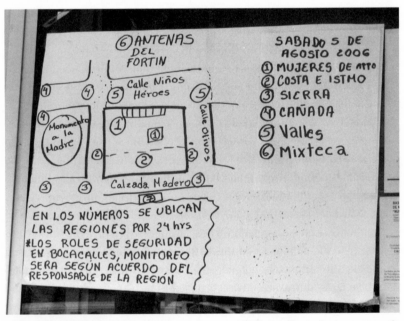

Figure 6.1 Security assignments for women occupying COR-TV in August 2006.
DOI: 10.7264/N3VD6WCT

cussing at length what kinds of programming, vision, and ideas should be projected on the radio and TV greatly intensified the experience for many women. Pilar Montenegro participated in the August 1 march and spoke on the radio about what she viewed as the transformative process going on for the women who were working together occupying the station: "Here in the installations of Radio Cacerola the energy is very visible. It is as if we are all playing one chord on the violin. . . . What is going on inside here is something incredibly rich. . . . We are discussing so many things that are so intimate but are also public at the same time." Pilar relayed her description passionately, with a look of rapture on her face. (I was in the station when she was speaking.) She was trying to convey the transformative process she was observing of women who had left their normal routines, families, and even children to secure and operate the TV and radio stations. Many had called their husbands to tell them that they were not going home. They asked their husbands to bring them clothing, food, and something to sleep on. For many women, this was the first time they had left their families for an unspecified period of time.

✳ VIDEOCLIP 6.2: http://dx.doi.org/10.7264/N3F18WNN

Rosario Romero,[2] who supported the teachers' occupation in the center of the city and then participated in the TV and radio station occupation, said:

The day that we took over Canal 9 [COR-TV], I spent the night there. I stayed there with other women. I asked one of them to loan me a telephone to call my husband. He said, "Where are you? You went to march and didn't return." I explained to him what I was doing at the station. I said, "Please bring me a sweater and two or three for the other women." I stayed until six in the morning and then went home for a while. He was okay. . . . I also got more respect from my father. He participated as well. He does his part to help out. For me, the rebellion has been marvelous. The kind of repression we lived through as women is hard. For me it has been a lot of work because four of my siblings don't support me and only one does. But it is worth what I have learned.

While Rosario's husband and father supported her participation in the occupation of COR-TV, not all women had this experience. At a conference of the organization Coordinadora de Mujeres de Oaxaca (Coordinating Committee of Women of Oaxaca, COMO) in August 2007—one year after the occupation began—some women in discussion groups shared experiences of the difficulties they faced in the occupation and in the COMO. The experiences described ranged from being castigated by mothers-in-law for abandoning their families and responsibilities to marriages that ended in separation or divorce because husbands were not ultimately understanding or supportive of the women's activism.

Patricia Jiménez, who became one of the spokeswomen for the group occupying the station, also recalled the intensity of the occupation and the importance of women being able to speak on the air and having their voices heard—the rights to speak and be heard: "When we occupied Canal 9 (COR-TV) we struggled with many difficulties. Many of the women who struggled together through those difficult times did so by joking and saying, 'In this movement we barely eat, we barely sleep, and just about barely do everything.' . . . Women who took over the station would say, 'We took over this station because we want our voices to be heard and we want to appear on TV.' . . . Those of us in charge of the production responded, 'Go ahead.'"[3] And they did, as did many other people.

✳ VIDEOCLIP 6.3: http://dx.doi.org/10.7264/N39884X9

From early in the morning until late at night, for most of the month of August 2006, Radio Cacerola and Televisión para el Pueblo Oaxaqueño became the chief means for people to voice their opinions, receive news, and have debates. This followed a trend that had begun in June at Radio Universidad, as explained below. Everyone—from the mototaxi association of six neighborhoods who were denouncing a corrupt licensing official to Zapotec vegetable farmers who were fed up with a corrupt local mayor—used the station to air their opinions. Regular radio shows discussed the murder of women in Ciudad Juarez and Oaxaca, celebrated local musical groups, and hosted discussions of indigenous rights in more than half a dozen of Oaxaca's sixteen indigenous languages.

When local municipal police refused to leave their barracks, the Oaxacan head of security and transportation, Aristeo López Martínez, put together an improvised police force of undercover "municipal" police that was rumored to include paramilitaries from outside the state. Radio Cacerola announced the locations where these police were seen and encouraged people not to lose faith. When leaders of APPO were detained without a warrant, Radio Cacerola relayed the kind of vehicle the police used and encouraged people in the neighborhood where the leaders had last been seen to search for the car. When APPO needed to gather supporters to reinforce groups of people holding more than twenty state government buildings, the call went out over Radio Cacerola. When fifty-year-old José Jiménez

Colmenares was shot dead in the middle of a peaceful protest march on the way to the TV station, Radio Cacerola broadcast the news and urged people not to be afraid and to continue to protect the station and other buildings that had been taken over by APPO. Throughout some of the tensest days and nights in August, the voice of a young woman told listeners, "Don't be afraid. We are not afraid. Do not abandon your posts. Do not be afraid to come down to help us to fight this intimidation. We are a pacifist movement; we have so many people they cannot force us out." The women behind the radio station did not appear to be militant fighters but rather longtime Oaxaca residents who had finally gotten fed up with their invisibility and bad treatment by the successive state governments that had been promising to improve their lives for decades. They were also tired of remaining silent in their homes and in the streets.

In her study of the ways Spanish-language radio engages listeners on the topic of immigration, Dolores Inés Casillas (2011) analyzes how listeners call in and share their frustrations with the immigration process and their feelings about increases in filing fees. Spanish-language radio stations can also serve as forums for on-air *migra alerts* that are "spontaneous, fleeting warnings to listeners that Immigration Customs Enforcement . . . has been sighted. The migra-alerts function as a subversive 'traffic report' for immigrants to avoid certain roads and highways in their commutes to work" (808). Like the analysis that follows, Casillas suggests the importance of testifying on the air as well as to the "experience of simultaneity" among a legion of listeners when sentiments of community are echoed and realized through sound (809). Ultimately she proposes that such broadcasts serve as spaces and opportunities for "live engagement among Latino listeners, essential components of cultural citizenship" (809). Her analysis has much to contribute to the discussion that follows as we see women articulate demands, rights, and finally a new sense of political subjectivity and belonging in the state of Oaxaca.

Radio Cacerola and Televisión para el Pueblo Oaxaqueño thus became testimonial forums where all of the disaffected of Oaxaca could share their stories. As a forum, the occupied stations became a container for the projection and assimilation of points of view not usually expressed in the media and a source of legitimation for those who were speaking and listening. People such as indigenous migrants to the city of Oaxaca from throughout the state, indigenous and nonindigenous rural farmers and ranchers, market vendors, single mothers, and the poor in the colonias of Oaxaca had previously been the objects of study or commentaries on COR-TV; now, through the medium of their testimonies on the occupied stations, these people gained subjectivity, dignity, and personhood. There is a world of difference between the way a TV report on malnourished children in the Mixteca done by a well-fed, tall, urban white female reporter is perceived and the perception of the same information when it is delivered by a Mixtec woman and her children describing their daily lives and routines. The Mixtec woman and her children shift from being an object of reportage and study to being active subjects describing their own experiences in their own terms. The information takes on a very different tone when there are no apologies and no filters.

Day and night, people flooded the station with calls and shared their past grievances. They also called in warnings about ongoing repression, conflict, and suspicious activities. The longer the women controlled the stations, the more the right to speak and to be heard was taken up by many and became generalized to a much larger public. The TV station also became the source of alternative political histories and interpretations of past and present events.

Because none of the women who took over the station was trained in television broadcasting and only a few had experience with community radio, they called on technicians from a local independent media collective known as Mal de Ojo TV. Mal de Ojo TV was formed just after the police attempted to evict the teachers from the center of Oaxaca City on June 14, 2006. Composed of fifteen individuals and two primary organizations, Mal de Ojo TV was born of the need to coordinate the independent media working to cover the movement in 2006. They agreed to coordinate editing, links to the Internet, and finding spaces to disseminate their material. They also shared photographs and radio reports that were put on the Internet. They worked to get video out on the Internet and on DVDs sold by pirate vendors. Their goal was to provide an alternative media perspective to that of the commercial media, which had given little coverage to the conflict in Oaxaca in June and July 2006. When the women called on them shortly after the takeover of COR-TV, Mal de Ojo TV made their engineers and video collection available to the women who were running the station. Their extensive video and DVD collection featured dozens of programs produced in indigenous communities in the native languages of Oaxaca, a collection of historical videos that reviewed key events in Mexican history from a leftist perspective, videos about events and movements in Mexico ranging from the EZLN in Chiapas to women's movements in Mexico City, and a growing set of self-produced videos about the ongoing repression against the movement in Oaxaca. Alternative news coverage was also provided through Mal de Ojo TV's coverage of marches, rallies, and press conferences that were either briefly profiled on Mexican commercial television or invisible in the mainstream media.

During the three-week period that the women occupied COR-TV and radio, long and difficult discussions ensued among them about what they were doing, what kind of programming they wanted to produce, and what kinds of rights they were asserting in the process. For many, the first way they experienced their rights as individuals—and particularly as women—was by speaking on the radio or in public. While we don't usually think of the right to speak as being gendered, many of the women who occupied the radio station were accustomed to being silent or soft-spoken, whether at home or in larger, mixed-gender grassroots organizations such as the teachers' movement. Although women are a majority of the membership of Sección 22, there are very few women in the public leadership structure of CNTE. Many teachers complained of sexism and exclusion from leadership positions within the union (see Stephen 2007b: 109–11). The right to speak was experienced by many women as a specifically gendered right because it was articulated within a group of several hundred women in a space where women held power and delegated responsibilities to each other and to men. If silence was the norm for many of the women from the grassroots movements and in their marginal political positions as poor, dark, and working class, then speaking as women and with women was experienced as a "woman's right" when they occupied the TV and radio stations.

Ruth Guzmán (real name), the wife of Ramiro Aragón Pérez (introduced in the previous chapter), recalled what it was like the first time she spoke in public in a press conference that was broadcast on Radio Cacerola, filmed, and attended by reporters. On August 12, when Ruth's brother Elionai was released along with his friend Juan Gabriel, they held a press conference. It was the first time Ruth had spoken in public about what had happened. She had not been an activist before. It was one of her moments of becoming a political actor. I asked her how she remembered feeling in that moment:[4]

The first time I spoke in public was on August 12, 2006. It was something more than personal at that point. It wasn't just the aggression against us. That had already passed. It was something more. Before that we were angry, but in that press conference . . . we made Ulises Ruiz [the governor] directly responsible for what happened. I said that it was he who had beaten Ramiro, my brother Elio, and Juan Gabriel. I said we were holding him accountable for anything

that happened to my family. My brother told me that they had taken every-
thing that had our addresses on it. He told me that they said that they were
going to come to the house to rape me and kill my children. They had our
addresses. So I accused Ulises Ruiz directly and that appeared in the press. . . .
I had spoken.

Ruth connects speaking with the right to hold the state governor responsible. She is asserting not only her right to speak but also her right as a citizen
to hold those who govern accountable. Ruth was heard not only in the national press but also locally and within her circle of family and friends. Her
speaking and the fact that she was heard by family and friends resulted in
a complete rearrangement of her life and the lives of those around her. She
decided to stop working and dedicate herself full time to the APPO movement and to getting her husband and others in the movement out of jail.

Initially some of the men in APPO and in Sección 22 could not believe
that women had successfully taken over COR-TV and radio. Some thought
it was a huge mistake and were not going to support the movement. Pedro
Cordova, a movement artist who participated in Radio La Ley, recalled com-
ments made by a few men in the leadership of Sección 22 when they heard
that women had taken over the station: "I remember one person who said
to another, 'Can you believe what these *pendejas estupidas* [stupid women,
literally pubic hair, but derogatory reference] have done? They have caused
even more problems for us. Look, they took over the radio station and now
they screwed themselves. The *magisterio* [teachers' union] is not going to
support them.' This was the attitude of the some of the people who were
leaders then. . . . The radios played a really major role in that they opened
up an expectation on the part of people that they could have a strong influence." Pedro was one of a small group of men who came to participate in
Radio Cacerola and also had a program on the air. He thought it was important that the women move beyond gender themes to include more general
themes in their programming, and they did.

Gradually APPO and Sección 22 leaders came to recognize that the takeover of COR-TV was a key strategic move that began to shift the local population in favor of the movement. Catalina Ruiz had a very vivid memory of
the men's responses. The fact that women were successful in gaining access
to mainstream media—a central problem endlessly discussed in the movement by male leaders—emphasized the importance of what the women had
accomplished by facilitating the right to speak and be heard for thousands
of people:

The men, the male teachers and others, they were shocked when we took over the station because it wasn't something they had thought up. A lot of times in our meetings they were always saying, "How do we get the official state station to carry our information?" They never could figure out how to do this. . . . After we did it, they supported us. We got a ton of calls on the radio from men who stated, "Bravo. These valiant women, these combative women, did what we couldn't do."

The identification of many women with being silenced and marginalized in multiple arenas of their lives amplified the importance to them of earning the right to speak and be heard through their occupation of COR-TV *and* their ability to facilitate this right for many others, both men and women, who also had been silenced. Catalina goes on to observe:

We hope that this is a lesson for the larger movement, for women, and for the media. We also hope that it is a lesson for the next governor so that it is clear the governor has to obey the citizens, and this includes women. Article 39 of our constitution says—and when you hear this being read in the voice of a working-class housewife it is clear—the article says we have the right to decide who will govern us. And if the person who is governing us doesn't work out, then we have the right to change that person.

In this portion of her narrative, Catalina makes the move from articulating the right of women to speak and be heard—particularly working-class women, which, in Oaxaca, invariably means women of indigenous descent—to the right of women as citizens to decide who will govern them. In this passage she links the rights to speak and be heard to the more general right of political citizenship for those who reside within a country (she makes reference to the Mexican Constitution) to remove from power those who govern ineffectively.

The Generation of Hybrid Racial, Ethnic, Class, and Location Identities in the Station

Another key participant in the station occupation and programming, Fidelia Vásquez, picks up on this theme in her narrative. She explicitly frames her identity as an Oaxacan working-class woman of indigenous descent and deliberately genders her description of what is going on. Fidelia is a teacher, a member of Sección 22, and a self-declared supporter of APPO. What is most striking about her testimonial is her claim that women who are "brown, short, and fat" are "the face of Oaxaca," represent the people, and have a right to a voice through their occupation of the TV and radio stations and also a right to decide who will govern them. I used part of this testimonial to open this book as it is very striking and summarizes some of the key ideas of the movement.

I am a woman born in Oaxaca of Zapotec and Mixtec blood. We Oaxacan women ask that a woman be treated with the same rights as a man. Our mission as women is to create, educate, communicate, and participate. That is why we are here occupying the state radio and TV station. . . . We are like a lot of the humble, sincere, working people of my state. From the countryside to the city, we Oaxacan women are tired of bearing this burden alone of the repression we are experiencing from a long line of people who have governed us and from our current governor, Ulises Ruiz. . . . We went out into the streets on the first of August to tell Ulises Ruiz that he had to leave Oaxaca. We are women who don't usually have a voice because we are brown, we are short, we are fat, and they think that we don't represent the people, but we do. WE are the face of Oaxaca. . . . It is too bad that the government doesn't recognize the greatness, the heart, and the valor of the women who are here. We are here because we want a free Mexico, a democratic Mexico, and we have had enough. . . . They will have to take us out of here dead, but we are going to defend the TV station and radio.

Fidelia's narrative is the most dramatic in terms of the stakes she sees for defending the rights she is claiming: the rights to speak and be heard, the right of women who are "brown, short, and fat" to represent "the face of Oaxaca," and the right to determine who governs. She is prepared to die to defend these rights. This narrative is a demonstration of the intense and passionate process that the women who occupied the stations went through.

In Fidelia's narrative we also see the complex process of hybrid identity formation that was articulated in the movement. Her narrative brings race, ethnicity, gender, and class categories into one hybrid label as Zapotec, Mixtec, brown, short, fat, female, and as a teacher or educator. The embodiment of this testimonial in the figure of Fidelia allows us to see the politics of identity formation in process. In a sense, her narrative opens up the broad, hybrid identity space that the radio station came to be—in

Figure 6.2 "Fuera Gachupines!" (Spanish get out!): graffiti sprayed in downtown Oaxaca, about eight blocks from the occupied radio station in August 2006. DOI: 10.7264/N3G44N6R

contrast to the identity space of the white, Spanish, upper-middle-class, tall, and slender, who were often the ones to publicly represent Oaxaca on television, in local beauty pageants, and elsewhere. As the many different kinds of people representing the different categories of identity Fidelia invokes marched into the radio station and spoke or appeared on television, public media spaces became spaces of assertion of hybrid identities, which reflected how the people in and around the city view themselves. They were the faces and voices of the real Oaxaca, as opposed to the "Gachupines," or Spanish, who had long dominated the politics and economics of Oaxaca City. The flip side to the reclamation of the public spaces by people who look indigenous was also reflected in the graffiti on the streets of central Oaxaca, which called for the Gachupines to leave the city.

Patricia Jiménez, a COMO leader, commented in an interview with Margarita Zires on some of the reactions to the appearance of women such as Fidelia on Television del Pueblo. Patricia stated that some people viewed the women as "really dirty. They said that we had not even bathed ourselves and that we should take a bath before we presented ourselves on television. . . . They saw us as *chimecas.* . . . We were [appearing] in opposition to the stereotypes because as Oaxacan women we were not the model of what is usually presented on TV. Instead we were another cultural reality and we said this on the air" (Zires 2009: 177). The term *chimecas* is a derogatory reference to the women's indigenous appearance. Deliberately projecting the racial and class identities that many Oaxacans were not accustomed to seeing and hearing on television was one of the most effective ways that the women's occupation began to challenge who belongs in the city.

As a speech form, testimonials are hybrid, interstitial, and flexible discursive spaces that reflect political and linguistic complexity (Beverly 2004; Maier and Dulfano 2004). When testimonials are deployed to claim rights in a specific political and cultural context, they are a part of real political practices that can literally let "the subaltern speak" and confer legitimacy (see Spivak 1988). For the twenty-one days that the women controlled the state TV and radio station and subsequently other radio stations, the subalterns were speaking in ways that had never been heard or seen before.

The 2006 broadcasts offered a striking example of the complex identities and subject positions of these new media practitioners. They challenged and unsettled the conventional categories of homogeneous ethnic or racial types that commonly circulate within the Mexican public sphere. Such types are often believed to define media audiences and producers as well. For example, state television stations such as COR-TV and commercial radio and television tend to use self-contained, hierarchical categories to distinguish "indigenous," "Spanish," and "mestizo" people.[5]

In order to describe these complex senses of identity expressed in the movement and on the television and radio stations, it is necessary to invoke a more complex frame that transcends linear or additive formulations of race, gender, class, and ethnicity and embraces subjective multiplicity. According to Michael Hames-García, multiplicity refers to how "memberships in various social groups (or categories of social identity) combine with and mutually constitute one another" (2011: 5). Further, "the subjective experience of any social identity always depends fundamentally on relations to other social identities" (6). This contrasts with an understanding of intersectionality that looks at how two identities conceptualized as discrete and unique categories (e.g., race, gender, class) come to intersect.[6]

In the city of Oaxaca, for example, urban, working-class women of Zapotec and Mixtec descent are not easily located within conventional local categories of race, class, and gender (see Stephen 2007b). Rather they simultaneously occupy multiple subject positions in relation to various interlocutors. Through radio testimonials, such contested subjectivities were asserted as politically legitimate. The complexity of the identities invoked by those in the Oaxaca social movement and broadcast on Radio Cacerola requires an effective form of subaltern speech capable of accommodating such multiplicity. Testimonials are ideal for such aspirations: they offer a space to synthesize personal, lived histories and to ground claims to certain subject positions within appeals to popular discourses of race, gender, ethnicity, and class (Latina Feminist Group 2001).

Broadcasting the Right to Speak, the Right to Be Heard, and the Right to Decide Who Governs to a Larger Public: Origins and Growth

The passion reflected in Fidelia's statement suggests the determination of women who occupied the station to extend to others the rights they had articulated for themselves. As radio and TV broadcasting from the redefined COR-TV moved into its second week, the opposition to the movement grew, as did the means to repress it. On August 10 events heated up: José Jiménez Colmenares (a mechanic who was married to a teacher) was killed in a peaceful march, several people were disappeared, and in the place of local Oaxaca police, paramilitary police who were not from the area appeared in civilian clothes and began to circulate in the late afternoon and at night in large convoys.

As stated earlier, Radio Cacerola became famous for the testimonial forum it offered for thousands of disaffected people in the state. Additionally people called in to the station and came in personally to denounce corruption and other things that they were dissatisfied with in the state and local governments. But Radio Cacerola was not the first station to air such views: two months earlier, on June 14, 2006, Radio Plantón was destroyed and broadcasters moved their operations to Radio Universidad that very day. There people began to arrive and call in as well.

Carmen López Vásquez, who participated in numerous radio takeovers and broadcasting experiments in 2006, recalled:

The phenomenon of people lining up to be on the radio didn't begin just with Radio Cacerola. People did this with Radio Plantón, earlier, but mostly through call-ins. And this happened on June 14 at Radio Universidad, where we were broadcasting during the desalojo. There, old people, invalids, handicapped people, all kinds of people arrived even in their wheelchairs and they wanted to talk on the air. . . . Long lines of people waiting to speak, and they waited for as long as necessary to speak. And people listened to them without any censure. . . . The way that people . . . participated in these different radios in Oaxaca is historic. . . . All of us who have not had a voice, this was one of the truly courageous and important things that the movement did, which was to give everyone a chance to listen directly to the people.

At Radio Cacerola (and later at other stations that were taken over) delegations arrived daily to denounce the governor or other corrupt officials on the air (see Stephen 2007b: 101–3). At one point at Radio Cacerola, the waiting list was so long that people were told to return several days later in order to ensure that their point of view would be heard. The parade of perspectives aired on the radio made a big impression on many in the city.

Josefina Reyes, a forty-year-old working-class mother whose husband had been in the United States for almost five years in 2006, reflected on the testimonial aspect of the radio:

The thing that happened with the women taking over the state radio station and TV and then on the other radio stations is that lots of people began to arrive and to go on the air. They would talk about what was going on in Oaxaca. And it wasn't just people from the city. People started to arrive from the towns and the ranchos from all over the state to say that they too were unhappy with things. They would go to the station or call in to say that they were in agreement with the movement, that they supported it.

✳ VIDEOCLIP 6.4: http://dx.doi.org/10.7264/N31V5BWK

In addition to facilitating the rights to speak and be heard by letting those who arrived go on the air, the women occupying the TV and radio stations also provided a direct communication channel for the movement and provided protection for people who might be in trouble. Ruth Guzmán recalled the time she was working at the station:

We had a lot of contacts and people would call us up. They would say, for example, that some blue trucks were nearby, coming toward the station. We always had these kinds of alerts. . . . We had lots of information, and people would call in from all over the city and we would put the information on the air.

Roberto Olivares, a participant in Mal de Ojo TV, felt that the takeover of COR-TV and the later takeovers of other radio stations demonstrated the central importance of the radio and its flexibility for the movement. He felt it was able to really compete with other forms of mass media:

Instead of the mass media, which only provides information in one direction, the radios [taken over by the movement] were functioning like walkie-talkies because everyone was speaking on them. Everyone had an opinion, everyone could talk, and everyone could hear them speak. Also, everyone heard about what kinds of actions were taking place. The radio stations had many functions. They also worked to introduce people to new ideas . . . and concepts from different angles.

☀ VIDEOCLIP 6.5: http://dx.doi.org/10.7264/N3X34VDM

Here Roberto highlights again the importance of the massive access the radio provided to many people to speak and be heard. He also emphasizes the importance of the movement-held radio stations to provide an open forum for different kinds of ideas—ideas that many people had never heard about before. This point was also emphasized by Josefina Reyes in her narrative:

There would be young people on Radio Cacerola who talked about neoliberalism and the people started to know more things. Before, we never heard about these things and we were not interested. But people started to know more and more, like about the Plan Puebla-Panama and other things that our government was involved in with other nations. People started to hear more and more from lots of people and to know more. They got more and more fed up with our government.

The effects of the movement-controlled radio and TV stations became obvious not only to those in the movement, who steadily increased their control of the city of Oaxaca in August 2006, but also to the governor and those in the state legislature. Unable to meet in their offices, which were controlled by APPO and Sección 22, state senators had to meet in hotels in the outskirts of the city. The governor made press appearances at resorts on the Oaxacan coast and then appeared on a national television show broadcast from Mexico City to assure everyone that things were under control in the capital city of Oaxaca. He made these appearances in these locations because it was so difficult for him to appear in the city of Oaxaca at the time.

During the dawn hours of August 21, 2006, a group of masked men shot out the transmission towers of COR-TV, rendering the stations inoperable. As soon as they began to destroy the towers, a group of APPO members spread out over the city and began to take over thirteen other commercial radio stations. The women who remained at the occupied COR-TV and radio stations decided to surrender the station buildings because they are unable to transmit without the antennas. They turned over the installations to federal police through a mediated dialogue. In the entire twenty days that the women had occupied COR-TV, not one mainstream TV station aired a report on their achievement. Outside of the state of Oaxaca, few people knew about the women's occupation or even that the state government of Ulises Ruiz had destroyed the transmission towers. Eventually the federal government accused the state government of Oaxaca of destroying the towers.

The State's Repressive Response to Occupied Media

Further analysis reveals that taking back the stations was part of a general ramping up of repression that began in mid-August and included a media strategy. On or about August 13 a website appeared titled Oaxaca en Paz (Oaxaca in Peace). It was designed with a police blotter's "most wanted" format and featured the names and addresses of supposed APPO activists. The website stated: "Estos son los delincuentes que te tienen secuestrado en tu ciudad. ¡Deténlos dónde los veas o buscalos en su casa!" (These are the delinquents holding you hostage in your own city. Detain them when you see them or look for them in their homes). By the end of August the photos of people such as José Jiménez Colmenares and Lorenzo San Pablo Cervantes (discussed below) were crossed out, signifying their deaths. Others, such as Germán Mendoza Nube and Erangelio Mendoza Gonzales, had been tortured, detained, and imprisoned; labels over their photos read "éste ya cayo" (this one has already fallen). Mendoza and Mendoza Nube were held in jail at the same time that Ramiro Aragón Pérez was. All three were released at the same time, on October 30, 2006, in Mexico City. Mendoza had been imprisoned in Tehuantepec, Mendoza Nube in Miahuatlán de Porfirio Díaz, and Aragón in Zimatlán de Álvarez. They were all transported to Mexico City to be released in a press conference.

On August 22, 2006, during a clean-up operation by four hundred ministerial state police and municipal police of Oaxaca to retake the thirteen commercial radio stations from APPO, police opened fire on APPO members guarding one of the newly occupied stations in Colonia Reforma. The architect Lorenzo San Pablo Cervantes, described in the Oaxaca en Paz website as "already fallen," was shot dead. Others were wounded. APPO ultimately held on to two of the stations, dubbed Radio La Ley and Radio ORO. Radio La Ley became the primary channel for the social movement from August 21 until October, 23, 2006, when its signal was blocked. Radio Plantón of Sección 22 began to broadcast with a limited range at the beginning of October 2006, and Radio Universidad began broadcasting in mid-October. Its range included the city of Oaxaca and some other regions to the south in the Sierra Sur and in some parts of the Mixtec zone (Zires 2009a: 185). The students were supportive of using Radio Universidad to support APPO and the social movement, and it became one of the last stands of the movement and the center of the resistance that fueled a temporary withdrawal of the PFP from UABJO of Oaxaca on November 2, 2006.

Carmen López Vásquez remembered vividly how the commercial radio stations were taken after the transmission towers of COR-TV were destroyed:

The first radio [station] we arrived at was La Ley 710. . . . When we arrived the night watchman was there. The door was open. Everything was very calm. We said to him, "Sir, where is the radio transmission room?" "What for? Why do you want to go there?" he asked. Some of the people with me explained to him what we were doing. The rest of us went up to the transmission room and they told me, "Sit down and start to talk." . . .

I went on the air and said, " . . . Instead of coming to the radio station where there are a lot of us, please go to help guard the transmission antennas in other places so that they will not deactivate them." From that moment, people went to occupy the antennas of each commercial radio station. So what happened on this first day, August 21, is that we took absolutely all of the radio stations in Oaxaca. But after the collective leadership of APPO discussed it, we decided to just keep two of the stations we occupied and turn in the rest.

Through September and most of October 2006, Radio La Ley served as a forum for a wide range of people to speak, be heard, and express their ideas about state government. It was also a space where new ideas for how to democratically govern the state and the meaning of citizenship were discussed.

Pedro Córdova, an artist born in Miahuatlán in 1962, is perhaps best known for his large puppets that dominated the Guelaguetza Popular. In 2006 he also participated in the occupation and programming of Radio La Ley. His show was known as *Café con Panela* (Coffee with Molasses), referring to the traditional sweetener used in rural and indigenous mountain communities. Shows like Pedro's were broadcast in the late afternoon as people headed to their barricades. He recalled one incident related to the show that demonstrated just how many people were listening:

Late afternoon I said something like, "Compañeros, prepare to go to your barricades tonight. Maybe some malendrines *[bad people, referring to the paramilitary convoys] will come. Have your fireworks, be ready. Have your cafecito with panela to keep warm. Oh how I wish I had a café with panela here in the station." The next day when we arrived at the station we found about half a ton of hard molasses here and many bags of coffee. Clearly people were tuned in to us.*

Pedro also told me that two years later, when he was spending most of his time restoring wooden saints and other wooden antiquities in indigenous communities outside of Oaxaca City, people would often refer to his show from Radio la Ley. "I would be out in a small town in the Sierra Juárez doing restoration work and people would tell me, 'I listened to your show *Café con Panela* on Radio La Ley.' 'Good,' I said. 'I am grateful that you paid attention.' That tells me that Radio La Ley carried its function, it reached people. It was reaching out into all parts of our territory in Oaxaca."

Radio La Ley also transmitted a program known as *La Hora de las Barricadas* (The Hour of the Barricades) from 3 to 5 a.m. All of the barricades tuned in to it and used it as a means to send greetings to one another. Zires described it as follows: "You could listen to urgent messages, information about what happened that day, and communiques . . . and calls from the people listening to the radio. . . . This show also built strong connections between the barricades: it permanently transmitted different kinds of greetings, 'fraternal,' 'combative,' . . . and 'revolutionary,' as well as ribbings and congratulations between different barricades" (2009a: 183, my translation). Many protest songs were also broadcast on this and other shows, including not only "Venceremos," but songs written specifically for the Oaxaca movement, such as "Son de la Barricada" (Musical dance son from the Barricada/ They Are from the Barricade/double entendre). Being a radio announcer was risky business in the fall of 2006.

René Trujillo Martínez, the announcer for *La Hora de las Barricadas*, was abducted from his apartment at gunpoint on November 7, 2006, brutally beaten, tortured, and held for two days incommunicado while being interrogated by federal authorities (Gibler 2009: 178). He was released on bail, but not until after being forced to hold guns and filmed, only later to be charged with the federal crime of possession of illegal firearms. Two friends of Trujillo were detained with him and faced similar charges. The entire incident bears a strong similarity to the abduction, torture, and false charges leveled against Ramiro, Elionai, and Juan Gabriel described in chapter 4.

Carmen and Pedro remembered the difficult conditions they worked under for two months. They were sure that the destruction of Radio La Ley was imminent, and the station location was constantly under surveillance.

Sometimes they didn't want to risk transmission from inside the actual station and would simulate transmission from elsewhere, close to the antennae. On October 23, 2006, their suspicions proved correct. Radio transmission of La Ley was stopped not by destroying the transmission towers but by blocking the station's signal. After they were unable to transmit, Carmen, Pedro, and others who worked at the occupied station decided to turn it back over to its owner. They turned in a notarized inventory of everything in the station and went on to work elsewhere. Both Carmen and Pedro spoke with pride about returning the station in exactly the same condition they found it in. Pedro recalled, "We acted with dignity. Not one photo, one drawer of a desk was violated. Not one cup was removed. There was even a refrigerator full of meat that they had left. We didn't touch it."

The shutdown of Radio La Ley was followed by another media strategy of repression. On October 26 a clandestine radio station called Radio Ciudadana began broadcasting, and at least initially all other radio stations went off the air. It featured support for the government of Ulises Ruiz and called for the removal of members of APPO and Sección 22 from the city. In its initiation transmissions, the station said it was guaranteeing that "the real voice of Oaxaca" would be heard and urged listeners to call in and share their feelings about "the abuses of the movement." People who called in to Radio Ciudadana insulted the teachers, "exhorted the governor to pull up his pants, and incited the people to remove the barricades" (Zires 2009a: 185).[7]

In a perverse recognition of the social movement's strategic use of radio, supporters of the governor replicated its strategy, creating a clandestine opposition radio station ironically named Citizen's Radio. Fueled by Radio Ciudadana, the conflict quickly escalated further. Zires (2009a: 185–86) and Diego Enrique Osorno (2007: 196) both link Radio Ciudadana to the death of the Indymedia reporter Bradley Will on October 27, 2006. Osorno wrote that an anonymous announcer on Radio Ciudadana reported that "the vecinos (neighbors) of Santa Lucía del Camino decided to take down the barricades and were attacked by the friends of Flavio Sosa" (a public APPO leader). Meanwhile the station incited listeners to "take up the example of Santa Lucía del Camino" (196). Shots were fired at fifteen different locations that day as PRI supporters, encouraged by Radio Ciudadana, took to the streets to tear down APPO barricades (Altamirano 2006). Radio Universidad, which had been silenced by an acid attack in July, was now back on the air with a new transmitter. On October 21 APPO sent out a call for help in Santa Lucia, where police and local officials opened fired on the barricade. More than a thousand people came out to push the attackers back, using rocks and bottles, and, as Gibler reports, "for the first time in the entire conflict, people on the APPO side drew guns, mostly low-caliber pistols, and fired back" (2009: 172).

Esteban Rodríguez Manuel was present at the scene where Will was shot and killed. He remembers it in detail and trembled as he retold the story, sitting on the edge of his seat in the headquarters of Sección 22 in Oaxaca City in July 2010:

I remember that exact moment when they asked for help. [Radio Universidad] requested that we come to Calicanto. I remember how Brad Will was laid down behind some street lights, how we were there on the sidelines like a lot of people who came to this barricade. . . . How we saw the journalists who were there and took great risks. . . .

From the sidelines we were advancing and then we turned left toward the city hall building of Santa Lucia when there was a panic. Everyone started running in reverse. We kept going to get to where the people were who were attacking the barricade. . . . Suddenly we started to hear shots from high-caliber weapons. Everyone began to run. I remember seeing a reporter running with a bottle that looked like it might have been a Molotov cocktail. When he fell, the glass cut his hand and he was bleeding. . . . I also remember seeing in that same street a White VW Bug [vocho] where the compañero [Will] was inside. He was already wounded when he was inside of that car and they were trying to take him to get medical attention. . . .

Then it started to rain very hard there in the Calicanto barricade. The rain poured out of the sky, and on the radio they said, "We are informing the people of Oaxaca that the journalist Ronald Bradley Will has just died from a frontal bullet wound received in Calicanto." A lot of people started to cry. . . . People considered him to be like another member of APPO who was working like everyone else for something different and better.

The "neighbors," as Osorno writes, who had taken up AR-15 rifles and fired on and killed Will and wounded the *Milenio* photographer Oswaldo Ramírez were soon identified. Photographs that were published in the national newspaper *El Universal* show police and officials from the Santa Lucía municipal government shooting at APPO protesters who were protecting the barricades right before Will was killed (Gibler 2009: 172).[8]

Although Oaxaca's state attorney general Lisbeth Caña initially said these men had been jailed, she soon let them go for "lack of evidence" (Gibler 2009: 173). She later made a presentation to the press in which she stated that Will had been shot at close range by an APPO protester. Almost two years after the murder, on October 16, 2008, Juan Martínez Moreno was arrested and charged with Will's murder. He was jailed for a year and a half and not released until February 2010. In March 2012, Oaxacan authorities detained Lenin Osorio Ortega and charged him with the murder. Oaxaca state officials worked with Mexico's national Attorney General's Office, the Procuraduría General de la República and with research carried out by the CNDH.[9]

On October 29, 2006, approximately 4,500 soldiers from the PFP undertook a large operation to push the movement occupation out of the center of the city. Using planes, helicopters, and tanks, they launched tear-gas canisters. They also used high-pressure water hoses and batons to move people. Dozens of people were wounded and twenty-three to thirty were detained. The PFP killed three people, according to Gibler (2009: 173): Alberto López Bernal, Fidel Sánchez García, and Roberto Hernández López. APPO and Sección 22 relocated their encampment to UABJO and in front of the Santo Domingo Cathedral. Radio Universidad became the primary communication forum for the movement on October 30, 2006. Radio Ciudadana continued its broadcasts.

One of the primary voices of Radio Universidad was Berta Elena Muñoz, a physician who initially set up a first-aid station for people wounded in the increasingly bloody confrontations that were occurring in the city. She, along with Alejandra and Miguel (radio names) and others, became the primary radio announcers for Radio Universidad. By October 29, when the PFP arrived, Radio Universidad, known as Radio de la Verdad (Truth Radio), was the logistical center of resistance.

On November 2 the PFP started to move toward UABJO. Soldiers took down the barricade known as La Barricada de Cinco Señores, which was located at the principal entrance to the university and its radio station. An all-day pitched battle that left participants from APPO injured, detained, and disappeared was run from Radio Universidad (Gibler 2009: 176–77). The station informed listeners about the advances of the PFP and where they were located. Broadcasters outlined strategic actions listeners could take: "Create a human chain around the university city; reinforce the barricades; videotape everything to document the aggressions of the police; stop up the water pipes supplying riot-armored personnel carriers; throw paint, burning oil, or any other material on the PFP to stop their advance" (Zires 2009a: 188). In the case of the radio going off the air, they urged people to communicate via the Internet and by phone trees and messages on cell phones (188).

The announcers kept the crowds mobilized and offered inspirational messages as they overcame their own fear of what would come next. Dr. Bertha shared with Diego Enrique Osorno how she felt as she reported the advances of the PFP toward the campus: "I was calm. . . . Did I feel fear? I was afraid. I am not crazy. And well, there came a moment when the tanks were going for the church, I said, 'they are going to grab us here. Here is where they are going to find us, in front of the microphones. So, I felt fear . . . but I never panicked" (Osorno 2007: 229, my translation). On the air, Dr. Bertha did remain calm, saying, "We are not going to confront them body to body, compañeros, no way. We do not want martyrs in this fight. We don't need any more. So what you need to do is come to Radio Universidad, in an intelligent way, to help protect the installations. . . . We have set an example for the world because of our peaceful resistance" (Zires 2009a: 189, my translation).

One of the other important voices broadcast that day was that of Francisco Martínez Neri, the rector of the university. He directed his words to the students, the PFP, the national government, the president of Mexico, and "those who have dreamed about the transformation of our people" (Zires 2009a: 191). He said, "We think that the public university has to be a space for debate . . . a place in which any person is free to express themselves, however they think. . . . There is no way that we can consent to letting the radio be an object of occupation [by the PFP] nor can the campus be an object of occupation" (190, my translation). Neri's words were supported by other academics, students, social organizations and NGOs, human rights organizations, and people from other parts of Mexico and other countries (190).

Gibler reported, "By 3:00 a.m., the police retreated and returned to the Zócalo, leaving the university in the hands of APPO. Some 20,000 people filled the streets and started to rebuild the barricades taken down that morning. More than 200 people suffered injuries during the fight" (2009: 177). On November 2 the people of Oaxaca succeeded in preventing the PFP from occupying the university and shutting down Radio Universidad. It is remembered by many as a highlight of the social movement of 2006, a time when a massive show of passive resistance coordinated from Truth Radio was successful.

Radio Universidad continued to be the central voice of the movement through November 25. On that day, after the station announced an APPO megamarch with the goal of encircling the PFP troops, the most violent clash of 2006 occurred.

As described at the end of chapter 3, November 25 was marked with violence that included injuries, assassinations, forced detentions, disappearances, and accusations of sexual assault by women who were detained. Gibler describes that night as characterized by extreme police violence: "a wave of violence not seen during six months of conflict: police beat men, women, and children unconscious in the middle of the street; police blasted machine guns at people running for cover; police entered hospitals throughout the night with their guns drawn, pulling wounded protesters out and piling them in trucks. That night the police grabbed 203 people—at most 30 people had participated in firing bottle rockets at police" (2009: 182).

Government offices were burned during the confrontation. The movement blamed provocateurs, who they said had infiltrated the movement and caused the damage. The police blamed members of APPO, and many were charged with property destruction and other crimes. APPO was removed from all the areas it occupied in the city. Two days later, 141 of the detained were shipped off to a federal prison in Nayarit.

I visited Mexico in October and met with women from COMO and APPO and with Sección 22 members who were carrying out a hunger strike in Mexico City. By November I was back in Oregon teaching classes. I remember listening to Radio Universidad on the Internet on November 25, in my study. I was anguished to be so far away and listening from such a distance. When I made calls to several friends in the city to see how they were, it became clear that I knew more than they because I was receiving a clear transmission. I told them what I was hearing. In Oaxaca City the transmission signal was being jammed by a rock song that played over and over again. I found it surreal that I was relaying information about what was going on in Oaxaca by cell phone from Eugene, Oregon, to people in Oaxaca. I also remember seeing a video shot from someone's cell phone in Oaxaca and instantly loaded onto YouTube: it showed prisoners being loaded into a helicopter and flown away. Relaying this and other information to friends in the moment made me feel connected but powerless. By this time many people outside the country were following Radio Universidad's broadcasts daily to keep track of the movement in Oaxaca.

A few days after November 25, those who ran Radio Universidad for the social movement turned it back to university authorities because they wanted to make sure that the station remained in good condition. University authorities had been supportive of their occupation of the radio station.

Amnesty International carried out an investigation and issued a report on the human rights violations committed in Oaxaca between June 2006 and April 2007. Of the mass arrests on November 25, 2006, the report states:

> At least four of those detained were minors, who were subsequently passed to the juvenile courts and later released. Many of the detainees were reportedly ill-treated, tortured, and denied access to legal counsel and adequate medical attention before being transferred to federal prison in Nayarit State, 1,000 miles away, preventing lawyers and family from reaching them for several days. The National Human Rights Commission (CNDH) concluded that at least 13 of the detainees were tortured by State Judicial Police and Federal Preventive Police. (Amnesty International 2007b; see also CNDH 2007)

Among those taken to the Centro Federal de Readaptación Social in San José del Rincón, Nayarit, were thirty-four women. The human rights activists Yésica Sánchez Maya, who worked for Limeddh in Oaxaca, denounced the treatment that the women and men received in transit and in the prison. Based on interviews with sixteen women and seventy men who were detained in Nayarit, Sánchez Maya stated in a press conference on December 10 that there were cases of sexual assault, including threats of rape by police during the transport of prisoners from Oaxaca to Nayarit (Olivares Alonso 2006; see also Castellanos Jurado et al. 2007).

Gender and the Rights to Speak, to Be Heard, and to Decide Who Governs

Daniela Aragón, a working-class single mother who sells clothing out of a stall in the market in the center of Oaxaca, recalls the importance of the movement radio broadcasts from August until the end of November, when the PFP destroyed the remaining APPO encampments, arrested hundreds of people in a massive operation, and finally forced the closure of Radio Universidad, which had been held by APPO:

We learned about so many things from the radios. We knew how many people were detained, what their names were, the names of the disappeared, all of this from the radio. When the government saw that what was going in Oaxaca was going to get national and international attention thanks to what we were able to communicate on the radios, when our governor went on Televisa [the national commercial channel] to tell us that everything was calm and nothing was going on in Oaxaca, that is when they took away all of the radio stations.

They left us without a means of communication. The radio was so influential and it gave the movement its main force. It was one of the main reasons that the movement could succeed. When they took the radios away and when they took Canal 9 back from the people, they began to take away our knowledge and our rights.

Daniela elegantly describes the communicative importance of the movement-held radio and TV stations, as well as making reference to the rights that people in support of the movement had gained through their occupation of the media. Her narrative allows us to see how information and rights were extended from the original group of women who occupied COR-TV and radio to a wide listening public.

One might suspect that the primary avenue of rights talk for the different kinds of women who came together to take over state television (and radio and later commercial radio) in Oaxaca would be feminism, but in fact feminism is just one strand of the discourse that entered their discussions. More central to the definition of a package of rights that emerged as the right to speak, the right to be heard, and the right to decide who governs was what Sally Merry (2006) and Richard Wilson (2007) refer to as the vernacularization of human rights discourses. Merry discusses both replication and hybridity in her work about how vernacularization functions in relation to gender violence. Of concern here is her discussion of hybridity in the vernacularization of human rights, which occurs "when institutions and symbolic structures created elsewhere merge with those in a new locality, sometimes uneasily" (2006: 46–48). In the context of the Oaxaca social movement, the merging of appropriated notions of general, universal human rights with particular, local injustices suggests a kind of denotative rights talk where "actors gesture towards aspects of human rights talk with very little specificity or actual content" (Wilson 2007: 358) in relation to specific human rights laws or treaties.

What interests me here is unraveling how the denotative appropriation of human rights talk in Oaxaca through the process of hybrid vernacularization was gendered. I used an event-based frame of analysis because I believe that it was through the process of their three-week occupation of Oaxaca state TV and radio stations that the women created their analysis. I am suggesting that for many (but not all) of the women involved, their gendered connection to human rights talk came not through their absorption of an initial gendered analysis of human rights influenced by feminist organizations and presence in the social movement circuit of Oaxaca, but through a different process. The experience of the women who organized to take over public and later commercial media in Oaxaca suggests that the ways human rights discourses became specifically gendered, in this example, emerged through the exercise of specifically defined local rights: the right to speak, the right to be heard, and the right to decide who governs. Many of the women who participated in the takeover of COR-TV and radio had long histories of silence. Some were silenced as daughters in their families growing up, some were quiet or silent in their relationships with adult men, and many were silenced when it came to assuming public leadership roles, even though they were the backbone and main support for Sección 22 and grassroots organizing in their communities.

This does not mean, however, that they were not leaders, that women did not speak to each other or did not have influence within the movements some participated in. Many have assumed the role of center-women, a concept articulated by Karen Brodkin (1988) in her analysis of union organizing at Duke Medical Center in her book *Caring by the Hour*. Center-women, Brodkin writes, gain their position from their ability to mediate and resolve conflicts by reconciliation and to provide emotional support and advice, skills they learned in their family but were able to deploy in organizing. In both the union analyzed by Brodkin and the Oaxaca social movement, there were gendered styles of leadership. Most people recognize only one aspect of leadership: that of the public and solo speakers. Women themselves can experience this as silencing but also can recognize that they provide other, less visible kinds of leadership in the movements they are in. Brodkin writes that in her initial analysis of Duke Medical Center workers, she missed the crucial aspect of network centers in her analysis: "Almost all the public speakers and confrontational negotiators were men. . . . Women were centers and sustainers of workplace networks—centerwomen or centerpersons—as well as the large majority of the union organizing committee" (132). Rather than just individuals following a popular orator, Brodkin writes, "leadership in the union drive involved already existing hospital-based social networks . . . around class and race-conscious or at least job-conscious values. . . . Centerwomen were key actors in network formation and consciousness-shaping" (133).

Like the organizing model at Duke Medical Center, most of the "public" speakers for APPO and the teachers' movement were men. In the takeover of the TV and radio stations, the leadership was women. Thus, while women were not the public spokespeople for Sección 22 and other organizations, they did have organizing skills. What was different about their experience taking over COR-TV was that they also became public leaders who were speaking and were heard "like men." For them, this was a new experience that was articulated as a new set of gendered rights. In enacting the rights to speak and be heard, Oaxacan women came to conceptualize what their rights were, thus creating their own localized culture of rights, which became a part of the larger movement ideology that washed over the city for a period of several months (see Speed 2007: 184). This gendered, local culture of rights became accessible to many other women and men, and through radio came to influence their views as well, at least temporarily.

It is unclear whether this new set of gendered rights articulated by women who took over the media in Oaxaca will have a lasting legacy. The Oaxaca social movement, APPO, and other organizations, such as the Coordinadora de Mujeres Oaxaqueñas, continue to exist and to struggle for some of the same rights they articulated during 2006. The right to speak and the right to be heard have been taken up in dozens of communities in Oaxaca. The model provided by the women who took over COR-TV in 2006 and then moved into other radio stations has spawned a multitude of forums on the air for people throughout the state to share their perspectives and generate discussions on a wide range of themes.

Summary

The story of the radio and television station takeovers allows us to see how the life of testimonials extends far beyond one event, one telling, or one context in terms of how they travel, work, and may resignify "the truth" and official and unofficial versions of history. For a sustained period of time, the public, political space of Oaxaca was significantly broadened via the open airwaves. Without a doubt one of the clearest legacies of the 2006 Oaxaca social movement is the proliferation of community radio stations since then, which offer alternatives to state-run and commercial media in many parts of Oaxaca.

The experience of the women and others who took over COR-TV and then went on to occupy commercial stations and Radio Universidad has much to tell us about processes of identity creation. The infusion of testimonials with emotion and their capacity to effectively represent hybrid identities, such as urban, indigenous, and working class, make them fertile terrain for analyzing the politics of complex identity formations in process. The case of the women in the radio and TV stations highlights the critical role that oral narrative can play in how political and ethnic identities are created in individuals, become shared in specific times and places, and sometimes help create new cultures, such as how to do politics, who can participate, and who is a citizen. Part of claiming rights in Oaxaca and elsewhere is creating a hybrid urban Indian identity and asserting this racialized identity in opposition to Gachupines, the central city elite and business owners.

What is also noteworthy about the identity-formation processes linked to the 2006 social movement is an engagement with the embodied category of race as opposed to ethnicity, which is usually the focus of identity in terms of self-identifying or being identified as *indígena* (indigenous) or mestizo. During 2006 the physical body (short, brown, and fat) was read into the self-identity of women making rights claims. In much of Oaxaca's recent history and in many other places, the primary axis of difference has been an ethnic identity built around language and ethnic-group affiliation, not an embodied sense of race. The visual-communication opportunity offered by the takeover and programming of COR-TV provided a critical opening for women to reclaim a positive, physical sense of race and to project it to others.

The women who took over the media in 2006 landed in various places. Several became announcers on radio stations, and some became personalities in their own right. La Maestra Carmen had to go into hiding after receiving death threats to her family. She went into seclusion outside of Oaxaca and later returned to teaching. A few other women left the country and have not returned. Many of the women who were teachers returned to their rural teaching posts. There some went into the regional leadership of the teachers' union—a new development. Many teachers still find, however, that they have to struggle for authority and recognition with local municipal authorities and with some of their male coworkers, but they have strong support from parents who acknowledge their leadership and importance (Cruz 2011). Organizations such as COMO continue to struggle for some of the same rights they articulated in 2006. This organization has split a couple of times and now is reorganized and continues to march every year on August 1 for democratic reforms, women's rights to political participation and leadership, and rights to housing, education, and medical services (see Radio Nhadía 2010).

The Oaxacan state government tried until December 2010 to engage in the political, physical, psychological, cybernetic, and broadcast annihilation of individuals and groups that were labeled criminals and ultimately terrorist threats (see Leyva Solano 2009). What appears to be harder to destroy, however, is the right to speak, the right to be heard, and the right to decide who governs. These rights are being articulated in ever-wider circles and have become vernacularized in many corners of Oaxaca as basic human rights and critical components of local conceptions of citizenship. Taking down radio stations and attacking those who work in them was a key strategy of the Oaxacan government in 2006 and continued until 2010. That year the PRI lost control of the governorship of Oaxaca after eighty years in power, and an opposition candidate, Gabino Cué Monteagudo, was elected as a product of a left-right coalition. It is unclear what his media policy will be with regard to the state-run TV stations. Programming appears to be somewhat more open than under his predecessor, but how this will develop is an open question.

7

The Economics and Politics of Conflict

Perspectives from Oaxacan Artisans, Merchants, and Business Owners

Founded in 1486, Oaxaca de Juarez, capital of the state of Oaxaca, Mexico, is one of the best-kept secrets in Mexican history. Here, strong pre-Hispanic roots coexist with a culture that changed radically after the Spanish conquest, and today both influences are visible throughout the city streets.

Oaxaca's historical center was declared a World Heritage Site by UNESCO. The city's colonial identity resides alongside a strong presence of traditions and customs of the many ethnic groups populating this area. Oaxaca also benefits from a profound respect for pre-Hispanic cultures, thanks to the proximity of two of the most important archeological sites in the country, Monte Albán, inherited from the Zapotec community, and Mitla, once a capital of the Mixtec and earlier Zapotec culture.

In Oaxaca, Oaxaca, folklore is everywhere and contributes to robust Oaxaca tourism. Local craftsmen, skillful masters of their art, come from villages deep in the state to fill the market and the shops

with their hand-made black clay pottery, textiles, and world-famous
alebrijes. Oaxaca also enjoys a varied cultural life, with many galleries
and art museums where photographers, painters, fine artists, musi-
cians, and writers display their wares.

—Mexico Tourism Board (2011)

Oaxaca City: There have been ongoing demonstrations and protests in
Oaxaca City due to civil unrest since June 2006. Several groups have
engaged in violent demonstrations in Oaxaca City, which resulted in the
death of an American citizen in October 2006. . . . U.S. citizens should
avoid participating in demonstrations and other activities that might be
deemed political by the Mexican authorities. The Mexican Constitution
prohibits political activities by foreigners, and such actions may result
in detention and/or deportation.

—U.S. Department of State, Bureau of Consular Affairs (2007)

The 2006 conflict between APPO, Sección 22, and the government of Ulises
Ruiz Ortiz laid bare the utter dependency of Oaxaca on tourism. Fueled by
bucolic descriptions of a powerful indigenous past and present, the mixing of Spanish colonialism with indigenous traditions, world-class food and
crafts, and unique cultural celebrations such as the Guelaguetza, tourism
has been the number one source of revenue in the state of Oaxaca for several decades. In the municipality of the City of Oaxaca, approximately 74
percent of the labor force works in the tertiary sector, which includes commerce, services, and tourism (Ramos Sánchez 2007: 29, table 12). Foreign
visitors to Oaxaca City's hotels fell by 43 percent between 2005 (169,000
visits) and 2007 (118,000 visits; Moon 2008). Three hundred businesses in
the historic center of Oaxaca shut down from the time the social conflict
began in June 2006 to July 2007, according to one source (Pedrero 2007).
The subsecretary of promotion and publicity of the Secretariate of Tourism
of the State of Oaxaca blamed the loss of 350,000 tourists and 950 million
pesos (about U.S.$83 million) in revenue on the conflict with APPO in 2006
(*Noticaribe* 2007). Regardless of the source, almost everyone agrees that international and national tourism in Oaxaca was negatively affected by the
social movement and conflict of 2006.

After 2007 increasing levels of drug violence, warnings from the U.S.
State Department about the violence, and the 2009 outbreak of swine flu
(the first reported H1N1 fatality was in Oaxaca) did not help the city and

state to recover from the 2006 downturn. Even by December 2010 hotel occupancy in Oaxaca was down significantly, at 42 percent, compared to rates of up to 85 percent earlier in the century. The headline for the newspaper story describing the low hotel occupancy rates read, "Tourismo de Oaxaca esta de rodillas" (Tourism in Oaxaca Is on Its Knees; Avendaño 2011).

Given such a prognosis, one would expect to find universal condemnation of the social movement of 2006 among those who make their living from tourism, but a range of opinions about the movement existed in and around Oaxaca City. Some businesses owners were bitterly opposed to APPO and joined in the governor's campaign to harass and repress the movement; others participated in their own initiative to engage with APPO, the state government, and the federal government to broker a settlement that would allow peace to return to the city. Artisans and smaller scale merchants had varied responses. Some supported the movement by providing food, fuel, and financial support; others expressed open hostility and bitterness toward Sección 22 and APPO and blamed them for the severe economic downtown that came with the conflict of 2006.

A survey by Jeffrey Cohen in 2007 found that in one community of artisans with the pseudonym El Arbol del Valle, "interviewees noted that the decline in tourism in the city had led to the collapse in the local market for goods as tour buses no longer visit the village." Those surveyed in this community also suggested that exporters were avoiding the area as well (Cohen 2007: 9). Interviewees there stated that over a hundred women had been laid off jobs, and the community's mayor maintained that over 250 people had left the community (10). Cohen only found 10 percent of El Arbol del Valle in support of the movement. Yet he also found people in other rural communities who were more supportive of APPO and Sección 22 or simply without information. Overall his research suggests a complex response by artisans, small merchants, and others in rural communities around Oaxaca who supported the goal of the movement but were likely to continue to oppose the strikes because of the consequences for children in school and the local economy (12–13). This analysis reflects many of the findings of the interviews highlighted here. The economic hardship produced by the social conflict pushed everyone to change their daily routines. Some lost jobs or, if they ran a business, suffered a significant decline in clients and customers. Daily roadblocks, the periodic commandeering of public buses by APPO, and the emergence of hundreds of barricades in and around the city decreased everyone's mobility significantly. The political lack of will on the part of the governor and the legislature and their failure to acknowledge the conflict, work to resolve it, or resign left a wide majority of citizens dissatisfied with the state government. Many were angered at the indifference of the federal government as well.

Artisan families and communities directly dependent on marketing campaigns and programs that stem from the Oaxacan state government were more likely to oppose the social movement and support the governor in the hopes of restored peace and business. Artisans from wealthier and more established craft-producing communities, such as the Zapotec weavers of Teotitlán del Valle, were more varied in their views of APPO, Sección 22, and Governor Ulises Ruiz Ortiz. Middle-aged and older weavers were often opposed to the movement, but some artisans who were university students or members of weaving cooperatives tended to be more sympathetic to the teachers and APPO. In some cases this perspective can be linked to prior exposure to ideas about social justice, human rights, and indigenous rights.

Among small merchants in the different markets of Oaxaca City, there was also a difference of opinion with regard to APPO and the teachers. Some vendors with rights to stalls in centrally located markets and those with rights to sell in special markets during holidays are aligned with the PRI. In conversations with the larger group of merchants who sell in the Mercado de Abastos on the outskirts of the city, I found more varied views, often tied to their family's political experiences and loyalties.

Owners of larger businesses such as hotels, restaurants, craft stores and jewelry shops, language schools, and tour operations were also varied in their perspectives. Some did support the governor, particularly those who were at the top of the business community, who received favors from him in return for their political support. But a surprising number did not, as his policies had not benefited them and they resented the blatant nepotism with which state business contracts were handed to friends and family of the governor and his administration. These entrepreneurs maintained a more independent political stance toward the state government. Some had participated in the Unión Social de Empresarios Mexicanos (Social Union of Mexican Businesses, USEM) and had already begun thinking about social problems and what they could do to resolve them. They began to try to talk with the governor and state officials, APPO representatives, and representatives of the national government, looking for a third path to resolve the conflict.

In their conversations with APPO, these entrepreneurs found some common ground in terms of things they wanted to change in state governance practices, laws, and organization. The group held a series of forums with APPO to exchange viewpoints. They also talked with the archbishop of Oaxaca to get him involved as well. They met with Mexico's secretary of the interior, secretary of state, and secretary of public security to push for a peaceful solution. The efforts of independent business owners to find a peaceful resolution to the conflict are an important part of the story of 2006. It also reveals the ways other members of the community—not only the poor and organized—were searching for new paths to political participation in Oaxaca.

Artisans and Small Merchants

San Antonio Arrazola is a neat, hillside town tucked in the shadows of Monte Albán, a large archaeological site that was a major Zapotec sociopolitical and economic center for more than a thousand years. Tourists may first meet people from Arrazola at Monte Albán, where they have been selling clay reproductions of pre-Columbian artifacts since the 1960s and 1970s (Brulotte 2006: 57), or at the community markets, where they sell the famous *alebrijes*, painted wooden animal fantasy figures (see Chibnik 2003). Earlier in the twentieth century, the community's revenue came primarily from agriculture and remittances from braceros, but by the 1980s the people became firmly entrenched in the tourist economy of Oaxaca. Arrazola is of fairly recent origin, becoming officially incorporated in 1937 as an *ejido* as a part of postrevolutionary land reforms (Brulotte 2009: 464, 2005, 2012). Before that time, residents worked as hired laborers on a small agricultural estate dating back to at least 1780, owned by the Arrazola Beita family. Included in that population were agricultural workers who spoke Chatino, Mixtec, and Zapoteco, but those languages faded out and Spanish became the lingua franca (464). Today artisans in the community walk a fine line between refuting and embracing ethnic and racial categorizations that define them as indigenous, even though they do not usually self-define as indigenous or manifest any of the characteristics associated with indigenous identity in the valleys of Oaxaca. I visited Arrazola for several days in 2010 and again in 2011 to talk with people about their experiences in 2006. I found that, unlike the artisans I had interviewed in Teotitlán del Valle, who were varied in their perspectives on the social movement of 2006, people in Arrazola were almost uniformly opposed to APPO, did not sympathize with the teachers, and were mildly supportive of the state government of Ruiz Ortiz.

Leticia Aragón Ramírez (real name) is a forty-year-old artisan who works

Figure 7.1 Leticia Aragón Ramírez and her sons in Arazola. DOI: 10.7264/
N3BG2KWB

with her husband, Catalino Carrillo Morales, and two sons, ages fourteen
and nineteen, to produce distinctive alebrijes. Their work is known for the
Zapotec designs (many found in archaeological sites and artifacts) painted
on their surfaces. Leticia learned the art of producing alebrijes when she
married her husband at age twenty in 1990. At that time, the market for
the wooden figures was booming. She and her family worked as fast as they
could to supply the six or seven intermediaries who came regularly to their
community, primarily from the United States. Tourism decreased after September 11, 2001, in the community of Arrazola and elsewhere, but began
to pick up again by 2005. The conflict of 2006, however, produced devas-
tating consequences for Leticia and her family. We spoke in August 2010 in
her home in Arrazola.

LYNN: *How did you see the conflict of 2006? How did it start? How did it affect you?*

LETICIA: *Well, it came about because the government was not in agreement with the requests made by the teachers and by APPO. But for me, APPO is a group of people who are only interested in having power, and they don't look out for the welfare of the people of Oaxaca. The people who have done the most damage to Oaxaca are APPO. They want the government to do as they say, and the government doesn't agree . . . so that is where the conflict comes from.*

The way that the conflict affected us personally is like this: There were some tourists through a university who were supposed to come here. My husband was going to give them classes and demonstrations for four hours a day here in his workshop. This exhibition and the workshop were cancelled. The professor from the university told me that she was forbidden to bring students from her university to Oaxaca because the U.S. government said not to [this is a reference to U.S. State Department warnings]. She said they couldn't come to Oaxaca. And they didn't come.

The governor of the state [Ruiz Ortiz] asked my husband to produce some wood figures for a convention that was going to take place in Oaxaca. But because of the conflict that there was between the government and APPO and the teachers, this convention didn't happen either. Instead, they had it elsewhere in another state. They returned the wooden figures my husband had made. The result of all of this was that we didn't have any source of income. That's when our economic problems began. . . .

Our biggest worry was our older son, who was in high school in Oaxaca. . . . He needed money for transportation and food. Since there was no tourism and thus no source of income, I started selling sweets, fresh fruit drinks, and fruit cocktails at the elementary school here to try to sustain my kids. My husband thought about migrating to the U.S., but we decided against it. He tried to keep working. . . .

I got up at four in the morning to prepare the fruit, the drinks, and to put together everything I was going to sell at the primary school. I had to sell everything between 10 and 10:30 in the morning. Once I finished there, I went into the city of Oaxaca every day to buy the fruit I was going to use. I would come back, rest a little, and then I would help my husband. . . . I would make maybe 120 or 100 pesos of profit per day [about U.S.$10 or less], and I would give about 40 pesos to my son for his school costs. That left us about 50 pesos *per day [U.S.$4–4.50] to feed my family. We usually bought tortillas and vegetables. . . .*

When I went into Oaxaca I went to the market on the outside of town [Mercado de Abastos] to buy what I was going to sell at the school and for us. But there were roadblocks. The teachers had blocked the roads. Imagine me carrying one hundred mangos, a watermelon, and a cantaloupe on my back. The police were on the roads making sure that those people from APPO didn't do anything wrong and to protect us. I felt more secure. When the PFP arrived, they also helped to take care of us, because there was a lot of delinquency. I suffered a lot carrying all that heavy fruit and I would have to carry it until the end of the roadblock. Sometimes I had to walk one or two kilometers to find a taxi home, depending on where the roadblocks were.

Leticia's negative experiences during the social conflict did not translate neatly into automatic support for the PRI. Instead she describes her family's dependence on the competence of state tourism officials. Our conversation continued:

LYNN: *So in general, how do people here relate to the government?*

LETICIA: *We always try to work with the government because they are the ones who support us. If, for example, there are expositions that are held outside of Oaxaca, it is the secretary of tourism who can help to support our trip.*

LYNN: *So how about political parties? Do people support particular political parties?*

LETICIA: *No. It doesn't have to do with political parties, but with the government. We depend on whoever is in the government. If the government produces good publicity, then we will have tourism here. But if they don't do any work on publicity, then we can't do anything. If the government supports us—whoever is in the position of the government—then that is good.*

LYNN: *What do you think of the government and what it did in 2006?*

LETICIA: *I think they did the right thing even though it really hurt all of the artisan communities. APPO and the teachers wanted to get rid of the government. Imagine if they had succeeded in removing the governor! They would have done that to any governor from any political party because they wanted the power to remove the government. So I think that if the government had not been ready, that they would have succeeded in getting rid of them and Oaxaca would be even worse off than it is now.*

Leticia's narrative reflects her family's position of relative powerlessness and dependence on state government officials for attracting tourists to her community through advertising and acting as gatekeepers to the craft expositions held in Oaxaca and elsewhere. The vast reduction in the number of tourists who arrived completely transformed her daily life. She went from working at home with her husband, sanding, finishing, and painting alebrijes to sell to intermediaries, to making an arduous daily trip to the Oaxaca Mercado de Abastos. She then had to carry a heavy load for one to two kilometers through roadblocks before she could take a taxi home. Her household's income was reduced by approximately 70 percent, and daily existence was precarious at best.

Interestingly she does not embrace the PRI, the party of Governor Ulises Ruiz, or any other political party. She simply wants to claim her entitlement as an artisan to have access to craft expositions and tourists. These entitlements stem from her identity as an artisan rather than from rights she feels entitled to because of her humanity or her identity as an Oaxacan citizen, woman, or rural inhabitant. She opposes APPO in part because she believes that APPO supporters are power-hungry and want to control the state but also because their actions disrupt her claims and entitlements as an artisan. Rather than a rights-based ideology, her narrative reflects the dissatisfaction of someone who has been denied services and entitlements. I will return to this distinction in the conclusion.

Leticia's dissatisfaction with the conditions created by the social conflict and the role of APPO and teachers in that conflict was shared by many small merchants in the city center, who have historically depended on the PRI to provide them with access to market stalls in exchange for political loyalty. Sara Rojas comes from a working-class Oaxacan family that lives on the outskirts of the city, in one of the *colonias* that was created through land occupations in the 1970s and became regularized over time (see Higgins 1983). Sara's family was strongly affected by the lack of transportation that resulted from the commandeering of buses by APPO and others. During the conflict period, her husband lost his job at a box factory, and the two of them resorted to making and selling hamburgers in their neighborhood to make ends meet. While Sara doesn't necessarily endorse any political party, she feels that for all its faults, the PRI at least provided consistent venues for her family to sell goods in. We spoke in August 2010, shortly after Gabino Cué Monteagudo was elected as governor:

SARA: *We live on the outskirts of town and the conflict first affected us in the case of the buses that go up to our house. The teachers commandeered the buses, and APPO did as well. Because many of the bus unions supported the governor—he uses the buses to cart around his supporters when necessary— they have to get along with him. So when APPO and others threatened the bus drivers and took the buses by force, then we would have to get off the buses and there was no way home. . . .*

We had one experience where we had a direct conflict with the barricada *in our neighborhood. My sister-in-law was pregnant and about to give birth. Her water broke at midnight and we had to get her to the hospital because she was going to give birth. My parents had a truck. My brother borrowed their truck and started to go in the direction of the hospital with my sister and me. We hit the first barricade in the neighborhood. My brother got out to explain to the people at the barricade that it was an emergency. He said he had to get by because his wife was about to give birth.*

The person who attended to him at the barricade was really rude. He said, "He's lying." He told my brother-in-law that the fact that his wife was about to give birth wasn't their problem. He started to say nasty words to my brother, and he kept trying to talk to them and convince them that they needed to let him get by. They still wouldn't let my brother get by, so he started to move the tree trunks out of the way that were blocking the road. When he did this, five or six men with machetes appeared and told him that if he didn't calm down he was going to get beaten up.

This was something terrible for us. When it is about the life and health of a baby, you don't mess around. My brother had to turn around and look for another way into the city so he could get to the hospital. Normally it takes about one half hour to drive from where we live to the hospital. On this occasion it took more than three hours to get there. . . . Everything turned out okay, and the little girl was born without any problems. But it was a very difficult experience for my family. . . .

LYNN: *How else did the social conflict affect you on daily basis?*

SARA: *For us the whole situation was terrible. We were afraid to go out of the house at night because of the danger. . . . We would go out as little as possible, and I really stopped going to see my parents. There was too much violence, too much insecurity. . . . The whole situation really got out of hand. It affected all of us as a society. The government never really gave an answer to them [APPO and the teachers] and it never really intended to negotiate with them. . . . It also affected us economically. . . .*

My husband lost his job at a box company in 2006 because it closed down due to the conflict. We were about four or five months without any work. After we spent the savings we decided that we would sell some food at night. So we started to sell hamburgers. We couldn't sell them at a high price because no one had any money. So we sold them as cheap as we could. We did this until my husband got another job, but the one he found was not like the other one. Before, he had health insurance for us, access to loans, a retirement fund, and a subsidy to help pay the utility bills. With his new job as a helper to a bricklayer, he doesn't have any of these benefits.

Like Leticia, Sara's daily life was significantly transformed by the physical and economic hardship brought on by the conflict. She remained circumspect about the possibilities for change, even with the election of a new governor. Like many, she also expressed distrust of political parties and the possibility that elections could produce significant change in her life:

The important thing to know about the political parties is that they just work for their own benefit or to win over people to vote for them. They don't work for the people. What they really have to do is also think about the merchants who need a form of income. It is the only thing we have. If the opportunity to sell is taken away from us, then it is like they are taking the bread out of our children's mouths.

I hope that the new governor [Cué Monteagudo] will be more flexible than the one we have now [Ruiz Ortiz] and that he will be able to arrive at an agreement and to lead a positive change like he said for Oaxaca. . . . We want a governor who will listen to the teachers and come up with proposals that work to avoid the marches, occupations, and all of that.

Sara's and Leticia's perspectives are in contrast to some of the responses I heard from weavers, who agreed on the terrible economic consequences of the social conflict but felt that the teachers and those in APPO were just in their actions and that the blame for the social conflict came not so much from them but from the actions of the governor and his administration.

Teotitlán del Valle is a town of Zapotec artisans who trace their presence as a distinct population site back more than two thousand years. After the

1950s, Teotitlán was transformed from a subsistence agricultural community supplemented by part-time textile production to dependence on tourism and textile production for export. By the mid-1980s agriculture was a pursuit carried out by only 11 percent of the population (Stephen 2005b: 103). A significant part of this transformation was also linked to migration, first within Mexico, then as braceros to the United States. Remittances helped locals to accumulate capital and build their weaving businesses. By the 1980s the community was marked by significant class differentiation between merchants and weavers. The booming success of the textile industry in the 1980s and 1990s raised the average standard of living in the community significantly, making it unique among indigenous communities in Oaxaca. Persistent inequality, however, has also accompanied that economic success. Another significant outcome of the textile boom was to support a cultural renaissance in the community that has nourished traditional and innovative forms of food, ritual, music, dance, language, and other arts (see Stephen 2005b).

I encountered a significant number of people in Teotitlán del Valle, particularly those fifty and older, who felt that APPO and Sección 22 were dangerous riff-raff who should get off the streets and go back to work. These people's perspectives were similar to those of Leticia's and Sara's. Here, I highlight the viewpoints of Mariana and Fernando to bring out some of the diversity of opinion I found among artisans. Unlike Leticia and Sara, they are generally supportive of the teachers and APPO.

Mariana Cruz Castro is a weaver from Teotitlán del Valle. She is approximately fifty years old and has been working with other women in a weaving cooperative for more than two decades. The cooperative pools the works of about sixteen women in Teotitlán del Valle and sells their products directly to consumers in Oaxaca, in Mexico City, and periodically at craft fairs elsewhere in Mexico (see Stephen 2005b: 215–30). Tourists who come to Teotitlán del Valle or to Oaxaca City are the primary source of income for the cooperative. The downturn in tourism that began in 2006 was a major blow to them. We spoke at the beginning of August 2007 about the impact of the social movement on the cooperative's business, and also about her impressions of the social movement.

Mariana sits in front of her treadle loom and wipes the sweat from her brow. It is late morning, and the sun has begun to pour into her weaving workshop. She is dressed in an embroidered white *blusa* with flowers ringing the neck. She speaks directly and with conviction:

MARIANA: *We are the most affected because we live from tourism. We have not sold anything. We can't go into the city of Oaxaca because of the conflict. So what this means for us is that we have to work every day to be able to eat, to buy food for our families. So it has affected us a great deal.*

LYNN: *How are sales this year [2007] for the cooperative in comparison to other years?*

MARIANA: *Well, we are selling very little right now. The people who used to come here to look for the cooperative don't come because of the situation in Oaxaca. Last year by this date we had sold enough to get by, because people would arrive to buy our products. But since last December, which is right after the conflict got to be really heavy, tourists have not been showing up here. It has been very hard to survive.*

We have been struggling in lots of ways just to survive. . . . We have been doing other things to help us get through these hard times. We are growing chickens to sell here, we have a place where we can sell local herbs, we are planting squash and other crops. . . . We are growing food that we can eat or sell. That is how we have managed to get by.

LYNN: *What is your perspective on the conflict? Do you have an opinion about what is happening and how it might be resolved?*

MARIANA: *I think that the conflict comes from the government and that the government should help to resolve it. Those in the government are not affected by it. We are the ones who are most affected by it. I also think that the teachers are right to ask for better schools. But since we are not given the opinion of the teachers [in the media], I took advantage of the opportunity to talk with a teacher and I asked her what the problem was that caused them to strike. She let me know that the situation was very difficult for those of them who work in rural areas of the state. She said that there are places where the children come to school without eating. The level of nutrition is very low. . . . They don't have access to healthy meals. So how are they going to improve their studies if they aren't eating well? So they asked for, or rather really demanded, that the government help out those remote communities. There are teachers who travel for a whole day in each direction to teach four days a week in very remote communities. So they have seen this situation. They have lived it. So I think they have the right and the need to help out these communities where they work. A lot of people around here say that it is the teachers who are making the situation so difficult.*

LYNN: *Do you see it that way?*

MARIANA: *No, I don't see it that way.*

LYNN: *Then who is making the situation more difficult?*

MARIANA: *It is the government of Oaxaca. . . . The functionaries of the government don't go out into the communities. . . . Maybe they visit once in a while, when they are campaigning during elections, but the people who live there with the children, who are out in the communities sharing the conditions present there, are the teachers.*

✳ VIDEOCLIP 7.1: http://dx.doi.org/10.7264/N3SB43P8

Mariana shares the deep concern and alarm expressed by Leticia and Sara about the depressed economy of Oaxaca associated with the social conflict of 2006. She relates how she and other women in the weaving cooperative had to look for alternative sources of income such as selling chickens and herbs and growing squash and other food to eat and sell. Mariana, Leticia, and Sara all resorted to survival strategies linked to food production and marketing. Mariana and Leticia experienced deep downturns in the markets for their work and in the number of tourists arriving in their communities to purchase their goods. The similarities end, however, when it comes to their perspectives on what the root of the conflict is, how they feel about the teachers in the Sección 22, and their feelings about the government of Ruiz Ortiz.

Mariana discusses her perception that the commercial media did not tell all sides of the story. As a result of her conversation with a local teacher and other exchanges, she believes that the demands of the teachers—for improvements in the schools they work in, for more breakfasts and lunches for children—are just. She suggests that the teachers are doing important and valuable work, and that it is government officials who have no idea what is going on in poor rural communities. While Mariana's town of Teotitlán del Valle is very well-off compared to other communities, she has traveled to and worked with women in other communities where there are high levels of poverty. And even though Teotitlán del Valle has an average standard of living that is significantly higher than that of many surrounding communities, the community is marked by the presence of very impoverished families as well as of very wealthy ones (Stephen 2005b; Wood 2008). Mariana directs her subtle disdain toward government officials and politicians, who she believes never visit or pay attention to the situation of children and others in isolated rural communities in Oaxaca unless it is election time. She sympathizes with the demands of the teachers and APPO, as she thinks they reflect the needs felt by many in the state.

✳ VIDEOCLIP 7.2: http://dx.doi.org/10.7264/N3NK3BZJ

Fernando Martinez, another artisan from Teotitlán del Valle, had a front-row seat to the social movement and social conflict of 2006. In addition to being a weaver, he was also enrolled as an undergraduate student at UABJO in 2006. On his daily walk from where he got off the bus to the university, he walked through one of the tensest conflict areas: around the set of barricades that protected the entrances to UABJO at the intersection of Cinco Senores. His perspective is significantly informed by fellow students and friends who actively participated in the movement. He also experienced the economic difficulties of the downturn in tourism as his family struggled to find outlets for their weaving production. We spoke in August 2007:

FERNANDO: *The social conflict of last year [2006] was very serious. It pulled in everyone in Oaxacan society. In my community we were strongly affected. Why? Because in my case I come from a family where my parents are artisans and the entire community is dedicated to producing textiles. More than anything else it affected us in terms of employment. We live from tourism. When the official Guelaguetza was cancelled last year, which is one of the biggest sources of tourism and income for us, we didn't sell any textiles. A lot of people from my community had to go and find other sources of income in order to survive.*

The conflict also affected people in the city of Oaxaca in a major way. They could not go out to buy things, take their kids out to play, and walk around because it was never safe. Another cause of the conflict was centered on the occupation of the university where I study. Because of this, the classes were cancelled. This affected all of us and our learning process. . . .

LYNN: *How did you see the conflict as a student? Did you feel a lot of tension?*

FERNANDO: *Well, as a student, some of my friends were in the movement. When they attempted to evict people from the university who occupied it [on November 2, 2006], the people I knew who were there told me that the media controlled by the government said that there were very few people from APPO defending the occupation of the university. My friend who was there told me that there were much larger numbers of people there defending the university than in the PFP. Because of the large numbers of people defending the UABJO, the PFP was prevented from entering the university. . . .*

LYNN: *What do you think was the origin of the conflict, and how can it be resolved?*

FERNANDO: *. . . Everyone says that it started with the attempt to evict the teachers, but I think that there were already a lot of emotions and resentment felt by many Oaxacans. A lot of people were ready to raise their voice and ask the government to pay more attention to the people. . . .*

LYNN: *Do you think that things have really calmed down now [in 2007]?*

FERNANDO: *I think that the people continue to have strong feelings. During this last phase of the movement a lot of people were disappeared. A lot of people died despite the fact that the government has hidden a lot of information about people who were disappeared, kidnapped, and tortured. There are people who right now up to this moment are still in jail. So I think that the families of these people want justice for them. . . .*

Ultimately I think that this situation we lived through reinvigorated people to see what is going on, to not be oblivious to the social problems we have in the state. The fact that one lives well and doesn't need anything doesn't mean that there are no other people who are suffering, starving, and lacking economic opportunity. I think it is very worthwhile to fight for these people.

Fernando's analysis parallels that of Leticia and Mariana in terms of documenting the huge economic losses his family and others in his community suffered with the cancellation of the official Guelaguetza in 2006 and the complete drop-off in tourism. Because of his role as a student at the UABJO, however, Fernando had another intense perspective on the social movement. Through his friends who participated and his daily path through the city, he saw the conflict up close. His sources of information were those who were participating in the occupation of the UABJO. He also received detailed information about torture, disappearances, kidnapping, and assassinations. This information gave him a very different perspective on the behavior of the state government.

The most strongly felt part of his narrative concerns the families of those who were the victims of human rights abuses. He points out that those people—including those who still had family members in prison in August 2007—will want to see justice for the violence and rights violations suffered by their loved ones. Thus, unlike Leticia, who had no direct contact with anyone who was a victim of violence and human rights violations, Fernando had intimate knowledge of the repression. His final thought is to hope that the social movement and conflict of 2006 opened many people's eyes to the profound inequalities and social problems in the state and that this experience will move them to act to assist those in need. This vision of social justice and responsibility was also reflected in the perspectives of independent business owners who attempted to build a third pathway for dialogue between APPO, the state government, and the federal government.

Independent Business Owners in the Conflict: Civil Society Promoting Dialogue

One of the untold stories of 2006 in Oaxaca was how middle- and upper-class Oaxacans attempted to mediate the conflict. During the summer and fall of 2006, a group of independent businessmen, the archbishop of Oaxaca, and local intellectuals and artists who identified themselves as part of *la sociedad civil* (civil society) created spaces of dialogue with APPO as well as with the federal government. They tried to include the state government as well, but with little success. By calling themselves a civil society, they were able to use their relatively privileged economic, social, and cultural positions to gain an audience and access to both political elites and leaders of the social movement.

As Chatterjee (2004) observes, it is important to make a distinction between liberal civil society and what he describes as "political society." I return to this point in the conclusion but want to clarify here what I mean by civil society. While Chatterjee is speaking of India, I believe that the same argument can be made for Mexico, where the majority of the population is not a part of the effective civil society:

> Ordinarily, governmental activity takes place within the stratified
> social structures of class, status, and privilege. Benefits that are meant
> to be available in general are effectively cornered by those who have
> greater knowledge of and influence over the system. . . . It happens
> well within the normal ambit of legality because some sections of peo-
> ple simply do not have the knowledge or the will to make the claims
> to what they are entitled. This is a common state of affairs, not only
> in countries like India where the effective civil society is limited to a
> small section of "proper" citizens. It is a well-known experience in . . .
> Western social democracies where the culturally equipped middle class

is much better able to use the system than the poor or underprivileged. When the poor in countries like India [become] mobilized in political society . . . we must say that they have expanded their freedoms by using means that are not available to them in civil society. (Chatterjee 2004: 66–67)

In Oaxaca the majority of people are not included in civil society, with its easy access to and knowledge of all the rights and political participation they are entitled to according to state and federal law. Many of those who joined in the Oaxacan social movement would fall into Chatterjee's category of "political society." They have traditionally been excluded. Some of them were a part of organizations and other movements, though many were not. What I want to focus on here are people who are representative of liberal civil society in Oaxaca. Their perspectives are interesting because they reflect thoughtful analysis from a position of privilege about the ways the economic and political marginalization of the majority contributed to the ability of APPO to form, grow, and be widely supported. Their narratives also reveal their firm belief in the rule of law and in the formal political process, which is centered on voting and elections.

Alfonso Rodríguez owns several stores in Oaxaca that depend heavily on tourism and a loyal local clientele. University-educated, he has been working and running businesses in Oaxaca for forty years and has traveled widely in Mexico and abroad. We talk in a pleasant second-floor room above one of his businesses in the late morning. He sits, relaxed, in a large leather chair and brushes his hair back from his forehead as the sun warms the room. He speaks candidly and openly:

What happened in 2006 is part of a longer story. . . . I think even before June 14 the circumstances were ripe for what happened. There has been a lack of respect for the dignity of the people of Oaxaca not just by this or the previous governor but for a long time.

I did a study for a thesis a long time ago in the 1970s. At that time I spoke with artisans and others in the countryside in Oaxaca. They told me their experiences of the politicians making fun of them. They said they promised them things that they took in good faith and then they never fulfilled those promises—again and again. So I think the problems began a long time ago. . . . I think people were feeling really tired of this long history of deception. I am talking about what I saw in the 1970s that has gone on for forty years now. So the moment arrived when the people just couldn't take any more. [The movement in] 2006 was the drop of water that filled the glass and knocked it over.

The attitude of the government was total disinterest and apathy about solving the problems. I think that the problem of the teachers and their demands just combined with everything to create one big problem.

. . . After June 14 the government showed a real incapacity to handle what happened. I am not saying that it is okay that the teachers go and occupy the center of the city every year. No, that isn't right. It is important for them to make their demands clear. But the government needs to engage in a transparent process of negotiation with them that everyone can understand.

The way the government conducted its attempt to remove the teachers was what unified everyone against the governor. . . . It was simply the opportunity people were waiting for to say, "Let's get rid of this government [of Ulises Ruiz]. We have had enough."

After that things started to get polarized. There was one group of business people who supported Ulises Ruiz. They said, "Bring in the army, repress the people." They said this without knowing anything about the history of the situation. I agreed that it wasn't right that the teachers were in the streets and blocking access to our businesses, but I also didn't think it was right to go out and beat them up either. We had to ask, "Why are the teachers doing what they are doing, and why did all the people come afterward to support them?"

LYNN: *Can you tell me how this situation affected your business? How did you decide to do something? What did you do?*

ALFONSO: *After things got more and more polarized we started to hear some talk that the teachers and APPO were going to burn down businesses. That is when a group of us who were not in favor of how the government was handling the situation and also were not in favor of what the teachers and APPO were doing decided to try to talk with them. We first went to the state government and said, "Hello, government, can we talk with people of APPO and try to look for another path for resolving this conflict?" They said to us, "Go ahead. Whatever you can do to lower the tension is a good thing." So then we went to APPO and we said, "We are a group of entrepreneurs who are worried about our businesses. We don't agree with what the government is doing, but we also don't agree with what you are doing. Why don't we sit down and see how we can help one another out?" . . .*

So we sat down with the leadership of APPO. We held the first meeting in the Graphic Arts Institute started by Francisco Toledo. It was on a Sunday and then continued over several days. It also was a chance for us to get together with each other, as entrepreneurs who had participated in an organization called the Unión Social de Empresarios Mexicanos [Social Union for Mexican Entrepreneurs, USEM]). We talk a lot about social responsibility, the importance of respecting the dignity of each person, and the principles of solidarity and sustainability. We also think about how we can change our businesses in ways that can help to promote more general social change. So this group of us had already been sensitized to social problems. Most of us who were involved in trying to construct a third way with APPO were participants in USEM.

LYNN: *How did the meetings go?*

ALFONSO: *They were very interesting. The first meeting was super tense. The first thing they [APPO leaders] said was that they wanted to get rid of Ulises Ruiz. We didn't agree that this was the first order of business. We said there are laws that we have to base our actions on. . . . We said that we had to do something together to lower the levels of violence we were seeing in our city. That was our proposal. And when we started to talk with them, we asked, "Well, if we leave Ulises Ruiz aside, what else do you want?" After that we began to find a series of points we agreed upon that left us somewhat disgraced by the lack of action by people in our position.*

For example, they said to us, "We have five different proposals that we have sent to the state congress in order to modify the public works law in terms of regulating the way that contracts are made." Then they asked us, "And you, how many proposals do you have?"

"None," we had to answer.

"Well then, does that mean that you are in favor of the way the state government has been handing out public works contracts, giving them to their friends, to their family members?" they said.

"No," we responded.

"Well then, how come you have not done anything about it?" they asked us.

Then they said, "Are you in favor of the way the legislative power in this state depends directly upon the executive power, as an appendage of the executive [governor's] power?"

"No," we answered, "we are not in favor of that."

"And have you done anything about it?" they asked us again. "Why not? And are you in favor of the fact that the State Commission for Human Rights is also directly dependent on and appointed by the governor?"

"No, we are not."

So what we found was that we really had a lot of ideas in common with them, and we said, "You are right. But we have to resolve this with another form beside violence."

The APPO leaders then said to us, "Well, they have not left us any other path. If we don't do what we are doing [occupying the streets, closing roads, etc.] then they won't pay any attention to us. This is what we have decided."

We responded again, "But this is not the path." After that conversation we began to put together working groups and we arrived at the conclusion that we needed to continue talking about the themes we had in common. APPO coordinated them and we also helped to promote them. This happened in August. We also began to talk with the archbishop, who was also very worried about the level of violence and also asked us to work to decrease the violence.

The civil society group also attempted to hold dialogues with the state government. Alfonso related that federal officials kept telling them, "This is for you to resolve in Oaxaca. Go tell your governor to work it out." According to Alfonso, the group tried to organize a forum to meet with people in the Oaxacan state government. On the day that they had scheduled a medium-size forum to talk with state officials, the event was hijacked by the PRI, who bused in hundreds of people claiming that the civil society group was going to endorse Gabino Cué Monteagudo. The civil society group of entrepreneurs, along with some people from APPO, tried to cancel the meeting when they realized what was happening, but they were only able to withdraw. The result harmed the political credibility of the civil society group with some in the city. After that, they concentrated their efforts on trying to influence officials in the federal government through a series of meetings. Alfonso recalled:

The secretary of the interior held a meeting with ex-governors [of Oaxaca], with important politicians, and with members of civil society. It was in August or early September.

After this meeting we began to see what we had in common with some of the thoughtful people within APPO. We saw how much there was to do. We also began to meet with others.

We went to speak with the minister of public security [secretaria de seguridad pública] and we tried, when things got really violent at the end of October, to make those in APPO see that the violence level was very high. We encouraged them to think about turning over the city through a peaceful process mediated by civil society. APPO itself recognized that there had been increasing influence by radicals inside and that some groups were taking advantage of the conflict to generate more violence. . . . Unfortunately, on the other side [i.e., of the governor], there were people who were calling the archbishop a communist. They were calling for the forced removal of APPO from the foyer of the church in Carmen Alto. . . . We went to talk with several ministries of the federal government. We proposed to the minister of public security that the city be turned over through a peaceful process. . . . He said, "Go ahead and make your proposal." We did, and I don't know what happened. Apparently Sección 22 or some part of it didn't accept this proposal. Then we got all of the violence and stuff that happened in late November. By that point we couldn't take any more. We could not hold out any more economically.

I interviewed another member of the same group who offered additional insights into the thinking of the civil society business people. His perspective also illustrates some of the entrenched social and cultural categories that permeate Oaxacan society, distinguishing between *la sociedad pensante,* or educated society, and the rest. The presence of these two categories and the association of educated society with civil society support Chatterjee's (2004: 67) assertion that civil society is limited to a small portion of "proper" citizens.

Julio Alonso owns a group of construction businesses in Oaxaca. He came to Oaxaca City from Mexico City in the 1980s. In addition to his businesses, he also has a long record of social service, working with homeless children and other disadvantaged sectors of Oaxacan society through several charities. When we spoke in 2010, it was shortly after the election of Gabino Cué Monteagudo, whom he had supported. Like many people, Julio traced the conflict between APPO, Sección 22, and the government of Ruiz Ortiz to a series of bad public policies from the past and from a general state of abandonment felt by a majority of Oaxacans. He provided an in-depth analysis of where the conflict came from and his role in trying to find a peaceful solution.

When we met in July, Julio looked relaxed. He wore a white button-down shirt slightly open at the neck and a light blue sweater casually draped over his shoulders. We sat outside at a table, with the late afternoon light washing over us. He sipped a glass of water as we spoke. A gentle and engaged man, he spoke thoughtfully, carefully choosing his words:

Oaxacan society was already very unhappy with Ulises. On the one hand there is educated society [la sociedad pensante], *those who think about*

what kind of criteria are needed to improve Oaxaca. On the other hand . . .
all over the state and including in the city, are Oaxacans who feel forgotten,
abandoned, outraged, and poor, and who have not known how to survive.
They feel that the state government has not given them any way to get ahead.
In Oaxaca, and all over Mexico, the people live with the sensation of not being
able to reach the levels of comfort that they yearn for and believe they deserve.

Without a doubt there has been a change in economic conditions all over
Mexico, and in Oaxaca as well. I remember when I was little how it pained me
to see people walking barefoot in the market. The indigenous men and women
were barefoot, and you would say, "Chihuahua [Wow]!" For me it wasn't
conceivable that people walked around barefoot in their daily lives. It was
something I saw that I didn't like. And now there are not so many barefoot
people, but the people have not been able to progress. They have not been
able to have the economic progress they desire. So for me, it seems like what
happened in 2006 was people saying, "I am going to have a change." And in
2006 the poor people came out to the barricades and the streets because they
wanted change so badly that they didn't care about dying. I don't have any
doubts about that.

There were two levels to this. There was the discontentment of the teachers
and of the intellectuals. And there were the people who were hoping that
something good would happen in their favor. Then came the terrible decision
made on June 14 to try and remove the teachers by force from the center. This
unleashed everything. . . . They could have quickly negotiated with the teachers before APPO formed and everything developed, but there wasn't anyone in
power with enough brains to think about how to do this.

. . . Instead what happened is that the different groups began to organize.
You know how civil society organizations, indigenous organizations, and
others exist in Oaxaca, and they have intelligent people working in them who
are waiting for political openings? Well, after the attempted removal of the
teachers from the center of the city, a political opening is created and these
groups move right into it and begin to act.

. . . We started to observe that people were REALLY unhappy and that
their discontentment ran very deep. We also saw that the ways the governor
messed up the situation and his stubbornness resulted in more and more
mistakes being made.

. . . In this context, a group of us began to meet to see what we could do. In
the business community, on one side are a group of people who are the leaders
of the chambers of commerce—those who represent the traditional business
elite who are manipulated by the governor. This group of people who are the

representatives in the chambers of commerce are those who have to accept what the governor says, because in one form or another, the governor pays them back economically with favors.

On the other side are the people I joined together with. We are not in this other group. We are business people, but we are not so close to the governor. We are more independent, and we have a different kind of vision. This gives us more possibilities in terms of what we can say politically. At the same time, myself and some others also wanted to recognize what the archbishop was saying.

I have participated in the church in Oaxaca for a long time. At this time [during the conflict of 2006], the archbishop was trying to help mediate the situation. I thought his voice was one of the saner ones we could hear in that moment. The archbishop invited me to participate in some meetings with the secretary of the interior. I am not sure, but we went several times to meet with Abascal, the secretary of the interior. I thought he was an ethical person who wanted to solve these problems differently than how they have traditionally been resolved in Mexico [by force]. He wanted to arrive at a series of agreements through negotiations. He realized the manipulation that the governor and his supporters were engaged in, but at the same time I don't think he had sufficient force or support from the president of the Republic to move forward [with the idea of negotiation]. . . . I don't think that Abascal was given enough time to work out a solution. The situation became much worse, to the point that they [the federal government] sent the PFP to Oaxaca.

Julio then talked for a moment about the arrival of the PFP in Oaxaca and how the emergence of Radio Ciudadana and the presence of Radio la Ley contributed, in his view, to the polarization of the city. Like many others in the city, he believed that the radio was a major factor in moving people to action, in support of both APPO and the governor. He began talking about Radio Ciudadana:

I think that Radio Ciudadana was an instrument of Ulises Ruiz to try to contradict what was being said on APPO radio, which was also very incendiary. This caused the citizenry to become very divided. People were very confrontational. [They were thinking things] like, "You are not my neighbor, you are my enemy." Then there was the shooting of the journalist Brad Will of the United States, and this really completely unwound everything and created the need to have the PFP enter Oaxaca. I have the impression that this journalist was killed by Ulises's people.

There is a very long pause in the conversation, and I wait through the silence for him to speak again.

Because of this, I think that the people were ready to die for the liberty of Oaxaca. They realized that they couldn't really do anything when the army arrived [a reference to the PFP]. They didn't have any other option than to hide themselves and appear to be submissive, at least for the time being.

Our conversation then turned to what happened in the elections of 2007, when there was an abstention rate of approximately 40 percent and the PRI won a majority of seats in the state legislature. We then moved to the radical turnaround in 2010, when the coalition candidate Gabino Cué Monteagudo won a majority of votes with an alliance joining the PRI, PAN, the Partido del Trabajo (Worker's Party), and his own political party, called Partido Convergencia (Convergence Party). Julio addressed this apparent change of heart about voting by stating that the underlying beliefs and desires of people remained the same in both elections. The difference in 2010 was the presence of a political coalition that made it possible to remove the PRI from power in the state after eighty years.

JULIO: *A lot of people said to me, "How is it possible that in 2007 people voted for the PRI.[1] . . . It was apparently what we call a* carro completo *[total victory]. But it was a victory based on fear. Also, many did not vote. Why? Because of fear.*

They also didn't vote because they were tired, they didn't feel supported, and they didn't believe in the institutions [that voting represents]. In the end the PFP came and created order, but it was not the kind of order that the people wanted. That is why people didn't vote.

LYNN: *So why did people vote in 2010 three years later? How do we explain that change?*

JULIO: *As I said, 2007 was a vote of fear. In 2010 the PRI would have won if there had not been a coalition. I was convinced that this coalition was necessary to get the PRI out of Oaxaca—specifically the PRI of Ulises Ruiz. . . . People voted because they wanted to get rid of the PRI. . . . Nevertheless my perception was that the people were still very afraid. People didn't openly declare themselves in favor of Gabino Cué until three weeks before the election. That is when you started to see how people were going to vote. You started to see more bumper stickers on cars. People started to say, "If you vote for the PRI, it will be another six years. If you don't vote, then don't complain."*

Others in the wider social and political circle of Julio and Alonso shared their analysis of how and why the social conflict started, what it cost businesses, and the importance of the participation of civil society in the process. Their use of the term *civil society* referred to the middle- and upper-class citizens who had political, personal, and social capital that they could mobilize to be listened to. As relatively privileged members of civil society, they also had confidence in legal processes and in the importance of political participation through elections. While they viewed the government of Ulises Ruiz as extremely inept and corrupt and agreed that those in power needed to be removed, they still had confidence in the institutions of the state and felt that if competent, honest people could be placed in political office and staff positions, the state would function well. This was their hope with the new administration of Gabino Cué Monteagudo.

Like the artisans and small merchants, these entrepreneurs and business people also suffered economic losses, as did those who ran educational enterprises that served students and tourists. Lucero Topete (real name), director of the Instituto Cultural de Oaxaca (Oaxacan Cultural Institute), spoke with me about the ways her school was affected by the conflict in 2006. Her analysis of the roots of the conflict was similar to that of Alonso and Julio. She felt that one of the most important things that happened during 2006 was the participation of civil society in the form of people like Alonso and Julio, which was a first in Oaxacan politics. For her, this indicated a significant and hopeful awakening of broader society to the importance of political processes. She continues to demonstrate faith in elections and in the importance of formal political participation.

We met for breakfast on an outdoor terrace. Lucero is a fashionable dresser who is direct, quick, and very insightful. She served as the director of the Instituto Nacional de Antropolgía e Historia (National Institute of Anthropology and History) before founding the language school she now runs. Born in Mexico City, she did her graduate studies in Paris and then returned to Mexico City before marrying and moving to Oaxaca, where she has lived for thirty-three years. When we talked in July 2010, she began by addressing the reasons for the conflict:

The first factor in what happened is that the people of Oaxaca don't have the economic, work, or educational opportunities that they have the right to as

Mexican citizens. Most are poor with little hope of advancement. People feel obligated to migrate, not only to the United States, but also to Mexico City and to other parts of Mexico. There is very little hope here for most people. So what happened in 2006 happened on fertile ground because most of the people were already dissatisfied. . . .

With this kind of situation of absolute economic and social marginalization, it is very easy for any social movement, no matter what the goals or the ends, to pick up steam. The people are going to listen. On the other hand, we have the PRI government, which has been in power in this state for many years and which has many deficiencies, like corruption, the placement of inept people who have no experience or preparation into important jobs, and there is also total impunity for what goes on. You combine this with high levels of marginalization and you have fertile ground for a social movement.

. . . The teachers have been occupying the zócalo for twenty-five or thirty years now on an annual basis. I have lost track of when they started this. They are there to demand labor rights and also to call attention to the situation of the schools and to let people know that they don't have the kinds of resources and tools they need for teaching. Because of this situation, every year they sit in and occupy the zócalo. They have marches, close down businesses, and occupy the public spaces. Because of this, a lot of people in Oaxaca don't like them. It is hard for me to understand these types of actions.

We are the ones who suffer—the ones who are not part of the government and also not part of the teachers. We are stuck in the middle. We suffer from the mistakes of the state government but also for the situation that is created by the forms through which the teachers protest. . . . We understand the reasons behind their protest, but we really don't like the way they carry it out. . . .

But what happened in 2006 is absolutely the responsibility of Ulises Ruiz. He did a terrible job in handling the teachers. Every year there are negotiations, and every year it is one or two months and then it's over. But in 2006, with the attempt to evict them and the other feelings there were, it became a much larger movement. The result was that all Oaxacans lost out . . . the rich, the poor, and the miserable. We all lost out from what happened.

LYNN: What was lost or gained from 2006 economically, socially, politically?

LUCERO: . . . There were negative results that resulted in impoverishment for everyone. We have a business that is more or less established, and we are middle class. But we were hit hard. We ran up debts that we still haven't paid.

We managed to survive. But there are many poor people and really poor people who are much worse off than they were before 2006. One example would be the artisans.

For example, I know that in Teotitlán del Valle there are families who are large merchant families. They buy the textiles that the small producers make. When tourism ground to a halt and no one came to Oaxaca in 2006 and later, these families had acquired huge reserves of textiles until they couldn't buy any more. They were not able to keep buying from the small producers because they had no business. The weavers kept producing, but no one bought their textiles. These are absolutely poor people who don't have any prospects for improving their lives. Who are they going to sell to? This is happening all over in the towns in the central valleys of Oaxaca. . . .

But there is one light at the end of the tunnel. Civil society began to organize in Oaxaca. This is something we should have done much earlier, but it never came together in a serious and meaningful form. We began to have a meaningful movement of civil society. At least it was a beginning. Out of this movement came some very important figures, like the young person who was just elected as the mayor of Oaxaca, Luis Ugartechea Begué. He is a very well-prepared young man who has a business, and, thanks to this movement of civil society, he stepped forward and realized he needed to do something. I don't think that he would have come forward if it were not for the work of civil society [the group described earlier] that emerged in 2006. Because of the civil society group he participated in, he began to speak and to see the necessities there are and to express himself.

LYNN: *What do you see resulting from the recent election won by Gabino Cué Monteagudo?*

LUCERO: . . . *I think that now that we have had an election, that we won, and that some of these people who participated in the movement of 2006 have had the opportunity to see a change, this should teach them that the election is important. From my point of view it should show them that marching in the streets, closing down businesses, and shouting in the street is not the way to go. It should show that it is really important and is effective when people go out and vote and that there are real and positive changes.*

Lucero remained very hopeful and optimistic that Gabino Cué Monteagudo could lead a clean government that would benefit the majority of Oaxacans. She did, however, end with a comment about the responsibility of each person to be vigilant and hold governments accountable, an idea she held in common with many: "It is our responsibility to make sure that things don't reach the extremes they did [in 2006 and earlier]. . . . We can't just blame the government."

Summary

The social movement and conflict of 2006 produced several years of economic hardship for many in Oaxaca, hitting hardest those directly connected to tourism. While some have begun to recover, dozens of businesses remain closed in the city, and artisan communities are still trying to recuperate. Attempts by the Cué Monteagudo government in the summer of 2011 to revive tourism produced interesting results. For the first time, the Guelaguetza Popular and the state-sponsored Guelaguetza were allowed to coexist. Sección 22 and what remains of APPO carried out the fifth annual Guelaguetza Popular with more than thirty thousand attendees in the soccer stadium of the UABJO. The accompanying *calenda* parade of the Guelaguetza Popular, featuring music, dancers, floats, and fireworks, was also widely attended in and around the zócalo. The culminating display of fireworks celebrating APPO and Sección 22 was shot off in front of a huge sound-and-light show projected on the cathedral by the state government. A huge standing-room-only crowd of thousands shouted, "Viva la Sección 22! Viva el APPO! Viva Oaxaca!" following the lead of the activists on the loudspeakers. Many were out-of-town Mexican tourists.

The official Guelaguetza was also well attended, primarily by national tourists who watched the dances and also populated other street events sponsored to coincide with the Guelaguetza celebrations. The Ferria del Mescal (Mescal Fair) during this same period also drew thousands nightly to listen to music and sample food, drink, and crafts in Llano Park.

For the first time since 2006, significant numbers of tourists arrived in Oaxaca for these activities. The state government reported that during the two-week period surrounding the Guelaguetza celebrations, ninety-seven thousand people visited the city. Ninety-three thousand were from Mexico and four thousand were foreigners, primarily from the United States and Canada. These tourists were reported to have spent 191 million pesos (about U.S.$16 million) in the city on hotels, restaurants, services, and crafts, a figure up 20 percent from the same period in 2010 (Rodríguez 2011). Hotel occupancy rates were reportedly at 91 percent during the first week and 74 percent during the second week of the Guelaguetza period (Rodríguez

2011). While the increase in national tourism was viewed by many as a positive sign, others noted that the tourists spent less and didn't support artisans and higher-end hotels and restaurants the way that international tourists tend to do. Thus tourism is not dead but perhaps is being reconfigured.

Most interesting was the peaceful cultural and political coexistence of the two Guelaguetza celebrations and their supporters. Parallel celebrations marked a new phase in the culture of the city and also the secure institutionalization of the Guelaguetza Popular in the tourist economy. Many Mexican national tourists chose to attend that Guelaguetza over the state-sponsored one for the simple fact that there was no entrance fee. Once inside, however, they spent liberally at the food, drink, and crafts stalls that were in the performance stadium. The state-sponsored celebration charged 400 pesos (about U.S.$34.50) for the best seating sections and also provided some complimentary seating, according to the website the state set up to promote tourist activities (ViveOaxaca.org 2011).

For some, the links between the social conflict of 2006 and the formal political outcomes of 2010 were a cause for optimism. The electoral victory of Gabino Cué Monteagudo in July 2010 through a coalition of supporting organizations removed the PRI from power in Oaxaca after eighty years—the longest single reign of the PRI in state power in Mexico. Interestingly a wide range of people supported the electoral process in July 2010, and some were further motivated to seek political office. While Sección 22 as an organization did not formally endorse the Cué Monteagudo's candidacy, many teachers worked in the communities they teach and live in to encourage people to get out and vote. Some also acted as poll watchers.

Some active participants in APPO launched their own political campaigns and were elected to office. A few were appointed to posts in the Cué Monteagudo administration. Flavio Sosa, one of the three hundred members of the provisional collective council of APPO in 2006 who were arrested and imprisoned from December 2006 until April 2008, was elected as a *diputado local* (local representative) to the Oaxacan state congress in 2010 through the same coalition that brought Cué Monteagudo to the governorship. Adán López Santiago (profiled in chapter 5), who was one of the founders of Radio Zaachila in 2006 and an active APPO participant, went on to be elected mayor of the town in 2010 through the same coalition. In naming his cabinet in December 2010, Cué Monteagudo drafted Rufino Domínguez Santos, former general coordinator of the FIOB—which had supported APPO in Oaxaca and Los Angeles—as director of the Instituto Oaxaqueño de Atención al Migrante (Oaxacan Institute for Attention to Migrants). Adelfo Regino Montes, a longtime Mixe intellectual, lawyer, and activist for indigenous rights, was appointed *secretario de asuntos indígenas* (secretary of indigenous affairs) of the state of Oaxaca. Regino Montes was present at the first APPO congress on November 12, 2006, and attended the Asamblea de los Pueblos Zapotecos, Mixe, y Chatino de la Sierra Juárez (Assembly of the Zapotec, Mixe, and Chinantec Peoples of the Sierra Juárez), which elected representatives to the Popular Council of APPO. As a public supporter of APPO, his appointment in the Cué Monteagudo administration was particularly notable.

In the colonia of Santa María—profiled in chapter 3 in the discussion of barricades—one of the key barricade leaders, Alberto Cordo Bautista, went on to be elected president of the Comité de Vida Vecinal (Neighborhood Life Committee). He was part of a slate that was elected to the positions of secretary, treasurer, two representatives, and leaders of local commissions for ecology, health, and security. Some of the young people who defended the barricade in Santa María in 2006 with slingshots participated as poll watchers in their neighborhoods during the elections of 2010. The Neighborhood Life Committee of Santa María works with the city government, led by the *presidente municipal* (mayor) Luis Ugartechea Begué, who was a member of the civil society group known as Movimiento Ciudadano por la Justicia, Paz, y Desarollo con Dignidad para Oaxaca (Citizens' Movement for Justice, Peace, and Development with Dignity for Oaxaca). Ugartechea Begué was elected through the same political alliance that brought Governor Cué Monteagudo to power and is a member of the PAN political party.

While many of those interviewed in this chapter expressed pessimism about political parties, a significant number nevertheless opted to participate in the formal political process of the elections of 2010. Some saw this as the only way to remove the PRI from power and to continue working for change through the political opening created in 2006. Others, however—including some inside APPO—never supported the idea of participating in formal electoral processes or of paying attention to political campaigns. Instead they remained committed to the search for new and more participatory models of governance that emphasized the concepts of autonomy (self-governance) and the use of consensus decision making through assemblies. Chapter 9 highlights one of these groups, VOCAL, and a related multipurpose cultural and political space, La Casota, whose participants attempted to live out in their daily lives and practice some of the ideas expressed in the 2006 social movement.

8

Indigenous Activism

The Triqui Autonomous Municipality, APPO Juxtlahuaca,
and Transborder Organizing in APPO-L.A.

*The assembly is the foundation of indigenous self-government and in it
is sustained all of the community's political system. Therefore, we claim
it and place ourselves present in the current struggle of the people of
Oaxaca against the bad government.*

—Assembly of the Zapoteco, Mixe, and Chinanteco Peoples of the Sierra
 Juárez, San Pablo Guelataõ de Juárez, Oaxaca, November 19, 2006

*Oaxaca aguanta, el inmigrante se levanta [Oaxaca endures and the
immigrant rises up]. APPO-L.A.*

—Sign from protest in front of Mexican Consulate in Los Angeles,
 October 2006

Indigenous Oaxacans throughout the state played important roles in the Oaxaca social movement, despite media and academic coverage that focused on urban, *mestizo* participants.[1] The Sierra Norte, the Mixtec and Triqui regions, the Isthmus of Tehuantepec, and the Oaxacan indigenous immigrant communities of Los Angeles were other important sites of participation (see

Hernández Díaz 2009). Pan-ethnic indigenous organizing, as well as indigenous alliance building with nonindigenous organizations and communities, urban-rural political collaborations, and transnational indigenous organizing were all important parts of the social movement. The organizational goal of the APPO to make decisions in local and regional assemblies that then get generalized to a statewide assembly in a process of participatory democracy owes much to indigenous forms of governance that have a long and varied history in Oaxaca. Indigenous claims to local governmental and legal autonomy through customary indigenous law were codified into Oaxaca state law and official election procedures in the 1990s. These legislative changes allowed municipal-level and lower authorities to be selected in traditional electoral systems, usually in open meetings known as *asambleas*, a concept reflected in the structure and name of APPO (see Hernández-Díaz 2007: 47–57).

This chapter focuses on organized indigenous participation and responses to the Oaxaca social movement in Juxtlahuaca, Oaxaca, and in Los Angeles. There are two interrelated forms of indigenous citizenship. The first is indigenous autonomy, claimed through the exercise of customary law and forms of governance. In Juxtlahuaca, Triqui and Mixtec men and women were integral agents of APPO's occupation of the city hall and the four-month effort to provide some city services while fending off paramilitary harassment and repression. The most significant outcome of indigenous participation in Juxtlahuaca was the creation of a regional APPO organization which gave way to twenty Triqui communities declaring San Juan Copala an autonomous indigenous municipality in January 2007. They did this by announcing a new Triqui organization called Movimiento Unificación Lucha Triqui Independiente (Independent Movement of Triqui Unification and Struggle, MULTI), splintering from MULT. MULTI's declaration of political and legal independence from MULT built on and produced a severe and violent retaliation. Nevertheless the declaration of San Juan Copala as an autonomous municipality was an important effort to reclaim unified Triqui Baja territory and forms of governance that had been subdivided and subordinated to mestizo municipalities in 1948 by the Mexican government.

Overall APPO in western Oaxaca functioned as a pan-indigenous organizing space that built on the work of organizations such as the FIOB, the newly created MULTI, and other local organizations. The process brought Mixteca Baja and Mixteca Alta communities and organizations together with Triquis on a temporary basis. Leaders from this regional assembly also participated in their home communities and in the statewide APPO assembly. APPO Mixteca was a temporary pan-indigenous organizing space that provided unique experimental opportunities for discourses about indigenous rights and autonomy to be put into practice as groups of indigenous allies temporarily occupied city halls, took control of the celebration of national holidays, and attempted to deliver some city services.

Within this four-month experiment, there were also important lessons about gender. These included confronting the limits on women's abilities to step into leadership roles outside of their communities due to cultural expectations about the gendered division of labor and the ongoing use of pejoratives against women as a still legitimate strategy for discrediting women's political activism. Within this organizational space, however, some women also gained important experience with participating in communal affairs. This experience spilled over into subsequent organizing, such as the establishment of the Autonomous Municipality of San Juan Copala, the creation of a Triqui radio station with women's participation, and a movement of Triqui women who occupied the zócalo of Oaxaca to draw attention to violence and displacement (De Marinis 2011, 2013).

The second form of indigenous citizenship highlighted here is transnational indigenous citizenship, combining traditions from Oaxaca with strategies for citizenship that cut across geographic, ethnic, legal, economic, and social borders. An analysis of APPO Los Angeles provides an important window on how transnational indigenous organizing and transborder communities were important vectors for APPO organizing outside of Mexico. The emotional intensity of rallies in MacArthur Park in Los Angeles, where speeches by APPO leaders were broadcast by cell phone to thousands listening in the park, speaks to the power of oral testimony to connect transborder citizens to their communities and motivate them to act. The organizing that APPO did between Los Angeles and Oaxaca also allowed immigrant Oaxacans to connect with their families and communities through financial donations and emotional and political support. I offer a case study of how the process of transnational indigenous citizenship can work through bridging local understandings of citizenship with postnational forms of political cooperation and participation.

Regional History and the Context of the MULT–MULTI Conflict

In 2005 the municipality (county) of Santiago Juxtlahuaca had an estimated population of 33,400 people. Of these, 71.3 percent spoke an indigenous language, primarily Mixtec and Triqui (nuestro-mexico.com 2013, INEGI 2005:

48). The city serves as a commercial center for the region, and the municipality includes over forty *agencias* (smaller administrative units) under its jurisdiction, as well as other smaller hamlets. The regional market is held every Thursday and Friday and is a major crossroads for the exchange of a wide range of goods from many different parts of the state of Oaxaca as well as from the neighboring states of Puebla, Veracruz, and Guerrero. Many of the forty communities under Juxtlahuaca's jurisdiction run transport and taxi services in and out of the city, making it a hub for politics as well as business. It has a thirty-two-bed public hospital that serves as the only significant place to seek medical treatment for many communities.

Before examining the process by which local alliances were formed to create APPO in 2006 and how they later blew apart in an ongoing conflict between MULT and MULTI, it is important to consider some of the relevant ethnic, political, and economic history of the region. I share this history specifically to provide important contextual information underlying the political conflict between MULT and MULTI. I begin in the nineteenth century.[2]

After Mexican independence, the administrative unit of the district of Juxtlahuaca was decreed in 1868. In 1889 the town of Juxtlahuaca was raised to the category of *villa*, the head of the district (Instituto Nacional para el Federalismo y el Desarrollo Municipal, Gobierno del Estado de Oaxaca 2009). In this capacity, it became a regionally important center of governance and justice as well as commerce. With its designation as a villa, the center of Juxtlahuaca became more populated with nonindigenous Mexicans, who typically worked in the commercial, legal, and government sectors. Unlike communities in the central valleys of Oaxaca, where indigenous peoples maintained control over administrative town centers, the center of Juxtlahuaca became dominated by nonindigenous families, some of whom continued to claim they were of Spanish descent. Many neighborhoods had and continue to have a strong Mixtec presence, but over time the Mixtec and Triqui people became concentrated in the towns and hamlets around the town of Juxtlahuaca.

In 1826, shortly after independence, San Juan Copala became a municipality, equivalent to the administrative category of county. López Barcenas argues that two new municipalities—San Juan Copala, which was created in the Triqui Baja territory in 1826, and Chicahuaxtla, created in 1825 in the adjoining Triqui Alta territory—"were not a concession of the new political class towards the Triquis, but rather a conquest on their part with their active participation in the War of Independence" (2009: 63). This important part of regional ethnic history established a base for administrative autonomy for the Triqui population after centuries of domination during both the pre-Hispanic and the colonial period. The idea of Triqui autonomy remained alive and well for almost two centuries. Unfortunately the Triqui themselves did not remain politically unified throughout this time.

Although the Triqui had successfully resisted Spanish colonialism and even defended their territory in two wars (1832 and 1843) against the independent Mexican state, by the late nineteenth century the Mexican state had successfully penetrated the region. Using a strategy of dividing the Triqui territory and fomenting political competition among different communities and leaders, the Mexican state focused much attention on controlling the Triqui region politically and economically. The postrevolution introduction and commercialization of coffee in the region created a private land market that existed alongside communal land tenure and increased economic competition among the Triquis. Coffee also brought mestizo merchants to the region. The merchants made handsome profits, according to López Barcenas, and paid Triqui producers with "cattle for their fiestas, with alcohol to get them drunk, and surely with arms. It is not a coincidence that the greatest number of armed conflicts exist in the same communities where the most coffee is produced" (2009: 89, my translation). As pointed out by James Daria (2013), the Mexican post-revolutionary state's focus on promoting ejidos led to the further marginalization of indigenous communities such as San Juan Copala whose land holdings were in the form of communal lands. Whereas the Copalenses struggled to preserve the integrity of their communally held territory, the ease with which surrounding communities were granted ejidos increased the occurrence and severity of conflict in the region as neighboring communities encroached on territory argued to belong to Copala. Daria's focus on the agrarian history of Copala adds much-needed information (2013).

The accounts of Tibón (1961), Huerta Ríos (1981), Martell Ramírez (1967), and López Barcenas (2009) leave no doubt that armed conflict, drinking, and competition for land and coffee profits fueled by mestizo merchants who provided arms and alcohol created high levels of robbery, violence, and revenge in the Triqui region during the first half of the twentieth century. Regional racism among mestizo merchants and authorities characterized the Triquis as "unos mañosos, mentirosos, ladrones y flojos" (obstinant, lying thieves and lazy; Martell Ramírez 1967: 94).

Apparently the increased local divisions and violence were not sufficient to dispel the fears of Oaxacan state political authorities about the potential threat of Triqui political unity and mobilization. In 1940 the municipio of

San Andrés Chicahuaxtla in the Mixteca Alta was subordinated and incorporated into the municipio of Putla de Guerrero. This placed the ceremonial center of the Triqui Alta region under the control of the mestizos who ran the government of Putla. Eight years later, in 1848, the municipality of San Juan Copala came to the same fate. After seventy-eight years as a unified ethnic and administrative unit, the historic Triqui Baja territory of San Juan Copala and its communities were divided among the three majority mestizo municipalities of Putla de Guerrero, Santiago Juxtlahuaca, and Constancia del Rosario.

The town of San Juan Copala itself was demoted from the status of a municipio head to an agencia (subcounty administrative unit) and put under the rule of mestizo authorities in Santiago Juxtlahuaca. San Juan Copala remained subordinated to Juxtlahuaca until January 2007, when the Autonomous Municipality of San Juan Copala was declared by MULTI. This declaration, however, was also a political declaration of exit by members of MULTI from MULT.

The story of the MULT begins in the 1970s in the community of San Juan Copala. The ongoing struggle for political control of San Juan Copala as a historic ceremonial and political center is at the root of the current MULT-MULTI conflict there. In 1975, in the community of San Juan Copala, a group of young Triqui leaders created the Cooperative Club and pledged to try to unify the region and bring peace. Their objective was to buy corn in bulk and sell it to Triqui consumers at a lower price than the mestizo intermediaries offered. In addition, they also sought to use cooperatives as a way of commercializing Triqui goods such as bananas and coffee. The group of men that formed this initiative appears to have had good intentions aimed at improving the economic situation of their community. The National Indigenist Institute had an office in San Juan Copala and supported the Cooperative Club. During this time the Cooperative Club also acted to defend the communal lands of San Juan Copala from mestizo invaders from neighboring communities—some of which were ejidos.

In 1976 a community authority who was a founder of the Cooperative Club was assassinated. That same year, a group of Triqui bilingual promoters affiliated themselves with the PRI. Other leaders sought protection within a national peasant organization, the Central Independiente de Obreros Agícolas y Campesinmos (Independent Federation of Agricultural Workers and Peasants, CIOAC). In 1978 the Mexican army established a permanent military post in San Juan Copala. In 1979 Triquis who were affiliated with the CIOAC also affiliated with the PRI, uniting the two groups.

That same year saw the emergence of the first Triqui political organization, the Comité de Lucha Triqui. This group affiliated in 1981 with the Coordinadora Nacional Plan de Ayala (National Coordinator "Plan Ayala," CNPA), a national confederation of leftist peasant groups. MULT was born in 1981, in affiliation with the CNPA and with the support of COCEI. According to several people I interviewed in 2008 from the Copala region, MULT was formed in part as a response to the violence and repression experienced by PRI-affiliated authorities in Copala and elsewhere. In the late 1980s MULT affiliated with the PRD, while some Triqui leaders opposed to the PRD remained affiliated with the PRI. The affiliation between the MULT and the PRD lasted until 2003, when, together with another organization, MULT created its own political party, called the Partido Unidad Popular (Popular Unity Party, PUP). Throughout the 1980s and into the 1990s political assassinations and revenge killings became commonplace in the Triqui region. During this time MULT also established a significant state and national political presence through large marches, rallies, and other events. During this two-decade period, MULT advocated for freedom for political prisoners, the resolution of land conflicts, and an equitable development of resources.

In 1994 leaders of the PRI Triqui faction formed the Unidad de Bienestar Social para la Región Triqui (Unity for the Well-Being of the Triqui Region, UBISORT). By this time the leadership of MULT had passed to a second generation of men who, according to many observers, appeared to be focused on gaining personal political power and channeling resources to their own pockets and those of their supporters. In 1996 Hector Sánchez, who would later lead PUP, and Heriberto Pazas Ortiz, a MULT leader in the city of Oaxaca, were wounded in a public ambush. After 2000 other leaders of MULT and of UBISORT were killed in ambushes, and revenge killings continued. While the ruthless control tactics exercised by the authorities over members of the MULT were open knowledge in local communities, they were seldom discussed outside.

On November 20, 2005, the sons of two Triqui leaders were killed: Misael Alejandro Merino, son of the MULTI leader and founder Timoteo Alejandro Ramirez from the community of Yosoyuxi, and Abel Francisco Herrera Martínez, whose father was a leader in UBISORT. Both had recently returned from the United States to participate in their communities' annual saint's day fiestas (López Barcenas 2009: 258–59). According to López Barcenas, the bullet that struck Misael Alejandro Merino was meant for his father. After Timoteo had buried his son, he went to MULT leaders to ask for the arrest of the people who killed his son and other compensation for damages.[3] After repeated encounters with MULT leadership with no results, Timoteo and others decided there was no room for them in MULT and decided to abandon the organization (265).

On April 20, 2006, at a press conference in Mexico City, MULTI announced its birth (López Barcenas 2009: 270–72).[4] The exit of MULTI members from MULT came with public accusations against MULT of channeling government resources meant for communities into the pockets of leaders and into the organization. MULT leaders denied the accusations and were angered (see López Barcenas 2009: 274).

After these political exchanges, new rounds of violence began. Adrian Bautista, a municipal authority of Yosoyuxi, was gunned down outside Juxtlahuaca on May 11, 2006. Then six-year-old Heriberto Ramírez Merino of Agua Fria was killed on May 20 while he and his father were near their house. May was also marked by gunfire exchanges between UBISORT and MULT in San Juan Copala, resulting in the death of another child, Albino Fuentes Martínez, who was playing chess at a table outside of the Agencia Municipal (López Barcenas 2009: 281).

Then this complex set of divisions took another turn. In the summer of 2006 UBISORT abandoned the PRI and joined in an alliance with MULTI in opposition to MULT. (This ended in November 2009, when UBISORT realigned with MULT against MULTI; see below.) The 2006–9 MULTI-UBISORT alliance against MULT resulted in substantial bloodshed. As described by Blanche Petrich (2008), a reporter for *La Jornada*, "Fourteen communities are aligned with MULT-PUP, and 18 with the autonomous [MULTI]. The cemeteries of each community receive, in equal parts, the bodies of new victims, from one of the other sides, fallen in terrible ambushes that are carried out by hired gunmen with machine guns."

The larger political conflict in Oaxaca between MULT and MULTI-UBISORT became even more complex when MULT gunmen were rumored to be helping Governor Ulises Ruiz Ortiz carry out his program of repression. Three of the first victims of the Oaxaca conflict were MULTI members who were on their way to an APPO meeting in August 2006.[5] MULTI leaders blamed the deaths on Ruiz Ortiz, a MULT leader, and the leader of PUP (Vélez 2006).

During the summer of 2006 MULTI joined APPO and marched in Juxtlahuaca in opposition to the governor. There they united with Mixtecs from FIOB and other organizations. Together, MULTI, FIOB, UBISORT, and other local organizations carried off a successful occupation of the Juxtlahuaca city hall that lasted almost four months.

The Birth of APPO in the Mixteca

Francisco Alfaro Arzola (real name) wipes his forehead to brush aside some hair and sweat as he sits down in the back room of the FIOB offices in Juxtlahuaca. The FIOB is a community-based organization and a coalition of indigenous organizations, communities, and individuals settled in the Mexican states of Oaxaca, Baja California Norte, and Baja California Sur and in the state of California in the United States—often known as the territory of Oaxacalifornia. Since its founding in Los Angeles in 1991, FIOB has focused on the promotion, training, and organization of the indigenous communities of origin of its membership as well as programs and organizing activities focused on the well-being of indigenous migrants who are outside of their home communities. In 2006 its mission statement stated that the purpose of the organization was to "contribute to the development and self-determination of the migrant and non-migrant indigenous communities, as well to the struggle for the defense of the human rights with justice and gender equity at the binational level" (FIOB 2006). The FIOB has regional offices in Oaxaca City, Juxtlahuaca, and Tijuana and in Los Angeles, Santa Maria, Greenfield, and Fresno, California.

✳ VIDEOCLIP 8.1: http://dx.doi.org/10.7264/N3HT2M77

It is a warm and humid afternoon, and sweat beads appear on his neck and begin to drip down to the collar of his blue button-down shirt. Francisco is a Mixtec schoolteacher, indigenous leader, and longtime participant in Oaxacan movements for social justice. At the time we talked in July 2007, he was the statewide coordinator for FIOB and a counselor in the APPO statewide assembly representing the Mixtec region. In Francisco's retelling of the history of APPO in the Mixtec region as well as in other areas of Oaxaca, such as the capital city, past indigenous and popular organizing played a crucial role in the formation of APPO in June 2006.

In the decades of the 1970s and the 1980s, there were social movement organizations, but we could count them on the fingers of both hands. Now we see more than five hundred social movement organizations. I really see APPO as the sum of these organizational experiences. Many of them were regional, and now we have seen how they were able to come together in a statewide movement.

Francisco is part of a group of Mixtec and Triqui movements and organizations that came together to form city and regional APPO committees in the summer of 2006, after APPO had been formally launched in Oaxaca City in June. The FIOB — long an ally in progressive causes and with a significant number of teachers in its ranks — published a manifesto on June 6, 2006, outlining its political position of support for the teachers' movement of Oaxaca, and urged the governor to answer their petitions for school lunches, classroom construction, and other demands. After the dramatic June 14 action in which poorly trained state police were unable to evict the teachers from their sit-in, FIOB and other indigenous and left organizations in the Mixtec regions took more decisive action. The FIOB had participated in the first megamarch on June 2, 2006, and in the second megamarch five days later. After the June 14 repression, some members of FIOB joined the growing sit-in in the center of Oaxaca and joined in the third large march, which took place on June 16, one day before the formation of APPO. According to Francisco:

We acted under the mandate of the resolutions of APPO. One of the resolutions was to broaden the struggle to other regions and sectors. So we in FIOB, along with others, decided to initiate takeovers of city halls. I participated directly in the takeover of the city hall of Huajuapan de León, together with other people from Juxtlahuaca, Tlaxiaco, and Nochixtlán. So what we did was to take over these city halls, get the word out about what was going on in the capital city, and get people involved. One of our key tasks was to inform people about what was going on. All mainstream media at that time was controlled by the state. The second thing that we knew we had to do was to begin forming the bases for popular assemblies in neighborhoods, in town, in counties, and in the region. We also knew that we had to figure out how to take over the media.

After the third large march on June 16, FIOB activists began to organize actively in the Mixtec region. Centolia Maldonado (real name), who was a longtime leader for the FIOB in the Juxtlahuaca region until the fall of 2009, became a key organizer, particularly of women in the region as well as in the communities where FIOB had a strong base.

After the third large march we were so indignant at the way the teachers had been treated and what was happening to them that we started to go from town to town to tell people in the communities what was happening. Everything people were hearing on the commercial radio stations was much manipulated. After we started to talk with people, we received a favorable response from people. Once they knew what was going on in Oaxaca City, they wanted to support the teachers. This was important because by the time of the fourth megamarch at the end of June, it was not only people from the FIOB who went, but also the municipal authorities from various communities went with us. The Mixtec region went to Oaxaca City in significant numbers to partici-pate in these and other marches. That is how we got started. Then we decided that we needed to organize in our own regions.

✳ VIDEOCLIP 8.2: http://dx.doi.org/10.7264/N3D21VHT

Organizers in FIOB, along with activists from MULTI, Sección 22, and other organizations, came together to organize occupations of city halls and to try to consolidate local APPO committees.[6] Their first target was the city of Huajuapan de León. At the end of September 2006 some FIOB organizers and others shifted their focus from Huajuapan de Léon to engineering an occupation of the city hall of Santiago Juxtlahuaca. There the mayor was a PRI stalwart and was viewed as a significant regional supporter of Governor Ruiz Ortiz. If APPO supporters could take and hold the city hall of Juxtla-huaca, it could be an important sign of the weakening of the PRI and of the governor's hold on the outlying regions of the state. This would help to un-dergird APPO's strategy of having the state declared ungovernable, which could facilitate the removal of the governor by the Mexican Senate (the only legal path to unseat a governor).

Occupation of the Juxtlahuaca City Hall and APPO Juxtlahuaca

At the end of September 2006 the occupation of the Juxtlahuaca city hall was supported by activists from FIOB, MULTI, and other organizations as well as by independent citizens and local authorities from a wide range of communities. One elected official who was in city hall when the occupation happened told me in 2007, "Well, they told me that they were going to take over the city hall, I closed my office. A lot of people came into the city hall after they announced the occupation and people just locked their offices. I was the last one here, but out of respect for the movement, I closed my of-fice. I continued to work outside in another location." The majority of the participants came from communities that work with FIOB and MULTI, in-cluding Yucunicoco, Agua Fria Juxtlahuaca, Agua Fria Copala, Santa Maria Asuncón, Vista Hermosa, San Juan Mixtepec, San Agustín Atenango, San Miguel Tlacotepec, Paxtlahuaca, San Juan Copala, Yusuyuxi, and San Juan Oaxtepec.

Because the city of Juxtlahuaca was run by officials elected from the PRI, the takeover was not easily maintained. After declaring themselves APPO Juxtlahuaca, activists had to initiate a serious security effort as well as begin to carry out the organizational responsibilities of the municipality, such as collecting garbage, administering the large regional market in town, and making sure that local buses and taxis were able to operate. While APPO occupied city hall, some of Juxtlahuaca's elected officials from the PRI set up shop in the local Casa de Cultura. In essence the town had two parallel governing groups attempting to maintain power and to at least partially administer the community. Unhappy with the loss of their administrative office, PRI officials also mounted a serious harassment and opposition campaign against APPO. From the first night of their occupation, APPO activists in Juxtlahuaca had to be on guard and work constantly to maintain the control they had gained. A majority of the people who were defending the city hall occupation and administering the work to be done were women from MULTI and FIOB, and representatives from Sección 22 in Juxtlahuaca. Triqui women were particularly important in these efforts.

People held the city hall around the clock. Their presence required an elaborate cooking operation, the maintenance of places to sleep, and a twenty-four-hour security detail in the town center and in the outlying neighborhoods. In order to prevent incursions by sympathizers of the PRI mayor and the governor, APPO activists set up barricades and blocked the entrances to the community every night. Ana Ruth Méndez (real name), who worked for FIOB at the time, described her participation in some of these activities.

Every night we made patrols around the community. We would meet in teams and go in a vehicle around town to see how the situation was. Some of us always slept in the city hall and others stayed there on guard all night long. We also had to close off the roads into and out of the community sometimes, when there were rumors that the governor was sending people to remove us from the city hall.

✳ VIDEOCLIP 8.3: http://dx.doi.org/10.7264/N38913SG

In addition to holding city hall and keeping the city secure, APPO activists were constantly organizing meetings, marches, and assemblies. As described by Centolia Maldonado, Triqui women from MULTI were very important to maintaining most of the operations of APPO in Juxtlahuaca:

Figure 8.1 Triqui women marching through Juxtlahuaca, 2006. DOI: 10.7264/ N3PN93H3. Photo by Jaciel Vallavicencio

"The MULTI was there and the majority of them were women. This is an organization that has a lot of organizational force and convocation power. They would send delegations of women from one community at a time that would stay for a whole week."

During October and November APPO Juxtlahuaca seemed to have won over a significant part of the regional community. At least one local PRI official who was ousted in the occupation of city hall expressed his sympathy for APPO in Juxtlahuaca, as well as his understanding of why the movement had formed. Mario Ruiz felt that the PRI under the governor had not done a good job in administering services and providing people in the state with what they needed. He hinted that even at the local level, corruption and mishandling of funds and resources was a common occurrence. If one didn't know better, the following testimony could have come directly from an APPO activist, not from a local PRI official:

I believe that APPO arose because the people were tired of being trampled on. They were tired of officials taking money that belonged to the municipality, of using government resources for things that don't help people and not focusing on the necessities of the population here. I think this is why we got an APPO here. I actually think that movements are good because the government doesn't pay attention if they don't go and sit in and occupy some of their offices. They don't give the people anything, and whenever we politely ask, we receive nothing. If the people don't demand a response, they don't get it.

While this official expressed heartfelt sympathy for the movement, others were overtly hostile and attempted to use their connections to the governor to throw the APPO activists out of the city hall. According to APPO activists, the local PRI mayor, who had been ousted from his office, continually organized against them. On one occasion he assembled a large group of PRI supporters from surrounding communities to confront them and try to root them out. APPO activists found out about the plans because some of the towns where there are APPO supporters also have PRI supporters. It is not hard to hear the news of what is going to happen the next day. Jaciel Villavicencio (real name), a teacher, radio host, and cultural activist in neighboring Tecomaxtlahuaca, was an integral part of the group of people who worked to maintain control of the occupation of the Juxtlahuaca city hall. He described learning of the attempt by the PRI to oust them and what they did to organize against it:

There were just a few of us who were together when we heard about this rumor. The other two were from the Triqui zone. We realized that they are going to try to forcibly evict us. So we said, "What are we going to do? We have to organize ourselves tomorrow with a lot of force so that they are not able to evict us." We went to the community of Yosoyuxi and spoke with the leaders there, and they said, "You know what, tomorrow we are going to mobilize people." . . . And boy, were they able to get people there! By eight or nine in the morning there were about eight hundred people there with us in the city hall. There we designed a strategy together to control all the entry points to the city. We set up barricades and checkpoints everywhere there was access to the city hall. . . . They didn't realize what we were doing. No sooner had they begun their march, when they saw that we had them barricaded in and they couldn't get anywhere near us.

✳ VIDEOCLIP 8.4: http://dx.doi.org/10.7264/N34M92GX

The Juxtlahuaca APPO continued to occupy the city hall through the month of November. At the beginning of November they set up an altar honoring the dead, in keeping with the custom of Todos Santos. The altar, which was set up in city hall, inspired widespread participation. Many in the community brought flowers, bread, and sweets and joined in maintaining the vigil. They lit candles for those who had died in the conflict with the state government. Many who visited the altar shared food, discussion, and more with one another. For some, it offered unique interethnic experiences of sharing. For Jaciel Villavicencio, who does not identify as indigenous, this was one of the most unifying and touching events of his experience in Juxtlahuaca:

We made our offering and set up our altar. People from the market brought us bread, and this was very satisfying. We lit candles for those who had already died in the conflict with the government. We lit the candles for their souls. We were there day and night. For all practical purposes we were living in the city hall at that point. I think at that moment was when we all really started to trust one another. I had one experience with the Triqui compañeras that really showed me how much they cared for me, someone who was not in their ethnic group or community.

They came with little bags of things like herbs. They took out copal incense, camphor, some aguardiente [liquor], and they began to pray over me and to carry out a limpia [ritual cleansing]. They were praying over me to protect me from the bad vibes of Ulises Ruiz Ortiz. They said they didn't want anything to happen to me. Then they all came to my house later and took a bath and relaxed a little bit. Then we went back to the occupation of city hall. This experience was very powerful for me. We don't often share these kinds of experiences in daily life.

Organizing as Women within APPO Juxtlahuaca, Radio Copala, and Beyond: Gender Equality?

While a majority of the participants in the marches, barricades, support teams, and occupation of the Juxtlahuaca city hall were women, their presence was often questioned by the opposition PRI activists. This was at the local level in Juxtlahuaca. Organizations like FIOB and MULTI encouraged women's participation at this level, but at the regional APPO meetings the presence of women was much sparser. Handling the insults that were often hurled at them by PRI activists, and their lack of adequate representation in APPO leadership meetings, were just two of the challenges facing FIOB female organizers and Triqui women from MULTI who participated in APPO.

During one march, a local employee who worked for the PRI government began to insult the indigenous people who were marching, particularly the Triqui women. Because a majority of the marchers were women,
one of the tactics used against them by PRI supporters was to yell insults at
them as they walked by. Anna Ruth Méndez recalled:

*They would always shout profanities at us, the women. They would say things
like "Damn whores, why don't you go back to your houses and do your house-
work? What are you doing here losing time instead of working in your houses?
Don't you have any husbands who can make you sit down and be quiet?" . . .
We in the FIOB always make a commitment to not respond to aggression,
because this is just what the government wants. They want to provoke us into
responding. There was one time where there was a confrontation. . . . Someone who worked for the PRI mayor of Juxtlahuaca shoved a Triqui woman
really hard and yelled a bunch of profanities at her. A man from Copala saw
what happened, and he pulled out a pistol. He was going to go and shoot him,
but he just hit him instead. We were glad that it was nothing more than a
punch.*

Gender issues came up at other times during APPO organizing in the
Juxtlahuaca region. Women provided food, protection, and support to those
maintaining limited services, such as garbage collection and the smooth
functioning of the market, but at APPO's regional meetings in Juxtlahuaca,
which leaders of different organizations would attend, the only women who
were present were usually from FIOB; none of the other organizations sent
women to the meetings.

According to Centolia Maldonado, larger meetings that covered the entire Mixtec region had very few women as well. The first statewide APPO
congress included many women, and they were interested in ensuring that
gender equity was taken seriously within APPO's representational structure.
While it was an exciting idea for Centolia in practice, it was very hard to
realize. Here she describes this process and her reluctant analysis of the difficulty of sending equal numbers of men and women to regional and statewide APPO meetings:

*When I went to the first statewide congress of APPO in October 2006, there
were more women. One of the things that impressed me was the presence
of some very strong women leaders in the debates who wanted to discuss
gender equity in APPO. They were proposing that APPO should be made up*

of 50 percent women and 50 percent men. . . . They wanted to have a shared leadership to avoid having all the responsibility fall on one person.

What happened when we broke the meeting down into smaller regional groups was that in my group from the Juxtlahuaca region people said, "No, we won't get 50 percent representation from women leaders." At first I said, "Yes, yes we can." But as we talked people said, "Well there are women from the FIOB, but where are the women leaders from the rest of the organizations?" Even the men from my own organization questioned this, saying, "When we go back to Juxtlahuaca, will we be able to get 50 percent of the leaders to be women?" I realized that the reality was that we could not. We have large numbers of women at the bases of our organizations, but we don't have very many leaders who can function outside of their own communities.

One year after their experience in APPO, several women leaders from FIOB collaborated in a research project with two anthropologists to determine what the obstacles were to better supporting and developing women and youth as a part of their leadership structure (Romero-Hernández et al. 2013). The research, based on focus groups and interviews, revealed that there are two kinds of leadership within the structure of the organization. One type is "political leadership," the charismatic public leader who is often a public spokesperson and knows not only how to function on a broad basis within the movement but can also relate to political parties, elected officials, and those in other social movements and organizations. The second type is "local community leadership," exhibited by those who have a high level of knowledge about local issues, strong networks of people at the local level, and who can mobilize these networks for a wide range of purposes, from community-development projects such as producing chickens for sale to organizing marches that put pressure on state and local political officials. While it is often assumed that the two types of leadership are gendered—with men serving as political leaders and women serving as community leaders—the research team found that in fact there are women who are political leaders and some men, particularly in Juxtlahuaca, who are community leaders. The challenge for the organization is to figure out how to integrate these two types of leadership and train young people—women and men—in both types.

The experience of Centolia and other women from FIOB in APPO led them to militate within their own organization for some rethinking of how leadership was learned, delegated, assumed, and acknowledged. One of the results of their research project is a plan for leadership schools to offer courses that take into account regional variations in gender roles. The curriculum of the leadership schools will work from the specific context in which ethnic, gender, and generational inequalities are played out in different geographical locations where the FIOB has members. The schools will train women and youth in local specifics, as well as in the skills defined as part of extralocal political leadership.

Another group (discussed in more detail below) in which women took on additional leadership as a result of their participation in APPO was the Triqui organization MULTI. They launched their community radio station on January 20, 2008, the one-year anniversary of the announcement of the Municipio Autónomo of San Juan Copala. Known as La voz que rompe el silencio (The Voice That Breaks the Silence), 94.9 Radio Copala was initiated with the help of the Centro de Apoyo Comunitario Trabajando Unidos, A.C. (Center for Community Support Working Together, CACTUS). With instruments donated by CACTUS, local youth and others built the station *cabina*, or broadcasting booth, in the rear of the city hall. A group of six young people, three women and three men, was formed to produce broadcasts and serve as hosts. According to Radio Copala's coordinator Jorge Albino Ortíz in an interview with John Gibler in 2007, "The radio station decided to have three men and three women working at the radio because one of its primary tasks was to encourage women's participation in the new autonomous municipality of San Juan Copala" (Gibler 2008). Yanira Vásquez, Felecitas Martínez Sánchez, and Teresa Bautista Merino were the three women in the production group. According to Yanira, "When we started, we felt really excited to have a radio station in Copala. . . . Women do not participate much and we were just beginning to promote women's participation in assemblies and meetings and to include their perspectives and interviews about how they see what is happening in the region" (Gibler 2008). On April 7 Teresa and Felecitas, who were in the backseat of a car driven by Felecita's cousin, Faustino Vásquez, were killed in an ambush when gunmen shot out the back of the car (Gibler 2008). Faustino was wounded, and three other passengers—Faustino's wife and two young children—survived. Police found twenty spent shells from AK-47s by the side of the road (Gibler 2008). The assassinations were roundly condemned by many human rights groups. According to most observers, the victims were further casualties in the MULTI-MULT conflict.

Natalia De Marinis conducted research in San Juan Copala in 2008 for a master's thesis, spending time every day in the radio station over a period of several months. When she arrived on May 3, 2008, Radio Copala was transmitting the Women's Revolutionary Law of the EZLN, which lays out a series of rights for indigenous women. According to De Marinis, women's rights were one of the themes featured regularly on Radio Copala broadcasts. Other themes included human rights, indigenous rights, interviews with local authorities of the autonomous municipio, stories told by elders to a younger person, and announcements about community fiestas and ritual activity (De 2009: 115–16). Young people also broadcast news summaries in Triqui in the morning and evening. Radio Copala functioned from 2008 until the beginning of 2010, when a state of siege was imposed on San Juan Copala by armed members of UBISORT, who broke ranks with the autonomous municipality and MULTI (see Paris Pombo 2010; Valle 2010).

The Triqui Autonomous Municipality of San Juan Copala and Further Conflict: 2007–2012

While Mixtec members of FIOB decided to hold on to the city halls of Juxtlahuaca and Huajuapan de León, Triqui members of MULTI and UBISORT of APPO Juxtlahuaca made a different decision. Once the city hall of Juxtlahuaca was lost in December 2006, they returned to their community and, after discussions with community elders, decided to declare their community an autonomous municipality, following the examples of dozens of communities in Chiapas and elsewhere. One of the significant ideas of autonomous indigenous municipalities is to unify ethnic communities that have been dispersed by administrative divisions which often pit people from the same ethnic group against one another. The architects of the autonomous municipality hoped to be able to unify dispersed communities and encourage them to work together to create grassroots development, media, and education projects. They also sought to eliminate the presence of the Mexican army and state police and introduce community policing. Finally, they hoped to reintroduce a council of elders as a significant form of governance, along with community assemblies.

On January 1, 2007, San Juan Copala declared itself to be an autonomous municipality that unified twenty of the thirty-six Triqui communities.[7] The combined population of indigenous Triquis in these communities is about fifteen thousand. The remaining population and communities are under the authority of MULT. On January 20 the indigenous municipality of San Juan Copala (at that time composed of MULTI and UBISORT leaders) installed its new government by presenting their political leaders with the traditional *bastones de mando*, ceremonial canes that signify community authority.[8] Representatives from FIOB, as well as from many of the other organizations that made up APPO Mixteca, were present.

Two of the most important projects of the autonomous municipality of San Juan Copala were their community police force and their community radio station. Jorge, a community spokesman for the autonomous government, said, "In Copala we had a military garrison, state auxiliary police, and ministerial police, but we never had peace in the region. That is why the community decided to get rid of them all because we didn't get any benefits from having them here. The auxiliary police became bodyguards for the leaders and caciques of the region" (Gasparello 2008). In an oblique reference to MULT, this spokesman signals the violence that wracked the area.

While San Juan Copala was unified as an autonomous municipality, it was also a political unit in opposition to MULT. San Juan Copala itself and some of the other hamlets and communities included in the autonomous municipality were divided between MULT and MULTI and engaged in a deadly series of conflicts. On a research trip I made to the region in the summer of 2008, and from interviews I conducted with five people who witnessed the MULT and MULTI conflict, I learned that MULT has been the source of significant violence for long periods of time and that MULTI activists were also not without blame, at least initially. According to these witnesses, in order to achieve unity in San Juan Copala, MULTI sympathizers removed MULT supporters from their houses and kicked them out of the community. Thus one result of municipal autonomy in San Juan Copala is a group of displaced families who have had to find other places to resettle.

The second important project of the San Juan Copala autonomous municipality was the formation of a community radio station, 94.9 FM Radio Copala, "The Voice That Breaks the Silence." Jorge Albino Ortíz, the coordinator of Radio Copala, had a program on Radio La Ley, one of the radio stations that APPO took over. During his experience with Radio La Ley, he realized the organizing power of radio. "We observed how the radio called people to participate in various actions of the movement and we wanted to do something like that in our region," he stated in an interview (Gibler 2009: 227). Since Teresa Bautista Merino and Felecitas Martinez Sánchez were murdered in April 2008, there have been many protests and calls for investigation. The crime has not yet been solved.[9]

The pattern of violence exhibited in the killing of Felecitas and Teresa is hauntingly familiar to anyone who lives in the region. During the past twenty years, violence has permeated the Triqui region. During the past ten years, it has come to increasingly include vengeance rapes and killings of women. In June 2008 two more Triqui women were disappeared near Juxtlahuaca. In interviews with people living in several Triqui communities in August 2008, I found that there was a common consensus, regardless of whether people sympathized with MULT or MULTI, that women and girls had become fair game in the escalating violence in the region. This is occurring at the same time that Triqui and other women have begun to establish a presence not only in the base of the organizations that make up APPO Juxtlahuaca and APPO Mixteca but also in terms of raising issues of gender equity in the leadership of such organizations and in the San Juan Copala community radio station.

The autonomous municipality of San Juan Copala continues to be an important symbol in the region of the possibilities for legitimizing grassroots indigenous government. Francisco Alfaro Arzola concluded that the experience of San Juan Copala was one of the most important gains by APPO in the region in 2006. He stated in 2007:

One of the other big gains we can point to in the Juxtlahuaca region is the declaration of municipal autonomy in San Juan Copala. This is probably the most important gain APPO made in the Juxtlahuaca region. The communities that belong to the municipality of San Juan Copala got together in their own congress, they disavowed the authorities they had who were from the PRI, and they named their own council. For us this was a very important political gain because one of the indigenous groups who are our brothers, the Triquis, were able to do this. We have not been able to accomplish this in any Mixteca municipality. They were only able to do it in some of the Triqui communities.

By late 2008 both the indigenous municipality of San Juan Copala and other organizations that had formed APPO Mixteca in Juxtlahuaca were feeling the consequences of a PRI victory in the Juxtlahuaca municipality. There PRI members and others affiliated with MULT took control of the municipal government in statewide elections held in August 2007. According to people I spoke with and other sources, the Copala municipality does not get any state resources because of the role of MULT in the Juxtlahuaca government, where decisions are made about how resources are to be given to communities (Petrich 2008; Paris Pombo 2010). APPO Mixteca held a second congress in 2007, and the people involved in it have continued to participate in some regional and statewide activities. The biggest impediment to continuing with a strong and unified APPO in the Mixtec region has been the decision of many of the organizations that formed the original group to go into electoral politics. This happened in 2007 and resulted in many tensions that still endure.

In midterm elections in Mexico in July 2009, which experienced low voter turnout, the PRI won the majority, consolidating its national political power. The opposition PRD, which some groups of APPO Mixteca had affiliated with in 2007 and again in 2009, lost both times. The lack of a cohesive political platform to distinguish the PRD from the PRI, internal party corruption and conflict, and a lack of inspiring candidates are partly behind the loss. For APPO Mixteca, participation in electoral politics seemed to have been a bust, leaving most activists to return to their local communities to strengthen their organizations.

By the fall of 2009 the alliance between the MULTI and UBISORT, which had been part of the declaration of autonomy of San Juan Copala, came apart. UBISORT realigned with MULT, reinvigorating the MULT-MULTI conflict that began in 2006. The broken MULTI-UBISORT alliance became clear to the outside world when, on November 28, 2009, UBISORT denied access to the community of San Juan Copala to a delegation visiting from San Salvador Atenco who came for a meeting with MULTI authorities.[10]

On November 29, 2009, armed members of UBISORT who had broken their alliance with MULTI named Anastacio Juárez Hernández to be the local governing authority. This act was intended to usurp the power of the MULTI elected leaders of the self-declared autonomous municipality. Along with this declaration of a new UBISORT political authority, a stream of violence was unleashed on San Juan Copala by UBISORT-MULT, directed against MULTI members who supported the autonomous municipality. Violence escalated in December 2009 and continued into the spring.[11]

A press report dated February 10, 2010, documents a group of more than thirty families leaving San Juan Copala due to "a paramilitary group of 50 people." The group reported that they did not want to "keep living in the community in the middle of shooting and tension and in which it is not possible to live and walk in the streets due to a paramilitary group which is strongly armed and which is patrolling the streets and nearby hillsides" (Valle 2010). Though many left, a group of mostly women and children and some leaders of the autonomous municipality remained. Power was cut, schools were closed, the medical clinic was closed, and food and water had to be snuck in at night past UBISORT-MULT gunmen. This state of siege continued throughout 2010, eventually forcing almost all MULTI sympathizers to leave San Juan and scatter to neighboring communities (Contralinea 2010).

During the month of April 2010 the tense situation and violence in San Juan Copala gained international attention when a humanitarian caravan carrying journalists, social activists, and international observers was attacked with high-powered weapons by UBISORT. Alberta Cariño Trujillo (nicknamed and known as Bety Cariño), who was the organizer of CACTUS, and Jyri Antero Jaakkolo, a native of Finland and an international observer, were killed (Paris Pombo 2010). Others were wounded, and two members of the press from the *Milenio* newspaper and several others had to remain in hiding for two days until they could successfully be rescued from the region.

On May 20, 2010, Timoteo Alejandro Ramírez, a founder and leader of MULTI and of the autonomous municipality of San Juan Copala, was gunned down in his home in Yosoyuxi, as was his wife, Tleriberta Castro. MULTI members accused the MULT of the assassinations. Ramírez had been the object of two other assassination attempts in early 2006. In the first attack, his son Misael Alejandro died; the second attack resulted in the death of another local authority in Yosoyuxi (Pérez et al. 2010).

On June 8, 2010, a second caravan attempted to deliver aid to San Juan Copala but did not successfully complete its mission due to the continued presence of paramilitaries in the area and the unwillingness of the state government to guarantee its security. The caravan was attempting to deliver over thirty tons of supplies. Unable to enter the town directly, the goods were left in a warehouse in Huajuapan de León and slowly brought in on foot to MULTI members, who were spread out in different communities.[12]

Beginning in August 2010 Triqui women from MULTI started a sit-in in the center of Oaxaca City to call attention to the ongoing violence and siege situation that their families were living in. They stated that they had to bring supplies to their families under fire. By the end of September all had escaped the siege, which was focused on women and children (De Marinis 2011, 2013).[13] De Marinis, who interviewed Triqui women in their Oaxaca City occupation during 2010, describes what happened to women who attempted to leave their homes while the siege went on:

> On September 3, Miriam and another woman, Teresa, went to buy food and when they returned they were intercepted by a group of armed men. In that ambush, Miriam was beaten with guns and raped

by many men. Teresa, when trying to run, was hit by a bullet in the back. Miriam was stripped of her clothes and, naked, they cut her long hair. After two days, they went to Oaxaca's sit in to report the violation and to seek protection. They did not return to San Juan Copala. (De Marinis 2011: 483)

Violence continued between MULTI and UBISORT-MULT into the fall of 2010 and after.[14] On October 23 a MULT founder and leader, Heriberto Pazos Ortiz, was gunned down in the municipality of Cinco Señores, adjacent to Oaxaca City, by two young men on a motorcycle. His personal bodyguard and two state preventative police assigned to protect him escaped harm.

Ongoing political conflict between MULTI and MULT and the intraethnic violence it has generated is one of the most historically and currently complex situations within Mexico. The area continues to experience high levels of paramilitary violence, the murder of men, women, and children, widespread sexual assault and rape, and "allowed violence" that provoked rupture and terror in Triqui communities and beyond in the larger region (De Marinis 2011, 2009: 76–89). Oaxaca state and national government officials seem incapable of creating the conditions necessary to open a road to dialogue and reconciliation. Instead many government officials seem tied to centuries-old racist thinking that blames the continued violence on indigenous ethnic warfare (De Marinis 2013, 2011, 2009). The complexity of this conflict also suggests the importance of taking a long historical view of ethnic-identity formation, alliances, and splits.

Transborder Citizenship: APPO Activism from Los Angeles to Oaxaca in 2006

Because FIOB is a binational indigenous organization, the leadership role it took on in Juxtlahuaca and Huajuapan de León in the formation of APPO Mixteca translated fairly quickly to the Los Angeles area. There are approximately seventy thousand indigenous Oaxacans living in the greater Los Angeles metropolitan area.[15] The majority of indigenous immigrants are Zapotecs from the Central Valleys and Northern Sierra of Oaxaca. Felipe López and David Runsten (2004: 267) found twenty-eight different Oaxacan-owned restaurants in Los Angeles, all owned by Zapotec families from those two regions. A thriving business culture that includes butcher shops, bakeries, food stores, and markets supports the restaurants and a broader Oaxacan population. Because Sección 22 has members from all over the state of Oaxaca, many teachers in Oaxaca who belong to Sección 22 have relatives in the Los Angeles area. There are also retired teachers, as well as some who are still active, living in Los Angeles.

Oaxacan migrants and immigrants have a rich history in the Los Angeles area, beginning with contracted braceros, who worked near the city, and multiple generations that have settled in and around the city from all over the state. During the 1970s significant Oaxacan migration networks were established and people settled in the area (López and Runsten 2004). Many Oaxacans gained legal residency in California in 1986 under the Immigration Reform and Control Act and the Special Agricultural Workers Program. This provided significant legal anchors for family members who remained in Mexico. From the 1990s to the present, the Oaxacan population has increased in Los Angeles as well as in other parts of California (Kresge 2007).

There are dozens of Oaxacan migrant associations in California, as well as several federations of these organizations, including FIOB, the Coalición de Organicaziones Indígenas de Oaxaca (Coalition of Indigenous Communities of Oaxaca), the Organización Regional de Oaxaca (Oaxaca Regional Organization), and the Union de Comunidades de la Sierra Juárez de Oaxaca (Union of Highland Communities of Oaxaca). There are also dozens of websites and radio stations linking communities in Los Angeles and Oaxaca.

Los Angeles is home not only to a large Oaxacan population but also to the largest concentration of Mexican immigrants and migrants in the United States. In 2008 the U.S. Census estimated that 47.7 percent of Los Angeles County's 9,519,331 residents were Latino. A majority of these are of Mexican origin. Among them, as well as among the non-Mexican population, are a number of progressive organizations dedicated to fighting for democracy in Mexico. These include the Comité Pro Democracia en Mexico (Pro-Democracy in Mexico Committee), the Frente Amplio Progresista de Los Angeles (Wide Progressive Front of Los Angeles), and the Otra Campana (The Other Campaign), associated with the Zapatistas.

The Comité Pro Democracía en Mexico defines itself as "a collective of individuals who are committed to the political, economic and social situation in Mexico, and Latin America as related to the United States" (Comité Pro Democracía en México 2012a). Their Facebook page states that the Comité is a collective organization which supports popular struggles in Mexico, Latin America, and the world and organizes protests, events, radio, fanzine, study circles, and other activities in order to promote a just world and to protect human rights (Comité Pro Democracia en Mexico 2012b). The Frente Amplio Progresista is the alliance linking the Party of the Democratic Revolution (PRD), the Worker's Party (PT), and the Citizen's movement (MC) that was formed in Mexico after the 2006 presidential elections. The left and center-left coalition supported the presidential candidacy of Manuel López Obrador in 2012. The branch discussed here is based in Los Angeles. Finally La Otra Campaña was formed in January 2006 as a political and networking strategy of the Zapatista Army of National Liberation to work outside of formal politics and elections to link groups throughout Mexico, the United States, and Europe who support Zapatista principles such as indigenous rights and community autonomy. Local groups of La Otra Campana have participated in a range of local and regional social movements in Mexico, including APPO in Oaxaca City. Prior organizing among California groups that were acting in solidarity with the Zapatista movement in the 1990s, the left PRD party of Mexico, and other political affiliations have resulted in a significant network of left and progressive organizations that these and other groups are a part of.

Soon after its inception, the APPO began to develop links with FIOB in the Los Angeles area because of strong historic links between teachers in Local 22 and FIOB in Oaxaca. Among the founders of FIOB are numerous teachers from Local 22, particularly from the Juxtlahuaca region. The membership of FIOB in Mexico has consistently included members of Local 22 in a variety of regions of Oaxaca.

The FIOB was one of the organizations in Los Angeles that was directly connected to Sección 22 and APPO through its membership, which includes significant numbers of teachers and indigenous leaders. As people in Los Angeles who had ties to Oaxaca became concerned about the heavy-handed action against the teachers on June 14, 2006, and saw the large mega-marches taking place in Oaxaca City, they began to talk with FIOB leaders and ask what they could do to support the movement.

Gaspar Rivera-Salgado (real name),[16] then general coordinator of the FIOB, explained in an interview in October 2009 how people from Oaxaca became involved and how APPO Los Angeles was formed:

At first people wanted more information, but then the people began to say to FIOB and our leaders, "We are going to do something. Now that we are interested, what can we do?" So first, people began to channel this solidarity into forming an APPO in Los Angeles. In this space of APPO-L.A., people who were not attached to organizations as well as the leadership of the FIOB and of other organizations began to think about what concrete actions we could take to support the movement in Oaxaca.

※ VIDEOCLIP 8.5: http://dx.doi.org/10.7264/N30V89R6

After the June 14, 2006, attempt to evict the teachers from the center of Oaxaca, FIOB members in Los Angeles quickly organized a series of marches. Marchers began at St. Thomas Church, walked through the Pico

Figure 8.2 APPO-L.A. march, 2006. The sign in front reads "Oaxaca Endures and the Migrant Rises Up." DOI: 10.7264/N3JW8BSC. Photo by Odilia Romero-Hernández

Figure 8.3 FIOB participation in APPO-L.A. march, 2006. The banner reads "Stop the Repression in Oaxaca." DOI: 10.7264/N3F769GP. Photo by Odilia Romero-Hernández

Union neighborhood, and ended across the street from the Mexican Consulate near MacArthur Park. These actions put FIOB organizers in touch with different groups that wanted to work in solidarity with the movement in Oaxaca. A group of people began to have meetings and plan events. One of the decisions the FIOB leadership had to make was to distinguish between the struggle for indigenous and migrant rights, which were front and center on the FIOB agenda in Los Angeles, and other, broader issues. Since not all FIOB members were in agreement with the other organizations who wanted to support APPO and Sección 22 in Oaxaca, it made sense to form a separate APPO in which FIOB members could participate.

The third march that FIOB participated in during the fall of 2006 was a joint FIOB-APPO march that drew about five hundred people. Participants in APPO Los Angeles decided that they would engage in a series of public mobilizations to call attention to the repression faced by the movement in Oaxaca. These mobilizations continued in Los Angeles through the fall of 2006 and into 2007.

A group of FIOB members from Los Angeles and Fresno made a trip to Oaxaca in August 2006 and met directly with APPO leaders, leaders of Sección 22, and others in Oaxaca City, Juxtlahuaca, and Huajuapan de León. Rufino Domínguez Santos, who was the general coordinator of FIOB at the time, met with Enrique Rueda Pacheco, who was the head of the teachers' union.

Odilia Romero, in her role at the time as coordinator of women's affairs of FIOB, also went on the trip. She met with Ezequiel Rosales Carreno and other members of Sección 22 in Oaxaca. In addition, she visited the women who occupied COR-TV in Oaxaca. In general, these FIOB leaders solidified already existing relations that they had with Sección 22 and established additional political ties with APPO members in a variety of cities. The California FIOB group was in Oaxaca when the conflict escalated in August; José Jiménez Colmenares was murdered on August 10, 2006, and a "clean-up" campaign was being conducted in the city of Oaxaca and nearby communities by a paramilitary force that circled in convoys of pickup trucks at night (see Osorno 2006, 2007: 96–97). With this sharp increase in violence, including the public shootings of those who supported APPO actions, the FIOB members visiting from California were quickly drawn into the tense situation in Oaxaca.

Odilia Romero was born in Zoogocho, Oaxaca, a Zapotec-speaking community in the Sierra Juárez region. She came to the United States at eleven and has lived in the Los Angeles area since that time. One of the key organizers of APPO Los Angeles, her trip to Oaxaca gave her direct experience with the social movement and solidified her commitment to continuing to organize support from the United States.

Going to Oaxaca had a big impact on me. I came here when I was eleven years old and I didn't know anything about Oaxaca until I started participating in the FIOB. Reading about the movement or seeing what is going on through the Internet or on television is not the same as being there and eating a tortilla with rice and chili, seated with APPO members who occupied the town hall in Huajuapan de León. It wasn't the same to read about it as it was to see compañerosos moving big stones to block the roads. This direct experience was how I was filled with energy to continue denouncing the atrocities that were happening in Oaxaca.

✳ VIDEOCLIP 8.6: http://dx.doi.org/10.7264/N3W37T87

The FIOB leaders from California returned to Oaxaca on August 30, 2006, and marched with others to the Mexican Consulate to deliver a letter to President Vicente Fox. "We are pained by the attitude of ignorance of the government and we ask that the President of Mexico, Vicente Fox, intervene to resolve the conflict in a peaceful manner," said FIOB's general coordinator Rufino Domínguez Santos as he gave the letter to the consul for protection of Mexicans, Marco Antonio Fraire (Salazar 2006a). The group of marchers, which included Oaxacans, Mexicans from other parts of the country, Salvadorans, and Chicanos, also called for the ouster of Ruiz Ortiz as governor, the liberation of political prisoners, and punishment of those responsible for the murders of participants in APPO such as Jiménez Colmenares. The group was accompanied by Aztec dancers and drummers, members of human rights organizations, the Association of Maestros de la Raza, the Center for Central American Resources, and members of the Koreatown Immigrant Workers Alliance, which joins together Oaxacan and Korean workers (Salazar 2006a).

As the situation became more intense in Oaxaca in the fall of 2006, APPO Los Angeles continued to organize public events. On October 3 about two hundred people marched again to the Mexican Consulate in Los Angeles to announce their support for APPO, demand the resignation of Ruiz Ortiz, and reject the presence of armed forces in the state of Oaxaca. They delivered another letter addressed to the president of Mexico, the Mexican secretary of state, the attorney general, senators, and the National Human

Figure 8.4 Young musicians playing in the APPOsada celebrated in Los Angeles in December of 2006. DOI: 10.7264/N39G5JRZ. Photo by Odilia Romero-Hernández

Rights Commission, calling for no use of armed repression or of federal forces in the conflict in Oaxaca. The protesters wanted the Mexican government to know that "the popular mobilization of the people of Oaxaca reflects sentiments shared not only by Oaxacans in Mexico, but also people in the United States, that Ulises Ruiz should renounce his office as governor. This would provide the first basis for a peaceful political solution to the ongoing conflict" (Salazar 2006b).

Other marches followed. On November 2, 2006, following the shootings of the American independent journalist Bradley Will and four Oaxacans and the arrival of 4,500 elements of the Federal Preventative Police in Oaxaca, APPO-L.A. unified 250 people to march through the streets of Los Angeles (Radford 2006). This coincided with the Mexican celebration of Days of the Dead. In preparation for the march, FIOB and other participants made coffins to represent those who had died in the Oaxacan conflict. The coffins were carried through the streets, and once again the group went to the Mexican Consulate. November 19, 2006, saw another march in solidarity with the people of Oaxaca sponsored by APPO-L.A.

On December 21, 2006, APPO-L.A. organized a sit-in in front of the Mexican Consulate at an event they called APPOsada. This event brought together the traditional *posada* marking the search of Mary and Joseph for shelter before Christ's birth with support for APPO. Held at St. Cecilia's Church in Santa Monica, APPOsada included cultural activities, food, and commemorations for the dead in the Oaxaca conflict (Rodríguez Santos 2009).

Protests continued into 2007. When former president Vicente Fox came to Los Angeles to receive recognition for his presidency and contributions to the Mexican economy, APPO-L.A. and FIOB were there to meet him at the Music Center in downtown Los Angeles. They asked him to remember the many people who had left Mexico during the six years of his presidency to find a better life in the United States and directed his attention to coffins the group bore to remind him of those who had died in the Oaxacan conflict (Morales 2007).

This series of marches, protest actions, rallies, and meetings at the Mexican Consulate intensified the network of relations not only between different parts of the Oaxacan community but also between Oaxacans and other Mexicans and Latinos in Los Angeles. In addition, the ways in which the marches were organized hinted at the power that simple telecommunications and electronic information sharing could have in binational organizing and mobilization. According to Rivera-Salgado:

The Oaxacan community began to carry out public demonstrations in the streets, asking for the support of Oaxacans and non-Oaxacans. These marches would arrive in front of the Mexican Consulate. This created a lot of interest, and so a lot of people began to unite behind APPO-L.A. The teachers' union of Los Angeles and other organizations began to participate. And then we also began to see a debate inside of the Oaxacan community about how we should interpret the movement going on in Oaxaca. As you can imagine, in a community where there are thousands of people there are many different positions. There were those who said that the teachers in Oaxaca were "good-for-nothings," that they were just cheating the kids there of their education, and there were others who said, "No, the teachers' movement is part of the struggle for democracy in Mexico and it is part of a better future our children and our community."

The APPO group in Los Angeles also began to raise money for the movement in Oaxaca. When FIOB and APPO leaders in Los Angeles asked APPO leaders participating in the mobilization in Oaxaca what they needed, their response was "We need money to buy phone cards for our cell phones." APPO marches, occupations of buildings, rallies, and other events were coordinated largely by cell phones and later, to some degree, by radio. Cell phone cards were very expensive. It made sense that the primary request from APPO organizers in Oaxaca City, Juxtlahuaca, Huajuapan de León, and elsewhere to FIOB was "money to subsidize communication," in the words of Rivera-Salgado. Women from FIOB and other organizations began to sell food in order to raise funds to send to Oaxaca.

Cell-phone communication not only played an important role in helping APPO leaders from different regions of Oaxaca communicate with one another; it also facilitated some of the most emotionally intense and dramatic moments of transborder organizing between APPO Oaxaca and APPO-L.A. After the first couple of L.A. marches, APPO leaders in L.A. began to establish direct connections with APPO leaders in Oaxaca. Once the Los Angeles marches had gone through Pico Union and arrived in MacArthur Park, APPO-L.A. participants would call APPO leaders in Oaxaca on their cell phones and then hold them up to microphones so that they would be broadcast throughout the park. Rivera–Salgado describes this:

> It was very interesting to hear these reports from Oaxaca at night in Mac-
> Arthur Park. When the leaders from Oaxaca were speaking, a great silence
> would go over the crowd because people were paying such careful attention.
> They were absorbing every word that was said, listening very carefully to
> the description of the movement in Oaxaca. This really united people here
> who were mobilizing. This would happen in the park in front of the Mexican
> Consulate here. And of course they would say, "Thank you so much for your
> solidarity in Los Angeles. Thanks for sending us money," and they would tell
> us what they were using it for. This was a really democratic practice, where
> they would tell us in detail how they were spending the money and give us
> information. It was a way of directly communicating with the people here.

Odilia Romero also remembers these moments of broadcast phone calls as having a great emotional impact on her and others:

> I think that for me, the moment that caused me the greatest personal impact
> was when we would hear the compañeros crying over the phone when we had
> our connections with them. I remember another time when a band from the
> community of Solaga played the Cancion Mixteco for them on the other end of
> the telephone and Ezequiel Rosales Carreno said, "This really moves me." And
> some of the people who heard this on the radio in Oaxaca wrote to us to say
> thank you. It was like we touched the tender side of one of these leaders. This
> was the most satisfactory moment for me.

The FIOB had conducted very effective transborder political actions in the past, such as a coordinated highway blockade in Huajuapan de León and

Juxtlahuaca, an occupation of the Mexican Consulate in Los Angeles, and a demonstration in Los Angeles—all on August 10, 1996 (Stephen 2007a: 302–3). Thus coordinating actions across borders was not something new for them. What seems to differentiate the transborder organizing of 2006 is its emotional intensity and the memory of that. Regular cell-phone communication between APPO in Los Angeles and APPO in Oaxaca City and elsewhere resulted in very strong emotional ties between leaders. These strong ties extended to the listening public at the L.A. rallies. They were also reinforced by previously existing political and personal ties between FIOB members and leaders and families and communities in Oaxaca. Listening to APPO leaders testify on the phone in public rallies in Los Angeles brought immigrant Oaxacans the "once-againness" of the lived experiences of their *paisanos* (countrymen). Even if some of the immigrant Oaxacans who were listening had political disagreements with APPO and Sección 22, many were moved to help.

Odilia Romero described ways people supported the Oaxacan social movement quietly, by sending donations. They were often motivated by family ties to the teachers, as she describes:

I remember one time there was a march of the teachers who were going to Puebla. They were stuck there with no money for food and they called us. We didn't have any money to send, so I called a leader in the Catholic community of Oaxacans. I said, "Listen, the teachers are without any food." He said to me "Odilia, if you promise not to use my name I will send money." He did this because he had family members who were in the teachers' union. He had first cousins that were there and also in the movement. It was these family ties and also the strong alliances that APPO had in Los Angeles that allowed things like this to happen.

Because of the large number of Oaxacans in the Los Angeles area, many people were intent on receiving information about the situation in Oaxaca. Those who had relatives in the movement talked to them regularly on the phone and also listened to Radio Universidad, Radio Cacerola, and some of the other radio stations the movement controlled. Some university students from Oaxaca created Internet pages and blogs to share information about the situation in Oaxaca. Gaspar Rivera-Salgado described this transborder network and how devastated people were when forms of communication were shut down after November 25, 2006:

> After the repression and when they closed the radio station in Oaxaca [Radio
> Universidad], people were very anxious to know what was going on. The
> repression had a psychological effect here in Los Angeles. Many people felt
> wounded that the government would act in this way. Because we didn't have
> information and communication was cut off, there was a lot of uncertainty.
> A lot of people had relatives participating in the movement and they didn't
> know what happened in November. They wanted to know if people had been
> taken prisoner, if they were okay, what was going on. So this really showed
> the connections and direct links that there were between this movement of
> APPO and the lives of migrants here. In the moments that the movement
> was growing there was a direct connection. People here listened to the radio,
> Radio Universidad, they read the papers, Internet pages, and they offered a
> lot of information. . . . So there was a strong network of people from different
> sectors here monitoring the situation of APPO.

The FIOB organizers in Los Angeles continued to support APPO activities, but late in 2007 they realized that it was impossible for them to maintain two organizations. Teachers from Sección 22 came to Los Angeles in
2007 and spoke of some of the emerging divisions in APPO in Oaxaca. In Los
Angeles some parts of the APPO coalition, such as the Comité Democratico
Por Mexico, wanted to broaden the struggle to include support for the Zapatista movement in Chiapas and other social movements in Mexico. When a
FIOB staff member suggested that they keep focused on Oaxaca, she was
told that the indigenous movement was "very narrow." Another part of the
APPO-L.A. coalition, the Unión del Barrio, wanted to keep on organizing sit-
ins in front of the Mexican Consulate in Los Angeles, but FIOB decided it did
not want to. According to Rivera-Salgado, "[In 2007 there were] differences
in how broad APPO should be and what kind of strategy we should take.
APPO-L.A. was really a temporary coalition. It didn't have a solid base. We
have continued our relationship with the movement through remembering
key events in October. We did that in 2009."

The story of APPO Los Angeles in 2006 is an important dimension of
the Oaxacan social movement and its transnational reach during that year.
Transnational connections continued to be important in the granting of political asylum to APPO supporters such as Ramiro Aragón Pérez and to those
fleeing the political violence of the Triqui conflict, such as a woman who,
with two of her children, was granted political asylum in a San Francisco
court in October 2010.

Summary

Indigenous participation in APPO in the Mixtec and Triqui regions of Oaxaca and in Los Angeles benefited from the prior gains of pan-ethnic indigenous organizing largely built by the FIOB. In 2005 and 2006 FIOB projects such as the Women's Regional Council integrated women's groups from Mixtec and Triqui communities in the Juxtlahuaca region that had organized themselves around income-generating projects. The Women's Council and, in particular, the participation of Triqui women were the backbone of the APPO occupation of the city hall in Juxtlahuaca. Ongoing political divisions in the Triqui region resulted in a temporary alliance in 2006. This provided an opening for a new form of political organization in January 2007, when a MULTI-UBISORT alliance declared the Autonomous Municipality of San Juan Copala. Longer held political tensions in the area, however, led to the fracturing of the alliance in 2009 and an escalation of violence in the region surrounding San Juan Copala. In late 2010, while MULTI struggled to hold on to the idea of indigenous autonomy in San Juan Copala, the besieged women, children, and few male leaders left in the Triqui homeland of San Juan Copala were simply struggling to survive. The Triqui conflict will take concerted, long-term efforts to truly resolve.

The FIOB membership of approximately five thousand tied to regional offices in Juxtlahuaca, Tijuana, Los Angeles, and Fresno provided the structure for transnational organizing of APPO. Strongest in Los Angeles during 2006, the pan-ethnic identity of FIOB was an ideological and cultural resource for building a coalition with other Los Angeles groups committed to human rights and democracy in Mexico. APPO-L.A. provided a public space in California in which family, relatives, and others connected to communities caught up in the social movement in Oaxaca could connect as either open allies or more subtle, under-the-table supporters. Rallies in MacArthur Park, sit-ins in front of the Mexican Consulate, and cultural events such as APPOsadas were also important for sharing news and emotional attachments.

Many members of FIOB and APPO Los Angeles are members of transborder communities. As a "hometown," this Oaxacan indigenous transborder community is both a real and a symbolic site that draws people back repeatedly in many senses, but that is also represented by multilayered forms of social and political organization that function in many different sites throughout Mexico and the United States. These discontinuous spaces are linked through kinship, ritual, cycles of labor, and individual and collective resources of material and symbolic means. A transborder community is full of people accustomed to living in multiple localities and discontinuous social, economic, and cultural spaces (Stephen 2007a: 19–23). The political activities of FIOB worked through the networks of indigenous transborder communities and provided a hybrid model of citizenship and participation as APPO-L.A. members responded to the rights and responsibilities of their local sense of citizenship as well as to transnational forms of political participation that worked across U.S.-Mexican national boundaries. This is further discussed in the concluding chapter in this book.[17]

9

From Barricades to Autonomy and Art

———

Youth Organizing in Oaxaca

While APPO and Sección 22 were important backbones of the Oaxacan social movement in 2006, the political and cultural space created by the social uprising also gave birth to other important organizations and forms of political participation. Once the movement began to root itself locally in neighborhood barricades, another style of participation and leadership emerged that challenged some aspects of the more vertical organizational model of the teachers' union. As people at the barricades networked with one another and coordinated their actions to protect key installations such as Radio Universidad, a different kind of political culture began to emerge—particularly among youth. This political culture, which many loosely identified with the concept of autonomy, has continued beyond 2006 in a range of organizations and collectives, many of which are tied to media, art, alternative development, and urban ecology models. The new political culture is characterized by horizontal relationships, consensus decision making, mutual aid, self-empowerment, self-sufficiency, and the belief that *how* something is achieved is as important as or more important than *what* is achieved.[1]

Two case studies of youth organizing in Oaxaca will demonstrate how the concept of autonomy is being theorized and practiced in experimental spaces and organizations. Public art involving graffiti and stenciling flourished in 2006 and after, largely fueled by youth organizing. The signature images, styles, context, and techniques associated with APPO and the wider 2006 movement have been partially legitimized through their entrance into the commercial art market and in museum exhibits. In my discussion of youth expression through public art, I use a case study of the Asamblea de Artistas Revolutionarios de Oaxaca (Assembly of Revolutionary Artists of Oaxaca, ASARO), which was founded in 2006. The artists of ASARO created important popular icons, such as the Virgen de las Barrikadas,[2] a hybrid symbol of youth activism on the barricades and popular religiosity. Another popular religious icon, El Santo Niño APPO, also recognizes the importance of youth activism in 2006.

Beyond creating unique organizational and cultural forms centered on ideas of autonomy, youth organizations helped to solidify politically and visually (through their art) the hybrid identity crafted by the movement in Oaxaca City of *Oaxaca popular*, which arose during the social movement of 2006 and lasted for some time afterward. The fusion of urban popular culture with indigeneity and working-class identity anchored in assertions of human dignity from below produced a unique political identity that created unity out of difference—at least during 2006 in Oaxaca. Youth activists were at the cutting edge of this process.

Political Participation and Governance outside of Electoral Politics: VOCAL

The Voces Oaxaqueños Construyendo Autonomía y Libertad (Oaxacan Voices Constructing Autonomy and Freedom, VOCAL) was formed in February 2007 by Ruben Valenzuela, David Vanegas, and others who felt that, after the second APPO constitutional assembly in February 2007, it was important to create an organizational space for the movement's participants who were not interested in electoral politics as their primary means of political participation. VOCAL included Zapatista sympathizers and adherents to the Zapatista La Otra Campaña,[3] anarchists, participants from the barricades, and those who, according to the VOCAL Manifesto, "worry about keeping our social movement faithful to its principles, autonomous and independent from political parties, and restoring the assembly model" (VOCAL 2007; see Neuhouser 2008). Several university-educated students were involved in the initiation of VOCAL.

Sonia Hinojosa is a young woman in her mid-twenties who studied social science at UABJO. In 2006 she became very involved in the barricades
that were set up to protect Radio Universidad. Like many young people,
she developed intense friendships as part of her participation in the barricades and further honed her ideas about political process, participation,
and social change. The kind of day-to-day political culture and the strategies that developed at the barricades went on to motivate her and others to
form VOCAL in 2007 and Casa Autónoma Solidaria Oaxaqueño de Trabajo
Autogestivo (Autonomous Oaxacan House Supporting Self-Managed Work,
CASOTA) in 2008. Sonia was arrested in 2007, when she was documenting
a march in support of the Guelaguetza Popular. She has since developed an
insightful analysis of the processes that led up to the formation of new organizations after 2006. In 2010 we talked about her experiences in 2006 and
the subsequent organizations she participated in. Here she describes how
she and other youth connected at the barricades:

SONIA: *VOCAL was formed in 2007, but almost all of us were part of the
movement of 2006. Some of us got to know one another in the barricades.*

LYNN: *Was this in the barricade at Cinco Senores?*

SONIA: *. . . What happened is that the barricade of Cinco Senores was not
just isolated. Since it had the objective of guarding the radio station, Radio
Universidad, to describe the barricade at Cinco Senores was actually to be
talking about everyone who was guarding the radio. That would include the
barricade of Soriana and the barricade of University City, and that is where
a lot of us got to know one another—in that context. . . . Radio Unviersidad
was transmitting all of October and November, and a lot of us were in the
radio and protecting it during that time period.*

David Vanegas, one of the founders of VOCAL, was born and raised in
Oaxaca City. He left to study agricultural engineering at the University of
Chapingo in Texcoco, in the state of Mexico. While there, he was caught up
in the repression against the farmers' movement in Atenco in 2002, when
the farmers resisted having their town relocated to make way for an airport.
Once he heard about the attempted removal of teachers from their occupation in the center of Oaxaca on June 14, 2006, he came back to the city
to participate in the emerging social movement. His initial incorporation
into the movement was, like Sonia's, through participation in a barricade,
according to his published testimony (Valenzuela and Vanegas 2008). Here

he describes in detail his experiences as part of a barricade and the kind of political culture that emerged through that experience and how those in the barricades came to participate in APPO assemblies and the APPO Constitutional Congress in 2006.

> The creation of the barricades was the response of the people for the defense and security of the spaces that had been appropriated or taken (buildings, radio stations, etc.). . . . The majority of the barricades were composed of people from the city, and in many cases they were people who had not participated in the organizations.[4] It was thought that because they had not participated (in other movements) that these people did not have a political conscience. They were regular townspeople—señoras (older, married women), young kids from different gangs. I had moved in different circles and I had this prejudice as well. We talked about how if it were not for the barricades we would not have gotten to know one another. A lot of us were neighbors. Our barricade was the biggest because it was almost a kilometer long. We used 25 trucks to close it off. Our barricade was on the road that was the entrance to Oaxaca, on the road that goes to Mexico City. It is a very large avenue. Our barricade was so large that the assassins could never take anyone away. When the "death squads" came to our barricade they couldn't remove us. This barricade was set up after the bad people sent by the state government destroyed the equipment at Canal 9 and forced people out. . . . There were 1,500 barricades and during the height of the struggle we were always there and we didn't leave.
>
> A lot of people didn't understand the kind of organization that had evolved and you don't find it theorized. What this experience of self-organization made clear is that yes, we can be governed by respect, as is done within the system of "usos y costumbres" (indigenous customary law relating primarily to governance and judicial practices) in indigenous communities.
>
> . . . In the barricades we had meetings structured like assemblies to discuss just about everything. I feel like this spirit of assembly came from the mountains (i.e., from indigenous communities). It came to us from the mountains and then arrived in the city.
>
> This is how things worked, by assembly. Nobody said or did something that others imposed on them. That included those who arrived in the name of APPO to the barricade and said to us, "We are

going to take down the barricades as a sign of detenté (to show a willingness to decrease tensions in the city)." But the group of people at the barricade didn't want to and didn't take it down. They (APPO) had to understand that you can't give orders and impose things on people.

APPO had to include (the people at) the barricades. If they had not, I don't know what kind of dynamic would have emerged. After they came to talk with people in the barricades we began to participate in APPO assemblies. We would elect two people from each barricade and little by little we entered APPO. . . . This became more regularized when the first statewide congress of APPO was held (in October 2006) and a lot of people from the barricades went. But there were only five elected barricade representatives, one from the east, one from the west, one from the north, one from the south, and one from the center. (Valenzuela and Vanega 2008: 94–98).

Sonia went to the second statewide assembly of APPO, which was held in February 2007. She and others who attended described to me a contentious assembly of clashing political styles between the more traditional leftists, who were attempting to push through their political agendas, and those who came from community assemblies and barricades, who were often new to politics. Their political experience was rooted in long discussions and attempts at consensus decision making. According to some who attended, the beginning of the assembly was marked by a heated discussion that lasted four or five hours about the nature of APPO. The debate focused on whether or not APPO should continue to exist and whether or not it should divide into different sectors. Herlinda Reyes, a twenty-five-year-old teacher I interviewed who was at the same congress, stated that the open conflict and heated, sometimes nasty debate discouraged people who came from rural and indigenous communities: "Many of the people who came from the communities were not accustomed to seeing this kind of situation and . . . they left, disillusioned. . . . At the end we didn't have council members from the Sierra Juárez region, from La Cañada, and also from Miahuatlán. It was a shame."

When I spoke with Sonia, she spent considerable time in our conversation outlining the strong conflicts concerning electoral participation that emerged at the second APPO statewide assembly in 2007 and how that led alienated youth to formulate their own organizational principles and structure.

In February, that is when we went to the [second statewide] APPO assembly. That is where they were talking about things that are very strange; ideas like taking APPO into elections. . . . The statutes from the creation of the Popular Assembly of the Peoples of Oaxaca have a certain tone. They are anti-electoral, suggest nonparticipation in political parties, are anticapitalist, and come from demands articulated by people a long time ago.

. . . There were a lot of us who were not "organized," and we said, "This is not what we want." This is why we left. This was before VOCAL was born.

We were really bothered by what went on in the meetings, and we decided to have some meetings of our own. We invited some youth to our meeting who had already been getting together. They were from the Soriana barricade. They had already held several meetings for youth. So we started to talk to them . . . and we realized that they [people in APPO] saw us as very young. In APPO they would say, "Well, you are very young. You don't have experience." So we reevaluated our ideas about seeing things in a different way. I think that it had to do with our age.

. . . I didn't represent anyone. In the APPO assembly they were looking for people who represented others. A lot of us didn't even agree with this idea of electing representatives.

So some of us said, "Well, we are not officially in APPO. Maybe we are in spirit, but not in a formal way." So we started to construct the idea of what we did want. . . . We started to work on an organizational proposal and to ground our dreams and our utopias. We started to look at what we had gotten from the experience of 2006 and what else we could do. We worked on the manifesto of VOCAL, and we made it public and we began to work on the principles that are in the document.

First published in March 2007, the VOCAL Manifesto captures a significant set of ideas about political participation that have important resonance with the Oaxacan youth who participated in the movement. These ideas reflect experiences from La Otra Campaña and anarchist collectives and the appropriation of and admiration for customary law and governing practice in many of Oaxaca's indigenous communities known as *usos y costumbres*. The focus on autonomy, creating intercultural spaces of plurality, and governance through assembly also resonates with the organizational forms and processes found in the worldwide Occupy movements of 2011 and in other recent Latin American social movements. What follows is my partial translation and editing of part of the Manifesto:

This space is proposed as a forum to bring together the autonomous forces of the mobilized people of Oaxaca—those of us who participate actively in the social movement that constitutes a formal part of, or not, the Popular Assembly of the People of Oaxaca. What we are concerned with is making sure that our social movement is loyal to its principles: autonomous and independent of political parties and reinvigorating the assembly as the most just and harmonious form to make ourselves understood, organize ourselves, and govern ourselves. [The assembly] is where the agreements of the people are not based on the competition of majority versus minority, nor forms [of governance] that are imposed by those in power from above, but in relation to mutual respect between all parts of the community.

Within this space we are fighting for the construction, strengthening, and connection of different forms of autonomy. We consider the autonomies of the peoples, groups, collectives, organizations, and everyone else as a real form of opposition to the authoritarian forms of formal government we have. Autonomy, as a process of the construction of other realities, shows that there is another way to change things from the root, [through a process] where the people can decide their own forms and modes of life. . . . It is for this reason that the work we do within this space will not be defined by elections [and electoral processes and calendars], because with or without elections, autonomy can advance in organization and [in the creation of] proposals for a new kind of society [*otro sociedad possible*]. . . .

The people of Oaxaca know the importance of mobilization and organization as a principal form for achieving victory. For this reason we believe that it is necessary to continue our mobilization in all of the state, joining together with all, between the different forms of understanding society and different forms of resistance with all of their characteristics of diversity and plurality. . . .

We want justice, dignity, to not have fear about expressing our ideas, to not be discriminated against for our color, way of thinking, languages, or tastes. We want healthy food earned through our own work. We don't want the rich to rob us. We want to use our creative energy for the greater good, and we want our prisoners to be liberated. We want the liberty to choose the form by which we live and we don't want lies, violence, and other forms of government imposed on us. We know that what we want is just and correct.

We are looking to join together in this struggle from below, with all of the men and women in the city and in the different regions who have offered resistance to the owners of money. We are looking to join our experiences of struggle with those of the most distant corners of Oaxaca. We are looking to talk and exchange ideas with the men and women of Oaxaca.

L@s Afromexican@s [Afro-Mexicans], Zapotec@s, Mixtec@s, Huaves, Triquis, Chatin@s, Chontales, Mixes, Mazatec@s, Chinantec@s, Cuicatec@s, Ixcatec@s, Choch@s, Nahuas, Amuzgos, Zoques, Tacuates, as well as *colonos* [neighborhood people], *barricader@s* [those from the barricades], boys, girls, teachers, workers, peasants, migrants, immigrants, young people, students, homosexuals, bisexuals, and lesbians. Everyone who is fighting for a better world.

The document very explicitly sends a message of inclusion and, in its orthography, challenges conventional gender designations in the Spanish language. In slight changes to the names of Oaxaca's sixteen indigenous ethnic groups and Afro-descendants, the text uses the symbol @ to neutralize an assumed male universal subject and include men and women. Thus what would conventionally be "Los Afromexicanos" and "Zapotecos" becomes "L@s Afromexican@s" and "Zapotec@s." The Manifesto also specifically references children, youth, different class sectors, immigrants, homosexuals, bisexuals, and lesbians. The social movement of 2006 was the first instance I can recall of public dialogue in Oaxaca, through forums such as El Foro Nacional: Construyendo la Democracia y la Gobernabilidad en Oaxaca (The National Forum: Constructing Democracy and Governability in Oaxaca), in which sexual identity groups were included in a broad list of diverse people to be respected, considered, and included. The VOCAL Manifesto firmly roots itself in the project of creating a new representation of who the face of Oaxaca represents. Like Fidelia, quoted at the opening of this book, Oaxaca includes all ethnic, race, class, gender, and age groups — and adds sexual orientation.

The VOCAL Manifesto also emphasizes the concept of autonomy, the use of assemblies as a form of governance and decision making over majoritarian voting, and ways of accommodating diversity and difference within one movement. The Manifesto clarifies that the organization's projects and processes are not driven by the electoral clock of formal party politics. And it emphasizes the ideology of alliance and inclusion. Many of these characteristics are consistent with the political culture developed in the barricades, in the radio stations, and in indigenous community governance, media stations, and projects, as discussed in previous chapters.

From Ideas to Practice: The Creation of CASOTA

In 2007 VOCAL created a silk-screening workshop. When a friend invited some of the *vocales* (members of VOCAL) to rent space in a house close to the historic center of Oaxaca City, they decided to move their silk-screen workshop there. In December 2008, a few months after they had installed the workshop, some Zapatista supporters who were working on promoting the first Festival de la Digna Rabia (Festival of Dignified Rage) in Mexico City came to Oaxaca. They carried out some activities, and some of them came back to stay at the house where the VOCAL members were. Some police followed them and tried to force their way into the house. After this, those living and working in the house decided to formalize the space they utilized in the historic center of Oaxaca. They called it CASOTA. Beyond serving as an acronym, the word *casota* can be seen as an antonym of *casita*, which denotes "a house (diminutive)" but also refers to the practice of married men keeping a mistress and often other children in a dwelling that exists apart from his main house, or *casa*. In this instance CASOTA also references inclusiveness and expansiveness as well as size.

From 2008 until mid-2011 CASOTA served as a multiuse venue that housed from eight to ten people and was composed of ten distinct spaces with particular purposes linked to the 2006 social movement. The themes and culture of how the house operated were organized around the principles of autonomy. Housed in a traditional Oaxacan home, which features a series of rooms built around a large central courtyard, the physical space of CASOTA was designed to embed those inside it in major intellectual and ideological traditions, as well as to commemorate specific people and events that were part of the 2006 social movement. To give readers a sense of the spatial and metaphorical dimensions of CASOTA, I include some notes about the parts of the house that explain the special meanings of their designations:

- *Multipurpose hall "Estela Ríos," Comandanta Cacerola (Commander Casserole Dish)*. Estela Ríos was born in San Jacinto Tlacotepec in 1934. As a child, she worked as a domestic worker and then was an active catechist who also received training as a human rights worker. She later became active in Organizaciones Indias por los Derechos Humanos de Oaxaca (Indigenous Organizations for the Human Rights of Oaxaca),

and was one of the women who took over COR-TV in August 2006—
hence the name Comandanta Cacerola, after the Women's March
(Marcha de las Cacerolas) that led to the takeover of COR-TV. The
designation Comandanta suggests her leadership and importance in
this process and beyond. She went on to lead the security detail that
protected the station and became one of the founders of COMO, which
was formed in September 2006. She died of cancer in 2008.

- *Community Dormitory "14th of June."* This name refers to the violent
  attempted eviction of the teachers from the center of Oaxaca on June
  14, 2006.

- *"Ricardo Flores Magón" Library* is named for the noted Mexican social
  activist and anarchist Ricardo Flores Magón (1874–1922), known as
  one of the major thinkers of the Mexican Revolution. CASOTA members sponsored a reflection and study circle focused on the writing of
  Magón in 2010.

- *Solidarity Store "Lorenzo Sampablo Cervantes."* Lorenzo Sampablo
  Cervantes was killed in the early hours of August 22, 2006, outside
  the radio station La Ley, which had been taken over by sympathizers
  of APPO and others who had participated in the takeover of COR-TV.
  He was a public works employee with a degree in architecture and the
  father of four children.

- *Soup Kitchen*

- *Documentation Center "Iván Illich."* This space was named for the
  Austrian philosopher Ivan Illich, famous for his article "Deschooling
  Society," which suggested that institutionalized education was not
  effective. He advocated self-directed learning and using advanced
  technology to enhanced "learning webs" built through peer-matching
  networks. CASOTA members were interested in his philosophy of
  learning and engaged in projects of self-directed learning and self-
  sustainability, such as a rooftop garden. They also produced videos
  and radio programming.

- *"2 de Noviembre" Central Patio.* This is a reference to the day that the
  Federal Preventative Police retreated from their intended occupation
  of the UABJO. Their retreat stands as the single most important strategic gain—in terms of defense of the city of Oaxaca and the coordinated power of the barricades, APPO, and the radio stations—achieved
  by the movement's working together in 2006. The Central Patio hosted
  concerts, discussions, poetry readings, and other events.[5]

- *Electronic workshop*. This room served as a base for the repair and recycling of electronic equipment.

- *VOCAL office*

- *Silk-screening Workshop "25 de Noviembre."* This is a reference to the day that the PFP entered into a major confrontation with APPO marchers, firing tear gas and rubber bullets. Police arrested more than 160 people. Dozens were also injured, and APPO encampments in front of Santo Domingo Cathedral were broken up. Confrontations continued on November 26. After that date, APPO members returned the radio station at the university to the rector and began to remove barricades in the city.

The spatial and process-oriented vision of autonomy reflected in CASOTA centers on the idea of promoting self-sufficiency and recuperating knowledge from nonmainstream sources and using workshops to repatriate that knowledge back to working-class urban neighborhoods and rural and indigenous communities. CASOTA sponsored free workshops on silk screening, editing and publishing, urban agriculture, recycling, and the repair of electronic equipment. CASOTA also served as a cultural hub for Oaxacan and visiting youth that generated a wide range of cultural production, study groups, art, publications, and significant solidarity for the Triqui Autonomous Municipality of San Juan Copala and MULTI. The doctoral dissertation of Mauricio Magaña explores and analyzes the wide range of activities carried out by CASOTA as well as by a series of related cooperatives and organizations that operated with similar ideals. What particularly distinguished the VOCAL and CASOTA ideologies was their interest in and study of experiences of indigenous and other forms of autonomy and self-determination. CASOTA sponsored a film series on the topic in 2010 (see figure 9.1).

VOCAL and CASOTA members were signifi-

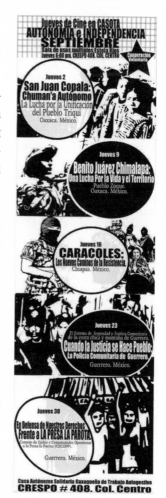

Figure 9.1 CASOTA poster for Autonomy Film Series, 2010. DOI: 10.7264/N35Q4T1N

cant participants in the caravan that journeyed to offer material support to members of the Autonomous Municipality of San Juan Copala in April 2010. When the Mexican human rights activist and indigenous leader Alberta ("Bety") Cariño and the Finnish human rights observer Jyri Antero Jaakkola were killed and several people wounded by paramilitary gunmen of UBISORT, the group of people running CASOTA and others in VOCAL became some of the primary people who pressed for bringing those responsible to justice. This work continues.[6]

Occupying Public Space through *Arte pa´ i Pueblo*: ASARO Stenciling and Graffiti

During the six months in 2006 that the city of Oaxaca was significantly controlled by the social movement, its physical presence was announced by widespread occupations of local, state, and federal government buildings as well as by an expanding corpus of what came to be known as *Arte pa´i Pueblo* (public popular art). Occupied government buildings were tagged as belonging to the social movement, and most walls in the downtown area became public galleries for a distinctive genre that also appeared in posters and on T-shirts. Detailed stencils emerged as one of the signature art forms that characterized the social movement of 2006 and became part of the formal art market in subsequent years. Movement art, like community and indigenous radio and media production, produces a strong cultural legacy that has thrived since 2006. In fact some of the key icons, such as La Virgen de las Barrikadas, were developed after the movement was significantly shut down in November 2006. The icons have become vehicles for the social memory and commemoration of key events of 2006. The production and proliferation of these icons, and the relative commercial success of some of the youthful artists who began in the street in 2006, suggest the centrality of culture in the continuity and social memory of the social movement in Oaxaca and elsewhere.

The role of art in social movements has been significantly overlooked by many. Ed McCaughan, however, offers important insights into the ways that the Zapotec, Mexican, and Chicano artists and artist collectives in Oaxaca, Mexico City, and California broadened the meanings of citizenship and democracy during movements of the 1960s, 1970s, and 1980s. His book offers important insights into the ways that local and popular culture is incorporated into the artwork of movement artists and helps to redefine "the meaning of national and patriotic symbols, civil liberties and democratic rights and processes" (2012: 23). His analysis has much to offer us in the study of art in the social movement of Oaxaca.

One of best-known artist collectives that emerged during the fall of 2006 is ASARO. Mario Guzmán is one of the unofficial spokespeople for ASARO. Mario has a warm smile that lights up his face as his sits in the sunlight in an interior courtyard of the ASARO working space, which is inside of a shared artist's space called Espacio Zapata (Zapata's space). The walls are painted brightly with stencil art featuring everyone from Frida Kahlo to Emiliano Zapata. On the walls are hung beautiful ASARO graphic prints and there are also stacks of prints to look through. Mario takes time to talk to me before departing for Europe and his young daughter runs in and out of our conversation. He explains that

> ASARO began in 2006 with the political turmoil in Oaxaca. . . . most of us who supported the popular movement as artists were young people. . . . We decided that ASARO could play an important social role in which art and different kinds of artist's expression could support the social movement.

✳ VIDEOCLIP 9.1: http://dx.doi.org/10.7264/N3RB72JW

The architect and anthropologist Iván Arenas joined and studied ASARO for an eighteen-month period in 2007–8. His 2011 doctoral dissertation, "Rearticulating the Social: Spatial Practices, Collective Subjects, and Oaxaca's Art of Protest," carries out an in-depth analysis of how political subjectivities are formed through their encounters and interactions with the material environment of the city. He writes eloquently of the impact that the collective of artists in ASARO had on the aesthetic and visual environment of Oaxaca and their crucial role in helping to articulate the political subjectivity of El Pueblo de Oaxaca as part of a specific political public:

> In stenciling their graphic messages on city walls, street artists gave visual form to a long history of the systemic marginalization of the Oaxacan people and, more importantly, to the Oaxacan people's courage in mobilizing to find a solution. Speaking from the perspective of shared experiences and struggles, images on city walls revealed common points of identification that interpolated the collective subject of *el pueblo* (the people). . . . This is rendered visible, for example, in how an anti-government stencil hailing *el pueblo* on the

¡LIBERTAD
DE EXPRESION!

Figure 9.2 "Libertad de Expresión!,"
by Adolfo Mexiac, 1968. DOI: 10.7264/
N3X63JTX

façade of a municipal building invites a different mode for inhabiting social and physical space from a billboard promoting tourism for foreigners framing the city as the heritage and patrimony of all Oaxacans. (2011: 2)

This contrast between grassroots images and government logos is discussed by McCaughan (2012: 20–21) in his chapter "Signs of Citizenship," where he analyzes two powerful images that resignify familiar logos and images. He begins with Adolfo Mexiac's "Libertad de Expresión" poster, which features the face of a man whose mouth has been chained and padlocked above Mexico's logo for the 1968 Olympics. The second image is Fernando Olivera's engraving *Resiste, voz libre del pueblo*, which shows market venders—primarily women—in the Zapotec town of Juchitán, which was occupied by the Mexican army in the 1980s.

The resignification of the Mexican Olympics logo by its juxtaposition with the gagged man (figure 9.2) works similarly to the way ASARO stencils produced in 2007 protested the official state-sponsored Guelaguetza in Oaxaca. Just as the gagged mouth questions the symbols of Mexican nationalism and legitimacy reflected in the Mexican Olympics logo, the figure of a traditional *danzante* (dancer) with a feathered crown from the Dance of the Conquest and a machine gun in his hand instead of the customary rattles questions the legitimacy of the Oaxaca state-sponsored folk festival known as Guelaguetza and the authority of those who organize it (figure 9.3).

The instantly recognizable *trajes* of the Zapotec market women who populate the forefront of Fernando Olivera's engraving, with the word "Resiste" in the background, let us know the importance of local language, dress, culture, and politics in the COCEI movement, which challenged the PRI as the first opposition-governed municipality in Mexico in the 1980s (figure 9.4). In direct conversation with Olivera's 1989 engraving is a print produced by

Figure 9.3 Stencil of Guelaguetza dancers with machine guns in July 2007. Text reads "Long Live the Guelaguetza Popular! Boycott the Commercial Guelaguetza." ASARO, 2007. DOI: 10.7264/N31Z4299

Figure 9.4 *Resiste, voz libre del pueblo*, engraving, by Fernando Olivera, 1989. DOI: 10.7264/N3SF2T3M

Figure 9.5 Resiste, engraving, by Beta of ASARO, 2007. DOI: 10.7264/N3NP22C8

Beta from ASARO that signals Mazateca female indigeneity associated with Huatla de Jimenez (figure 9.5). The bandana suggests her readiness for tear gas associated with APPO encounters with PFP and police. The mushrooms signal the sacred rituals associated with hallucinogens. The "Resiste" echoes the word on the wall in Olivera's engraving of women in Juchitán.

Guillermo Pacheco, one of the artists in ASARO, described the collective in the following way in early 2007: "ASARO was organized as a part of the different levels that the social movement of Oaxaca has. We are an assembly of artists who are unified by the goal of liberty in expression. We denounce

Figure 9.6 ASARO artists creating a *tapete* in front of the PFP, October 2006.
DOI: 10.7264/N3J1012K. Photo by Hank Tusinski

the problems in a broken system. Our objective is to propose an alternative
counterculture to the one that has been planted in Oaxaca, with a central
focus on graphics. Most of us are between 18 and 28 years old" (Aguilar
Orihuela 2007).

In the fall of 2006 ASARO began painting and stenciling on public walls
and performed in situ art, such as the *tapetes* (sand paintings) they produced at the security line of the PFP. The tapetes are modeled on the commemorative art form in Oaxaca that uses colored sand and flowers to honor
the dead in November and in ritual ceremonies performed thirty days and
one year after a loved one dies (see figure 9.6).

Itandehui Franco Ortíz was one of the few women who began working
with the ASARO collective in the fall of 2006. In addition to creating stencil
art, Itandehui also documented much of the ASARO street art and gallery
shows. She was studying for her B.A. in 2006 and also going to art school
in the afternoons. After Brad Will was killed, she and other ASARO artists
decided to incorporate their public art into the tradition of making sand
paintings known as tapetes in the streets. Itandeui spoke with me in Mexico
City in 2012, where she is now enrolled in a doctoral program. We spoke
over coffee at a well-known bookstore and then at a home where I was stay-
ing. She relaxed into our conversation, crossing her legs and cocking her

head as she thought and talked with me. She said of the tapetes created in October 2006:

> When the typical celebration came around [referring to Todos Santos or Days of the Dead] we decided that we were going to fill the entire tourist corridor in downtown Oaxaca with tapetes. This is the street that runs down the middle of Oaxaca. . . . We made tapetes all through this street and various members of ASARO were there as well as other artists collectives and students from the art school. We were making work that reflected the skeletons since they are very traditional in the imaginary of Oaxaca. We even made some drawing and portraits of Brad and we also made slogans from the movement in our work. The people supported us, they brought flowers, dyes for us to use in our work. We had the support of a lot of people.

❋ VIDEOCLIP 9.2: http://dx.doi.org/10.7264/N3GT5K3V

ASARO built a presence on the streets of Oaxaca with its high-contrast stencils featuring inspirational revolutionary slogans. Some of the initial images centered on children and women. One of the most powerful icons

Figure 9.7 "Ni un Explotado mas," by Beta of ASARO, 2006. DOI: 10.7264/N3D798B9. Photo by Itandehui Franco Ortiz

Figure 9.8 "Educacion primero al hijo del obrero," by Ikne of ASARO, 2006. DOI: 10.7264/N38G8HMK. Photo by Itandehui Franco Ortiz

was of a bent-over male child, which appeared with several slogans, including "Ni un explotado mas" (Not one more exploited person) (figure 9.7). "Not One More Exploited Person" suggests the death of childhood through work and the killing off of the potential of youth in a life or marginality. The downward-looking boy is using his finger to trace out a message, which may or may not be the one the viewer reads on the wall. A link is created between the viewer and the child who inhabits the wall. The child's dress and sandals suggest a working-class, urban identity.

"Educación primero al hijo del obrero" (Education first to the child of the worker) reflects a demand for equal access and, in fact, priority in the educational system for the children of physical laborers. The mother with a baby and another, smaller boy suggests an absent father who may be a laborer (figure 9.8). The right to education was one of the underlying demands in the teachers' strike, which strove to improve access to school and conditions in the schools for the most marginal children. Having this message repeated on public walls, coupled with the image of a working-class urban or rural family, helps to create a sense of identification for those passing by who might be in a similar situation. For those Oaxacans who can send their children to private schools and don't identify as workers, it is a reminder of the life circumstances of the majority.

Women figure prominently in images of resistance, as do *calaveras,* or skeletons. Calaveras in graphic arts was popularized by the satirist and illustrator Jose Guadalupe Posada in his political drawings published in Mexico City in the late nineteenth and early twentieth centuries. Calaveras are also prominently featured in popular art and cultural productions associated with the Day of the Dead. The use of women as signs of resistance in ASARO art can be linked to the women who occupied COR-TV, marched to Mexico City, and continued to have a strong presence in the radio stations through the fall of 2006. Armed women in resistance as a motif also builds on popular Zapatista icons and other revolutionary art, such as the famous photograph of a Sandinista women cradling a baby in her arms with a gun slung over her shoulder. The ASARO artist Beta has placed images of an armed calavera woman, with a child slung on her back in a *rebozo* (shawl), on a wide range of public walls, where the images are accompanied by various slogans. The woman is dressed in the garb of an urban working-class mother and has a bandana over her mouth, suggesting a protective measure against tear gas and a means to hide her identity. The bandana is a well-known feature of dress in Zapatista communities, which some describe as "covering our faces so that we can be seen." The interplay between the stencil of the woman and layers of graffiti creates a multipronged message. The same image, with different text and in a different context, conveys a different message each time.

In figure 9.9, Beta's armed calavera woman with a baby is a figure of power and protection, as suggested by the slogan "All the power to the people, long live Oaxaca!" It conveys energy and hope and serves to recognize and validate "the people" as a public political identity. Figure 9.10 shows "We don't forget our dead, evil assassins," stenciled onto a *petate.* The image evokes the dead watching over the assassins responsible for their deaths, in this context a serious and ominous figure. The petate, from the Nahuatl word *petatl,* connects with Oaxaca's indigenous cultures, where it is widely used for sleeping, sitting, and drying seeds and other foods. Those who are too poor to afford coffins are often buried in petates. The calavera woman can inhabit the petate as one of the dead. She is watching over those who killed her and letting the viewer know that impunity will not be tolerated: "Our dead are not forgotten." In a public space, this image sends a strong message to remind all of the people who have died.

Figure 9.9 *Mujer calavera*, "Todo el poder al pueblo," by Beta of ASARO, 2006. DOI: 10.7264/N34Q7RWV. Photo by Itandehui Franco Ortiz

Figure 9.10 *Mujer calavera*, "Nuestros muertos no se olivden," by Beta of ASARO, 2006. DOI: 10.7264/ N30Z715X. Photo by Itandehui Franco Ortiz

ASARO was invited by the Oaxacan artist Francisco Toledo to hold its first public art exhibit in the Instituto de Artes Gráficas (Institute of Graphic Arts, IAGO) in Oaxaca City. It opened on January 2, 2007. As described by Iván Arenas, the discussions that followed the invitation nearly broke up the collective. Some felt that the street was the only site they should paint in, but others wanted to open up the doors of museums to the street (Arenas 2011: 211–12). One artist collective, Arte Jaguar, left ASARO over their decision to take Toledo up on the invitation and participate in the exhibit. The move from the street into formal exhibitions brought internal discussions of how to think about authorship and inspiration. César Chávez, a graphic artist who began working with the original ASARO group, describes the work of ASARO artists as a "licuadora visual" or "visual blender." He describes the first exhibit in the IAGO as a pivot point in the life of ASARO and how people thought about their art moving from the street into galleries. César spoke with me while printing up T-shirts in the Espacio Zapata.

He commented:

It has been a learning process for ASARO. . . . When we had the exhibition in the IAGO in 2006; there was a stencil that had been painted in the street. There was the person who painted the original stencil and then there was a person who took a picture of it. In the exhibit they included the photograph and not the original stencil. The photograph came with a photo credit, but we had to wonder about whether he was the really the one who should be considered the "author" of the work. . . . But if you are going to fight about your rights of authorship then you shouldn't put your work in the street. . . . I think about it as a visual bender. We go taking pieces of things, adopting them.

✳ VIDEOCLIP 9.3: http://dx.doi.org/10.7264/N3C24TCF

Titled *Grafiteros al paredón* (Graffiti Artists to the Big Wall/Graffiti Artists Write on the Big Wall), the exhibit turned the walls and ceilings of the gallery into the artists' canvas. The exhibit featured images of the repression by the PFP in November as well as many images of political prisoners. While the streets of Oaxaca were militarized, many were still in prison, and the movement was silenced in the streets. But inside of the IAGO, ASARO set out a display of images that became foundational in the construction of the collective social memory of the 2006 movement and the severe repression it met.

The images in figure 9.11 evoke a multilayered message built on the

Figure 9.11 "Malburro" box / Political prisoners, by Irving of ASARO, 2007.
From the IAGO exhibit *Grafiteros al paredón.* DOI: 10.7264/N3W66HPJ. Photo by
Itandehui Franco Ortiz

juxtaposition of the logo and colors on a Marlboro cigarette box. It shows
a woman, a man, and a child behind bars, representing political prisoners.
The cigarette brand is deliberately misspelled "Malburro" (bad burro), with
the prisoners inside the box, incarcerated. The faces peer out at the viewer
with proud yet serious gazes. The image of the Marlboro man has been
turned on its head as the box features the prisoner, not a free-roaming cow-
boy. Grafitti that reads "La APPO Vive" (APPO Lives) is on one side of the
image, providing the message that even in prison, APPO continues.

The January 2007 IAGO exhibit was the first of many in which ASARO
has participated. It has had exhibitions in multiple venues in Mexico City
and Xalapa Veracruz, including universities, museums, and art galleries. In
2007 ASARO artists painted a wall at the U.S.-Mexican border, on the Tijuana side. International exhibits include a silk-screen exhibit in Riverside,
California, in 2007, a woodblock print show in the Little Fish Gallery in San
Francisco in 2007, a woodblock print exhibition at the the Fowler Museum
at UCLA in 2008 (see Johnson 2008), a print exhibition at the Glass Gallery

Figure 9.12 El Heces Ruiz (The Feces Ruiz): The innocent, the autocrat, the thief, the murderer, the pimp, woodblock print, ASARO, 2008. DOI: 10.7264/ N3RF5RZT. Photo by Kevin McCluskey

in North Adams, Massachusetts, in 2011, an exhibit titled *Prints from the Resistance* at the Cultural Center for Latino Arts in San Francisco's Mission District in 2011, and a graphic print exhibit titled *ASARO: Art and Activism* at the Bernstein Gallery at Princeton University in 2012.

Figure 9.12 illustrates the woodblock technique developed by several ASARO artists which was the basis for a number of exhibits. *El Heces Ruiz (The Feces Ruiz): the innocent, the autocrat, the thief, the murderer, the pimp* suggests the many different types of corruption and crimes for which ASARO artists and others held the governor of Oaxaca responsible. The different aspects of Governor Ruiz Ortiz were originally stenciled on the walls of buildings in downtown Oaxaca by ASARO artists. The woodblock incorporates the stencil images and adds the perspective of two horrified young people who are retreating from the death and ruin Ruiz Ortiz has caused in Oaxaca. The piece is a powerful comment on the depth of destruction and pain ASARO artists associate with the repression of the social movement in

2006. The woodblock print also serves as a visual testimonial of the different kinds of human rights and legal violations many people held the Ruiz Ortiz government accountable for.

These exhibitions have launched ASARO into the international art world and have also helped disseminate the unofficial story of the Oaxaca social movement of 2006. In Oaxaca, ASARO was one of the elements that forged a temporary unity out of difference, through the visual representation of El Pueblo in public spaces. This unity in difference did not come easily, as Arenas explains: "It has only been through the process of learning to debate, deliberate, and craft the commons at assemblies and through collective art practices that ASARO has been able to articulate together a collective and to demonstrate ways in which practices of struggle may continue to articulate social formations across difference" (2011: 304).

La Virgen de las Barrikadas:
ASARO Artists Launch a Religious Icon

One of the key icons that ASARO created, which was widely disseminated within the movement, built on popular religiosity and the importance of the icon of the Virgen de Guadalupe. Harnessing popular religion was another successful strategy that worked at least temporarily to create unity out of difference. The icon, known as La Virgen de las Barrikadas, also helped to legitimize the efforts of the many Oaxacan youth who guarded barricades and kept the PFP at bay on November 1, 2006, when they attempted to enter UABJO.

Life on the barricades in Oaxaca during the 2006 conflict was intense, and in October and November it became fraught with danger. As noted by Margarita Zires (2009b: 9), altars were built in some of the most dangerous barricades, such as the one guarding Radio La Ley and in the series of barricades around Cinco Senores that guarded access to Radio Universidad and UABJO. These altars often contained images such as the Virgen de Guadalupe (the patron saint of Mexico), La Virgen de Juquila (a patron saint of Santa Catarina de Juquila, considered very powerful in Oaxaca), and La Virgen de la Soledad (the patron saint of the state of Oaxaca). People working at the barricades would ask the virgins to protect them and to remove Ruiz Ortiz from office. Petitions to remove the governor could take the form of silent prayers or lighting candles and leaving flowers on the altar—all common elements for making requests to the saints.

According to Zires (2009b: 13), La Virgen de las Barrikadas (original

Figure 9.13 La Virgen de las Barricadas, by Line of ASARO, 2012 version. DOI: 10.7264/ N3MS3QNT

spelling, also later spelled with correct Spanish grammer, barricadas) was created by two design students, Line and Won, who belonged to ASARO. The image, a virgin modeled after the Virgen de Guadalupe, wears a gas mask and features burning tires on her cloak (figure 9.13). The image here is a later version printed and gifted to me by Line in August 2012 where the logo has changed slightly. The original version bore the logo "Protegenos Santisima Virgen de las Barrikadas" (Protect us Holy Virgin of the Barricades).

The image incorporates elements from the barricades (burning tires) and a gas mask to represent protection from the tear gas sprayed at protesters in many confrontations. The deliberate and stylized misspelling of *barricadas* as "barrikadas" in the original provokes the theme of resistance that is reflected in the image. There is resistance to proper orthography.

Line is an affable young man with an infectious laugh and engaging manner. He continues to work at ASARO, taking shifts printing T-shirts of the Virgen de las Barrikadas (his image above) and other prints that are sold in Espacio Zapata. Like other ASARO artists, he was young when he became involved in the movement.

Well in 2006 I was working making graffiti and stencils and I got involved in the 2006 movement because my parents were teachers. They lived through the repression that happened on June 14, 2006. I am also a graphic designer. So my way of supporting the movement was to make posters and also stencil art that had social themes. . . . I got involved in ASARO at the end of 2007 at the invitation of Mario and JESCA. That is how I got involved in the collective and began to produce some images for them.

✳ VIDEOCLIP 9.4: http://dx.doi.org/10.7264/N3MK69T5

La Virgen de las Barrikadas debuted in the exposition *Grafiterros al paradon* at IAGO in early 2007. While formally unveiled in the exhibit, one of her creators, Line (originally Line Marker), traces the Virgin's origins to the barricades themselves: "Part of sharing life on the barricades was that you would arrive and see a lot of people. They would come and say, 'Virgin, please make sure that nothing happens today, that when we wake up tomorrow everything is OK.' So that is how the idea emerged for a virgin we would devote ourselves to. That is how the Virgen de las Barrikadas was born" (Zires 2009b: 14).

After the exhibit, the Virgin began to appear on banners in marches, as she was adopted by teachers in Sección 22 and other parts of APPO. Zires (2009b: 15) documented her image on T-shirts, bags, stickers, postcards, posters, and other paraphernalia that were sold in Oaxaca and Mexico City and in the United States to raise funds for the artists to keep working to finance movement events. The image is not copyrighted; the artists who created her, Line and Wons, are not in favor of patenting the image. "It belongs to everyone, even though we created it," stated Line in an interview (Zires 2009b: 15). Since La Virgen de las Barrikadas is in the public domain, we incorporated it into the website Making Rights a Reality, a project that was developed in tandem with this book.

El Santo Niño APPO: Symbol of Youth Resistance and Popular Religion

El Santo Niño APPO appeared through a different trajectory than the Virgen. A second type of popular icon found on home altars in Oaxaca and other parts of Mexico is of the Niño Díos (the little God Child), who is venerated at Christmas and is carried from house to house as a part of the posadas ritual. The Niño Dios is honored with a large celebration on Christmas Eve (which ends the posadas) and on February 2, Candlemas. In Mexico people traditionally take their Niño Dios to mass on February 2 to be blessed. This date marks forty days from Jesus's birth, when his parents were said to have brought him to a temple to present him to the rabbis/religious authorities. The presentation of the Niño Dios in a mass requires a new outfit for the image. A popular version of the Niño Dios in Oaxaca and elsewhere in Mexico is the Santo Niño de Atocha, who is seated on a chair and carries a staff. Preparations for the veneration of the Santo Niño can begin on January 6, which is Día de los Reyes, when families traditionally share a ring-shaped sweet bread that has several miniature plastic infants hidden inside. Family members who find one of the infants in their piece of bread are supposed to buy tamales and drinks for others on Candlemas. If they choose to make a more serious commitment, they can take on sponsorship of the celebration for the Santo Niño on Candlemas, including purchasing a new outfit.

One of the families who participated in the Santa María barricade highlighted in chapter 3, along with an artist who worked closely with Sección 22 and APPO, decided to create a Santo Niño APPO. Pedro Cordova, one of the producers and announcers of Radio La Ley, is also a visual artist who works in multiple mediums. Working with Jorge Luis Martínez and Remedios Antonio, Pedro made the clothing and implements of the Santo Niño APPO (figure 9.14). Pedro explained in an interview in 2009 where he got the idea for the Niño APPO: "When they attacked the radio stations, we went to Radio 'La Ley' in the Colonia Reforma. Inside of the station there was an image of the Virgen de Guadalupe. A lot of my compañeros venerated her, they respected her" (García Morales 2009). Once Pedro observed how much faith people had in the Virgen de Guadalupe, he was motivated to create the Santo Niño APPO at the end of July 2006.

The Santo Niño APPO sits on a small chair, resembling that of the Niño

Figure 9.14 El Santo Niño APPO with a member of the Barricada Santa María.
DOI: 10.7264/N3H12ZXD

Antocha. In place of a staff, El Santo Niño APPO carries bottle rockets in one hand and a shield with APPO written on it in the other. He carries a slingshot over one shoulder, and a bazooka is slung across his back. El Santo Niño often sports a *pasamoñtana* (a black, open-faced ski mask made famous by the EZLN) and is dressed blue jeans. He wears a red T-shirt with APPO written on it and often red tennis shoes. He has a halo on his head. In explaining the symbolism of the figure, Pedro Cordova explicitly links it to the importance of youth in APPO and in the defense of the city from the PFP:

> The red is the color of social struggle; the blue jeans represent the youth who were attacked the most during our struggle, particularly in the barricades. The slingshot together with marbles were the only weapons they used to defend themselves. The *cohetes* [bottle rockets] symbolize the way we alert the people when there is a difficult situation and also to frighten the enemy. The ski mask was used by those in the movement to avoid being identified. (García Morales 2009)

Remedios Antonio, a teacher, and her husband, Jorge Luis Martínez, saw the Santo Niño APPO and, according to Cordova, wanted to take it to be blessed. Cordova gave it to them. Remedios and Jorge took the Santo Niño APPO to be blessed by a priest, but disguised it as a regular Santo Niño. Afterward Jorge and Remedios decided to take him out into a large march in February 2007, the ninth megamarch since June 14, 2006. In preparation, the couple decided to take his picture and to write a prayer for him. One of their sons created a religious stamp using his picture and the prayer. This was passed out during the parade and began to circulate on the Internet (Zires 2009b: 18). The prayer reads: "From this humble home, I ask you, Niño APPO, that you don't permit that this struggle be in vain, that the death of our compañeros not be met with impunity, that our compañeros who are prisoners be freed and that those who are persecuted and exiled have the freedom to return to their homes. All of these petitions that we make are for peace and democracy in Oaxaca" (Hernández 2011).[7]

After its debut on February 4, 2007, the Santo Niño APPO continued to make appearances in APPO marches and at commemorative events. The Santo Niño APPO is given credit for the liberation of many of the political prisoners who were taken in 2006, for the return of exiles, such as Dr. Bertha (profiled in chapter 6), and for protecting widows and orphans (Hernández 2011). Like La Virgen de las Barrikadas, El Santo Niño APPO was disseminated in multiple ways. When Sección 22 took up its occupation in the zócalo again in June 2007 and led a series of protest marches, the largest on July 29, a group of teachers set up a shrine known as the Campamento al Santo Niño APPO in front of the main cathedral of Oaxaca, on one side of the zócalo. Members of Sección 22 cared for the Santo and also provided spaces for people to write messages to him (Zires 2009b: 23). The Santo Niño APPO and La Virgen de las Barrikadas continued as important religious icons in APPO marches from 2007 forward.

Both images have been incorporated into pubic ritual activities that combine traditional elements of Oaxacan religious rituals with actions to create social memory and commemorate past events. On November 25, 2008, after a large march commemorating the day the PFP shut down the movement and arrested dozens of people, the Comité de Familiares de Desaparecidos, Asesinados y Presos Políticos de Oaxaca (Committee of Families of the Disappeared, Assassinated, and Political Prisoners of Oaxaca), along with Christian-based communities and, reportedly, ten priests sympathetic to the moment, walked in procession. They stopped at places in the city where police violence had been particularly brutal. This is similar to the processions held during Holy Week, which stop at the Stations of the Cross, or Oaxacan funeral processions, which also stop at the Stations of the Cross mapped onto local community geography. At each spot the procession stopped on November 25, 2008, prayers were said while copal (an indigenous religious incense) was blown in the four cardinal directions and someone read a description of what had happened in that spot (Zires 2009b: 30–31). The Santo Niño APPO was a part of this procession. The anthropologist Kirsten Norget has characterized the type of spirituality shown that day as based in the values and practices derived from indigenous cultural traditions. She states that these characteristics have evolved into a singular popular urban-hybrid culture in Oaxaca (2009: 315). Indigenous elements, along with those of folk Catholicism, permeated the social movement of 2006 and found strong resonance with the inclusion of symbols like the Virgen de las Barrikadas and the Santo Niño APPO. Norget (2008) has pointed out elsewhere how APPO incorporated many representations of indigeneity in the urban context of Oaxaca.

Summary

The contributions that were made by Oaxacan youth in groups such as VOCAL, CASOTA, and ASARO to create a new blueprint for what "the face of Oaxaca" looks and feels like in the eyes of the majority should not be underestimated. While the collective subject of a multiclass, ethnically hybrid, multigenerational, and gender-and-sexuality-inclusive pueblo de Oaxaca was most likely a temporary achievement, the broadening of the Oaxacan social imaginary to include this subject cannot be undone. Organizational, visual, processual, and strategic experimentation by youth and women, in particular, have changed the perspectives and experiences of many individuals, families, and neighborhoods in Oaxaca. Although Ulises Ruiz Ortiz stayed in office until the formal political system removed him, the widespread participation of youth in nonelectoral forms of cultural and political change was part of the broader context that resulted in the election of Gabino Cué Monteagudo in 2010. At the end of the day, the contributions of Oaxacan youth documented here helped to produce new political subjects. As I discuss in the conclusion, the enduring legacies of the Oaxacan social movement and of others like it enable the marginal majority to recuperate personal and collective dignity, to articulate important sets of rights and identities, and to broaden the concept of citizenship. These processes are fundamental to facilitating participation in political systems. They can work in tandem with formal electoral systems if the right circumstances emerge to foster significant improvements in the quality of life for the majority—the 99 percent.

Conclusions

Every Oaxacan was profoundly affected by the events of 2006. The social conflict revealed in stark terms the lack of rights (in practice) and political participation that the majority of Oaxacans had. It also revealed the potential power and strategic effectiveness of testimony and of the political identity forged around El Pueblo de Oaxaca.

Following the shutdown of the Oaxacan social movement by the PFP in November 2006, the different parts of the movement became less visible but continued and in some cases flourished. Sección 22, for example, continued to organize for better salaries, basic school infrastructure, and improved conditions for students. The teachers also institutionalized the Guelaguetza Popular, which was held alongside the official Guelaguetza for the fifth and sixth consecutive years in 2011 and 2012 and was a great success. Indigenous and community radio stations proliferated and even expanded. Youth organizing took off in different directions: VOCAL continued to support the movement for Triqui autonomy through MULTI; ASARO mounted many exhibitions and continued their public art production. The women's organization COMO split into several parts and then partially came back together. The businessmen and entrepreneurs of Oaxacan civil society formalized an NGO dedicated to peaceful change: Movimiento Ciudadano por la Justicia, Paz, y Desarollo con Dignidad para Oaxaca. Ulises Ruiz Ortiz left office after Gabino Cué Monteagudo assumed the governorship and named several active supporters of APPO to his cabinet. Ramiro Aragón Pérez and Ruth Guzmán Sánchez received political asylum in the United States. The Oaxaca state government formed a special commission to look into human rights abuses and passed a law in January 2012 making the state Human Rights Commission independent of the state government and in August 2012, Governor Gabino Cué Monteagudo presented the Oaxacan legislature with a proposal to form a truth commission to investigate human rights violations committed in 2006 and 2007.

The APPO still exists in principle, but has not held a successful state-wide assembly for several years. In the words of Iván Arenas, "That APPO marches, assemblies, and barricades succeeded in uniting socialist and anarchist factions, wives, homemakers, and street youths, and was able to articulate together the collective subject of *el pueblo* is remarkable and was unforeseen" (2011: 298). By 2012, however, the solidarity and promise of APPO had largely unraveled (298), the Triqui autonomy movement through MULTI came under heavy repression, and families were unable to return to San Juan Copala (as of February 15, 2012). Did the social movement of 2006 succeed? Did it fail? Or are we asking the wrong question?

Rights and Identities

The lasting legacy of the 2006 social movement can be found in the words of Fidelia: "We are brown, we are short, we are fat, and they don't think that we represent the people, but we do. WE are the face of Oaxaca." While APPO as a unified movement has not endured in the strategically powerful way that it functioned in 2006, it has left many important legacies. The Oaxacan social movement gave birth to a new set of political subjects—not only those who identify with the words of Fidelia but others as well. They include the middle-class entrepreneurs and business people who felt that they had to step up and participate in new ways in politics in Oaxaca; they include women and youth, who were central players during the most powerful periods of the movement and whose personal transformations were probably the most significant. These two sectors were the driving forces behind the hybrid urban popular identities that emerged and endure.

The women who took over and ran COR-TV and subsequently other radio stations were personally transformed by their experience and created a new gendered discourse of dignity and human rights centered on the rights to speak, to be heard, and to decide who governs. The repeated categories they used, the specific rights they claimed, and the symbols they deployed offer insights that broaden the study of human rights. Their experience highlights the importance of looking at the processes of local vernacularization of "universal" rights and the reverse: how the local can come to influence the universal (see Merry 2006; Goodale and Merry 2007).

The mobilization of human rights categories and symbols by these women likely influenced the formal outcome of a new piece of state legislation, La Ley de la Defensoría de los Derechos Humanos del Pueblo de Oaxaca (Law on the Office of the Human Rights of the People of Oaxaca), approved in January 2012. The work of human rights organizations and human rights defenders such as Yésica Sánchez Maya, were also important influences on this new law. The law created an autonomous, citizen-based, secular office that will include perspectives on gender and multiculturalism and on ways to prevent discrimination. This new office is completely independent from Oaxaca's state executive, legislative, and judicial branches of government, and will have financial, organizational, and administrative autonomy. These characteristics are particularly important given that, during the violence and repression of 2006, the state organization charged with defending human rights, which was dependent on the government of Ulises Ruiz Ortiz, did nothing to intervene when violence and abuses occurred (Olor a mi tierra 2012). The law states in part that the new office shall include "mechanisms of early alert, for the attention of serious cases without the possibility of reparations, when there has been knowledge of alleged violations of the rights of the physical and psychic integrity of journalists, defenders of human rights, migrants, indigenous peoples, women, persons with disability, girls, children, adolescents or any person who has a great degree of risk or vulnerability" (Olor a mi tierra 2012). The law also requires that all 570 municipalities in Oaxaca create offices for the defense of human rights.

Such a requirement will add new *cargos* to municipal systems of governance and justice, which will no doubt undergo a period of adjustment. Local systems of *usos y costumbres* are often built around different understandings of rights, justice, punishment, and security than those of the state. Experiences such as the community policing system of Guerrero (Sierra 2009, 2010, 2013) and instances of community-based models of security and justice can coexist with and overlap state-mandated systems. They can also, however, result in clashes, such as when different sectors of the same community have opposing visions of what shared rights and responsibilities are and invoke conflicting authorities to bear out their particular visions (see Stephen 2005a).

The women who took over COR-TV also had an effect on assumptions about who belongs in Oaxaca. Through their claims as urban, indigenous, working-class, and poor people who had rights to be heard, to speak, and to decide who governs, they recentered who represents the majority. By profiling on the TV and radio women who looked, sounded, and behaved in ways that were rooted in the daily lives of women in the city and challenged the prevailing images of a white, Spanish, upper-class elite, they put forward new conceptions of who is Oaxaqueña. By giving a media platform to women in blue jeans and T-shirts who were brown, had short hair, and spoke urban Spanish, and also to self-defined Zapotec women speaking in their own language, with long braids, aprons, and *huipiles* (indigenous women's blouses), they produced compelling images of active Oaxaqueñas. Youth organizers and artists built on this legacy.

The visual images of people represented on public walls and later in art galleries by the artists of ASARO, Arte Jaguar, and other youth collectives took the same kind of hybrid, urban identity projected by the women who took over COR-TV and broadened it to include men and children as well. Using visual cues such as *huarachas* (sandals), blue jeans, huipiles, bandanas, T-shirts, and hairstyles from indigenous women's braids to punk cuts, urban youth artists added another layer of visibility and permanence to the hybrid popular identity that emerged in 2006. With their entry into the commercial and museum-based art world in Mexico and internationally, ASARO artists and others participated in globally recentering the image of what Oaxacans look like and act like.

In Juxtlahuaca APPO succeeded in temporarily forging pan-indigenous solidarity between Mixtec and Triqui activists and building alliances with nonindigenous people in the region. The declaration of the Triqui Autonomous Municipality of San Juan Copala in early 2007 was an attempt to build on this pan-indigenous solidarity and use it to reclaim the traditional territory and capital of lowland Triqui culture and politics. In 1948 the Triqui capital of San Juan Copala was changed by the federal government from a *municipio* (county) head to an *agencia* (subcounty administrative unit) and put under the rule of mestizo authorities in Santiago Juxtlahuaca. The pan-indigenous solidarity that was solidified in 2006 by APPO Juxtlahuaca was not able to endure in the same form beyond early 2007. The experience of operating and defending an APPO government in Juxtlahuaca, however, resulted in strong ties between some Mixtec and Triqui communities that continue through the work of FIOB in the region, particularly in the work of the Consejo Regional de Mujeres (Women's Regional Council) in the Juxtlahuaca region (see Stephen 2009b). The Consejo sponsors a number of ongoing projects, such as rotating savings clubs and small production and distribution projects for crafts, organic vegetables, mushrooms, and traditional foods, with the goal of supporting local economies and the "right to not migrate."

The Autonomous Municipality of San Juan Copala has been the center of severe conflict between different Triqui organizations in recent times. The fragility of the coalition that existed between UBISORT and MULTI at the time of the formation of the autonomous municipality suggests the complexity of forming a unified ethnic identity in Oaxaca and elsewhere. Ethnic solidarity is anything but automatic when regional ethnic histories such as that of the Triqui are permeated by militarization, state intervention, commercialization of crops (such as coffee), the presence of political bosses, and agrarian conflict. Even in this situation of conflict, however, displaced Triqui women from MULTI who set up and occupied an encampment in the center of Oaxaca City for more than two years beginning in 2010 resisted their historical framing as victims and demonstrated amazing creativity and resilience in reconstructing family, economic, and social relations. A number of these women also became vocal leaders of the encampment and spokespeople for the cause of Triqui autonomy (De Marinis, 2013). Thus while the 2006 social movement resulted in the formation of new political subjects in Oaxaca by creating unified identities out of diverse elements, in San Juan Copala a temporary unified ethnic identity was initially fragmented, but reconstituted in part through the efforts of Triqui women who emerged from the margins to be the motor of ongoing effort to establish a Triqui autonomous municipality.

Dignity and Rights

For those who suffered directly from repression and violence in 2006—and for the circle of family, friends, neighbors, coworkers, and colleagues close to them—the conflict revealed that the "rights" that people were supposed to have were a farce. As Juan Gabriel said of the torture suffered by himself, Elionai Santiago Sánchez, and Ramiro Aragón Pérez, "We had to declare again and again what happened. We have pictures, infinity of photos showing what they did to us. And in spite of all this, the government says, 'You are accused of a crime, you are guilty, and that's the end of it.'"

The doubts that Elionai had about the capacity of the Oaxacan state or federal justice system to defend the human rights of Oaxacans and to truly impart justice are shared by many. Elionai said of the justice system: "After the death of José Jiménez Colmenares we understood what was going on. There were more than twenty other deaths after that. This has put us in a situation of despair with the Mexican system of justice, the federal as well as the state. . . . We are profoundly disillusioned with the system we live under. We have seen so many injustices committed in the light of day, and now this situation has become normalized." Their experiences and those of many others who were tortured, assassinated, and imprisoned revealed the fact that "rights"—even those specified in the state and federal constitutions—were not inherently bestowed on all citizens of Oaxaca but were selectively bestowed upon the population by the small group of political elites who held power (Mignolo 2011: 214).

For many, the result of the social conflict of 2006 was a desire to recuperate personal and collective dignity, a process that comes from below and usually occurs prior to the claiming of rights. In the case of the women who took over COR-TV, the recuperation of their dignity began on the air and was a significant part of the process that led them to author a gendered discourse of rights. In indigenous and community radio, the recuperation of dignity is also an important precursor to the declaration of rights. Walter Mignolo's differentiation between rights and dignity is instructive here: "'Rights' are attributed to us by someone who has the right to attribute rights; dignity cannot be attributed, but is taken by the non-person whose rights are being defended. The colonial difference is the main factor that extracts dignity from people: being racialized and seen as inferior by the dominant discourse makes us believe in our own inferiority. That is what taking away our dignity means" (2011: 214).

Although Mignolo is highlighting this difference to clarify what he sees as one of the primary theoretical contributions of the Zapatista movement, the difference between rights and dignity is useful for reflecting on the longer term outcomes from the Oaxacan social movement. Taking or claiming human dignity is the primary path to declaring rights from below and then pressuring for their realization. Recuperating dignity and then a capacity to name and claim rights and entitlements are cornerstones in the creation of new political subjects and in broadening definitions of citizenship.

Political Participation and New Forms of Citizenship

Many scholars have focused on the ways that those who are disenfranchised from political participation through a lack of formal citizenship may participate through transnational or nonnational political spaces and strategies

(Levitt 2001; Bosniak 2000; Sassen 1999). In her more recent work, Saskia Sassen has suggested important ways in which, even inside capitalist democracies, there is "the emergence of a type of political subject that does not quite correspond to the notion of the formal political subject who is the voting and jury-serving citizen" (2006: 321). Her argument is that processes of globalization have produced a growing distance between the state and the citizen. Some of this distance involves the ways states have accommodated global ideas and institutions, such as the rule of law and respect for private authority from the inside, reinscribing the global within the national. These changes, she argues, can take place without dislodging citizenship from "its national encasement" (320). The other paths for changes in how citizenship is structured and understood are related to what she calls "postnational citizenship, transnational identities, and formalized innovations" such as "the European passport and the increasingly institutionalized human rights regime" (320). What makes Sassen's argument interesting is her insistence that global processes producing transnational identities and forms of political participation also result in critical changes happening inside the national state. "The critical assumption here is that citizenship is inevitably an incompletely specified contract between the state and the citizen, and that in this incompleteness then lies the possibility of accommodating new conditions and incorporating new formal and informal instrumentalities" (21).

Sassen's theoretical insights provide a useful framework for understanding the transborder organizing that FIOB did through its participation in APPO Los Angeles and the subsequent role it played in the electoral organizing and campaigning for the Oaxaca governorship in 2010. The existence of transborder Oaxacan communities in multiple locations throughout Mexico and the United States, and their organization by FIOB, permitted the U.S.-based FIOB members to participate in the Oaxacan social movement of 2006 from Los Angeles. While some members of FIOB are formal citizens of Mexico, others, born in the United States, are not. The definition of citizenship that was operative in the organizing that FIOB and APPO-Los Angeles carried out in 2006 was not centered around the contract between the state and the citizen, but rather on the sense of citizenship that emerges from Oaxacan transborder communities that is practiced within FIOB as an organization, both in form through service to the organization through cargos and in process through following the model of the participatory assembly to make decisions. This sense of citizenship is articulated through specified rights and responsibilities to the collective community, wherever it is located and in FIOB to the binational organization and its local and regional committees. The transborder communities represented within the structure of FIOB permitted their 2006 participation in APPO to encompass the larger territory in which FIOB operates. Known as Oaxacalifornia—a term coined by anthropologist Michael Kearney (1995b), this territory includes Oaxaca, Baja California Sur, and Baja California Norte in Mexico and the state of California in the United States (Rivera-Salgado 1998).

Citizenship in both Oaxaca and California was constructed both outside the framework of the national, through transborder solidarity and the inclusion of people living outside Mexico who were not citizens, and also within the framework of the national politics as Oaxacans abroad participated in formal and informal political processes centered in Mexico. The case of FIOB binational political participation in the Oaxaca social movement from Los Angeles suggests how we can learn from indigenous models of citizenship that have responded in creative ways to a transborder and multisited reality. Through a hybrid model of citizenship that combines local Oaxacan understandings of the rights and responsibilities of local citizenship with national strategies of dialoguing with the Mexican state but not engaging solely through the contract between the state and the citizen, FIOB activists have successfully inhabited national, binational, and multisited local spaces of political participation. Such a model provides an important epistemological example of the ways that indigenous knowledges can enrich and complicate modernist notions of democracy, and political participation.

The election of Gabino Cué Monteagudo, Oaxaca's first non-PRI governor, who ran as a candidate of the opposition (PRD-PAN-Convergencia) alliance in 2006, was helped by the strong ties forged by FIOB with Sección 22, APPO, and other Oaxacan organizations. Cué Monteagudo invited one of FIOB's founders, Rufino Domínguez Santos, to serve in his administration as director of the Oaxacan Institute for Attention to Migrants. Domínguez Santos had been residing in California for more than two decades. His acceptance of the post signaled a new era in FIOB's relationship with the Oaxacan state government which has developed its own challenges.

The fact that Cué Monteagudo campaigned in California for the governorship of Oaxaca and incorporated a California-based FIOB leader into his government suggests important ways that the Mexican state has changed as a result of globalization and collaborates in the production of new kinds of political subjects.

While Sassen writes about processes taking place primarily within modern liberal states, Partha Chatterjee's book *The Politics of the Governed,* on "popular politics in most of the world," takes as its subject "those parts of the world which were not direct participants in the history of the evolution of institutions of modern capitalist democracy" (2004: 1). Chatterjee writes that this refers to well over three-fourths of contemporary humanity. His interest lies in understanding the forms of political participation that disenfranchised groups of people have engaged in.

Chatterjee's focus is on "political society," the entry of the rural and urban poor and disenfranchised into a different form of political engagement with states that permits them to negotiate entitlements by being defined as "populations" that become the targets of specific policies. Using the Foucauldian concept of governmentality, Chatterjee argues that even if people do not have formally defined rights—such as those rights that belong to the numerical minority in India, who, he states, are the ones who really constitute "civil society"—they have entitlements such as to assistance in rebuilding a home if they have been displaced. Refugees, day laborers, homesteaders, and people living below the poverty line are all demographic categories of governmentality. Based on their categories, they can define claims.

In order to make claims effectively, however, Chatterjee argues that a population group produced by governmentality must be invested with the moral content of a community. Thus, for example, a technically illegal colony of refugee migrant populations resulting from the partition of India in 1947 who occupied land owned by the national railroad mobilized metaphors of kinship and family "to give the empirical form of a population group the moral attributes of a community" (2004: 57). By successfully constituting themselves over time, people in the colony were able to resist removal and negotiate a wide range of services and welfare benefits, such as immunization for children, schools, counselors, negotiating with power and electrical companies after illegally tapping electrical lines, and housing assistance. In this and other cases, the politics of the governed involved the government's obligation to look after the poor and those who form political society using the moral rhetoric of community to stake their claims.

Chatterjee argues that the concept of governmentality can create conditions, as in the case of the railroad colony, for an expansion of democratic participation. While some of this indirectly involves working with people in political parties who participate in electoral politics, much of the negotiating is done by brokers and representatives and with government agencies and NGOs. Chatterjee suggests, finally, that the "paralegal then, despite its ambiguous and supplementary status in relation to the legal, is not some pathological condition of retarded modernity, but rather part of the very process of the historical constitution of modernity" (2004: 75).

I find Chatterjee's framing of political society versus civil society instructive in analyzing forms of organizing and political participation in the Oaxacan social movement of 2006. The business people and entrepreneurs who identified themselves as civil society formed an NGO, and many also went on to participate in Cué Monteagudo's campaign for governor. Others ran for political office and won, such as Luis Ugartechea Begué, who became the *presidente municipal* (mayor) of Oaxaca City. Their belief in the electoral system and their middle- and upper-class standing and cultural capital allowed them to successfully mobilize inside the narrow space of a select Oaxacan civil society. In many senses, this group also represents what Sassen calls "the voting and jury-serving citizen" (2006: 321).

On the other hand, El Pueblo de Oaxaca, or *Oaxaca popular*, the hybrid urban, indigenous, working-class, and poor people who came together strategically in marches, barricades, and occupations and on the air correspond to Chatterjee's political society—at least in a temporal sense. The short, the brown, and the fat exercised a massive physical and symbolic presence during 2006 and also came to exist as a moral community, particularly after the state government ramped up repression and violence. Claims staked in the name of El Pueblo de Oaxaca for the rights to speak, to be heard, and to govern, sustainable development, social stability and justice, and economic, human, social, cultural, and ecological rights (articulated at an APPO forum held in August 2006) came from a moral community in which a range of differences was blended into one identity. The different pieces of that identity (indigenous, youth, female, gay and lesbian, poor and working class) can be seen in part as corresponding to different categories of governance that, through the establishment of state policy, lend legitimacy to the claims of individuals in the category. When these identity categories came together in the political opening of the 2006 movement and achieved legitimacy as a moral community, the people's ability as political society to negotiate services and even changes in the law gained capacity. Even though APPO did not continue to function with the same level of unity and force as it did in 2006, after that time the constituent pieces of the coalition and the political subjects known as El Pueblo de Oaxaca were able to continue to be politically effective through their partial entry into formal state power in the liberal wing of the Cué Monteagudo government. The inclusion of indigenous leaders such as Adelfo Regino (secretario de asunto indígenas del estado de

Oaxaca) and Rufino Domínguez Santos (director del Instituto Oaxaqueño de Atención al Migrante) in the Cué Monteagudo government allows them to function as brokers for the political society of El Pueblo de Oaxaca.

In October 2011, at their Seventh General Assembly, FIOB elected new leaders and developed binational policy and strategy in a series of discussions and a plenary assembly. What was most notable at the opening ceremonies of the assembly was the open embrace of FIOB by representatives of the progressive wing of the Oaxacan state government. While prior congresses and FIOB participation in APPO were received with veiled hostility at best and attempts at repression at worst, the Seventh Assembly signaled the Cué Monteagudo government's open support of FIOB. This is an example of the ways political society can gain access to state power and also suggests ways that political participation is broadened. For leaders like the former FIOB general coordinator and founder Rufino Domínguez Santos, their position can be double-edged, as they try to provide better access for organizations such as FIOB and many others that were previously shut out of conversation with the state government. At the same time, they must also represent the interests of the state, which will no doubt produce situations of conflict with members of the political society of El Pueblo de Oaxaca.

Why Testimony Matters in Social Movements

In the Oaxaca movement of 2006, testimonials were broadcast on the radio and television, shared at public demonstrations, in the streets, at barricades, around kitchen tables, in prisons, in human rights offices, and in front of soldiers, police, and government officials. Testifying significantly repositioned many previously excluded speakers as active citizens who can speak, be heard, claim rights, and develop as new political subjects. One of the key organizing tasks taken on by many sectors of the movement either consciously or unconsciously was to create venues where people could tell the story of how they came to realize what was wrong, conceive of themselves as people capable of recognizing what was wrong and articulating what should be, and create a community of others who have been wronged in similar ways and can dream in similar ways of what to do to make things right (Stephen 2010: 80). This community of others, in the case of Oaxaca, became El Pueblo de Oaxaca.

Testimony is a crucial vehicle for creating experiences and feelings of passionate politics that are central to how people live and feel collective struggle. The experience of testifying, and also of witnessing others as they testify (directly and indirectly), is an important part of how political identities develop in individuals, how those individuals seek to provide others with the knowledge and confidence to analyze the world from their particular social locations, and how groups of people participate in the ideological work of shifting public political discourses and perceptions. This requires scaling down to reveal the pivotal, emotive moments for individual activists in their own personal development. It also requires scaling up to look at how collective identities move beyond specific individuals and organizations and take on an independent ideological life in relation to other public political discourses and ideologies (see Brodkin 2007).

The analysis that activists create can be legitimized in temporal and/or structural circumstances (such as that in Oaxaca in 2006) that create an opening for a new political narrative to emerge and be heard and validated by other political actors. By studying the forms of knowledge production that activists engage in and the processes by which they become inserted into the political and cultural mainstream, we can understand how public discourses change or are challenged. Testimony as a form of knowledge production and its archiving on audiotape or videotape, in text, or in the brain is an important epistemology for understanding the formation of new political identities that are behind processes of rights claiming and the broadening of concepts of citizenship and political participation.

Politics is a multifaceted and multilayered archive; our understanding of political processes is greatly enriched if we are able to access the broadest range of experiences in that archive. The unofficial stories of El Pueblo de Oaxaca in all of their diversity and beauty are offered here in the hopes that their entry into the archive will allow multiple truths to emerge and enrich the social memory of the movement that rocked Oaxaca in 2006.

NOTES

Chapter 1

1. For the United Nations system, "transitional justice is the full range of processes and mechanisms associated with a society's attempt to come to terms with a legacy of large-scale past abuses, in order to ensure accountability, serve justice and achieve reconciliation. It consists of both judicial and non-judicial processes and mechanisms, including prosecution initiatives, facilitating initiatives in respect of the right to truth, delivering reparations, institutional reform and national consultations" (United Nations 2012).

2. For descriptions and photos of the people on the website team, see http://pages.uoregon.edu/mrarOaxaca/bios.htm.

3. Here the words of David Graeber are instructive:

Almost every time I'm interviewed by a mainstream journalist about [Occupy Wall Street], I get some variation of the same lecture: "How are you going to get anywhere if you refuse to create a leadership structure or make a practical list of demands? And what's with all this anarchist nonsense—the consensus, the sparkly fingers . . . ? You're never going to be able to reach regular, mainstream Americans with this sort of thing!"

It is hard to imagine worse advice. After all, since 2007, just about every previous attempt to kick off a nationwide movement against Wall Street took exactly the course such people would have recommended—and failed miserably. It is only when a small group of anarchists in New York decided to adopt the opposite approach—refusing to recognize the legitimacy of the existing political authorities by making demands of them; refusing to accept the legitimacy of the existing legal order by occupying a public space without asking for permission; refusing to elect leaders that could then be bribed or co-opted; declaring, however nonviolently, that the entire system was corrupt and they rejected it; being willing to stand firm against the state's inevitable violent response—that hundreds of thousands of Americans from Portland to Tuscaloosa began rallying in support, and a majority declared their sympathies. (Graeber 2011b)

Chapter 2

1. The Movimiento Revolucionario Magisterial (Revolutionary Teacher's Movement) of the Communist Party was involved in both of these struggles. One took place in Mexico City between 1956 and 1960. This struggle, like CNTE, involved the integral relationship between economic demands and the development of new forms of struggle (Street 1992: 91). The other prior struggle took place in Chihuahua at the beginning of the 1970s; teachers of Sección 8 of SNTE were trying to democratize their union but were unable to agree on how workers' control should be implemented within the state. Ultimately they were co-opted (Street 1992: 92).

2. See Victor Raúl Martínez Vásquez 2004 for a different perspective.

3. Since 1970 more than 150 teachers have been killed or disappeared by thugs working for the SNTE or by government security forces (Monroy 1997: 3). Many more have been disappeared or imprisoned (Hérnandez Navarro 2011: 22).

4. A telesegundaria is a secondary school (junior high school) that was created in the late 1960s to service isolated rural communities with low numbers of students, where it was not possible to sustain a full-scale middle school. The schools use a televised curriculum but also include at least one and often more teachers on site. In the late 1990s telesegundarias averaged one teacher for every two grades, with an average of twenty-two students per grade. The number of students who attended was almost a million by the year 2000 (Castro et al. 1999).

5. San Juan Copala is the site of a current conflict between two organizations, discussed in chapter 7.

6. In 1981 the Movimiento de Unificación y Lucha Triqui (Movement for Triqui Unification and Struggle, MULT) was born in affiliation with the Coordinadora Nacional Plan de Ayala (National Coordinator Plan de Ayala, CNPA) and with the support of another indigenous leftist organization in Oaxaca, the COCEI. MULT is described in greater detail in chapter 7.

7. The agrarian conflict between Santo Lorenzo Texmelucan and Santo Domingo Teojomulco has been called one of the gravest agrarian conflicts in the state. It was finally resolved through federal and state government intervention in 2006 (see Grupo Misófilo 2011: 34).

8. The guerrilla movement was organized by the Unión del Pueblo and later through the Liga comunista 23 de Septiembre. The other half of the movement formed COCEO and these other organizations: Central Campesina Independiente (Independent Peasant Central), El Movimiento Revolucionario del Magistereo (Revolutionary Teachers' Movement), El Movimiento Sindical Ferrocarrilero, (Railroad Workers' Movement), the Sindicato de Trabajadores Electricistas (Union of Electrical Workers), and a peasant group from Santa Gertrudes, an agricultural community about forty minutes south of the city of Oaxaca (Martínez Vásquez 1990: 133).

9. The structure of COCEO, according to Martínez Vásquez (1990: 133n11),

was an assembly of representatives who were primarily the secretary-generals of the participating organizations. Each had specific tasks to realize.

10. As noted by Martínez Vásquez (1990: 142–43) and in my earlier work (Stephen 2002), the ideological aspects of revolutionary-era Zapatismo were alive and well in Oaxaca beginning in the 1920s and were particularly strong during the 1930s, under the presidency of Lázaro Cardenas. In 1973, for example, when lands were occupied in La Ciénega on April 10, local peasants shouted "Tierra y Libertad" (Land and Liberty) as well as "The land belongs to those who work it," in commemoration of the death of Emiliano Zapata (Mártinez Vásquez 1990: 143).

11. Although three slates of independent candidates won in Santa Gertrudis, El Trapiche, and Zimatlán in 1974, these electoral victories were annulled by the new governor.

12. Some of the many strikes in 1974 included the meat industry, led by the Sindicato Independiente de Obreros de la Industria de la Carnes de Oaxaca (Independent Union of the Works of the Meat Industry of Oaxaca); the Choferes del Sur (Bus Drivers of the South); the municipality of Oaxaca, La Dirección de Obras Públicas del Gobierno de Oaxaca (Secretary of Public Works of the government of Oaxaca); the Navarro y Reforma businesses; bakeries; El Instituto de Investigación e Integración Social del Estado de Oaxaca (Institute of Investigation and Social Integration of the State of Oaxaca); and La Universidad Autónoma Benito Juárez (Martínez Vásquez 1990: 150–55)

13. This group was the Federación Independiente de Obreros Agrícolas y Campesinos de Oaxaca (Independent Federation of Agricultural Workers and Peasants of Oaxaca).

14. Also at this time, four COCEI leaders were imprisoned: Leopoldo de Gives, Carlos Sánchez, Manuel Vásquez Nicolás, and Jesús Vicente Vásquez. The first three were in prison until 1985; the last was released at the end of 1986 (Martínez Vásquez 1990: 232).

15. These organizations included COCEI, the Unidad de Comunidades Indígenas de la Zona Norte del Istmo (Union of Indigenous Communities of the Northern Zone of the Isthmus), and Servicios del Pueblo Mixe, (Services of the Mixe People).

16. In the 1980s Grupo de Estudios Sobre la Mujer, Rosario Castellanos A.C. sponsored weekly radio shows, conducted workshops on health, and worked to bring women's rights to state and city politics. In 1991 it opened La Casa de la Mujer Rosario Castellanos (Rosario Castellanos Women's Center) and in 1995 began giving scholarships to young indigenous women to help them continue their education in high school and university.

Chapter 3

1. See Poole 2007a for a description of the contemporary Guelaguetza and the alternative Guelaguetza Popular.

2. Indigenous organizations such as Servicios del Pueblo Mixe (Services of the Mixe People), under the leadership of Adelfo Regino, and the Unión de

Organizaciones de la Sierra Juárez de Oaxaca (Union of Organizations of the Sierra Juárez of Oaxaca), as well as part of the democratic teachers' movement and the liberation theology branch of the Catholic Church in Oaxaca, were also influential (Hernández Díaz 2007: 50; Yescas 1996: 449).

3. The massacred peasants belonged to Organización Campesina de la Sierra Sur (Campesino Organization of the Southern Sierra).

4. According to a report published by Servicio Internacional por la Paz (International Service for Peace, SIPAZ: 2011), there were "at least 200 illegal detentions, 150 cases of torture, 32 unlawful entries, 22 extrajudicial executions, 22 forced disappearances, 127 people imprisoned for political or conscience reasons and innumerable cases of sexual abuse, harassment, threats of death and unlawful penal processes in later years."

5. Founded in 1997, CIPO-RFM is a grassroots organization of indigenous communities based on the philosophy of Ricardo Flores Magón, the Oaxaca-born anarchist revolutionary who was an important figure in the Mexican Revolution (Kolhatkar 2006). According to Raúl Gatica Bautista of San Miguel, Tlaxiaco, a founding member of CIPO-RFM, who is a Mixtec writer and a primary school teacher:

CIPO-RFM is searching in a peaceful manner for the resolution of problems regarding health, housing, education, and work for the indigenous people in Oaxaca. We also demand the community ownership of our land and recognition of our rights as individuals and as a group. We have our own language, our vision of the world, self-determination, and autonomy. We also fight for the respect of indigenous nations, for the preservation of forests and the environment. (Kolhatkar 2006)

6. Sánchez López, who was the candidate of the Partido Unidad Popular (registered by Heriberto Pazos Ortiz, leader of the MULT), received 40,000 votes. Heriberto Pazos Ortiz, one of the founders of the MULT and the statewide leader of the Partido Unidad Popular, was assassinated in Oaxaca City in October 2010.

7. This organization was the Confederación Revolucionaria Obrera Campesina (Revolutionary Confederation of Workers and Peasants).

8. The case of the CIPO-RFM and Raúl Gatica Bautista was discussed earlier. A partial list of other organizations affected includes indigenous leaders associated with local struggles for municipal autonomy and elections following usos y costumbres. Well-publicized examples include the *comuneros* of Santiago Xanica, who resisted a PRI mayor imposed by the governor and then were detained after a meeting with a representative from the Comisión Nacional de Derechos Humanos in Mexico City, and the Ayuntamiento Popular de San Blas Atempa, which had ten leaders detained and one assassinated (SIPAZ 2010a: 8). Another indigenous leader who was affected was the head of the Organización Indígena de Derechos Humanos de Oaxaca (Indigenous Organization of Human Rights of Oaxaca), who was detained during a meeting. Under Murat, the leaders of the Frente Amplio de Lucha Popular (Broad Front of Pop-

ular Struggle), Germán Mendoza Nube and Bertín Reyes, were also detained (Martínez Vásquez 2007: 37–38). A long list of groups had complaints against Ruiz Ortiz. These complaints were articulated by a petition presented to the governor by Sección 22 on June 7, 2006.

9. The competing political currents include La Unión de Trabajadores de la Educación (Union of Education Workers, UTE), Organización Revolucionaria de los Trabajadores de la Educación (Revolutionary Organization of Education Workers), Coordinadora Democrática del Magisterio (Democratic Council of Teachers, CODEMO), Grupo Praxis (COCEI), Cuadernos Sindicales (Union Notebooks), Organización de Izquierda Revolucionaria-línea de masas (Organization of the Revolutionary Life-Line of Masses), Promotora de la Organización Democrática Revolucionaria del Magisterio del Comité de Defensa de los Derechos del Pueblo CODEP (Democratic Revolutionary Organization of Teachers of the Committee in Defense of the People's Rights, CODEP), Bases Magisteriales (Rank and File Teachers), Coordinadora de Bases Magisteriales (Council of Rank and File Teachers), Solidaridad Campesina Magisterial de Oaxaca (Peasant Teacher Solidarity), and others (see Cortés 2006; Martínez Vásquez 2007: 55).

10. The most important of these groups were CODEMO, UTE, and Grupo Praxis.

11. As explained in detail by James Daria, in Oaxaca "teachers are paid differently according to the zoning patterns established by the federal government. The zones range from Economic Zone One, the lowest, to Economic Zone Three, which is the highest. Rezoning from Economic Zone One to Economic Zone Three, however, necessarily involves the intervention of the federal government" (2010: 154). Significant numbers of teachers in Oaxaca in 2005 were receiving Zone One salaries, despite the fact that the cost of living in Oaxaca is high due to the large numbers of tourists who visit all areas of the state. In the period 1995–97, all the state's teachers were rezoned to Zone 2.2. From 1998 to 2001, Zone 2.5 was achieved (Daria 2010: 154), raising salaries. In 2005 between 2.67 and 2.9 was achieved resulting in a significant increase for all.

12. After some saw Ruiz Ortiz as caving to the teacher's demands, corruption charges intensified against Secretario-General Enrique Rueda Pacheco and Secretaria-Técnica Alma Delia Santiago Díaz. Both were accused of receiving illicit payments, and Rueda Pacheco was accused of receiving an automobile. An investigative committee of Sección 22 was formed and ultimately found that the accusations were false. The rift temporarily healed, and the union focused on combating neoliberalism and creating alliances with other movements (see Daria 2010: 101–8).

13. The structure of APPO developed at this first congress reflected the influence of Sección 22 in terms of geographic and sectorial representation. Sección 22 had more representatives than any other sector, with twenty-eight people at the APPO Constitutive Congress. The accords approved by the congress included the following points:

- At least 30 percent of the representatives should be women.
- Communities and towns from all of the different regions of Oaxaca should be represented, as well as all different groups, unions, organizations, collectives, and other entities found in the state.
- Political party participation would be respected only if and when it does not interfere with the principles of APPO.
- The term for a representative to APPO is two years.
- The site for meetings of the APPO State Council will be the governor's palace, located in the zócalo of Oaxaca.
- The congress will name honorific ambassadors who will help to disseminate information about APPO at a national and international level. (APPO 2006)

Chapter 4

1. Martínez Vásquez (2009) provides an excellent summary of the findings of different human rights reports relating to the social conflict in Oaxaca in 2006.

2. See points 10–20 in the conclusions of the report of the CCIODH (2007).

Chapter 5

1. Mototaxis are a relatively new form of motorized transportation in Oaxaca. They are about the size of golf carts and run on a small motor. Their costs are low, so they are generally cheaper to run and maintain than cars. This lowers the cost of fares, which has made them attractive to poor and working-class people in the city. They have had ongoing problems with other taxi unions as a result of their lower fares.

2. This is a local system of governance based on more than 250 unpaid jobs that include a mayor, judges, police and school committees, irrigation committees, firefighters, committees regulating the use of communal land, and jobs caring for the local Catholic church. Groups of people are proposed by outgoing officials and confirmed or contested through a recorded voice vote in community assemblies in Zapotec. Such assemblies are attended primarily by men, but by some women as well. Women are also named to some of the volunteer governance and staffing positions, or cargos. Agreeing to serve in civil cargo positions throughout one's adult life is part of the citizenship requirements for living in many indigenous communities in Oaxaca (see Stephen 2005a).

3. Migration to the United States from Teotitlán del Valle began in the 1940s with the Bracero program, which by the late 1940s had brought about 25 percent of the male population to the United States as braceros. About 25 percent of households continued to send people as part of the Bracero program until 1964. Some remained in the United States. From the mid-1980s until the present, there has been a steady flow of migrants from Teotitlán del Valle to the

United States, with many settling. About 25 to 35 percent of the Teotitlán del Valle community is consistently living outside of their home base in many U.S. locations as well as in Mexico (see Stephen 2005b: 96–108).

4. This refers to the *baston*, or cane, that police used to carry, which is a symbol of authority in Teotitlán del Valle and other indigenous communities in Oaxaca. Other local authorities serving high-level cargos also carry canes. The contrast here is with the weapons carried by those the police often have to confront. Several years after this assembly, a decision was made to arm the municipal police with pistols.

5. Ojo de Agua offers media production and training to indigenous communities in Oaxaca. During the 2006 takeover, they provided technical assistance to the women who took over COR-TV.

6. For a thorough overview of indigenist radio policy in Mexico from the 1950s to the present, see Castells-Talens 2004.

7. See Warman et al. 1989 for a detailed look at some of these criticisms and advocacy for indigenous autonomy.

8. For a list of the FM stations, see Wikipedia 2011.

9. Zaachila has two ejidos within its municipality, which has a total of 1,694 hectares of land and approximately 871 *ejidatarios*, referring to those people who have land rights in the ejido (INEGI 2006). Ejidos were created after the Mexican Revolution to satisfy the demands of landless peasants who had seen their communal village lands eaten up by large agricultural estates or who served as laborers on those estates. *Ejido* refers to territory, the actual land tied to a particular community. The first ejidos were granted after the Revolution through a process of petitioning the government. Zaachila has two *nucleos agrarios*, which are ejidos, Barrio San José Zaachila and Santa María Zaachila. The Procuraduría Agraria (Office of the Agrarian Attorney) estimates that there are 871 ejidatarios in these two ejidos in the Municipio of Zaachila (INEGI 2006: 129).

10. A video titled *Zaachila recorrida por el librameiento sur* documents ejidatarios confirming their agreement to not let the roadway pass through their ejido lands (http://www.youtube.com/watch?v=wgizfbxZSko). This is one of six parts. The video is produced by El Punto/Zaachila en linea and is dated April 4, 2009.

11. This estimate was given by Roberto Olivares in an interview on December 3, 2009, at Ojo de Agua Comunicación.

12. Interview with Juan José Garcia on December 4, 2009. See also Ojo de Agua Comunicación 2013.

13. The video *Zaachila: Tradiciones de mi pueblos* demonstrates some of the local cultural traditions in Zaachila emphasized by Adán López Santiago (http://www.youtube.com/watch?v=T41r3QMpYkk). It was produced by Miguel Aragon Mendoza and is dated October 5, 2009.

14. The YouTube video *Zaachila: Día de muertos en el panteón* provides good footage of this celebration as well as of the sand-art sculptures that commem-

orate those who have died (http://www.youtube.com/watch?v=okuox8yaj4o &feature=related). If you look closely you can see one for Radio Zaachila at about 1:04–1:29. There are others making reference to the social movement and conflict of 2006. The video is produced by Ciber Café / El Punto and dated November 7, 2007.

Chapter 6

1. These numbers are based on estimates provided by women I interviewed who participated directly in the march and the takeover of the state media stations on August 1, 2006. While some press reports spoke of higher numbers of women—up to ten thousand—these women provided more modest numbers.

2. Rosario was interviewed on August 1, 2007, one year after the occupation of the station.

3. Statement made by Patricia Jiménez on August 1, 2007, at a conference commemorating the first anniversary of the takeover of the station. I recorded the conference speeches.

4. Ruth Guzmán was interviewed in July 2007.

5. After the Mexican Revolution (1910–20), the promotion of *mestizaje* (supposed mixing of Spanish and Indian) as a nationalist ideology was pushed in tandem with policies focused on incorporating the indigenous population. Writers such as Manuel Gamio (1916), who called for the fusion of the races, and José Vasconcelos's (1956) writings about "the cosmic race" reinforced the nationalist idea of Mexico as a one-race nation. This one race, the mestizo, required the erasure of the Indian and Afro-descendants.

6. María Lugones argues that we cannot look for actual people at the intersection of two discrete identities because there is no one there—it is an empty space: "The logic of categorical separation distorts what exists at the intersection. . . . We have ahead of us the task of reconceptualizing the logic of intersection so as to avoid the reparability. It is only when we perceive gender and race as intermeshed or fused that we actually see women of color" (2007: 193). Arguing that it is impossible to perceive human experience at the intersection of discrete, separate categories within colonial realities, Lugones proposes that we use the concept of a "fractured locus" as a way to understand the politically agentive identifications of subjects such as the actors in the Oaxacan social movement.

7. Free Speech Radio News broadcast the following on October 26, 2006:

This news from Oaxaca, Mexico: As of this morning, every radio station on the FM and AM dial has gone off the air . . . with one exception. Using the name "Radio Ciudadana" [Citizen Radio], 99.1 FM is the only station broadcasting in Oaxaca City at the moment. It first appeared on the dial last night. The programming is a mix of traditional music, talk, and pro-government propaganda. The hosts have been calling for a crackdown on striking teachers and members of the state's popular assembly movement.

8. The following day, October 28, *El Universal* published the following:

In the photographs obtained . . . by El Universal appear the Public Security Counselor of Santa Lucía del Camino, Abel Santiago Zárate, the chief of personnel of the same PRI local government, Manuel Aguilar, who is also a leader of the CROC [Confederación Revolucionaria Obrera Campesina (Revolutionary Confederation of Workers and Peasants)], David Aguilar Robles, who is a local PRI representative. . . . Also appearing is the municipal police officer Juan Carlos Soriano Velasco, alias El Chapulín. Testimonies also identify Pedro Carmona, ex-presidente of the neighborhood of Felipe Carrillo Puerto, of Santa Lucía. (Altamirano 2006)

9. The newspaper *Milenio*, which reported on the story, cited the Attorney General's Office as stating that "Osorio was found on the day of the shooting on top of a house forty meters up where he shot at the victim from a distance of 43 meters" (Rodríguez 2012).

Chapter 7

1. This is a reference to state elections in 2007, when the PRI won in a majority of districts and continued to dominate the state congress.

Chapter 8

1. It should be noted, of course, that a significant percentage of Oaxaca's teachers are indigenous.

2. Xiuxtlahuaca, the Nahua name for Juxtlahuaca, is one of the oldest communities in the Mixtec region of Oaxaca. Xiuxtlahuaca was founded by kings from the kingdoms known as Ciki-ntaha y Yucu-yu'gua, most likely between the twelfth and fourteenth centuries (Instituto Nacional para el Federalismo y el Desarrollo Municipal, Gobierno del Estado de Oaxaca 2009). The name Xiuxtlahuaca may come from Xiucóatl, which means "Sacred Cape of the God of the Wind," or from Xiuhpohualli, which means "summary of the years" (Instituto Nacional para el Federalismo y el Desarrollo Municipal, Gobierno del Estado de Oaxaca 2009). The Triqui ethnic group was subordinate to the Mixtec rulers of Xuixtlahuaca, who paid tribute to the Mexica or Aztec (López Barcenas 2009: 50). Between 1521 and 1522 Xuixtlahuaca was conquered by Pedro de Alvarado and subsequently missionized by Dominicans, who established the first Catholic church of Santo Domingo in 1539. The Triqui ethnic territory was part of the Juxtlahuaca colonial jurisdiction as well. There is ongoing evidence that indigenous Mixtec *cacicas* and *caciques* (royal lords) continued to rule in Juxtlahuaca in the sixteenth and seventeenth centuries. These lords periodically contested Spanish rule and battled legally with other regional caciques, such as those in neighboring Tecomaxtlahuaca.

3. Other requests were that compensation be paid for the car that was destroyed when Misael and Abel Francisco were assassinated and that Rufino Merino Zaragoza be asked to resign from the city council (Consejo municipal)

of San Juan Copala, since he was also a state representative in the leadership of the MULT (López Barcenas 2009: 260–61).

4. Because the MULT had previously aligned itself with the EZLN and its civil society organization, known as La Otra Campaña, the newly formed MULTI addressed the announcement of its birth to Delegado Zero (Subcomandante Marcos of the EZLN), La Otra Campaña, and other social organizations in Mexico (see López Barcenas 2009: 270–72).

5. Andrés Santiago Cruz, one of the victims, was mayor of the community of Paraje Pérez and a member of the Commission for Security and Order of APPO's indefinite sit-in based in Oaxaca's historic center. The other two victims were the seventy-year-old MULTI leader Pedro Martinez and a twelve-year-old (Vélez 2006).

6. Other groups included in this effort were the Frente Popular Revolucionario (Popular Revolutionary Front), Centro de Apoyo Comunitario Trabajando Unido A.C. (Center for Community Support Working Together), Frente Nacional Indígena Campesina (National Indigenous Peasant Front), and Frente Civico de Juxtlahuaca (Juxtlahuaca Civic Front).

7. The autonomous municipality included the towns of San Juan Copala, Yosoyuxi, Santa Cruz Tilaza, Guadalupe Tilaza, Tierra Blanca, Paraje Pérez, El Carrizal, Sabana, Yerba Santa, San Miguel Copala, Yutazani, Uníon de los Angeles, Río Metates, Río Lagarto, Cerro Pájaro, Cerro Cabeza, and others.

8. In addition to the mayor, the community installed other civil *cargo* authorities, including a *suplente* (alternate) to the president, an *alcade* único *constitutional* (a judge), a secretary, and a six-member council of elders (all men; Olivares Alonso 2007; López Barcenas 2007).

9. Faustino Vasqúez identified the gunman as someone working for the MULT leader Heriberto Pazos Ortiz (Gibler 2009: 228). Some people, including the Oaxaca state attorney general, have stated that the two women were not the target, a theory I heard repeated by some people in July 2008. Others are sure that the women were the targets because of their media activism and their continued support of APPO and of the San Juan Copala autonomous municipality. The station coordinator Jorge Albino Ortiz stated after the assassinations, "People from the government of Ulises Ruiz contacted us to threaten us. They said that if we talked, we would be in danger. They said if we were silent then we would receive economic resources" (Petrich 2008).

10. The visitors were from the Frente de Pueblos en Defense de la Tierra (Peoples United for the Defense of the Land), which was part of the Zapatista-aligned La Otra Campaña, formed in 2005 as a grassroots alternative national network to formal political parties and campaigns. The Frente planned to have a last political act to end a campaign to free their political prisoners in San Juan Copala but were never granted access to the community.

11. According to Francisco López Barcenas, a writer and congressman, an assault on the local shelter for youth in December 2009 resulted in the death of one child and the injury of two others. A volley of bullets unleashed by the UBISORT cascaded over the community. UBISORT members also set up a road-

block in the nearby community of La Sabana, restricting access to San Juan Copala. On December 10, 2009, a group of UBISORT gunmen forcibly removed MULTI authorities and others from the city hall they occupied. The UBISORT members then maintained a permanent presence there for three months, until March 10, 2010, when a group of women from MULTI took advantage of a breach in the security and retook the city hall (López Barcenas 2010).

12. On July 29, 2010, violence again erupted in the region when the imposed UBISORT political leader of San Juan Copala, Anastasio Juárez Hernández, was killed. UBISORT claimed he was shot by MULTI members; MULTI members said that he was killed in a gunfire exchange with disgruntled taxi drivers in Santiago Juxtlahuaca. Following his death, the Policía Estatal Preventiva (State Preventative Police, PEP) and agents from the Agencia Estatal de Investigación (State Agency for Investigation, AEI) entered San Juan Copala, accompanied by dozens of UBISORT paramilitaries, to "recover" the body. MULTI supporters claimed that Juárez's body was planted in the San Juan Copala city hall after being transported from Juxtlahuaca. MULTI members provided an account of what happened that contradicts that of UBISORT-MULT members. During the operation in San Juan Copala carried out by AEI and PEP agents and UBISORT-MULT gunmen, two female MULTI members were seriously injured and hospitalized in Oaxaca City. For an account by UBISORT of what happened, see Aguilar and Carrera Pineda 2010. For a MULTI account of events leading up to the shooting and following it, see "400 militantes de UBISORT y 300 policías estatales entran a San Juan Copala: Convocamos una movilización urgente HOY para detener la represión," Autonomía en San Juan Copala, July 31, 2010, http://autonomiaencopala.wordpress.com/2010/07/31/400-militantes-de-ubisort-y-300-policias-estatales-entran-a-san-juan-copala-convocamos-una-movilizacion-urgente-hoy-para-detener-la-represion/.

13. For an account of what it is like for women to bring in supplies in mid-August, see "Denuncian Mujeres de San Juan Copala Nuevo Ataque, cuando llevaban viveres en su comiunidad," Publicado por Frida, August 16, 2010, http://fridaguerrera.blogspot.com/2010/08/denuncian-mujeres-de-san-juan-copala.html.

14. Another planned aid caravan from Mexico City to San Juan Copala was suspended after the three men in charge of organizing operations were murdered on August 23, 2010.

15. Ed Kissam (2012) estimates that there are approximately 1.4 million residents in Los Angeles County born in Mexico based on the 2010 American Community Survey data and approximately 52,000 Oaxacan indigenous migrants in Los Angeles County. This is calculated using Survey data and correcting for an undercount and racial misclassification. In addition there are likely another approximately 17,000 U.S.-born children of Oaxacan indigenous migrants. This makes a total of 69,000 indigenous Oaxacans in Los Angeles County. Other estimates suggest that there may be as many as 200,000 Zapotecs living in the Los Angeles area (Takash et al., 2005; Kresge 2007: 7).

16. Gaspar Rivera-Salgado, general coordinator of the FIOB, was interviewed

on October 28, 2009, and on April 15, 2010, in Los Angeles. I also conducted an interview with him in October 2007 in Mexico City.

17. In Oaxacan indigenous communities where customary law is practiced, citizenship consists of a collective set of rights and responsibilities that guide the governance of the community in its many locations in Mexico and the United States (Stephen 2005a). These responsibilities usually include:

1. Participation of primarily adult men, and increasingly some women, in the local system of civil cargos. This is a local system of governance in which community members perform governmental duties without pay. Tasks are divided among more than 250 positions, or cargos, that range from mayor, judge, and police officer to school and irrigation committee member.

2. Participation of adult men and women in the religious cargo system. These cargos are integrated with the practice of *mayordomías*, in which community members sponsor the celebrations of the feast days of saints venerated in the local Catholic church (see Stephen 2005b: 230–81).

3. Participation of adult men and women in *tequio* (communal labor).

4. Payment by adult men and women of specific quotas or amounts of money for community projects or celebrations, known as *cooperación*.

Citizenship rights include:

1. Access to communal land for farming or house construction.

2. Access to community forests, water, sand, minerals, plants, and wild game.

3. The right to burial in the community cemetery.

4. The right to express opinions and vote in the decision-making process that takes place in community assemblies.

Citizenship is thus commonly understood as constituted by the responsibilities and rights outlined above, most of them collective responsibilities.

Chapter 9

1. Mauricio Magaña's (2013) dissertation focuses in depth on the practices, organization, and norms of urban youth in the southern state of Oaxaca. Magaña's research suggests that youth in Oaxaca, as is the case in many other recent social movements such as the Occupy movement, Arab Spring, and youth protests in Greece, Spain, and Chile, have "injected existing traditions of organizing with a new energy, logic, and unique practices whose aims go far beyond electoral change, posing a serious challenge to dominant political regimes and traditional opposition politics."

2. Not all participants in the organizations discussed here and in other chapters are Catholic. The number of people who identify as Protestant grew significantly in Oaxaca from 1980 to 2000, to slightly more than 10 percent of the population (Dow 2005: 13). Images such as the Virgen de Guadalupe are

not only signs of Catholic faith but are also broader symbols of cultural nationalism in Mexico. Thus La Virgen de las Barrikadas and the Niño APPO are created and received by many in the spirit of a Oaxacan popular identity, not as symbols for Catholics.

3. La Otra Campaña (the Other Campaign) was launched by the EZLN in January 2006 to create connections among Zapatista groups in different parts of Mexico and other groups in opposition to neoliberal capitalism and policy. Their goal was to create a constitutional convention that would rewrite the constitution to guarantee indigenous rights and autonomy—including many aspects of the San Andrés Accords on indigenous rights and culture—that were not legislated by the Mexican government. Subcomandante Marcos and other members of the EZLN traveled throughout Mexico to meet with indigenous organizations, trade unions, teachers, students, women's groups, gay, lesbian, and transgender organizations, environmental activists, fisher people, youth, and others. La Otra Campaña was not a political campaign but was created with the idea of establishing a different kind of political force that could influence politics but would not work through traditional political parties. This idea also permeates the thinking of some members of VOCAL.

4. This is in reference to the organizations that made up APPO, such as Sección 22, other unions, human rights organizations, indigenous organizations, student organizations, and others.

5. To see a video of a hip-hop concert in the central patio of CASOTA in May 2009 featuring local performers followed by BocaFloja, see http://www.youtube.com/watch?v=LGaTaK5jVHk. (The video quality is low.) BocaFloja, Aldo Villegas, is a Mexico City–based poet, spoken-word artist, and hip-hop musician. As of January 2012, he had released seven albums and eight videos.

6. The VOCAL-APPO website's section on the Autonomous Municipality of San Juan Copala is http://vocal.saltoscuanticos.org/?page_id=125.

7. "Desde este humilde hogar, te pido a ti, Niño APPO, que no permitas que esta lucha sea en vano, que la muerte de nuestros compañeros no quede impune, que nuestros compañeros presos sean liberados y que los perseguidos y exiliados tengan la libertad de regresar a sus hogares. Todas estas peticiones que te hago son para la pacificación y democracia de Oaxaca."

REFERENCES

Acevedo Conde, María Luisa, and María Teresa Pardo. 1993. "Reformas constitucionales y derechos culturales de los pueblos indígenas de Oaxaca." *Cuadernos del Sur* 2(4): 89–97. (May–August), p. 1A, 5A.

Aguilar, Lesli, and Andrés Carrera Pineda. 2010. "No cesa balacera en Copala." *El Imparcial*, July 31.

Aguilar Orihuela, Alonso. 2007. "En el Instituto de Artes Gráficas de Oaxaca Inauguran exposición Grafiteros al paredón." ASARO Blogspot, http://asar-Oaxaca.blogspot.com/search/label/PRENSA.

Alafita Méndez, Leopoldo. 1979. "1970–1976: Lucha pólitica y sindicalismo independiente en México." In *Anuario*. Jalapa: Centro de Investigaciones Históricas, Instituto de Investigaciones Humanísticas, Universidad Veracruzana.

Altamirano, Genaro. 2006. "Identifican a regidor en una de las balaceras: Registros fotográficos ubican a policías y jefes de un ayuntamiento." *El Universal sábado*, October 28. http://www.eluniversal.com.mx/nation/144774.html.

Álvarez, Sonia, Evelina Dagnino, and Arturo Escobar. 1998. "Introduction: The Cultural and the Political in Latin American Social Movements." In *Cultures of Politics / Politics of Culture: Re-visioning Latin American Social Movements*, ed. Evelina Dagnino, Sonia Alvarez, and Arturo Escobar. Boulder, Colo.: Westview Press.

Amnesty International. 2007a. "Amnesty International Calls on Mexican Officials to Probe Alleged Torture in Oaxaca." August 1. http://www.amnestyusa.org/document.php?lang=e&id=ENGUSA20070801002.

———. 2007b. "Oaxaca: Clamor for Justice." July. http://www.amnesty.org/en/library/info/AMR41/031/2007.

Anaya Muñoz, Alejandro. 2002a. "Governability and Legitimacy in Mexico: The Legalisation of Indigenous Electoral Institutions in Oaxaca." Ph.D. diss., University of Essex.

———. 2002b. "Amoltepec, ya van tres muertos y 12 heridos. Un polvorín

Oaxaqueño (otro más)." Ojarasca, La Jornada, 9 Julio 2002, http://www
.jornada.unam.mx/2002/06/09/mas-alejandro.html.

Anderson, Benedict. 1983. *Imagined Communities: Reflections on the Origin and Spread of Nationalism*. London: Verso.

Anderson, Kurt. 2011. "The Protester." *Time*, December 14. http://www
.time.com/time/specials/packages/article/0,28804,2101745_2102132_
2102373,00.html.

APPO (Asamblea Popular de los Pueblos de Oaxaca). 2006. "Relatoría y Acuerdos Preliminares del Congreso Constitutivo del APPO." November 13.
http://ebookbrowse.com/relatoria-y-acuerdos-preliminares-del-congreso-
constitutivo-de-la-1-doc-d206495884.

APPO-CODEP (Asamblea Popular de los Pueblos de Oaxaca-Comité de Defensa de los Derechos del Pueblo). 2006. "Resumen final del Foro Nacional Construyendo la Democracia y la Gobernabilidad." August 16–17. http://
codepappo.wordpress.com/2006/08/17/resumen-final-del-foro-nacional-
construyendo-la-democracia-y-la-gobernabilidad/.

Aquino Casas, Arnulfo. 2011. *Imágines de rebelión y resistencia: Oaxaca 2006*.
Mexico City: Centro Nacional de Investigacion, Documentación e Información de Artes Plásticas, Instituto Nacional de Bellas Artes, CONACULTA.

Arenas, Iván. 2011. "Rearticlating the Social: Spatial Practices, Collective Subjects, and Oaxaca's Art of Protest." Ph.D. diss., University of California, Berkeley.

Arias, Arturo, ed. 2001. *The Rigoberto Menchú Controversy*. Minneapolis: University of Minnesota Press.

Arias, Arturo, and Alicia del Campo. 2009. "Introduction: Memory and Popular Culture." *Latin American Perspectives* 36(5): 3–20.

Arriaga, María de la Luz. 1981. "El magisterio en lucha." *Cuadernos políticos* 27: 85–101.

Auyero, Javier. 2003. *Contentious Lives: Two Argentine Women, Two Protests, and the Quest for Recognition*. Durham: Duke University Press.

Avendaño, Olga Rosario. 2011. "Turismo en Oaxaca está de rodillas: Secretario." *El Universal*, January 27. http://www.eluniversal.com.mx/
notas/740510.html.

Barton Kranz, Thomas. 2010. "Visual Persuasion: Sixteenth Century Tlaxcalan Pictorals in Response to the Conquest of Mexico." In *The Conquest All Over Again: Nahuas and Zapotecs Thinking, Writing, and Painting Spanish Colonialism*, ed. Susan Schroeder. Eastbourne, U.K.: Sussex Academic Press.

Bauböck, Rainer. 2003. "Towards a Political Theory of Migrant Transnationalism." *International Migration Review* 37(3): 700–723.

Bellinghausen, Hermann. 2006. "Torturó la policía a dos maestros acusados de portación de armas: Reaparecen en Oaxaca dos profesores con huellas de torturas." *La Jornada*, August 13. http://www.jornada.unam.mx/2006/
08/13/index.php?section=sociedad&article=040n1s.

Bennett, Drake. 2011. "David Graeber, the Anti-Leader of Occupy Wall Street." *Bloomberg Business News*, October 27. http://www.businessweek

.com/magazine/david-graeber-the-antileader-of-occupy-wall-street-10262011.html.

Beverly, John. 2005. "*Testimonio*, Subalternity, and Narrative Authority." In *The Sage Handbook of Qualitative Research*, ed. Norman K. Denzin and Yvonne S. Lincoln. Thousand Oaks, Calif.: Sage.

———. 2004. *Testimonio: On the Politics of Truth*. Minneapolis: University of Minnesota Press.

Blas López, Cuauhtémoc. 2007. *Oaxaca ínsula de rezagos: Crítica a sus gobienos de razón y de costumbre*. Oaxaca: Editorial Siembra.

Bosniak, Linda. 2000. "Citizenship Denationalized. Symposium: The State of Citizenship." *Indian Journal of Global Legal Studies* 7(2): 447–510.

Bouvard, Marguerite Guzman. 1994. *Revolutionizing Motherhood: The Mothers of the Plaza de Mayo*. Wilmington, Del.: Scholarly Resources.

Brodkin, Karen. 2007. *Making Democracy Matter: Identity and Activism in Los Angeles*. New Brunswick, N.J.: Rutgers University Press.

———. 1988. *Caring by the Hour: Women, Work and Organizing at Duke Medical Center*. Urbana: University of Illinois Press.

Brulotte, Ronda. 2012. *Between Art and Artifact: Archaeological Replicas and Cultural Production in Oaxaca, Mexico*. Austin: University of Texas Press.

———. 2009. "'Yo soy nativo de aquí': The Ambiguities of Race and Indigeneity in Oaxacan Craft Tourism." *Journal of Latin American and Caribbean Anthropology* 14(2): 457–82.

———. 2006. "Revealing Artifacts: Prehispanic Replicas in an Oaxacan Woodcarving Town." Ph.D. diss., University of Texas.

Burkhart, Louise. 2010. "The Destruction of Jerusalem as Colonial Nahuatl Historical Drama." In *The Conquest All Over Again: Nahuas and Zapotecs Thinking, Writing, and Painting Spanish Colonialism*, ed. Susan Schroeder. Eastbourne, U.K.: Sussex Academic Press.

Campbell, Howard. 1994. *Zapotec Renaissance: Ethnic Politics and Cultural Revivalism in Southern Mexico*. Albuquerque: University of New Mexico Press.

Campbell, Howard, Alicia Barabas, and Leigh Binford, eds. 1993. *Zapotec Struggles: Histories, Politics, and Representations from Juchitán, Mexico*. Washington, D.C.: Smithsonian Institution Press.

Casillas, Dolores Inés. 2011. "Sounds of Surveillance: U.S. Spanish-Language Radio Patrols La Migra." *American Quarterly* 63(3): 807–29.

Castellanos Jurado, Aline, Ana María Hernández Cárdenas, Leticia Cuevas Rossette, Mariana Vásquez Marcial, Soledad Jarquín Edgar, and Yésica Sánchez Maya. 2007. *Voces de la valentía en Oaxaca: Violaciones a los derechos humanos de las mujeres en el conflicto social y político*. Oaxaca: Consorcio para el Diálogo Parlamentario y la Equidad Oaxaca, Comunicación e Información de la Mujer, Liga Mexicana por la Defensa de los Derechos Humanos, Ciudadanía, Trabajo y Familia.

Castells i Talens, Antoni. 2004. "The Negotiation of Indigenist Radio Policy in Mexico. Ph.D. diss. University of Florida."

Castro, Claudio de Moura, Laurence Wolff, and Norma García. 1999. "Tele-secundaria de México: Televisión educativa en zonas rurales." Sustainable Development Technical Paper. Washington, D.C.: Inter-American Development Bank.

CCIODH (Comisión Civil Internacional de Observación por los Derechos Humanos). 2007. "Conclusiones y recomendaciones preliminares sobre el conflicto social de Oaxaca de la Comisión Civil Internacional de Observación por los Derechos Humanos (cciodh)." January 20. http://cciodh .pangea.org/?q=es/taxonomy_menu/3/30/68.

CDDHO (Comisión para Defensa de los Derechos Humanos de Oaxaca). 2008. "¿Que es la Comisíon para Defensa de los Derechos Humanos de Oaxaca?" http://www.cedhOax.org/home/cedho.html.

Cerda García, Alejandro. 2011. *Imaginando Zapatismo: Multiculturalidad y autonomía indígena en Chiapas desde un municipio autónomo.* Mexico City: Universidad Autónoma Metropolitana, Miguel Ángel Porrúa.

Chatterjee, Partha. 2004. *The Politics of the Governed: Reflections on Popular Politics in Most of the World.* New York: Columbia University Press.

Chibnik, Michael. 2003. *Crafting Tradition: The Making and Marketing of Oaxacan Wood Carvings.* Austin: University of Texas Press.

CIPO-RFM (Consejo Indígena Popular de Oaxaca "Ricardo Flores Magón"). 2003. "Testimonio de experiencias en México: Día a día sufrimos la represión." May 6. http://chiapas.laneta.org/desmilitarizacion/ encuentro/ponencias/Oaxaca.htm.

Clarin. 2006. "México: El fallo electoral confirmó la ventaja de Calderón sobre López Obrador." Clarin.com, August 28. http://edant.clarin.com/ diario/2006/08/28/um/m-01261040.htm.

CNDH (Comisión Nacional de Derechos Humanos). 2007. Informe especial sobre los Hechos Sucedidos en la Ciudad de Oaxaca del 2 de junio de 2006 al 31 de enero de 2007. http://www.cndh.org.mx/sites/all/fuentes/ documentos/informes/especiales/2007_oaxaca.pdf.

CNTE. 1982. "Tácticas para la democratización del SNTE." Folleto de Educación Sindical, Delegación D-III-24, SNTE. INAH, ed. Vol. 9. México D.F.

Cobacho, Ana, and Gerd Schwartz. 2002. *Mexico: Experiences with Pro-Poor Expenditure Policies.* Washington, D.C.: International Monetary Fund.

Cohen, Jeffrey H. 2007. The Effect of Political Unrest on Migration Decisions: New Evidence and Preliminary Findings from Oaxaca, Mexico. San Diego: The Center for Comparative Immigration Studies. University of California, San Diego. (Report No. Working Paper 154). http://ccis.ucsd .edu/wp-content/uploads/2012/07/wrkg154.pdf.

Comisión Nacional para el Desarollo de Los Pueblos Indígenas. 2008. "Sistemas de Radiodifusoras Culturas Indígenas." December 31. http://www.cdi .gob.mx/index.php?option=com_content&task=view&id=180&Itemid= 99999999.

Comité Pro Democracía en México. 2012a. "CDM Facebook page" [online]. Available at: http://www.facebook.com/comiteprodemocracia.

———. 2012b. "Comité Faq. What Is the Comité?" [online]. Available at: http://www.geocities.ws/comite_pro_democracia_en_mexico/

Contralínea. 2010. "Copala: Zona de Guerra." In April 11. http://www.you tube.com/watch?v=TlzoEjooClo&feature=related\.

Cook, Maria Lorena. 1996. *Organizing Dissent: Unions, the State, and the Democratic Teachers' Movement in Mexico*. State College: Penn State University Press.

Cornelius, Wayne, Ann L. Craig, and Jonathan Fox. 1994. "Introduction: Mexico's National Solidarity Program. An Overview." In *Transforming State-Society Relations in Mexico: The National Solidarity Strategy*, ed. Ann L. Craig, Wayne A. Cornelius, and Jonathan Fox. La Jolla: Center for U.S.-Mexican Studies, University of California, San Diego.

Cortés, Joel Vicente. 2006. *Educación, Sindicalismo y Gobernabilidad en Oaxaca, Mexico*. Mexico City: Sindicato Nacional de Trabajadores de le Educación.

Cruz, Anna. 2011. "Gender in Spaces of Resistance: The Role of Oaxacan Teachers Post–2006 Uprising." M.A. thesis, Department of Anthropology, University of Oregon.

Cué Monteagudo, Gabino. 2004. *Oaxaca: Transición democrática o regresión autoritaria (La lucha contra el fraude y la elección de Estado en el sur de México)*. Oaxaca: Coalición Todos Somos Oaxaca.

Dalton, Margarita. 2007. "Los organismos civiles en Oaxaca y el movimiento ciudadano: Causas y consecuencias." *Cuadernos del Sur* 11(24/25): 63–79.

Daria, James. 2010. "The Oaxacan Conflict: Social Movements and the State in Southern Mexico." Master's thesis, Latin American Studies, University of Chicago.

———. 2013. "Written in Blood and Ink: Agrarian Reform, Intercommunity Conflict, and the Struggle for the Communal Lands of San Juan Copala." Master's thesis, Department of Anthropology, University of Oregon.

Davies, Nancy. 2006. "Denuncia formal de juicio político y revocación de mandato al Gobernador Constitucional del estado libre y soberano de Oaxaca, C. Ulisis Ernesto Ruiz Ortiz." July 22. http://narcosphere.narconews .com/node/186.

de Burgoa, Fran Francisco de. (1670) 1989. *Palestra Historial*. Mexico City: Editorial Porrua.

de Certeau, Michel. 1988. *The Writing of History*. Trans. Tom Conley. New York: Columbia University Press.

De Marinis, Natalia Leonor. 2013. "Desplazamiento forzado y construcción de (in) seguridad: Voces y perspesctivas de mujeres triquis de San Juan Copala, Oaxaca." Ph.D. diss. Centro de Investigaciones e Estudios Superiores en Antropología Social (CIESAS). Mexico City, Mexico.

———. 2011. "Breaking the Silence: State Violence toward Triqui Women of Oaxaca, Mexico." *Development* 54: 480–84.

———. 2009. "Entre la guerra y la paz: La intervención política partidista, el conflicto armado y la autonomía como paz entre los Triquis de San

Juan Copala, Oaxaca." Master's thesis. Centro de Investigaciones y Estudios Superiores en Antropología social (CIESAS), Mexico City, Mexico.

Dezalay, Yves, and Bryant G. Garth. 2002. *The Internationalization of Palace Wars: Lawyers, Economics, and the Contest to Transform Latin American States*. Chicago: University of Chicago Press.

Dow, James W. 2005. "The Growth of Protestant Religions in Mexico and Central America." Paper presented at the Society for the Scientific Study of Religion, annual meeting, Norfolk, Virginia, October 23–26, 2003. http://www.prolades.com/cra/regions/cam/Dow_sssr_2003.pdf.

Durazo Herrmann, Julián. 2010. "Neopatrionialism and Subnational Authoritarianism in Mexico: The Case of Oaxaca." *Journal of Politics in Latin America* 2(2): 85–112.

Earle, Duncan, and Jeanne Simonelli. 2011. "Occupy Wall Street, Consensus General Assembly and the Zapatistas: Into the American Zócalo." *SAA News*, November 1. http://sfaanews.sfaa.net/2011/11/01/occupy-wall-street-consensus-general-assembly-and-the-zapatistas-into-the-american-zocalo/.

El Universal. 2010. "Conflicto agrario deja 5 muertos en Oaxaca." February 21. http://www.eluniversal.com.mx/estados/74885.html.

Elizalde, Trianfo. 1999. "Zapotecos buscan apoyo en el DF para liberar a sus presas políticas." *La Jornada*, August 2.

Englke, Matthew. 2007. *A Problem of Presence: Beyond Scripture in an African Church*. Berkeley: University of California Press.

Enlace Zapatista/CACTUS. 2006. "La Otra Campana 2006 Urgente desde CACTUS." November 26. http://enlacezapatista.ezln.org.mx/denuncias/596#cactus48.

Esteva, Gustavo. 2008. *Crónica de un movimiento anunciado: Cuando hasta las piedras se levantan. Oaxaca, Mexico 2006*. Buenos Aires: Editorial Atropofagia.

———. 2007. "Oaxaca: The Path of Radical Democracy." *Socialism and Democracy* 21(2): 74–96.

Farriss, Nancy. 1984. *Maya Society under Colonial Rule: The Collective Enterprise of Survival*. Princeton: Princeton University Press.

Faudree, Paja. 2013. *Singing for the Dead: The Politics of Ethnic Revival in Mexico*. Durham: Duke University Press.

Felman, Shoshona, and Dori Laub. 1992. *Testimony: Crises in Witnessing in Literature, Psychoanalysis, and History*. New York: Routledge.

FIOB (Frente Indígena de Organizaciones Binacionales). 2006. About Us. Mission. http://fiob.org/en/about-us/.

Flores, Richard, and Rina Benmayor. 1997. "Introduction: Constructing Cultural Citizenship." In *Latino Cultural Citizenship: Claiming Identity, Space, and Rights*, ed. William V. Flores and Rina Benmayor. Boston: Beacon Press.

Flores Cruz, Cipriano. 2002. "El sistema electoral de los pueblos indígenas de Oaxaca." In *Dilemas de la democracia en México: Los actores sociales ante la representación pólitica,* ed. Aline Hémond and David Recondo. Mexico City: Centro Francés de Estudios Mexicanos Centroamericanos.

Fox, Jonathan. 2005. "Unpacking Transnational Citizenship." *Annual Reviews in Political Science* 8: 171–201.

———. 1994. "Targetting the Poorest: The Role of the National Indigenous Institute in Mexico's Solidarity Program." In *Transforming State-Society Relations in Mexico: The National Solidarity Strategy,* ed. Ann L. Craig, Wayne A. Cornelius, and Jonathan Fox. La Jolla: Center for U.S.-Mexican Studies, University of California, San Diego.

Franco Ortíz, Itandehui. 2011. "El deleite de la transgresión: Graffiti y gráfica política callejera en la ciudad de Oaxaca." Bachelor's thesis, Escuela Nacional de Antropología e Historia.

Free Speech Radio News. 2006. "Radio Stations Disappear from Oaxaca Airways." October 26. http://fsrn.org/content/thursday,-october-26,-2006/1814.

Galo Samario, Agustín. 2010. "Se indagarán asesinatos cometidos en el conflicto de Oaxaca de 2006: Gabino Cué." *La Jornada,* July 2. http://www.jornada.unam.mx/2010/07/10/opinion/010n1pol.

Gamio, Manuel. 1916. *Forjando Patria.* Mexico City: Editorial Porrúa.

García Morales, Ismael. 2009. "Encabezara 'Santo Niño APPO' la movilización de este día." *Noticias,* November 25, p. 8A.

Gasparello, Giovanna. 2008. "Los retos de un Nuevo municipio autónomo: San Juan Copala." March 1. http://www.anarkismo.net/article/7621?print_page=true.

Gibler, John. 2009. *Mexico Unconquered: Chronicles of Power and Revolt.* San Francisco: City Lights Books.

———. 2008. "Death Squads in Oaxaca: The Mexican Government Ignores the Assassination of Two Community Radio Activists." *In These Times,* June 10. http://www.inthesetimes.com/article/3740/death_squads_in_Oaxaca/.

Global Exchange and Alianza Cívica. 2000. "Mexican Federal Elections 2000: Electoral Observation Report." http://www.globalexchange.org/sites/default/files/MXElectionReport.pdf.

Gobierno del Estado de Oaxaca. 2010. "Porque Gabino?" Gabino Cué website. February 10. http://www.gabinocue.org/hemeroteca/2010/02/12/porque-gabino/.

Goodale, Mark. 2007. "The Power of Right(s): Tracking Empires of Law and New Modes of Social Resistance in Bolivia (and Elsewhere)." In *The Practice of Human Rights: Tracking Law between the Global and the Local,* ed. Mark Goodale and Sally Engle Merry. Cambridge: Cambridge University Press.

Goodale, Mark, and Sally Engle Merry, eds. 2007. *The Practice of Human Rights: Tracking Law between the Global and the Local.* Cambridge: Cambridge University Press.

Goodwin, Jeff, James M. Jasper, and Francesca Polletta, eds. 2001. *Passionate Politics: Emotions and Social Movements*. Chicago: University of Chicago Press.

Graeber, David. 2011a. *Debt: The First Five Thousand Years*. Brooklyn: Melville Publishing House.

———. 2011b. "Occupy and Anarchism's Gift of Democracy." *Guardian*, November 15. http://www.guardian.co.uk/commentisfree/cifamerica/2011/nov/15/occupy-anarchism-gift-democracy.

———. 2009. "Debt: The First Five Thousand Years." http://www.eurozine.com/articles/2009-08-20-graeber-en.html.

Grandin, Greg, and Thomas Miller Klubock. 2007. "Truth Commissions: State Terror, History, and Memory." *Radical History Review* 97: 99–101.

Greer, Thomas. 1969. "An Analysis of Mexican Literacy." *Journal of Inter-American Studies* 11(3): 466–76.

Grupo Mira. 1988. *La gráfica del 68: Homenaje al movimiento estudiantil*. 2nd ed. Mexico City: Ediciones Zurda, Claves Latinoamericanas, El Juglar.

Grupo Misófilo. 2011. "Estudio de Ordenamiento Territorial Comunitario en Santo Domingo Teojomulco, Sola de Vega, Oaxaca." http://www.grupomesofilo.org/pdf/proyectos/OTC/OTC_Sto_Domingo_Teojomulco.pdf.

Hale, Charles R., and Lynn Stephen. 2013. "Introduction." In *Otros Saberes: Collaborative Research on Indigenous and Afro-Descendant Cultural Politics*, ed. Charles R. Hale and Lynn Stephen. Santa Fe: School of American Research Press.

Hames-García, Michael. 2011. *Identity Complex: Gender, Race, and Sexuality from Oz to Abu Ghraib*. Minneapolis: University of Minnesota Press.

Harvey, Neil. 2001. "Globalization and Resistance in Post–Cold War Mexico: Difference, Citizenship, and Biodiversity Conflicts in Chiapas." *Third World Quarterly* 22: 1045–61.

Hernández, O. 2011. "Conservan culto a Santo Niño APPO." *Noticias*, January 5. http://www.noticiasnet.mx/portal/principal/conservan-culto-santo-nino-appo.

Hernández Díaz, Jorge. 2009. "Las demandas indígenas en el movimiento de la Asamblea Popular de los Pueblos de Oaxaca." In *La APPO: ¿Rebelión o movimiento social? Nuevas formas de expresión ante la crisis*, ed. Victor Raúl Martínez Vásquez. Oaxaca: Instituto de Investigaciones Sociológicas, Universidad Autónoma "Benito Juárez" de Oaxaca.

———. 2007. "Las dilemas en la construcción de ciudadanías diferenciadas en un espacio multicultural: El Caso de Oaxaca." In *Ciudadanías diferenciadas en un estado multicultural: Los usos y costumbres en Oaxaca*, ed. Jorge Hernández Díaz. Mexico City: Siglo XXI editores.

Hernández Navarro, Luis. 2011. *Cero en conducta: Crónicas de la Resistencia magisterial*. Mexico City: Fundación Rosa Luxemburgo y Para Leer en Libertad.

———. 2007. "Oaxaca y los derechos humanos." *La Jornada*, November 20.

http://www.jornada.unam.mx/2007/11/20/index.php?section=opinion &article=023a1pol.

Herrera, Jorge, and Arturo Zárate. 2006. "Señalan las entidades donde habrá recuento. *El Universal*, 5 Agusto, 2006. http://www.eluniversal.com.mx/ notas/366899.html.

Higgins, Michael James. 1983. *Somos Tocayos: Anthropology of Urbanism and Poverty.* Lanham, Md.: University Press of America.

Hill Boone, Elizabeth. 1994. "Aztec Pictoral Histories: Record without Words." In *Writing without Words: Alternative Literacies in Mesoamerica and the Andes*, ed. Elizabeth Hill Boone and Walter D. Mignolo. Durham: Duke University Press.

Huerta Ríos, César. 1981. *Organización sociopolitica de una minoría nacional: Los Triquis de Oaxaca.* Mexico City: Instituto Nacional Indígenista, Series Antropología social, México.

Huizar Murillo, Javier, and Isidro Cerda. 2004. "Indigenous Mexican Migrants in the 2000 U.S. Census: Hispanic American Indians." In *Indigenous Mexican Migrants in the United States*, ed. Jonathan Fox and Gaspar Rivera-Salgado. La Jolla: Center for U.S.-Mexican Studies, Center for Comparative Immigration Studies, University of California, San Diego.

INEGI (Instituto Nacional de Estadística, Geografía e Informática). 2006. "Nucleos Agrarios: Tabulados por municipio, Oaxaca." http://mapserver. inegi.org.mx/geografia/espanol/cartcat/tabulados/PDF/tbe_Oax.pdf.

———. 2005. INEGI. Perfil sociodemográfico de Oaxaca II Conteo de Población y Vivienda. http://www.inegi.org.mx/prod_serv/contenidos/ espanol/bvinegi/productos/censos/conteo/2005/perfiles/Perf_Soc_Oax2 .pdf.

Iturbide, Graciela, Elena Poniatowska, and Pablo Ortiz Monisterio. 1989. *Juchitán de las Mujeres.* Mexico City: Ediciones Toledo.

Jelin, Elizabeth, and Susana G. Kaufman. 2000. "Layers of Memories: Twenty Years after in Argentina." In *The Politics of War Memory and Commemoration*, ed. G. Dawson, M. Roper, and T. G. Ashplant. New York: Routledge.

Jën Poj. 2013. Quienes Somos? Radio Jën Poj, Tlahuitoltepec, Oaxaca. http:// radiojenpoj.info/quienes-somos.

Jiménez, Eugenia. 2008. "Balean a dos integrantes de Radio Zaachila, Oaxaca." *Milenio.* July 28. http://www.milenio.com/cdb/doc/impreso/ 8084940?quicktabs_1=0.

Jimeno, Myriam. 2006. "Citizens and Anthropologists." *Journal of World Anthropology Network* 1(2): 59–73. http://www.ram-wan.net/documents/ 05_e_Journal/journal-2/8.Jimeno.pdf.

Johnson, Reed. 2008. "Urgent Posts from Oaxaca." *Los Angeles Times*, July 20. http://articles.latimes.com/2008/jul/20/entertainment/ca-Oaxaca20.

Jordan, Glenn, and Chris Weedon. 1995. *Cultural Politics: Class, Gender, Race and the Postmodern World.* Oxford: Blackwell.

Juris, Jeffrey. 2008. "Performing Politics: Image, Embodiment, and Affective

Solidarity during Anti-Corporate Globalization Protests." *Ethnography* 9(1): 61–97.

King, Linda. 1994. *Roots of Identity: Language and Literacy in Mexico*. Stanford: Stanford University Press.

King, Mark. 1994. "Hearing the Echoes of Verbal Art in Mixtec Writing." In *Writing without Words: Alternative Literacies in Mesoamerica and the Andes*, ed. Elizabeth Hill Boone and Walter D. Mignolo. Durham: Duke University Press.

————. 1988. "Mixtec Political Ideology: Historical Metaphors and the Poetics of Political Symbolism." Ph.D. diss., Department of Anthropology, University of Michigan, Ann Arbor.

Kissam, E. 2012. Rough Population Estimates—Indigenous People in Los Angeles County. Personal communication, January 30.

Kissam, Edward, and Ilene J. Jacobs. 2004. "Practical Research Strategies for Mexican Indigenous Communities in California Seeking to Assert Their Own Identity." In *Indigenous Mexican Migrants in the United States*, ed. Jonathan Fox and Gaspar Rivera-Salgado. La Jolla: Center for U.S.-Mexican Studies, Center for Comparative Immigration Studies, University of California, San Diego.

Kleinman, Arthur, Venna Das., and Margaret Lock. 1997. *Social Suffering*. Berkeley: University of California Press.

Kolhatkar, Sonali. 2006. "An Interview with Raúl Gatica." Z *Magazine*. http://www.zcommunications.org/an-interview-with-ra-and-250–1-gatica-by-sonali-kolhatkar.

Kresge, Lisa. 2007. "Indigenous Oaxacan Communities in California: An Overview." National Center for Farmworker Health. Buda, Texas. http://www.ncfh.org/?plugin=ecomm&content=item&sku=7340.

LASA (Latin American Studies Association). 2008. Violaciones contra la libertad académica y de expresión en Oaxaca de Juárez Informe presentado por la delegación de la Asociación de Estudios Latinoamericanos encargada de investigar los hechos relacionados con el impacto del conflicto social del año 2006. *Desacatos*, núm. 26, enero–abril, pp. 151–66. http://www.ciesas.edu.mx/desacatos/26%20Indexado/Testimonios3.pdf.

Latina Feminist Group. 2001. *Telling to Live: Latina Feminist Testimonios*. Durham: Duke University Press.

Laub, Dori. 1992. "An Event without a Witness." In *Testimony: Crises of Witnessing in Literature, Psychoanalysis, and History*, ed. Shoshona Felman and Dori Laub. New York: Routledge.

Levitt, Peggy. 2001. *The Transnational Villagers*. Berkeley: University of California Press.

Leyva Solano, Xochitl. 2009. "Nuevos procesos sociales y políticos en América Latina." In *Repensar la Política desde América Latina: Política, Cultura, Democracia Radical y Movimientos Sociales*, ed. Raphael Hoetmer. Lima: Programa Democracia y Transformación Global.

Limeddh (Liga Mexicana por la Defensa de los Derechos Humanos). 2006. "Relato de Torturo en Oaxaca: Relato de Elionaí Santiago Sánchez y Juan Gabriel Ríos." August 14. http://espora.org/limeddh/spip.php? article48.

López, Felipe H., and David Runsten. 2004. "Mixtecs and Zapotecs Working in California: Rural and Urban Experiences." In *Indigenous Migrants in the United States*, ed. Jonathan Fox and Gaspar Rivera-Salgado. La Jolla: Center for U.S.-Mexican Studies, Center for Comparative Immigration Studies, University of California, San Diego.

López Barcenas, Francisco. 2010. "San Juan Copala: Crónica de una repression anunciada." *La Jornada*, April 29. http://www.jornada.unam.mx/ 2010/04/29/index.php?article=009a1pol&section=opinion.

———. 2009. *San Juan Copala: Dominación Política y Resistencia Popular, De las rebeliones de Hilarión a la formación del Municipio Autónomo*. Mexico City: Universidad Autónoma, Unidad Xochimilco, División de Ciencias Sociales y Humanidades.

———. 2007. "Viaje al centro de la autonomía triqui." *La Jornada*, January 2. http://www.jornada.unam.mx/2007/01/26/index.php?section=opinion &article=024a2pol.

Lugones, María. 2007. "Heterosexualism and the Colonial/Modern Gender System." *Hypatia* 22(1): 186–209.

Magaña, Maurice. 2008. "Articulating Social Networks in a Mexican Social Movement: The Case of the Asamblea Popular de los Pueblos de Oaxaca (APPO) in Oaxaca." Master's thesis, University of Oregon.

———. 2013. "Youth in Movement: The Cultural Politics of Autonomous Youth Activism in Southern Mexico." Ph.D. diss., Department of Anthropology, University of Oregon.

Maier, Linda S., and Isabel Dulfano. 2004. *Woman as Witness: Essays on Testimonial Literature by Latin American Women*. New York: Peter Lang.

Mantilla Falcón, Julissa. 2005. "The Peruvian Truth and Reconciliation Commission's Treatment of Sexual Violence against Women." *Human Rights Brief* 12(2): 1–15.

Martell Ramírez, Ricardo. 1967. "Problemas del Estado de Oaxaca: Los indios triques de Oaxaca." Bachelor's thesis. Self-published, Mexico City.

Mártinez López, Felipe. 1983. *El crepúsculo del poder, Juchitán, Oaxaca, 1980–1982*. Oaxaca: Instituto de Investigaciones Sociales, Universidad Autónoma "Benito Juárez" de Oaxaca.

Martínez Vásquez, Víctor Raúl. 2009. "El movimiento popular y los derechos humanos en Oaxaca." In *La APPO: ¿Rebelión o movimiento social?*, ed. Víctor Raúl Martínez Vásquez. Oaxaca: Instituto de Investigaciones Sociológicas, Universidad Autónoma "Benito Juárez" de Oaxaca.

———. 2007. *Autoritarismo, movimiento popular y crisis política: Oaxaca 2006*. Oaxaca: Instituto de Investigaciones sociológicas, Universidad Autónoma "Benito Juárez" de Oaxaca, Centro de Apoyo al Movimiento

Popular Oaxaqueño, Servicios para la Educación Alternativa, Consorcio para el Diálogo Parlamentario y la equidad.

———. 2004. *La educación en Oaxaca*. Oaxaca: Instituto de Investigaciones Sociologicos de la UABJO.

———. 1990. *Movimiento popular y política en Oaxaca: 1968–1986*. Oaxaca: Consejo Nacional para la cultura y las Artes, Dirección General de Publicaciones.

McCaughan, Edward J. 2012. *Art and Social Movements: Cultural Politics in Mexico and Atzlán*. Durham: Duke University Press.

McElmurry, Sara. 2009. "Indigenous Community Radio in Mexico." Americas Policy Program. http://www.cipamericas.org/archives/1744.

Merry, Sally. 2006. *Human Rights and Gender Violence: Translating International Law into Local Justice*. Chicago: University of Chicago Press.

Mexico. 2006. *Constitución Política de los Estados Unidos Mexicanos*. Mexico City: Editorial Porrua.

Mexico Tourism Board. 2011. *Oaxaca: Culture, History, and Tradition Come Together in This Colonial City*. Mexico City: Mexican Tourism Board. http://playazipolite.blogspot.com/2012/05/oaxaca-culture-history-and-tradition.html.

Michel, Victor Hugo. 2009. "Mexicanos colman el sistema de asilo de Estados Unidos." *Milenio En Línea*, July 19. http://impreso.milenio.com/node/8610590.

Mignolo, Walter D. 2011. *The Darker Side of Western Modernity: Global Futures, Decolonial Options*. Durham: Duke University Press.

Monaghan, John. 1994. "The Text in the Body, the Body in the Text: The Embodied Sign in Mixtec Writing." In *Writing without Words: Alternative Literacies in Mesoamerica and the Andes*, ed. Elizabeth Hill Boone and Walter D. Mignolo. Durham: Duke University Press.

———. 1990. "Performance and the Structure of the Mixtec Codices." *Ancient Mesoamerica* 1: 133–40.

Monroy, David. 1997. "Mexican Teachers and the Struggle for Democracy." San Francisco: Global Exchange. This pamphlet is available from Global Exchange, 2017 Mission Street, Suite 303, San Francisco, CA 94110.

Monsiváis, Carlos. 1983. "Crónica de Juchitán." *Cuadernos Políticos* 37 (Julio–Septiembre): 46–55. http://www.scribd.com/doc/52666300/Carlos-Monsivais-Cronica-de-Juchitan-Cuadernos-Politicos-37-julio-septiembre-de-1983ra.

Moon, Freda. 2008. "Mexican Artisans Try to Survive Oaxacan Unrest." *Womennews*, September 22.

Morales Almada, Jorge. 2007. "Protesta en Los Angeles por la presencia de Fox." *La Opinion*, January 30. http://codepappo.wordpress.com/2007/02/04/protesta-en-los-angeles-por-la-presencia-de-fox/.

Nathán Pérez, Raúl. 2003. "SNTE-XXI, al desnudo." *El Imparcial*, December, p. 1.

Neuhouser, Joshua. 2009. "Looking Back on the Oaxaca Rebellion." Libcom .org.

Newdick, Vivian Ann. 2012. "'To Know How to Speak': Technologies of Indigenous Women's Activism against Sexual Violence in Chiapas, Mexico." Ph.D. diss., Department of Anthropology, University of Texas, Austin.

Norget, Kirstin. 2009. "La Virgen de las barricadas: La iglesia católica, religiosidad popular y el Movimiento de la Asamblea Popular de los Pueblos de Oaxaca." In *La APPO: rebelión o movimiento social (nuevas formas de expresión ante la crisis)*, ed. Victor Raúl Martínez. Oaxaca: Instituto de Investigaciones sociológicas, Unviersidad Autónoma Benito Juárez.

———. 2008. "A Cacophony of Autochthony: Representing Indigeneity in Oaxacan Popular Mobilization." *Journal of Latin American and Caribbean Studies* 15(1): 116–43.

Noticaribe. 2007. "Se recupera el turismo en Oaxaca, tras conflicto social." September 15, p. 1.

Nuestro-mexico.com. 2013. Santiago Juxtlahuaca. Información y datos sobre el municipio de Santiago Juxtlahuaca. (Based on 2005 Census by INEGI.) http://www.nuestro-mexico.com/Oaxaca/Santiago-Juxtlahuaca/.

OAS (Organization of American States), Department of International Law. 1969. "American Convention on Human Rights Pact of San Jose, Costa Rica." http://www.oas.org/juridico/english/Sigs/b-32.html.

Oaxacalive.com. 2008. "Guelaguetza 2008." http://Oaxacalive.com/guelaguetza.htm#anchor443537.

Ojo de Agua Comunicación. 2013. Audioteca. http://www.ojodeagua comunicacion.org/index.php/audioteca.

———. 2009. "Didhza Kieru." http://www.ojodeaguacomunicacion.org/index.php/videoteca/87-ojo-de-agua-comunicacion/programas-de-ojo-de-agua/espacios-de-comunicacion-comunitaria/151-didhza-kieru.

Olivares Alonso, Emir. 2007. "Asumen cargos autoridades triquis autónomas de San Juan Copala." *La Jornada*, January 21. http://www.jornada.unam .mx/2007/01/21/index.php?section=politica&article=006n1pol.

———. 2006. "Mujeres detenidas en Oaxaca padecen vejámenes en el Cefereso de Nayarit." *La Jornada*, December 10. http://www.jornada.unam .mx/2006/12/10/index.php?section=politica&article=014n1pol.

Olor a mi tierra. 2012. "Organismo autónomo sobre DDHH en Oaxaca." January 13. http://www.oloramitierra.com.mx/nueva/?p=9774.

Olvera Romero, Gregorio Moisés. 2008. *La construcción de espacios públicos en México: Las radios comunitarias y su participación en la democratización de los medios electrónicos*. Mexico City: Facultad Latinoamericana de Ciencias Sociales.

Osorno, Diego. 2007. *Oaxaca sitiada: La primera insurreción del siglo XXI.* Mexico City: Random House Mondadori.

———. 2006. "Operación 'Limpieza' en Oaxaca. *Narco News Bulletin*, August 27. http://www.narconews.com/Issue42/article2026.html.

Paris Pombo, Maria Dolores. 2010. "San Juan Copala: The Roots of the Violence." CIP Americas, May 10. http://www.cipamericas.org/archives/2187.

Parra Mora, León Javier, and Jorge Hernández Díaz. 1994. *Violencia y cambio social en la región triqui.* Oaxaca: Universidad Autónoma "Benito Juárez" de Oaxaca y Consejo Estatal de Poblacion de Oaxaca.

Pedrero, Fernando. 2007. "Turismo, el más afectado por conflicto en Oaxaca." *El Universal,* July 20. http://www.eluniversal.com.mx/estados/65353 .html.

Pennick, Tom. 2009. "1996 EPR Attack on Huatulco and 6 Other Towns." November 20. The Pacific Coast of Mexico. http://www.tomzap.com/epr1 .html.

Pérez, Matilde U. 2006. "Acepta Canadá a indígena de Oaxaca como refugiado político." *La Jornada,* March 1. http://www.jornada.unam.mx/ 2006/03/01/index.php?section=politica&article=024n2pol.

Pérez, Matilde, Octavio Vélez, and Agustín Galo. 2010. "Matan al líder Triqui Timoteo Alejandro Ramírez: Culpan a miembros del MULT." *La Jornada,* May 21. http://www.jornada.unam.mx/2006/03/01/index.php?section= politica&article=048n1pol.

Petrich, Blanche. 2008. "Balas impunes silencian la voz Triqui." *La Jornada,* April 21.

Polletta, Francesca. 2006. *It Was Like a Fever: Storytelling in Protest and Politics.* Chicago: University of Chicago Press.

———. 2002. *Freedom Is an Endless Meeting: Democracy in American Social Movements.* Chicago: University of Chicago Press.

Poniatowska, Elena. 1975. *Massacre in Mexico (La noche de Tlatelolco).* Trans. Helen R. Lane. New York: Viking.

Poole, Deborah. 2007a. "Political Autonomy and Cultural Diversity in the Oaxaca Rebellion." *Anthropology News* 48(3): 10–11.

———. 2007b. "The Right to be Heard." *Socialism and Democracy* 21(2): 113–16.

———. 2004. "An Image of 'Our Indian': Type Photographs and Racial Sentiments in Oaxaca, 1920–1940." *Hispanic American Historical Review* 84(1): 37–82.

Prieto Beruiristáin, Iñigo. 2009. "Radio Ñomndaa, the Word of Water." Americas Policy Program. http://www.cipamericas.org/archives/1728.

Rabasa, José. 2010. *History: Subaltern Studies, the Zapatista Insurgency, and the Specter of History.* Pittsburgh: University of Pittsburgh Press.

Radford, Leslie. 2006. "¡Oaxaca Valiente!" *Indymedia,* November 6. http:// la.indymedia.org/news/2006/11/186729_comment.php.

Radio Nhadía. 2010. "Comunicado de prensa: Las mujeres convocamos a marcha festiva el 1° de agosto y a construir una realidad con justicia social, política y económica." July 24. http://radionandiafm.radioteca .net/leer.php/449176.

Ramos Sánchez, Otoniel Jairzhinio. 2007. "Evaluación Económica de la

Producción y Comercialización Jitomate Saladette (Lypercopersicum Esculentum Mill) de Invernadero en el Municipio Oaxaca de Juárez." Bachelor's thesis, Universidad Tecnológica de la Mixteca. http://jupiter .utm.mx/~tesis_dig/10047.pdf.

Rappaport, Joanne, and Tom Cummins. 2012. *Beyond the Lettered City: Indigenous Literacies in the Andres.* Durham: Duke University Press.

Recondo, David. 2002. "Etat et coutumes électorales dans l'Oaxaca (Mexique): Réflecions sur les enjuex politiques du multiculturalisme." Ph.D. diss., Université Montesquieu Bordeaux IV.

Renique, Gerardo. 2007. "Subaltern Political Formation and the Struggle for Autonomy in Oaxaca." *Socialism and Democracy* 21(2): 62–73.

Rivas, Silvia Chavela. 2011. "La primera Guelaguetza bajo techo." *Noticias*, July 20. http://www.noticiasnet.mx/portal/principal/56039-primera-guelaguetza-bajo-techo.

Rivera Salgado, Gaspar. 1998. "Radiografía de Oaxacalifornia." *Masiosare: Política y Sociedad en La Jornada*, August 9.

Rodríguez, Óscar. 2012. "Lenin Osorio Ortega disparó contra el camarógrafo el 27 de octubre de 2006 a una distancia de 43 metros." *Milenio*, May 23. http://www.milenio.com/cdb/doc/noticias2011/c84ec533b3a22e5ff3c71 efcd8bddb62.

———. 2011. "Guelaguetza deja ganancias por 191 millones de pesos." *Milenio*, August 5. http://www.milenio.com/cdb/doc/impreso/9003972.

Rodríguez Santos, Bertha. 2009. *Indigenous Communications in the Global World: Strategies Used by the FIOB in the United States and Mexico.* Washington, D.C.: Center for International Policy, Americas Program.

Romero-Hernández, Odilia, Centolia Maldonado Vásquez, Rufino Domínguez-Santos, Maylei Blackwell, and Laura Velasco Ortiz. 2013. "Género, generación y equidad: Los retos del liderazgo indígena binacional entre México y Estados Unidos en la experiencia del FIOB." In *Otros Saberes: Collaborative Research on Indigenous and Afro-Descendant Cultural Politics*, ed. Charles R. Hale and Lynn Stephen. Santa Fe: School of Advanced Research Press.

Rosaldo, Renato. 1997. "Citizenship, Inequality, and Multiculturalism." In *Latino Cultural Citizenship: Claiming Identity, Space, and Rights*, ed. William V. Flores and Rina Benmayor. Boston: Beacon Press.

Ross, Fiona. 2003. "Using Rights to Measure Wrongs: A Case Study of Method and Moral in the Work of the South African Truth and Reconciliation Commission." In *Human Rights in Global Perspectives: Anthropological Studies of Rights, Claims, and Entitlements*, ed. Richard Ashby Wilson and Jon P. Mitchel. London: Routledge.

———. 2002. *Bearing Witness: Women and the Truth and Reconciliation Commission in South Africa.* London: Pluto.

Rubin, Jeffrey. 1997. *Decentering the Regime: Ethnicity, Radicalism, and Democracy in Juchitán, Mexico.* Durham: Duke University Press.

Ruiz Arrazola, Víctor. 2005. "La CIDH revindica la defensa de garantías de los indígenas en Oaxaca." *La Jornada*, March 10. http://www.jornada .unam.mx/2005/03/10/index.php?section=estados&article=040n1est.

Ruiz Arrazola, Víctor, Guadalupe Ríos, and Juan Balboa. 1996. "Ataca EPR en seis estados." *La Jornada*, August 29. http://www.jornada.unam.mx/ 1996/08/29/epr.txt.html.

Ruiz Cervantes, Francisco José. 1978. "La lucha de clases en Oaxaca: 1971–1977." In *Oaxaca, una lucha reciente, 1960–1978*, ed. Rene Bustamente V. et al. Mexico City: Ediciones Nueva Sociología.

Salazar, Margarita. 2006a. "'Nos duele represión en Oaxaca,'" afirma Mixteco durante protesta frente al consulado Mexicano en LA." Narconews, August 31. http://narconews.com/Issue42/articulo2035.html.

_____2006b. "Los Angeles Mobilizes in Support of People of Oaxaca." October 4. El Enemigo Comun. http://elenemigocomun.net/2006/10/ angeles-mobilizes-support-Oaxaca/.

Salomon, Frank, and Mercedes Niño-Murcia. 2011. *The Lettered Mountain: A Peruvian Village's Way with Writing*. Durham: Duke University Press.

San Andrés Accords on Indigenous Rights and Culture. 1996. Trans. Rosalva Bermudez-Ballin. January 18. http://flag.blackened.net/revolt/mexico/ ezln/san_andres.html.

Santibañez Orosco, Porfirio. 2004. "Voto de calidad o voto ciudadano: La disyuntiva en la elección de gobernador de Oaxaca en 2004." In *Voces de la transición en Oaxaca*, ed. Claudio Sánchez Islas. Oaxaca: Carteles.

SARH (Secretaría de Agricultura y Recursos Hidraúlicos-Comisión de Río Balsas). 1977. *Anteproyecto para la instalación de una radiodifusora en Tlapa, Guerrero*. Mexico City: SARH.

Sarkar, Bhaskar, and Janet Walker. 2010. *Documentary Testimonies: Global Archives of Suffering*. New York: Routledge.

Sarlo, Beatriz. 2005. *Tiempo pasado: Cultura de la memoria y giro subjetivo. Una discusión*. Buenos Aires: Siglo Veintiuno.

Sassen, Saskia. 2006. *Territory, Authority, Rights: From Medieval to Global Assemblages*. Princeton: Princeton University Press.

———. 1999. *Guests and Aliens*. New York: New Press.

Schirmer, Jennifer. 1993. "The Seeking of Truth and the Gendering of Consciousness: The CO-MADRES of El Salvador and the CONAVIGUA Widows of Guatemala." In *"Viva": Women and Popular Protest in Latin America*, ed. Sallie Westwood and Sarah A. Radcliffe. London: Routledge.

Schroeder, Susan, ed. 2010. *The Conquest All Over Again: Nahuas and Zapotecs Thinking, Writing, and Painting Spanish Colonialism*. Eastbourne, U.K.: Sussex Academic Press.

Seider, Rachel. 2001. "Rethinking Citizenship: Reforming the Law in Postwar Guatemala." In *States of Imagination: Ethnographic Explorations of the Postcolonial State*, ed. T. B. Hansen and F. Stepputat. Durham: Duke University Press.

Sierra, María Teresa. 2013. "Desafiando el estado desde los márgenes: Justicia y seguridad en la experiencia de la policía comunitaria de Guerrero." In *Justicias indigenas y Estado: Violencias contemporáneas. Justicia, pueblos indígenas y violencia en México y Guatemala*, ed. María Teresa Sierra, R. Aída Hernández, and Rachel Sieder. Mexico City: Centro de Investigaciones de Estudios Superiores de Antropología Social (CIESAS).

———. 2010. "La fuerza de la justicia indígena frente al Estado: La experiencia de la policía comunitaria de Guerrero, México" *NACLA* 43(4): 34–38.

———. 2009. "La experiencia de la policía comunitaria de Guerrero La Seguridad Pública en México: Balance y perspectivas." *Seminario Experiencias de Seguridad y Derechos Humanos*, CIESAS, 2009.

SIPAZ. 2011. IN FOCUS: Impunity in Oaxaca—Report on Human Rights 2006–2010. http://www.sipaz.org/en/reports/91-informe-sipaz-vol-xvi-no-1—marzo-de-2011/279-enfoque-impunidad-en-Oaxaca-balance-de-derechos-humanos-2006–2010.html.

———. 2010a. "Oaxaca: Fechas Claves." http://www.sipaz.org/crono/ocrono_esp.htm.

———. 2010b. "Oaxaca en Datos." http://www.sipaz.org/ofini_esp.htm.

Speed, Shannon. 2007. "Exercising Rights and Reconfiguring Resistance in the Zapatista Juntas de Buen Gobierno." In *The Practice of Human Rights: Tracking Law between the Global and the Local*. ed. Sally Engle Merry and Mark Goodale. Cambridge: Cambridge University Press.

Speed, Shannon, and Xochitl Leyva Solano. 2008. "Introduction." In *Human Rights in the Maya Region: Global Politics, Cultural Contentions, and Moral Efficacy*. Durham: Duke University Press.

Spivak, Gayatri. 1988. "Can the Subaltern Speak?" In *Marxism and the Interpretation of Culture*, ed. Cary Nelson and Lawrence Grossberg. London: Macmillan.

Stengel, Rick. 2011. "Person of the Year Introduction." *Time*, December 14. http://www.time.com/time/specials/packages/article/0,28804,2101745_2102139_2102380,00.html.

Stephen, Lynn. 2011. "The Rights to Speak and to Be Heard: Women's Interpretations of Rights Discourses in the Oaxaca Social Movement." In *Gender and Culture at the Limit of Rights*, ed. Dorothy Hodgson. Philadelphia: University of Pennsylvania Press.

———. 2010. "Karen Brodkin and the Study of Social Movements: Lessons for the Social Movement of Oaxaca, Mexico." *Critique of Anthropology* 30(1): 1–29.

———. 2009a. "Elionai Santiago Sánchez: Video Testimonial 7 July 2007." In *Making Rights a Reality: The Oaxaca Social Movement, 2006–Present*. University of Oregon, digital ethnography. http://www.mraroaxaca.uoregon.edu/chapterthreelionai.html.

———. 2009b. "Women and Social Movements in Transborder Communities: Mexico and the United States." In *Rural Social Movements in Latin*

America, ed. Carmen Diana Deere and Frederick S. Royce. Gainesville: University of Florida Press.

———. 2007a. *Transborder Lives: Indigenous Oaxacans in Mexico, California, and Oregon*. Durham: Duke University Press.

———. 2007b. "'We Are Brown, We Are Short, We Are Fat. . . . We Are the Face of Oaxaca': Women Leaders in the Oaxaca Rebellion." *Socialism and Democracy* 21(2): 97–112.

———. 2005a. "Negotiating Global, National, and Local 'Rights' in a Zapotec Community." *Political and Legal Anthropology Review* 28(1): 130–50.

———. 2005b. *Zapotec Women: Gender, Class, and Ethnicity in Globalized Oaxaca*. Durham: Duke University Press.

———. 2002. *Zapata Lives! Histories and Cultural Politics in Southern Mexico*. Berkeley: University of California Press.

———. 2001. "Gender, Citizenship, and the Politics of Identity." *Latin American Perspectives* 28(5): 97–112.

———. 1999. "The Construction of Indigenous Suspects: Militarization and the Gendered and Ethnic Dimensions of Human Rights Abuses in Southern Mexico." *American Ethnologist* 26(4): 1–22.

———, ed. 1994. *Hear My Testimony: María Teresa Tula, Human Rights Activist of El Salvador*. Boston: South End Press.

Stern, Steve J. 2010. *Reckoning with Pinochet: The Memory Question in Democratic Chile: 1989–2006*. Durham: Duke University Press.

———. 2006. *Battling for Hearts and Minds: Memory Struggles in Pinochet's Chile 1973–1988*. Durham: Duke University Press.

———. 2004. *Remembering Pinochet's Chile: On the Eve of London 1998*. Durham: Duke University Press.

Stoll, David. 1999. *Rigoberta Menchú and the Story of All Poor Guatemalans*. Boulder, Colo.: Westview Press.

Street, Susan. 1992. *Maestros en Movimiento: Transformaciones en la burocracia estatal (1978–1982)*. Mexico City: Centro de Investigaciones y Estudios Superiores en Antropología Social, Ediciones de la Casa Chata.

Takash, Paula Cruz, Raúl Hinojosa-Ojeda, and David Runsten. 2005. *Investment of Remittances for Development in a Migratory Economy*. Los Angeles: UCLA North American Integration and Development Center.

Taylor, Diana. 2003. *The Archive and the Repertoire: Performing Cultural Memory in the Americas*. Durham: Duke University Press.

Taylor, Julie. 1994. "Body Memories: Aide Memories and Collective Amnesia in the Wake of Argentine Terror." In *Body Politics: Disease, Desire, and the Family*, ed. Michael Ryan and Avery Gordon. Boulder, Colo.: Westview Press.

Theidon, Kimberly. 2007. "Gender in Transition: Common Sense, Women, and War." *Journal of Human Rights* 6: 453–78.

Tibón, Gutierre. 1961. *Pinotepa nacional: Mixtecos, triquis y negros*. Mexico City: Universidad Nacional Autónoma de México.

UNESCO Institute for Statistics. 2002. "World Adult Literacy Rates, Latin America and the Caribbean, Selected Countries." http://www.uis.unesco .org/en/stats/statistics/ed/g_lit_amerique%201atine.jpg.

United Nations. 2012. "Transitional Justice." United Nations Rule of Law Unit. http://www.unrol.org/article.aspx?article_id=29.

United Nations General Assembly. 2007. "Report of the Special Rapporteur on Extrajudicial, Summary, or Arbitrary Executions. Phillip Alston. Addendum. Summaries of Cases Transmitted to Government and Replies Received." March 12. http://www.geneva-academy.ch/RULAC/pdf_state/ Extrajudicial-executions-report-Ireland-2007.pdf.

United Nations Office of the High Commissioner for Human Rights. 1966. "International Covenant on Civil and Political Rights." http://www2 .ohchr.org/english/law/ccpr.htm.

Uribe, Carlos. 1997. "A Certain Feeling of Homelessness: Remarks on Estebon Krotz's 'Anthropologies of the South.'" *Critique of Anthropology* 17(3): 253–61.

U.S. Census Bureau. 2008. "State and Country Quick Facts, Los Angeles County." http://quickfacts.census.gov/qfd/states/06/06037.html.

U.S. Department of State, Bureau of Consular of Affairs. 2007. "Spring Break in Mexico: 'Know Before You Go.'" http://travel.state.gov/travel/ cis_pa_tw/spring_break_mexico/spring_break_mexico_5014.html.

Valadés, Diego. 1579. *Rhetorica christiana*. Perugia.

Valenzuela, Ruben, and David Vanega. 2008. "Conversaciones con Ruben Valenzuela y David Vanegas." In *Hasta la piedras se levantan: Oaxaca, México 2006*, ed. Norma Giarracca. Buenos Aires: Editorial Antropofogia.

Valle, Roger. 2010. "Triquis denuncian arribo de armamento para grupo paramilitar en Cópala: Familias se desplazan a otros lugares por la tensión que vive en la zona." MIT/Texcoco Mass Media, February 24. Mixteca Hag.

Vargas, Jorge. 2008. "Rights and Obligations of Americans in Mexico under Immigration Law and Other Areas of Foreign Law." *University of Richmond Law Review* 42(4): 839–90.

Vasconcelos, José. 1956. "Raza cósmica." In *Obras Completas*. Mexico City: Librero Mexicanos Unidos.

Vaughn, Mary Kay. 1997. *Politics in Revolution: Teachers, Peasants, and Schools in Mexico, 1930–1940*. Tucson: University of Arizona Press.

———. 1982. *The State, Education, and Social Class in Mexico, 1880–1928*. DeKalb: Northern Illinois University Press.

Vélez, Octavio. 2006. "Matan a 3 indígenas miembros de la Asamblea popular." *La Jornada*, August 10. http://www.ainfos.ca/06/aug/ainfos00080 .html.

Vélez Asencio, Octavio. 2011. "Crean en Oaxaca fiscalía y comisión para investigar la represión de 2006." *La Jornada*, March 10. http://www.jornada .unam.mx/2011/03/10/estados/036n2est.

ViveOaxaca.org. 2011. "Guelaguetza 2011 (25 de julio y 1 de agosto)." *Boletos y Sede.* http://www.viveOaxaca.org/2011/04/guelaguetza-2011-25-de-julio-y-1-de.html.

VOCAL. 2007. "VOCAL Manifiesto." http://argentina.indymedia.org/news/2007/08/540670.php.

Warman, Arturo, Margarita Nolasco Armas, Guillermo Bonfil Batalla, Mercedes Olivera de Vásquez, and Enrique Valencia. 1989. "Políticas y Tareas Indigenistas (1989–1994)." *Boletín Indigenista* 2(4): 2–5.

Werbner, Richard. 1998. *Memory and the Postcolony: African Anthropology and the Critique of Power.* London: Zed Books.

Wikipedia. 2011. "Sistema de Radiodifusores de Culturas Indígenas." http://en.wikipedia.org/wiki/Sistema_de_Radiodifusoras_Culturales_Indigenistas.

———. 2010. "List of Mexican States by Literacy Rate." http://en.wikipedia.org/wiki/List_of_Mexican_states_by_literacy_rate.

Wilson, Richard Ashby. 2007. "Tyrannosaurus Lex: The Anthropology of Human Rights and Transnational Law." In *The Practice of Human Rights: Tracking Law between the Global and the Local,* ed. Mark Goodale and Sally Engle Merry. Cambridge: Cambridge University Press.

Wood, Warner. 2008. *Made in Mexico: Zapotec Weavers and the Global Ethnic Art Market.* Indianapolis: Indiana University Press.

Wortham, Erica Cusi. 2013. *Indigenous Media in Mexico: Culture, Community, and the State.* Durham: Duke University Press.

———. 2004. "Between the State and Indigenous Autonomy: Unpacking Video Indígena in Mexico." *American Anthropologist* 106(2): 363–68.

Yescas Martínez, Isidoro. 1996. *Los costumbres de ayer, los usos de hoy: Coloquio Sobre Derechos Indígenas.* Oaxaca: Instituto Oaxaqueño de las Culturas.

———. 1979. "El movimiento popular en Oaxaca." Professional thesis, Instituto de Investigaciones Sociológicas, Universidad Autónoma "Benito Juárez" de Oaxaca.

Zafra, Gloria. 1979. "El movimiento campesino en Oaxaca: Las invasiones de tierras en el valle de Zimatlán, 1972–1974." Bachelor's thesis. Instituto de Investigaciones Sociológicas, Universidad Autónoma "Benito Juárez" de Oaxaca.

Zires, Margarita. 2009a. "Estrategias de communicación y acción política: Movimiento social de la APPO 2006." In *La APPO: ¿Rebelión o movimiento social? (nuevos formas de expresión ante la crises),* ed. Victor Raúl Martínez Vásquez. Oaxaca: Instituto de Investigaciones Sociológicos, Universidad Autónoma "Benito Juárez de Oaxaca.

———. 2009b. "Imaginarios religiosos y acción Pólitica en la APPO: El Santo Niño de la APPO y la Virgen de las Barrikadas." *Estudios Cultures*: 131–69.

INDEX

Arrazola, San Antonio Arrazola, 182
Arte pa'i Pueblo (public popular art),
256. *See also* Asamblea de Artistas
Revolucionarios de Oaxaca
(ASARO)
artisans, apolitical identity, 186
Asamblea de Artistas Revolucionarios
de Oaxaca (ASARO): art exhibitions, 266–69, *267, 268*; César
Chávez on *licuadora visual* (visual
blender), 266, *266*; creation of
icons, 245–46; "Educación primero
al hijo del obrero" (Education
first to the child of the worker)
stencil, 263–64, *263*; female *calaveras* (skeletons) in resistance art,
264, *265*; Guelaguetza dancers
with machine guns stencil, 258,
259; legacy of, 279; "Libertad de
Expresión" poster (Mexiac), 258,
258; Line and César Chávez on
participation in ASARO, 271, *271*;
Mario Guzmán on emergence of
ASARO, 257, *257*; "Ni un Explotado
mas" (Not one more exploited person) stencil, 262–63, *262*; *Resiste*
engraving, 258, *259*; *Resiste, voz
libre del pueblo* engraving, 258–60,
260; *tapetes* (sand paintings),
261–62, *261, 262*
Asamblea Popular de los Pueblos
de Oaxaca (APPO): APPO Los
Angeles, 25, 30–31, 211, 282–83;
APPO Mixteca, 229–30; author's
documentation of, 17–18, 22–27,
84–87; barricaded neighborhoods,
87–90, 92–93; and civil society
dialogues, 196–99; confrontation
with government-sponsored
dancers in El Llano park, 67–68,
68; conversations with business
owners, 181–82; Guelaguetza
celebration and occupation of El
Llano park, 66–68, *67*; June 2006

emergence of, 3, 7, 28, 80–81;
merchants' opinions of, 180–81,
182, 184, 186–87, 188, 189; Oaxacan state government and social
movements, 1986–2006, 68–75,
94; occupation of public spaces,
83–84, *83*; official government
account of, 6–7; participant
accounts of, 7–8; participatory
democracy and indigenous forms
of governance, 210; post-shut-
down existence, 276–77; and
presidential election of 2006,
81–84; repression and shutdown
of, 6, 28–29, 57, 84–87, 92–93,
169–72; respect for teachers and
birth of APPO, 80–81; separate
police forces of, 84; structure,
governance, and political plans,
90–92, 293–94n13; student
views of, 192–94; 2007 statewide
assembly, 249–50. *See also* APPO
Juxtlahuaca; community and
indigenous radio stations; Coordinadora Nacional de Trabajadores
de la Educación (CNTE); indigenous activism; teachers
asamblea, rural community governance, 29, 125–26, 210, 294n2
ASARO. *See* Asamblea de Artistas
Revolucionarios de Oaxaca
(ASARO)
assassinations: of farmers in Santiago
Textitlán, 73; of José Jiménez
Colmenares, 22, 86, 101, 152–53,
236, 280–81
Assembly of Revolutionary Artists of
Oaxaca. *See* Asamblea de Artistas
Revolucionarios de Oaxaca
(ASARO)
Assembly of the Zapoteco, Mixe, and
Chinanteco Peoples of the Sierra
Juárez, San Pablo Guelataõ de
Juárez, Oaxaca, 209

Autonomous Benito Juarez University of Oaxaca. *See* Universidad Autónoma "Benito Juárez" de Oaxaca (UABJO)

Autonomous Municipality of San Juan Copala, 30–31, 210, 214, 227–32, 280

Autonomous Oaxacan House Supporting Self-Managed Work. *See* Casa Autónoma Solidaria Oaxaqueña de Trabajo Autogestivo (CASOTA)

Autonomous Oaxacan House Supporting Self-Managed Work (CASOTA), 32

ayuntamiento popular (people's government), 59

Aztec pictorial histories, 14

barricadas: Barricada Santa María, 88–90, 92–93, 179; La Barricada de Cinco Señores, 169; *La Hora de las Barricadas* (The Hour of the Barricades) radio show, 166; La Virgen de las Barrikadas icon, 269–72, *270*; merchants' opinions of, 185, 187; neighborhood barricades, 64; and youth engagement, 247–49

Bartolomé Carraso Regional Center for Human Rights, 62

bastones de mando (ceremonial canes), 227–28

"Battle of Seattle", 34

Bautista Merino, Teresa, 226, 228

Bermejillo, Eugenio, 135

bilingual education and CNTE, 43

Binational Front of Indigenous Organizations. *See* Frente Indígena de Organizaciones Binacionales (FIOB)

Blas López, Cuauhtémoc, 43

Boca de Polen, 135

Bolivian National Commission on

Inquiry into Disappearances, 8–9

Bracero program, 294–95*n*3

bufete popular (people's attorney's office), 53

building of schools, teacher and community effort, 47–49

Cabañas, Lucio, 58

caciques (political bosses), 39

caciquismo (political bossism), 50–51

CACTUS (Centro de Apoyo Comunitario Trabajando Unidos, A.C.), 226

caerse el sistema (system crash), 2004 governors' election fraud, 74–75

Café con Panela (Coffee with Molasses) radio show, 165–66

calaveras (skeleton) imagery in resistance art, 264, *265*

Calderón, Felipe, 81, 82–83, 93, 104

Campesina, Antorcha, 70

Caña, Lisbeth, 168

caracoles (points of communication), Juntas de Buen Gobierno (Good Governance Councils), 136–37

caravanas de la muerte and barricaded neighborhoods, 87

Cárdenas, Lázaro, 38

Caring by the Hour (Brodkin), 174

Cariño Trujillo, Alberta "Bety", 231, 255–56

Carraso Altamirano, Diódoro, 69–71, 74

Carrillo Morales, Catalino, 182–83

Casa Autónoma Solidaria Oaxaqueña de Trabajo Autogestivo (CASOTA) and autonomous youth political culture, 32

Castro, Tleriberta, 231

CCI (Central Campesina Independiente), 290*n*8

CCIODH (Comisión Civil Internacional de Observación por los Derechos Humanos), 114–15

Echeverría, Luis, 56, 68
economics and politics of conflict: Alfonso Rodríguez on APPO and civil society dialogues, 195–99; effects of civil unrest on Oaxacan tourism, 30, 179–81, 190, 205; Fernando Martinez on student experience at UABJO, *192*, 192–94; Leticia Aragón Ramírez on effects of APPO movement, 182–86, *183*; Lucero Topete on effects of APPO on Instituto Cultural de Oaxaca (Oaxacan Cultural Institute), 203–6; Mariana Cruz Castro on effects of APPO movement, 189–92, *191*; pre-Hispanic cultures and tourism in Oaxaca, 178–79; Sara Rojas on effects of APPO movement, 186–88; Teotitlán del Valle artisans, 188–94; 2010 election results, 207–8; 2011 tourism revival, 206–7; U.S. State Department on civil unrest in Oaxaca, 179. *See also* civil society
education: bilingual education and CNTE, 43; democratic teachers' movement, 39–44; "Educación primero al hijo del obrero" (Education first to the child of the worker) stencil, 263–64, *263*; mestizos and public education, 37–38; and teachers organizing, 37–38
Ejército Guerrillero de los Pobres (Guerrilla Army of the Poor), 58–59
Ejército Zapatista de Liberación Nacional (EZLN): and APPO Los Angeles, 233–34; community and indigenous radio stations, 141–44; emergence of, 34, 35; Juntas de Buen Gobierno (Good Governance Councils), 136–37; *mandar obedeciendo* (lead by obeying) ideology, 64; and Radio Copala, 226–27;

and San Andrés Accords, 60–61, 132–33, 135; Teotitlán del Valle community assemblies, 125–27; Vivian Newdick's ethnographic positionality and, 19. *See also* Voces Oaxaqueñas Construyendo Autonomía y Libertad (VOCAL)
ejidos (communally owned and managed lands), 99, 182, 295*n*9
Ejutla de Crespo jail, 100–103, *102*
El Ejército Popular Revolucionario (EPR), 70
El Foro Nacional: Construyendo la Democracia y la Gobernabilidad en Oaxaca (The National Forum: Constructing Democracy and Governability in Oaxaca), 90–91
El Llano, Guelaguetza celebration and occupation of El Llano park, 66–68, *67*, *68*
el pueblo de Oaxaca political identity, 27, 277
elections: civil society dialogues, 198; and CNTE, 41; election of Cué Monteagudo, 6, 199, 202–3; elections fraud, 74–75, 82–83; and governmental reforms, 69–70
embodiment, Elionai's *zocalo* press conference, 110
emotional power and importance of testimonials, 27, 31–32, 286–87
engaged politics, 31–32
EPR (El Ejército Popular Revolucionario), 70
Escuela Normal Federal Superior de Oaxaca, 47
Espacio Zapata, 257, 266
EZLN. *See* Ejército Zapatista de Liberación Nacional (EZLN)

factuality vs. other forms of testimonial knowledge, 12–13
Federación Estudiantil Oaxaqueña (Oaxacan Student Federation), 53

López Vásquez, Carmen: childhood, 50–51; "Maestra Carmen," Radio La Ley 710, 45, 49–50; teacher training and early career, 51–52; and women's media takeover, 161, 165, 166–67, 176

Loxicha region militarization and repression, 70–71

Luis Martínez, Jorge, 273–74

MacArthur Park rallies, 211, 235–36, 240

Madrazo, Roberto, 82

Madrid, Miguel de la, 59

Making Rights a Reality website, 18, 23–24, 26, 271–72

Mal de Ojo TV, 24, 128, 148, 154–55

Maldonado, Centolia, 218–19, *219*, 220–21, 224–25

mandar obedeciendo (lead by obeying), 64, 136

Martínez Alvarez, Jesús, 74

Martinez, Fernando, *192*, 192–94

Martínez, Gabriela, 26

Martínez Luna, Jaime, 133–34

Martínez Moreno, Juan, 168–69

Martínez Neri, Francisco, 170

Martínez Sánchez, Felicitas, 226, 228

mayordomías, 22

The Memory Box of Pinochet's Chile (Stern), 11

memory, social truths and alternative understandings of collective trauma, 11

Menchú, Rigoberta, 12

Méndez, Ana Ruth, 220, *220*, 224

Mendoza Nube, Germán, 99, 101

mestizos and public education, 37–38

Mexican Federal Constitution: and cultural rights, 60–61; and foreign researchers, 18–19; and INI radio programming, 129–32; Ramiro's testimony on voting absurdities, 104–5; and rights discrepancies, 96, 115–20

Mexican League for the Defense of Human Rights (Limeddh), 22, 62–63

Mexican Revolution, 37–38

Miller, Alina Padilla, 26

Ministry of Agriculture and Hydraulic Resources (SARH), 128

Ministry of Public Education (SEP), 37–38

Mitla, 178

Mixtec codices, 13–14

Mixtec communities: APPO Mixteca, 229–30; and birth of APPO, 217–19, *217*; and indigenous activism, 209–11; videotape testimonials, 25

Monte Albán, 178, 182

Montenegro, Pilar, 124–25, 150–51

Morales, Magali, 26

Morelos, Avenida, 124

mosquetón weapons charges, 103–4, 109

Mothers of the Plaza de Mayo of Argentina, 97–98

Movement for Triqui Unification and Struggle. *See* Movimiento de Unificación y Lucha Triqui (MULT)

Movimiento Ciudadano por la Justicia, Paz, y Desarollo con Dignidad para Oaxaca (Citizens' Movement for Justice, Peace, and Development with Dignity for Oaxaca), 208, 276

Movimiento de Unificación y Lucha Triqui (MULT): and San Juan Copala Autonomous Municipality, 228–32; and San Juan Copala community, 47

Movimiento Revolucionario Magisterial (Revolutionary Teacher's Movement) of the Communist Party, 290n1

Movimiento Unificación Lucha Triqui Independiente (MULTI): formation of, 210–11, 216; Juxtlahuaca regional history and MULT–MULTI conflict, 211–16; and Radio Copala, 226–27; Triqui Autonomous Municipality of San Juan Copala and 2007–2012 conflicts, 227–32; Triqui women and APPO Juxtlahuaca, 220–21; Triqui women marching through Juxtlahuaca, 221

MULT. See Movimiento de Unificación y Lucha Triqui (MULT)

MULTI. See Movimiento Unificación Lucha Triqui Independiente (MULTI)

multiple forms of transmission of testimonies, Elionai's *zocalo* press conference, 111

Multipurpose hall "Estela Ríos," Comandanta Cacerola (Commander Casserole Dish), CASOTA, 253–54

Muñoz, Berta Elena, 169, 170

Murat, José, 71–72, 73–74

National Action Party. See Partido Acción Nacional (PAN)

National Autonomous University (UNAM), 53

National Commission for Human Rights (CNDH), 61, 71, 96, 105

National Commission for the Development of the Indigenous Peoples of Mexico (CDI), 131, 135

National Coordinator Plan de Ayala (CNPA), 215

National Council of Education Workers. See Coordinadora Nacional de Trabajadores de la Educación (CNTE)

National Indigenist Institute. See Instituto Nacional Indigenista (INI)

National Peasants Confederation (CNC), 38, 56

National Union of Education Workers. See Sindicato Nacional de Trabajadores de Educación (SNTE)

Newdick, Vivian, on researcher positionality, 19

Nichols, Jesse, 24–25, 26

Noticias, government takeover, 75

Nuevo Acuerdo para los Pueblos Indígenas (New Agreement for Indigenous Peoples), 69

Nuñez, Conchita, 77–78, 85, 147

Oaxaca Agenda for Gender Equity, 63

Oaxaca City: militarization of, 6; and tourism, 179–80; Triqui women's sit-in at City Hall, 231; World Heritage Site designation, 178

Oaxaca (Cué Monteagudo), 74–75

Oaxaca en Paz (Oaxaca in Peace) website, 164

Oaxaca, Mexico: central locations map, 4; general location map, 2; human rights and cultural citizenship, 18; Juxtlahuaca and Huajuapan de León and Mixtec Baja region, 5; primary locations map, 3; state government and social movements, 1986–2006, 68–75, 94. See also Asamblea Popular de los Pueblos de Oaxaca (APPO)

Oaxaca Network for Human Rights, 62

Oaxaca popular identity, 246, 285–86

Oaxacalifornia, 282–83

Oaxacan Constitution modifications, 68–69

Oaxacan Corporation of Radio and Television. See Corporación Oaxaqueña de Radio y Televisión (COR-TV)

telesegundaria (middle school with televised curriculum): described, 44, 290*n*4; teaching career of Esteban Manuel Rodríguez, 46, 47–49

Televisión para el Pueblo Oaxaqueño (Television for the People of Oaxaca), 150, 152, 153

Tello, Carlos, 134

Teotitlán del Valle: artisans, 188–94; community assemblies, 125–27; weavers, 30, 181, 188–91, 205

tequio, 22

testimonials: alternative and contested historical truths, 9–10; and APPO movement, 8; barricaded neighborhoods as cultural centers, 87–90; community assemblies, 122–28; emotional power and importance of, 27–28, 31–32, 286–87; factuality vs. other forms of knowledge, 12–13; and human rights consciousness in Oaxaca, 97; inclusion of marginalized people, 10–12; and individual transformations, 10–11; and Latin American truth commissions, 8–9; and participatory democracy, 31–32, 121–22, 136–39, 144; performance aspects, 1–2, 13–17; and political participation, 1–3; research effects on, 17; and rights claiming, 160; and social movements, 15–17; testimonial archive and performance, 8; and testimony in documentary films, 12–13. *See also* community and indigenous radio stations; women's media takeover

testimony and human rights violations in Oaxaca: Elionai's arrest and beating, *102*, 106–9; Elionai's *zócalo* press conference, 109–12; function and social context of testimonials, 112–13; human rights theories, 96–99; Juan Gabriel's arrest and beating, *102*, 106; overview, 95–96, 120; and political asylum, 115–19, 242; Ramiro's arrest and beating, 99–106, *100*, *102*; reports of violations in Oaxaca, 2006–2007, 113–15; repression of APPO and protestors, 95–96

testis, 2

Theidon, Kimberly: factuality vs. other forms of knowledge, 12–13; on truth commissions and inclusion of marginalized peoples, 10–11

Tlapa, Guerrero, 128

Tlatelolco student massacre, 53

Tlaxiaco, Oaxaca, 70

TMA (Transferencia de Medios Audiovisuales a Organizaciones y Comunidades Indígenas), 132, 134–35

Todos Santos customs, 222–23

Topete, Lucero, 203–6

tourism: effects of civil unrest on Oaxacan tourism, 30, 179–81, 190, 205; pre-Hispanic cultures and tourism in Oaxaca, 178–79; 2011 tourism revival, 206–7

Transferencia de Medios Audiovisuales a Organizaciones y Comunidades Indígenas (TMA), 132, 134–35

transitional justice, 289*n*1

transnational indigenous citizenship, 211, 232–44, *235*, *238*

Tribunal Electoral del Poder Judicial de la Federación (Electoral Tribunal of the Federal Judiciary), 2006 presidential election, 82

Triqui Autonomous Municipality of San Juan Copala, 30–31, 210, 214, 227–32, 280

Triqui communities: and CASOTA and VOCAL, 255–56; and indigenous activism, 209–10; regional history, 211–14; videotape testimonials, 25. *See also* Movimiento Unificación Lucha Triqui Independiente (MULTI)

Trujillo Martínez, René, 166

truth and truth commissions: alternative and contested historical truths, 9–10; factuality vs. other forms of knowledge, 12–13; social truths and alternative understandings of collective trauma, 11; and testimony in documentary films, 12–13

truth commissions: historical truth and reconciliation goals, 9–10; and human rights violations in Oaxaca, 7–8; inclusion of marginalized people, 10–12; Latin American, 8–9

Tsotsil and Tseltal-Maya women's activism in Chiapas, 19

2010 election results, 207–8

2011 tourism revival, 206–7

"2 de Noviembre" Central Patio, CASOTA, 254

UABJO. *See* Universidad Autónoma "Benito Juárez" de Oaxaca (UABJO)

Ugartechea Begué, Luis, 205, 208, 285

UNAM (Universidad Nacional Autónoma de México), 53

Unidad de Bienestar Social para la Región Triqui (UBISORT): alliance with MULT, 230–32; alliance with MULTI, 216; formation of, 215; violence in San Juan Copala, 230–31, 298–99nn11–14

Union de Comunidades de la Sierra Juárez de Oaxaca (Union of Highland Communities of Oaxaca), 233

Unión de Trabajadores de la Educación (UTE), 293n9

Unión del Barrio, 242

Unión del Pueblo (People's Union), 58–59, 290n8

Union of Education Workers (UTE), 293n9

Unión Social de Empresarios Mexicanos (USEM), 181, 196–97

Unity for the Well-Being of the Triqui Region. *See* Unidad de Bienestar Social para la Región Triqui (UBISORT)

Universidad Autónoma "Benito Juárez" de Oaxaca (UABJO): and formation of FUCUPO, 56–57; and student movements in the 1970s, 53–54; student views of APPO movement, 192–94

Universidad Nacional Autónoma de México (UNAM), 53

U.S. State Department on civil unrest in Oaxaca, 179

USEM (Unión Social de Empresarios Mexicanos), 181, 196–97

usos y costumbres (customs and traditions), rural community governance, 30, 69, 250, 278

UTE (Unión de Trabajadores de la Educación), 293n9

Valenzuela, Ruben, 246

Vanegas, David, 246

Vargas Garfías, Rogelio, 40–42, *40*

Vásquez, Faustino, 226

Vásquez, Fidelia, 1, 157–59, 277

Vásquez, Martínez, 36

Vásquez, Yanira, 226

vernacularization of human rights discourses, 173

victim narratives and individual transformations, 10–11

video indígena (indigenous video), 134

Villavicencio, Jaciel, 222–23, *222*

violence and killings, Triqui region, 228–32

visual and alphabetic indigenous literacy, 13–15, 27–28

Voces Oaxaqueñas Construyendo Autonomía y Libertad (VOCAL): and autonomous youth political culture, 31; David Vanegas on youth engagement, 247–49; formation of, 246; Manifesto of, 250–53; Sonia Hinojosa on barricades and Radio Universidad, 247; Sonia Hinojosa on 2007 statewide APPO assembly, 249–50

voter intimidation, August 2000 elections, 72

voto de castigo (punishment vote), 82

Warman, Arturo, 129–32

water privatization attempts in Bolivia, 34

Will, Bradley, 86, 88, 167–69, 201, 238

witnesses, Elionai's *zocalo* press conference, 111

women: female *calaveras* (skeletons) in resistance art, 264, *265*; Fidelia Vásquez's testimony, 1, 157–59, 277; indigenous activism and leadership roles, 211, 223–27; as majority members of CNTE, 43; Triqui women marching through Juxtlahuaca, *221*; women organizing within APPO Juxtlahuaca and Radio Copala, 223–27; women's activism in Chiapas, 19; women's groups and defense of human rights, 63

women's media takeover: Carmen López Vásquez on importance of radio testimonials, 161; Carmen López Vásquez on Radio La Ley, 165, 166–67; Catalina Ruiz on COR-TV takeover, 148–49; Catalina Ruiz on men's response to womens' COR-TV takeover, 156–57; Conchita Nuñez on COR-TV takeover, *147*; Daniela Aragón on Radio Universidad, 172–73; Fidelia Vásquez's testimony, 1, 157–59, 277; "Fuera Gachupines!" (Spanish get out!) graffiti, *159*; and gendered construction of rights in COR-TV, 150–56; and gendered rights to speak and be heard, 173–75, 176–77; and hybrid identity formation, 158–60, 175–76; Josefina Reyes on importance of radio testimonials, *162*, 163; lack of mainstream media coverage, 163–64; legacy of, 277–79; La Marcha de las Cacerolas (the March of the Pots and Pans), 147–49, 253–54; Mariana Gómez on COR-TV takeover, 147–48; overview, 1, 29–30; Patricia Jiménez on formation of COMO, 151–52, *152*; Patricia Jiménez on reaction to women occupiers, 159; Radio Cacerola testimonials, 150–51, *152*–54, 155–56, 161–63; Roberto Olivares on importance of media takeovers, 162–63, *163*; Rosario Romero on takeover of COR-TV, 151; Ruth Guzmán's testimony and political engagement, 155–56, 162; security assignments for women occupying COR-TV, *150*; testimony on occupation of COR-TV, *151*; testimony and political engagement, 145–47

Women's Regional Council, indigenous activism, 243

woodblock prints, 268–69, *268*